CANADA HOME

CANADA HOME

Juliana Horatia Ewing's

Fredericton Letters

1867–1869

EDITED BY

Margaret Howard Blom & Thomas E. Blom

University of British Columbia Press

VANCOUVER

CANADA HOME
Juliana Horatia Ewing's Fredericton Letters, 1867–1869

© The University of British Columbia 1983

This book has been published with the help of a grant from the Canadian Federation for the Humanities, using funds provided by the Social Sciences and Humanities Research Council of Canada, and with the assistance of the Canada Council. Also financially assisted by the government of British Columbia through the British Columbia Cultural Fund.

This book is printed on acid-free paper

CANADIAN CATALOGUING IN PUBLICATION DATA

Ewing, Juliana Horatia, 1841–1885.
Canada home

Includes index.
ISBN 0-7748-0174-3

1. Ewing, Juliana Horatia, 1841–1885 -
Correspondence. 2. Ewing, Juliana Horatia,
1841–1885 - Homes and haunts - New Brunswick-
Fredericton. 3. Authors, English - 19th
century - Correspondence. 4. Authors, English -
19th century - Homes and haunts - New Brunswick -
Fredericton. 5. Fredericton (N.B.) - Social
life and customs. I. Blom, Margaret Howard,
1934–   II. Blom, Thomas E. (Thomas Edgar),
1933–   III. Title.
PR4699.E85Z48 1983   823'.8   C83-091394-7

International Standard Book Number 0-7748-0174-3
Printed in Canada

CONTENTS

ILLUSTRATIONS

ACKNOWLEDGEMENTS

We thank the Hunter Archaeological Society and the Gatty family for permission to publish Mrs. Ewing's Fredericton letters. Members of the Gatty family generously assisted in our research: we are grateful to Mr. Jonathan Gatty, Mrs. Pamela Gatty, Mr. and Mrs. Patrick Johnson, Mrs. Elizabeth Orpwood, Mrs. Juliana Prosser, Mr. David Scott-Gatty, Mrs. Hester Smallbone, Miss Joyce J.P. Smith, Captain and Mrs. Alexander Swann, Mr. George Ward, Miss Hermione Moir, and Miss Marion Ward. The Reverend Ralph Mayland, past vicar of the Ecclesfield Parish Church, and his wife, Jean, introduced us to Ecclesfield and shared our interest in the Gatty family. Mrs. Connie Marcroft of Sheffield and Mrs. Lucy McNeill of Fredericton opened their homes to two traveling scholars: we thank them for their kindness. And we thank our editor, Dr. Jane Fredeman, for her wisdom, patience, and skill.

Librarians and archivists on both sides of the Atlantic were of immense help to us. It is a pleasure to express our gratitude to the Sheffield Central Library, the Provincial Archives of New Brunswick, the New Brunswick Museum, the Harriet Irving Library of the University of New Brunswick, the York-Sunbury Historical Society, the Charlotte County Historical Society, the University of British Columbia Library, the Osborne Collection of the Toronto Public Library, the Public Archives of Canada, and the British Library. Special thanks are due the Wakefield District Library for permission to publish drawings and water-colours in its possession.

We are grateful to the Social Sciences and Humanities Research Council of Canada and to the University of British Columbia for grants which enabled us to work on this book.

INTRODUCTION

The *David Weston* steams its way against the current of the St. John River. To the right, rolling evergreen hills rise behind the small farms which skirt the water's edge. To the left, bluffs confine willow, elm, and poplar to a narrow margin of riverbank, but as the river turns, these bluffs subside, revealing a vista of church spires, white houses, and shady, tree-lined streets. This is Fredericton, New Brunswick, 3:00 P.M., 28 June 1867. For a newlywed couple aboard the *David Weston*, a journey which began in Liverpool some three weeks earlier is over.

The bride is Juliana Horatia Ewing, and this book presents 101 of the letters she wrote from Canada to her Yorkshire home. Ecclesfield, north of Sheffield, has the hard, cold, limited charm of a village devoted to the manufacture of nails, files, and forks. It is a flint-grey place, which forms a ragged apron around three sides of a knoll crested by the twelfth-century church of St. Mary, the Minster of the Moors. Mrs. Ewing's father, the Reverend Alfred Gatty – scholar, editor, and religious controversialist – held the living of St. Mary's for sixty-three years, and in the vicarage beside the churchyard, he and his wife Margaret raised eight children.[1] Theirs was an amazing family, even for Victorian times. Margaret Gatty – a woman of formidable energy, intellect, and talent – was the daughter and biographer of Dr. Alexander John Scott, chaplain to Nelson aboard the *Victory*; she wrote the popular *Parables from Nature:* five volumes of moral and religious lessons drawn from her own scientific observation and from contemporary natural history. She also compiled *British Seaweeds*, an illustrated taxonomy held in scientific favour for almost a century. And in her last years, she edited *Aunt Judy's Magazine*, one of England's finest publications for children.

Like their parents, the Gatty children were *virtuosi*: one became chief justice of Gibraltar; another, Garter King-at-Arms, distinguished both for his knowledge of Welsh genealogy and his songs for schoolroom and music hall; yet another, a clergyman whose collection of early oak furniture strengthened the holdings of the British Museum and whose belief that pygmies once populated England contributed a curious page to nineteenth-century eccentric scholarship.

Today, the achievements of the Gatty family are almost forgotten, save for those of Juliana Horatia. For over half a century her prose and poetry enriched childhood for millions of English-speaking people. Her talent revealed itself early. As a young child, she amazed and entertained her family with improvised nursery stories. Indeed, her narrative skills inspired Margaret Gatty's *Aunt Judy's Tales* and *Aunt Judy's Letters*, "Aunt Judy" being Juliana's family nickname. Today, she is best remembered for *Jackanapes*, *Lob Lie-by-the-Fire* (both illustrated by her friend Randolph Caldecott), *A Flat Iron for a Farthing*, and *The Story of a Short Life*, but all of the more than thirty books she wrote reveal the accurate observation and flexible style which enable her to capture experience in memorable, moving language.

During the late nineteenth and early twentieth centuries, individual titles of her works exceeded 200,000 sales and won the approval of Ruskin, Charlotte Yonge, Henry James, Kipling, and Arnold Bennett. Indeed, when Bennett discovered her books in 1927, he wrote, "I conceive that Rudyard Kipling must have read Mrs. Ewing when he was young, and I wish I had." Ten years later, Bennett's guess was confirmed by Kipling in his autobiography: "I have still, a bound copy of Mrs. Ewing's *Six to Sixteen*. I owe more in circuitous ways to that tale than I can tell. I knew it and I know it still, almost by heart. Here was a history of real people and real things."

Mrs. Ewing's Fredericton letters offer just such a history and thus make a valuable addition to the library of travel literature. Mark Twain's title *Innocents Abroad* suggests what is indeed the case: travel literature is a literature of initiation, in which strangers in strange lands pass from innocence to experience. In the tales of innocents abroad, we find deeper insight into *otherness* than natives, blinded by familiarity, can give. But insight into *otherness* is always confined to travelers' particular interests and coloured by their assumptions. Mrs. Ewing's letters are no exception. She is not concerned with the immensity of the wilderness or the rigours of frontier life; instead she takes Fredericton as her subject, and she describes this city during an important stage of its transition from a pre-Confederation, imperial garrison to a post-Confederation, middle-class, Maritime city.

Settled in 1783 by Loyalists driven from the United States following the War of Independence, Fredericton became the seat of New Brunswick government (the provincial legislature first met there in 1788); the home of the University of New Brunswick, known as King's College when it opened in 1829; and from 1845, the Cathedral City of the See of New Brunswick. But above all else, from 1784 to 1869, Fredericton was an army town, as the original, 1785 town plat attests: it takes the garrison as its primary point of reference. Visitors to Fredericton are still impressed by the handsome stone barracks bordering one side of Queen Street, the "Main Street" of the old city.

From 1866 to 1869, Fredericton was headquarters of the 1st Battalion of Her Majesty's 22d (Cheshire) Regiment, to which Juliana's husband, Captain Alexander Ewing (1830–1895), was attached in June 1867. Alexander–or "Rex," as Juliana called him–was an ardent musician, remembered today for his setting for the hymn "Jerusalem the Golden;" a writer of children's literature (he wrote a serial, *The Prince of Sleona*, for his future mother-in-law's magazine while he was courting her daughter); a student of foreign languages, who later published translations of Richter's *Flower, Fruit, and Thorn Pieces* and Hoffman's tales.

The newlyweds arrived in Fredericton the week of Confederation. An officer in the Commissariat and therefore responsible for the security of British military property, Captain Ewing remained in Fredericton for three months following the withdrawal of British troops from New Brunswick in the spring of 1869. He was the last British officer to leave the city, and his wife's descriptions of the deserted garrison create an apt and moving image for the end of a colonial era.

Mrs. Ewing's home letters bring her Fredericton to life. The instalment of *Mrs. Overtheway's Remembrances* which she completed just prior to her wedding, opens with the observation, "Pity, that pleasant impressions – pity, that most impressions – pass away so soon!" The perception that inspired this remark illuminates all of Mrs. Ewing's writing, for she was, above all else, able to capture experience impressionistically, infusing it with the humour, warmth, and sensitivity of her loving spirit.

Written almost at the moment the events she describes occur and while her feelings are at full flood, Mrs. Ewing's letters chronicle concerns which often go unrecorded or – if recorded – unpreserved. Her letters, which form a domestic social history, accordingly reduce Fenian threats, *Alabama* matters, and Red River rebellions to hazy presentiments, noteworthy only insofar as they might impose upon an army wife's duty and destiny. Her caricatures of Yankees and Irishmen are as broad as her sketches of New Brunswick Indians are picturesque, but between these extremes we find her witty, affectionate descriptions of the Fredericton society which attracted a woman of her background, class, and interests. A neophyte housewife, a professional writer, and a devout Christian, Mrs. Ewing tells us a great deal about her household chores, her creative endeavours, and her religious concerns, but she also enjoys depicting the sleighing and canoeing parties, the picnics and balls, the musical evenings and choral concerts which enlivened mid-nineteenth century Fredericton life.

Mrs. Ewing was an avid gardener and student of natural history; accordingly, references to Fredericton weather occur throughout her correspondence. But all English immigrants stood in awe of the harsh Canadian climate, warding it off with health-conscious caution and simultaneously embracing it with enthusiastic wonder. Here was a realm quite *un*English, where overnight summer's intense heat gave way to killing frost and soon thereafter to the freezing of the St. John River. Winter was a spectacle of snow-burdened evergreens, seen only in Christmas pantomimes back home. And spring, sudden and short-lived, offered the *grand finale* of the freshet – the break-up of the St. John, which plunged a swirling mass of ice and water to the sea, scouring the riverbanks and flooding low-lying areas of town. For most English visitors, weather was the common denominator of Canadian experience. Mrs. Ewing is no exception.

So much is unambiguously clear. But it is not possible to determine the extent to which she is aware of – but chooses not to comment on – other aspects of Fredericton life. Her account certainly suggests that the ethos of Fredericton was conservatively "English" – based on eager endorsement of the British military presence and commitment to high Anglicanism. But Fredericton in the 1860s (population: 6,000) also supported a thriving economy based on farming and lumbering. Indeed, one contemporary report describes wharves groaning under stacked lumber, rivers "choked up by rubbish" and "streams paved several feet deep with decomposing sawdust and rubbish."[2] Mrs. Ewing seems uninterested in the commercial life of Fredericton and unaware of the pollution (perhaps, compared to industrial Yorkshire, New Brunswick *was* a paradise). And she is also – until the brutal murder of a British soldier in October 1868 – apparently ignorant of the ambivalent, even hostile attitude of many local people to the presence of Imperial troops in Fredericton. Music of the military band at morning parade, the muffled thunder of firing from the rifle range, the sight of neatly uniformed red-coats – all of these undoubtedly enhanced city life. But there were also complaints that the military presence in Fredericton was an unwelcome reminder of irresponsible colonial government, and that a "miasma of immorality" seeped from the barracks to poison local youth.[3]

Certainly, Mrs. Ewing sometimes does shade the truth in a loving attempt to protect her family from worry. Knowing her mother's fear that the New Brunswick climate will prove too much for her daughter's delicate constitution, Mrs. Ewing insists throughout her first Canadian winter that she and Rex are wonderfully warm in their rambling, riverbank house, but following a move to snugger quarters, she speaks frankly and humourously of the inadequate stratagems by which she had previously attempted to defeat the cold. As long as there seems no foreseeable end to Rex's tour of duty, she insists she is delighting in her every experience, yet she breaks into a paean of joy when orders for England seem imminent.

Mrs. Ewing's biography explains why sometimes she is less than honest. At twenty-six, she was the first Gatty child to marry, the first to establish a home of her own. The sorrow attending this break in an unusually close family circle was intensified for Mrs. Gatty by the fact that her favourite daughter, who had never been strong, was leaving not just the Ecclesfield vicarage, but England, and journeying across the Atlantic to a world of which the family knew nothing.

Though she was eager for her daughter to find happiness in marriage and knew how deeply Rex and Juliana were in love, Mrs. Gatty initially opposed the marriage because she feared that her daughter could not endure the hardships of army life. In April 1867, when it seemed Alexander might be sent to the Canadian frontier, Mrs. Gatty wrote to a friend, "she cannot *rough* it. She needs comforts and £250 will not give them.... Picture them marrying now on £250 – he out on the frontier in camp – she in Quebec or Montreal, alone among strangers with those means."[4] Then, unexpectedly, Captain Ewing was posted to New Brunswick. There was a likelihood of more pay. Family opposition gave way, and the lovers were urged to marry at once, so that Juliana could accompany Rex when he sailed in June. After months of waiting and hoping, Juliana suddenly found herself in such a flurry of activity that she was "obliged to Joke & not to think."[5]

On 1 June 1867 Juliana and Rex were married, and a week later they were on the Atlantic. Juliana then had time to think, and despite her great happiness with Rex, she grieved. The pain of separation was intensified by her knowledge of her mother's heartache and failing health.[6] In April 1867 Mrs. Gatty had written to a friend,

the lovers are so devoted that they must marry as soon as there are tolerable means. He can't rest out of her sight & she is much deeper over head and ears than she is aware of herself. I like all this, but when I think of bidding her good-bye for Canada, I feel as if it were the last time I should ever see her– And what does that matter? He will certainly guard her from all evil if he can, & if my time is over before they return, *that* will not signify. But goodbyes are horrid

things in families—however one may theorize & be reasonable.[7]

Intuiting the specific apprehension behind her mother's courage,
Mrs. Ewing determined to build a bridge of words over which her
mother's thoughts could travel to Canada. And she succeeded. Her
mother found her daughter's letters "perfectly delightful" and declared that the family drew from them "the sunniest thought of our
lives—the happiness of those two."[8]

But for Mrs. Ewing, letter writing was not just a way to solace
her mother and maintain home ties. The activity was also a workshop where she could practise her craft. Training the eye to see,
the ear to hear, the heart to comprehend, is lifelong labour. Juliana
embarked upon an artist's career early; she published her first book
when she was twenty-one. Her correspondence, diaries, and jour-
nals—to say nothing of her many poems and stories—reveal her
professional commitment. Here is Mrs. Ewing, near the end of her
life, describing the creation of a scene in *Daddy Darwin's Dovecot:*

> I cannnot tell you what work I spent upon the fugue scene!
> Brain work excites and exhausts me so preposterously, I
> prowl up and down till every limb aches fit to come off, and
> I cry like fifty fools, and rub my hair up on end, and break
> or crush anything that is between my fingers for its
> sins—and am so found by the maid who announces callers
> or some other detail of sub-lunary existence! Dignified!!
> and then I feel inclined to throw turnips at my own head
> and ask myself—if you're played out like this over a tale the
> length of a halfpenny tract, whereabouts would you be
> with a novel? I had special difficulties with that scene. I re-
> membered the anthem as performed. . . in my childhood. It
> had very poetic and affecting associations in memory, but I
> felt that it was too likely that it might be a poor thing in
> fact. Then not one of my family or the existing choir could
> recall it, and accused me of having invented it! At last I did
> trace it—then came the difficulty of conveying its effect
> without music, to the readers who knew it not. The
> Wilberforce's best paper knife got between my fingers in

an evil hour, and I beat time and wrote, and wrote and beat time, and cut and altered and tried again, and broke the paper knife!!

And here is the product of her efforts:

The parson's daughter struck a chord, and then the burly choir-master spoke with the voice of melody:

"My heart is disquieted within me. My heart – my heart is disquieted within me. And the fear of death is fallen – is fallen upon me."

The terrier moaned without, and Jack thought no boy's voice could be worth listening to after that of the choirmaster. But he was wrong. A few more notes from the organ, and then, as night-stillness in a wood is broken by the nightingale, so upon the silence of the church a boy-alto's voice broke forth in obedience to the choirmaster's uplifted hand:

"*Then*" I said – I said —— "

Jack gasped, but even as he strained his eyes to see what such a singer could look like, with higher, clearer notes the soprano rose above him – "Then I sa-a-id," and the duet began:

"OH that I had wings – O that I had wings like a dove!" *Soprano.* – "Then would I flee away." *Alto.* – "Then would I flee away." *Together.* – "And be at rest – flee away and be at rest."

The clear young voices soared and chased each other among the arches, as if on the very pinions for which they prayed. Then – swept from their seats by an upward sweep of the choirmaster's arms – the chorus rose, as birds rise, and carried on the strain.

It was not a very fine composition, but this final chorus had the singular charm of fugue. And as the voices mourned like doves, "Oh that I had wings!" and pursued each other with the plaintive passage, "Then would I flee away – then would I flee away —— ," Jack's ears knew no weariness of the repetition. It was strangely like watching

xvi

the rising and falling of Daddy Darwin's pigeons, as they tossed themselves by turns upon their homeward flight.

After the fashion of the piece and period, this chorus was repeated, and the singers rose to supreme effort. The choirmaster's hands flashed hither and thither, controlling, inspiring, directing. He sang among the tenors.

Jack's voice nearly choked him with longing to sing too. Could words of man go more deeply home to a young heart caged within workhouse walls?

"OH that I had wings like a dove! Then would I flee away–" the choirmaster's white hands were fluttering downwards in the dusk, and the chorus sank with them–" flee away and be at rest!"

Following the completion of *Daddy Darwin's Dovecot*, Mrs. Ewing wrote one last novelette, *The Story of a Short Life*. What more she might have achieved as a writer in the course of her own short life–if her economic circumstances had been better, if her health had been stronger–one can only guess. In the late 1870s she suffered a series of illnesses which drained her strength and which, when Rex was posted abroad in 1879, led to an extended separation. Though she longed to accompany him, her precarious physical condition made travel impossible. Alone in England, she strove to manage on a minimal allowance, supplemented by her own earnings. Immediate necessity made it impossible for her to try her hand at adult fiction, though she wished to break out of the field of children's literature, which provided a ready but painfully ill-paying market. In 1883 Rex returned to England, and the Ewings settled in Taunton, their first real home in years, but Mrs. Ewing's health continued to deteriorate, and in 1885 she died at the age of forty-four.

Juliana Horatia Ewing's Fredericton letters were written during the happiest years of her life. Amusing, perceptive, and sympathetic, they reflect their author and her varied interests; they also describe Fredericton in the twenty-seven months following the establishment of the Dominion of Canada. Here, indeed, is a history of real people and real things.

BIBLIOGRAPHIC NOTE

AVERY, GILLIAN. *Mrs. Ewing*. London: The Bodley Head, Ltd., 1961.

EWING, JULIANA HORATIA. *Complete Works*, 18 vols. London: SPCK, 1894–1896.

GATTY, HORATIA K[ATHARINE] F[RANCES]. *Juliana Horatia Ewing And Her Books*. London: SPCK, 1885.

HUTCHINS, MICHAEL, ed. *Yours Pictorially: Illustrated Letters of Randolph Caldecott*. London: F. Warne, 1976.

LASKI, MARGHANITA. *Mrs. Ewing, Mrs. Molesworth, and Mrs. Hodgson Burnett*. London: Arthur Barker, 1950.

MARSHALL, MRS. [EMMA]. "'A.L.O.E.' (Miss Tucker) Mrs. Ewing," *Women Novelists of Queen Victoria's Reign: A Book of Appreciations*, by Mrs. Oliphant, Mrs. Lynn Linton, *et al*, pp. 291–312. London: Hurst & Blackett, Ltd., 1897.

MAXWELL, CHRISTABEL. *Mrs. Gatty and Mrs. Ewing*. London: Constable, 1949.

TUCKER, ELIZABETH S. *Leaves from Juliana Horatia Ewing's "Canada Home."* Boston: Roberts Brothers, 1896.

Maxwell is the only full-length biography; Avery and Laski provide some biographical as well as critical information, and both include bibliographies. The only full bibliography is in Gatty; this work is reprinted with excerpts from 25 of JHE'S Canadian letters under the title *Juliana Horatia Ewing And Her Books* [*with a selection from Mrs. Ewing's Letters*], vol. 18, *Collected Works*. Hutchins reprints 13 letters from JHE to Caldecott and 40 from him to her, written between 1879 and 1885. Tucker gives local recollections of JHE's life in Fredericton and prints excerpts from 20 of her Canadian letters.

Among the finest and most popular of Mrs. Ewing's works are the following:

Mrs. Overtheway's Remembrances. London: Bell & Daldy, 1869.

The Brownies and Other Tales. London: Bell & Daldy, 1870.

A Flat Iron for a Farthing. London: Bell & Sons, 1872.

Lob Lie-By-The-Fire; or The Luck of Lingborough and Other Tales. London: Bell & Sons, 1873.

Six to Sixteen. London: Bell & Sons, 1875.

Jackanapes. London: SPCK, 1883.

Daddy Darwin's Dovecot. London: SPCK, 1884.

The Story of a Short Life. London: SPCK, 1885.

A NOTE ON THE TEXT

The originals of Juliana Horatia Ewing's Fredericton letters are the property of the Hunter Archaeological Society and are in the archives of the Sheffield Central Library, Sheffield, England (HAS 60).

Our editorial policy is based on a desire to promote readability without sacrificing either scholarly accuracy or a sense of the ease and irregularity of informal correspondence. Because space limitations do not allow us to print more than three-quarters of the letters, our edition concentrates on what Mrs. Ewing has to say about Canada and about her activities as an author. Our deletions consist primarily of those letters and sections of letters in which Mrs. Ewing discusses Ecclesfield matters or briefly comments on the contents of *Aunt Judy's Magazine*. We omit the following letters: To Margaret Gatty, 18 February, 16 June, 3 November 1868; August 1869?. To Alfred Gatty, April? 1868. To Eleanor Lloyd, 23 August 1867, 22 January, 2 June, 11 August, 14 December 1868; 11 March 1869. Ellipses mark deletions from the letters we print, and all ellipses are ours.

With the exception of the first pages of Letter 1, which are written in blue pencil, the letters are written in ink on both sides of a variety of thin papers. Mrs. Ewing's hand is remarkably legible, but at times the porosity of what she calls her "vile" paper causes her ink to bleed considerably, and in a few places, tearing or cutting of a page has destroyed a word or words. When context makes the identity of blurred or missing words unmistakable, we introduce them silently into our text, but when we must guess, we place our conjectures in square brackets. In Letter 91 a blank space enclosed in square brackets indicates one word which defied all our guesswork.

We silently correct both careless spelling errors and eccentric use of the apostrophe in possessives and contractions (Mrs. Ewing habitually writes *was'nt, is'nt, wo'nt*), but we do not regularize inconsistent spellings (she alternates freely between *color* and *colour*, for example), nor do we correct misspelled proper nouns, for we think her letters are enlivened by the difficulties she has spelling words she first encounters in Canada (on occasion she writes *Fredicton, Maguadavie, moccasons, rampacks*). In our notes, however, we use the accepted spellings of such words.

We have chosen not to expand Mrs. Ewing's ampersands and her abbreviations (*Xmas, shld, cld, wld*): these seem to us to contribute significantly to the informal tone of her letters. Mrs. Ewing occasionally follows an abbreviation with a period, but she is just as apt to use a colon or to omit punctuation entirely, and here we follow her practice. We lower superscript letters in forms of address.

Distinguishing between Mrs. Ewing's upper and lower case letters is not always possible, nor is it always possible to determine her intention in word division (*fire flies, fireflies*): in both instances, we rely on our own judgement. She almost never uses hyphens to indicate compounds, so we have chosen not to add them to our text – though, of course, they will be found at printer's line breaks. Where we today might use a hyphen to indicate a compound, she is apt to use a colon; we reproduce these colons where they occur in her letters.

Type cannot accurately render Mrs. Ewing's written punctuation. We transcribe her obvious commas as commas, her obvious periods as periods, and her obvious – and numerous – dashes as dashes, but we transcribe ambiguous, downward-slanting pen-strokes (ˎ) and brief dashes (-) as full dashes (–), in order to preserve the sense of rapid, informal composition which the original letters convey. We alter punctuation in complex series to achieve consistency, and occasionally we add a comma or a dash to eliminate ambiguous phrasing.

We reduce multiple underlings to one, and italicize underlined words. When a clause or sentence ends at the right-hand margin, Mrs. Ewing usually omits punctuation. We supply it. We follow the paragraphing of the original letters, with one exception: when the end of a sentence falls noticeably short of the right-hand margin, we indent the following line if a new paragraph seems appropriate.

Many of the drawings and water-colours which Mrs. Ewing sent as gifts to her family were pasted in an album, now part of the Yorkshire Collection of the Yorkshire and Humberside Libraries Joint Services Consortium, based at the Wakefield District Library Headquarters (Sketchbook [Ewing-Gatty Collection], acc. no. 7/99083). We reproduce these drawings and water-colours as well as other pen-and-ink sketches which were cut from Mrs. Ewing's letters and pasted in the same album. The following pages contain material from Wakefield: pages 6, 7, 19, 20, 46–47, 52, 54, 76, 88, 90, 95, 98, 106–7, 113–14, 121, 145, 163–64, 167, 177, 179, 182, 231, 297; plates 4–8. We also reproduce the sketches which appear on the pages of the original letters. We enter the notation "[missing sketch]" when a letter makes an otherwise confusing reference to a sketch cut from a letter and currently lost.

PHOTO CREDITS

"Juliana Horatia Ewing" (Webster Collection #3184) and "The Charles Fisher Family" (Acc. #24832–35; C.P.F. #000156), courtesy New Brunswick Museum.

"Queen Street" (P5/881), "Reka Dom" (P5/882), "The Ewings and Hector" (PI/0016), and "Bishopscote" (P5/17), courtesy Provincial Archives of New Brunswick.

"The Bishop and Mrs. Medley" (PA-51550), courtesy Public Archives of Canada.

"Amateur Theatricals" (5405), courtesy York-Sunbury Historical Society.

"Canoe Scene" and "Portage Crossing" (Acc. 7/99083), courtesy Wakefield District Library Headquarters.

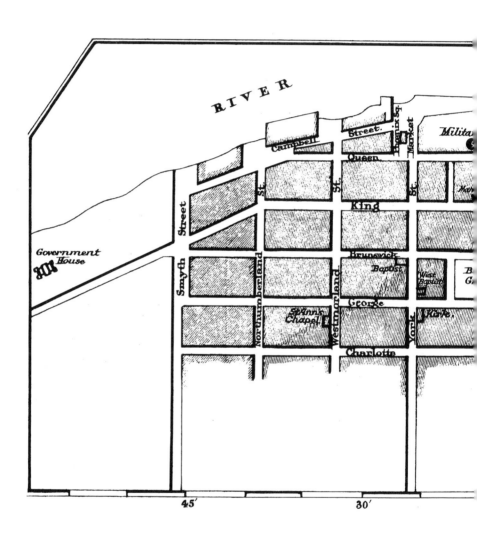

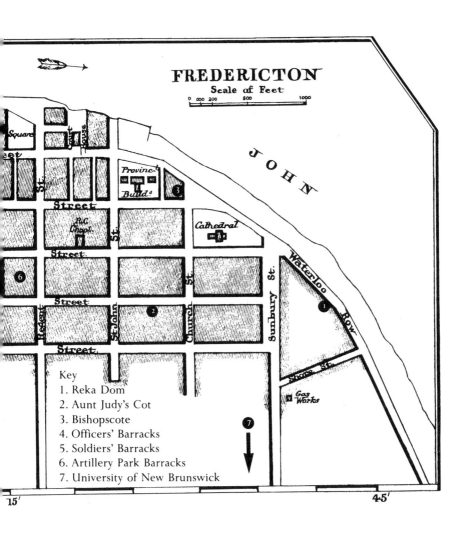

FREDERICTON

Scale of Feet

JOHN

Key
1. Reka Dom
2. Aunt Judy's Cot
3. Bishopscote
4. Officers' Barracks
5. Soldiers' Barracks
6. Artillery Park Barracks
7. University of New Brunswick

The Fredericton inset from McMillan's *Map of New Brunswick* (1867). Key added.

CANADA HOME

Some Homes are where flowers for ever blow,
 The sun shining hotly the whole year round;
But our Home glistens with six months of snow,
 Where frost without wind heightens every sound.
  And Home is Home wherever it is,
   When we're together and nothing amiss.

—Juliana Horatia Ewing

LETTER
I

Tous droits réservés!!!!!   14 June 1867. S.S. "China"[1]
Not to be published.   Mid Atlantic!! –

My darling Mum –

As it is cold and rainy on deck, I have not got up as yet, & write in my berth with Alex's blue pencil. We are having a very good passage, thank GOD, & hope to be in Halifax on Monday, if not sooner. I have been very seedy. In fact today is the 1st day I could do *this*, but I feel very comfy today. Though it has not been really rough, the chief steward says he has never had such an invalid crew, so I am not singular. It seems the more strange, as this is the 1st good passage they have had since last November, so we are fortunate. I cannot say *how* thankful I am not to have had to make this voyage alone. The helpless look of the ladies who either have no husbands or whose husbands are ill, being helped staggering hither & thither by stewards, is irresistibly ludicrous, but really awfully wretched. *I* have had the best & most capable of nurses in my husband!! He *has* been good! I have not been able to help myself with a finger, & he has dressed & undressed me like a baby, dragged me up into the air & brought me down again, read to me the little I have been able to bear it – made me laugh when I was so sore I *couldn't* bear it – made himself a beast of burden with quilts, rugs, & wraps – & fed me nightly with gruel out of a spoon!!! I cannot say that I am any more converted to the delights of sea travelling than in Antwerp days,[2] but though I have been one of the most ill – I have certainly been *the* most fortunate in being so splendidly cared for! "It has been observed" to him that if his wife doesn't

I

get well, it won't be for want of good nursing! – One day I got very bad, stiff & shivering, & he fetched a nice little army surgeon, whom he knew at Aldershot, & who is on board. He was very jolly – gave me chlorodyne (he had none but happily *I* had!) & ordered me beef tea. I have lived on beef tea ever since with great benefit – till this morning I have actually breakfasted on broiled ham & toast & tea!!! When I was very ill once I begged him to go, & send me a stewardess. I did not like him to be bothered, to which he replied that he didn't mean to let any stewardess come near me; & really I have been very thankful – for the little I have had to do with her has not prepossessed me – She is the coldest – most lugubrious – & perfunctory female I ever saw. A steward "Tom" chiefly waits on us – makes the beds &c. – a very jolly kind man, who comes into one's cabin with the air of John or Addy³ – when catching us hairdrying by the kitchen fire! – One day I was too bad to get up, so he came in to make Rex's bed (which is the shelf above mine!!) Rex declares he put his head in at the door, & saw me in bed, & Thomas with his foot apparently in my eye, bedmaking in a sort of flying attitude. Amid all the discomfort, some of our misfortunes have been awfully absurd. The day I was most ill, & Rex in an awful state of mind – I eating nothing but iced champagne – & everything "lost" & not to be found – I unable to move in my berth – when with one fatal shock – over went the iced champagne into my berth – & I lay like what's his name in the butt of Malmsey. Poor Rex nearly lost hope at this juncture – he piled everything on to the floor in a frantic heap – tore off his coat & hat – & flung them down in despair. I could hardly help laughing. We couldn't find a clean nightdress – & the cold bath not being fortuitous I struggled into a chemise – & Rex lifted me into his berth – whilst imperturbable Thomas came in like a genie – to refurnish mine! Hunting wildly for my nightdress – Rex knelt upon a tumbler! Another day lying on deck – a roll of the ship sent my beef tea gently meandering round Rex's mattrass on which I was! – The people have been awfully kind. One man sent me a tumbler of concentrated beef tea – another twice brought me strawberries (oh *so* grateful!) – & the ladies have offered me hot water bottles &c. &c. & been awfully kind. They are chiefly a sort of moving colony of Boston people – awfully

curious & characteristically Yankee—but kindhearted & lively in
the extreme. They all seem to know each other & to wish to know
everybody else. One old gentleman, very proud of a large Scotch
cap he bought in Scotland, has devoted his life to sick people in
general, & his own in particular. The day I lay on deck—all his people were grouped round too, & he went about chaffing incessantly.
The striking feature by the bye of the sick Bostonians is that they
never seem too ill to chatter & chaff each other. Imagine—the
Materfamilias wrapped like a mummy by her attentive spouse &
her face *tied up* as a finale in a brown veil (all the Yankee ladies
seem chiefly afraid of the sea air
on their skins) motionless & silent—her daughter near with
her head in Regie's oak chair
(which another sick friend opinionated had come out of the
Ark) being waited on by her father, and ordering him very
much as if he were her "young
man" but with no end of chaff
and affection—friends & cousins in all stages—advising each
other to try pork—guessing it

The Belle of Boston

wld be long before they tried another trip &c.—discovering each
other in unexpected heaps—& going into fits of laughter—"That
you—Tom? 'thought 't was a bundle o' wraps" &c. Paterfamilias loq.
in loud tones "Dinner's at 4 precise, & I 'xpects all you ladies to be
dressed in good time & look bright & spry." At intervals of 10 minutes or so he used to go up to his wife's effigy, & stooping over about
that part of the heap where her nose might be supposed to be—enquire "And *how's* the Belle of Boston?" He's a splendid old fellow at
the bottom, & they seem a devoted family party. He's awfully
civil to me—& wears this Scotch bonnet—which Rex says is a type
not to be bought nearer than Inverness, & only worn by Scotch
shepherds—as the latest European fashion!— Some of the ladies
are strange—transcendental:looking specimens—awfully clever &
managing with invalids. Dr. Den (R.'s friend) thinks one of them

must have a medical diploma. Another marvellous old party
... in a yellowish wideawake & cotton gloves, sits happed up in a
chair all day – which he moves & turns with the wind – & reads
Pepys' Diary!!! He had the place next Rex at dinner & R. asked him
to change with me – he declined very politely saying that he was
sensitive, & had chosen the seat to avoid draughts!! It matters the
less as I have never dined at table yet.

A shoal of porpoises has been seen & some mother Carey's
chickens & whales but not by *me!* But last night after Rex had
put me to bed (it being very cold during the day) he went on
deck – & found it a very mild night & lovely moonshine – so he came
down & dressed me up, & took me up on deck – & I did my 1st bit of
walking since I gave in. It really was *lovely* – You would have gone
wild over it – on one side the pale green & red streaked sky where
the sun had just set – & on the other – the sea rushing by (we were
going about 13 knots) *really* like "molten silver" – in the moonlight.
Otherwise – there is nothing to be seen, & except for being now &
then lovelily *blue* the Atlantic is not taking. Rex says he never went
a less agreeable voyage, & so says another man on board who has
been many other voyages but never this one. We have been going
splendidly but tonight a fog has come on, so we have slackened. I
hope we shall be in Halifax in good time at least on Monday. We
may have to move on to S. John's – but we hope not. I shouldn't
care much for another packing up & a day or two on the Bay
of Fundy. However even if we have – S. John's is a nice place I believe. *Trinity Sunday* [16 June]. Friday night was "really very unpleasant" – the ship *rolled* over the Newfoundland banks – & all
yesterday I was good for nothing again. Today I am better again,
but there is a fog – which will probably prevent our getting in quite
so soon as we expected. However – D. V. we shall be in tomorrow.
I staggered up yesterday morning to have my 1st sight of an *iceberg* – made a giddy sort of memorandum from which I hope to
make a sketch. The sea was dark blue, a low line of land (Cape
Race) was visible – & the iceberg stood in the distance *dead white*,
like a lump of sugar. This is done on my back in berth – so under
difficulties – but A is really like the iceberg – sea quite as deep blue

4

[as shown by JHE's blue pencil]. B line of coast. It is cold & damp – & the saloon not agreeable so I keep to my berth. Dear old Rex has read the service to me – Athanasian Creed & all – but at one point one of Inkey's[4] hysterical fits took him, I am shocked to say! – There seem to be no general prayers today. I suppose the Captain is busy with the fog &c. The fog signal is a hideous yell – like a monster pitch pipe – vainly trying to "give the note." Imagine this – alternating or making a duett with the turning out of the ashes – (a sound like coals being carted at your bedhead.) – a crashing of crockery suggestive of nothing but a saturnalia of sarvint gals with all their Missuses' china cupboards – but no! words is powerless to describe the noises of a steamship!!! Rex is a regular sailor – can't feel the motion – enjoys his wittles – (there is plenty, & nothing to complain of – but critically speaking – ship's fowls seem to be a race allied with ancient extinct species – & the amazing amount of black on everything suggests a black cook who lives with the stoker – keeps provisions in the funnel – & cooks everything in one of those infernal looking places "aft" regardless of expense in the matter of coal!!) On a voyage to Australia once – he & the Captain were the only 2 who sat at table – the ship rolled so. Rex had his chair lashed to a mast & they sat with a sherry bottle in one pocket & a glass in the other!! –

Dear old Mother – I hope to have a jollier letter to write soon from my new Home. It is a great trial to be so far from you all, but I have so much to thank GOD for, one must not dwell on this. The voyage has been so far most favorable – & the penance is nearly over which any sea passage is to me. My *dearest* love to all, & 10,000 thanks to the dear girls for all they did for me. I shld like Liz to know with my love that her quilt has been in constant operation – & old Eleanor's bag hangs aloft – Let somebody tell Mrs. Wake too, that the eau-de-cologne bottle in her bag which she filled, has been in my berth constantly while I was ill. Tell Regie – we found that everybody brings their own travelling chairs to sit on deck – so Rex determined to have mine put up. I was waiting feebly on deck when he arrived like one distraught – "*Do you know Jow how that chair is put together* – there are about 15 men at work on it below!!!" I went below, & found a selection of the ship's company struggling with crossbars – arms – back &c. &c. as you can imagine!! It was rigged up eventually however – & has been much used. Monday Evening [17 June]. Halifax. Arrived – safe & well thank G O D. Sunday was a wretched foggy day, so I stayed in my berth. We ought to have been in on Sunday evening – but the fog put us on 1/2 speed & kept us back. Then towards dark the fog suddenly lifted – & we were told we might be "in" about midnight!!! I had just turned seedy again so poor Rex had to pack – & help me to dress. However the fog came down again – we slept in our clothes ready for a start – but did not get in till about 9.A.M. Happily there was no wind – so though we lay kicking about all night – we invalids were none the worse – & a little before 8.A.M. (after fog signals – & firing guns for a pilot – & no end of weary waiting) the fog lifted, & Rex got me on deck. I was too muddleheaded to enjoy it at first, but the air revived me, & I think the first sight of Halifax was one of the prettiest sights I ever saw. When I first came up, there

Boatt — in t Halifax. June 17. 1867. 9 AM.

was no horizon: we were in a sea of mist. Gradually the horizon line appeared – then a line of low coast – muddy looking at first – it soon became marked with lines of dark wood – then the shore dotted with grey huts – then the sun came out – the breeze got milder – & the air became *strongly* redolent of pine woods – Nearer, the coast became more defined, though still low, rather bare & dotted with brushwood & gray stones low down, & crowned always with "murmuring pines." As we came to habitations which are dotted – & sparkle along the shore – the effect was what we noticed in Belgium – as if a box of very bright new toys had been put out to play with – red roofs – even red houses – cardboard looking churches – little bright wooden houses – & stiffish trees mixed everywhere. It looks more like a quaint watering place than a city – though there are some fine buildings. It is built of wood – & I should imagine that once set alight 6 & 30 hours would about see the last of it!!! We took a great fancy to the old place – which was like a new child's picture book, & I was rather disappointed to learn it is not to be our home. But Fredricton (where we are going) has superior advantages in some respects – & will very likely be quite as pretty. It is not so liable to fogs – house rent is cheaper – Rex will have sole command there – & it is a nice quiet place. It entails 45 miles of rail & 8 hours more steamer – but then we settle! – A com-

missariat officer met us – & was awfully civil – had got a carriage for us – & arranged what hotel we were to go to. (We get ^{s}10/- a day extra the 3 days we are detained here for accidental expenses.) My 1st effort was to have a good wash – & put on all the clean things I could find – & then the view from the window was one too many for me & with the spinning head & valour which Regie will remember at Antwerp – I began to sketch with Mrs. B.'s new block & paint box – (By the bye. Do let somebody tell her they are *charming* – the blocks take color so well – & the box so handy.) I felt very bad though – & rather down. It is all so strange – & I was so weak – when up came the sarvint – with a cup of tea & toast saying it was too long to wait till luncheon. It was so good – & the taste of *real* toast – & clean victuals & fresh butter – so jolly I fairly cried! It freshened me up no end – & I have really made a very fair sketch of the harbour – & Rex & I have had a long walk — & when we came back our glass was stuck over with cards of callers!! Rex's chief & wife & daughter – the one who met us ditto ditto – & another, who has called again since, & asked us to dine with him tomorrow on the other side of the harbour. We are to go about 3 & I shall take my sketching things. It is very hot & jolly, & the intense smell of pine ought to be a universal panacea! I must tell you a Major Graham & his wife – & their brother & sister in law Capt. Irvine & his wife – are destined for Fredicton too. They are in this house now, & will be nice neighbours. We start again on Wednesday at 7. A. M. & shall be glad to rest on our oars. I must stop darling Mother. Please remember – that things sent to us will come best & cheapest by sailing vessel, but nothing is to be sent without directions from us. I shall leave a tiny corner for my dear old Boy to scribble. He gets better & dearer every day. *I am all right now. Circumstances* were not favorable you know – & seasickness made matters worse. But I am very well – & no discomfort whatever – but the weakness of that *ojus* thing a sea voyage!! N.B. Rex & I overheard a Yankee saying to a friend with much fervour on Sunday night "You don't ketch me coming *this route* (pronounced *rout*) again!!" I laughed aloud! Dear love to Pater & all. Your own daughter

J. H. E.

8

I have got a short thing in my head for A.J.M. shall come soon.[5]

(Rex's Postscript.) The dear child has managed to give you rather a lugubrious idea of things in general, but then she has been very seedy till now, and has been quite knocked over by the sea voyage. It so happened that a swell came on just as we left port, and knocked over 5/6ths of the passengers in such a way that they never fairly recovered. Julie was *among* the worst, though there were many others quite as ill as she was; but, owing to many circumstances, she had less reactive power than some others, and as the Atlantic is a nasty sea to cross, her experience of seafaring, so far, has been most unfavorable.

We have, notwithstanding, been very happy, and now that we are on shore, I fancy all will be well with her. This place is *much less* of a foreign country than anywhere I have previously been, and we have been very much pleased with what little we have seen of it to-day.

We are lucky (as it appears) in going to Fredericton for many reasons. I shall be very happy to come to an anchor! I have not had my things unpacked for over six months. Julie has been sketching all day very jollily – there is a pretty view from our window, and she has done the first of what, I hope, will be an extensive and charming collection, for you all to look over with us when we come home. Please address to her as follows

Mrs. AE
Fredericton
New Brunswick

Ever afftly yrs AE.

[JHE's Continuation]

Monday Night [17 June].

Mr. Routh (R.'s Chief) & his daughter, & another officer have been in again. I like them all very much. Mr. R. is most kind & jolly, & has asked us to tea on Wednesday, for we are not to be moved now till Friday, & then are to go to S. John's for a few weeks to take another man's place, before going forward to Fredericton. Mr. R. says F. is very pretty. S. John's very nice too. I expect I shall sketch my head off! The one care on my mind amid all these changes – is the Dixon's porcelain card-dish!!!! Hitherto I have preserved it unbroken, & now we have so many cards to put in it, it wld be 1000 pities if it fell a victim to the changes of military life!!! Such a warm moonlight night, with such a strong smell of pines! – I am very glad we stay till Friday in some ways. I want to get 2 or 3 sketches of the place before we leave it. But I pity poor old Rex & his baggage – (& indeed am not perfect in that line myself – living at present on my oldest hat & one garter!) – We tried for some linen collars today, but are far behind the Atlantic Wave of Civilisation – "We sell nothing but *paper* now Sir!" — Good night dearest Mum. Yr loving & very jolly – J. H. E.

(Rex:) Certainly Civilisation has not come Westward as regards *collars*!

I did not say before how marvellous it feels to me to have my *Home* always with me; so that it is immaterial *where* our tent is pitched. I am glad Jowie likes this country thus far – in the *sketching* line it is a *grand* new field – and I pointed out a *red* house by the water which certainly *was* REKA DOM'[6] –
Paper done –

ADieu   AE

[JHE's Continuation]

Wednesday. 19. June. Rex is out, so I write a bit more dear Mum, before this goes. We are getting on capitally, & liking it all better than at first – even. I think it does capitally for us. We are in a private hotel, the best in the place – a small queer *looking* wooden house, but very comfortable inside – & *capital* grub. Mr. Routh says it is rather expensive, but we get our extra $10/- till we leave – & I believe Mr. R. is going to try & continue it till we leave S. John's.

(We shall be there probably about a fortnight or 3 weeks) Our room here was high up, but today some people have cleared out, & we are down in a jolly one looking out on trees, with some splendid arm chairs & awfully comfy. Yesterday I had a grand *tidy* of all Rex's things whilst he was out – & my own too! – Our dressing table looks very swell. I put out all Mr. Hawthorn's bottles from the dressing case &c. &c. & Rex's & my photo.s in their frames stand on each side! We feed table d'hôte, & hitherto have had no sitting room, the house being too full, & now this room is so very jolly, I think we shall hardly need one. Breakfast at 8.30 when Miss Lovett (whom we secretly call Todgers – she being a good specimen – & a splendid "Bailey Junr" waiting at table under her orders.) presides.[7] Very good breakfasts – broiled salmon & hot rolls &c. Lunch at one. Dinner at 6 – & then tea. Yesterday we drove in a cab to call on the McKinstreys, & drove on over the Common where reviews are held – & saw the rink where they skate in winter – & I got Rex to stop the cab, & we got out to hunt on the boggy ground for flowers. I found two lovely ones I never saw, & having no means of preserving – I have made coloured drawings of them. Rex has given me his big note:book – & I am going to devote it to drawings of plants. I have made a successful beginning I think, & we are very proud of this new "collection." One flower is a pale blue 4 pointed star with yellow centre. The other a low growing dark leaved thing, the actual flower being like a single blossom of white hawthorn. Neither have scent. Also I found a pale pink lichen. As this is early summer I hope I shall pretty well see all the flowers through. I hear there is one like white wax & sweet – the "May Flower" – we are going to look for it. (Queen's accession [20 June].) I have discovered that there are daily prayers at S. Luke's at 9.15. So this morning Rex & I went to Church. Plain reading, but chanting, & a hymn – "Holy, Holy, Holy." No great "performance" – but *very* blessed & pleasant somehow to hear the familiar Lord's Song in a strange land! The last 2 Sundays were wretched enough – & I have not been to Church since All Saints in London.[8] I *did* feel thankful dear old Mum, as you will understand, for all my happiness – to be here safe & sound, my Boy *so* good & kind – & such a hopeful lookout before us, & so many little pleasures by the way. I pray every day that we may all meet happily in old England after a while – & I believe we shall, & I even now look forward to all we shall have to show you. I think you will almost like my *new* sketchbook (the flowers) best of all – I do *the* flower in colours – & accessory bits of grass &c. in pencil. Rex says one *bud* is the loveliest thing I have ever done!!!! But he likes all I do – GOD bless him! Excuse promiscuous information, but washing is dear. ^{S}2/- a dozen. House rent *here* is awfully dear – but cheaper at Fredricton. Another happy fact is that the oldest of old clothes pass muster – & from all we hear – I think a young couple who want to live cheaply, & at the same time keep up the imperial dignity of an Alexander & a Juliana could not have a more fortunate destination. A *sole command* – in a quiet lovely place – where you may wear anything, & I fancy living is cheap. We know 4 nice people there to start with. We are to succeed a man who was very fond of a *garden*, so if we get his house I shall have a bit to grub in in summer, & to crown all though *here* Church matters are dull looking enough they say the Cathedral at Fredricton is beautiful,[9] & the service musical & good: so you will probably hear of Rex in connection with it – & we shall speak of practise nights as composedly as if we were in Ecclesfield. I have begun my little legend for A.J.M. but somehow my hands seem full – & we are going out for the afternoon to some jolly people — the Mannings. N.B. *She* came out as a bride, & was ill the whole way, & *they* were a fortnight coming!! *She* had a throat, & is now strong & well. So the Rouths tell me. We went there to tea last night, & they were awfully jolly & kind. Rex & the young ladies flirted at the piano, & I chatted to Mr. R. & his wife. Nothing could be kinder than they were. We walked home in the moonlight about II. We are rather lucky in being here tomorrow, as it is *the* grand day of the year in Halifax. The birthday of the city. 100 salutes are to be fired at sunrise, & 100 at sunset, & all sorts of festivities through the day, which will be fun.[10] My cursory judgement of shops here, is that everything is *dearer* & *inferior* – like a mushroom watering place. I see no prospect of engraving our plate, & wish we had left it – *I* believe it will be cheaper to send home for anything we want. By the bye tell Madge that unfortunately *her* old winter dress was sent instead of mine. It lasted the voyage, but will do no more. Tell her that *mine* is I know in much better condition, & that when we *do* have a parcel I had better have it. It will last me the winter for common, in this out of the way region – will probably not fit her well – & she had much better have a new one than I, as Ecclesfield requires much better dressing than Nova Scotia!!! Rex just came in – has been to the fish market he tells me to tell you – & it is a wonderful sight – awfully fine salmon, one – 24 lbs weight — & ᵈ6 a pound!! If we get very low in the world we must live on fish! – *Such* dear old black Dogs "go about the city"!! – Best love to all the doges – including dear Trotus.[11] P. M. Rex & I went down to the fish market that I might see it. Splendid fish certainly! Coming back we met an old N. American Indian woman – such a picturesque figure. We talked to her, & R. gave her something. I do not think it 1/2 so degraded looking a type as they say. A very broad – queer – but I think acute & pleasant looking face. Since I came in I have made 2 rather successful sketches of her.[12] She wore an old common striped shawl, but curiously thrown round her so that it looked like a chief's blanket – a black cap embroidered with beads – black trousers stuffed into moccasins – a short black petti-

coat – & a large, gold colored cross on her breast, & a short jacket trimmed with scarlet, a stick & basket for broken victuals. She said she was going to catch the train! It sounded like hearing of Plato engaged for a polka!! – I have got notes of a nigger – & a gentleman carrying a fish nearly as big as himself – but I wish I had Maggie's fingers for the figures! Am I not industrious? But I feel that though I have years before me in Fredricton we *may* never come here again. I think I must now say Goodbye dear old Mum. You will hear again in a fortnight – & it will take you nearly that time to read this . . . . My – *Our* dear love to all. We are very well and very very very happy,

> & your ever most loving children
> J. H. E.   AE.

LETTER
2

> Fredericton. New Brunswick.
> [ca. 25] July. 1867.

My dear Mrs. Ewing –

Thank you very much for all the kind messages you have sent to me through Alexander. *I* am going to write you our news this time. I do not know what he has told you already, & he is out just now, so I can't ask him. You must forgive me if I send you old news!

Since we must be "abroad" somewhere – I do not think we could well have been more fortunate in a station than we are in being sent here. There is that most disagreeable Atlantic between us & Great Britain — but otherwise it is in many respects very like Home. We hear rather appalling accounts of the winter, but we were told awful things of the summer heats; & yet (except for occasional oppressive days) we have found it delightful. It is rather blazing in the morning often, & makes one rather giddy if one attempts to walk much – but the evenings & nights are delicious, & quite cool. Fredericton is on the river, & all by the riverside it is lovely, & we have not yet been able to decide by what lights, & at which time of day it looks most beautiful. Very fine willows grow on the bank – & the fire flies float about under them like falling stars. The moonlight & starlight nights are splendid, & the skies are particularly beautiful. We were detained for some days both at Halifax and at S. John: but we are very glad that our lot has fallen here rather than in either of those places.[1] Halifax has lovely country near it, but S. John is a *town* pure et simple, & I think if one must live in a town, one likes it to be as highly civilized a city as possible, & S. John is more like a watering place without the shore. I suppose the New Brunswickers would be duly indignant at my not calling Fredericton a town – for it is a *city!*[2] but it is all in lovely country, & the streets are planted with trees, & have no names & *very* few lamps to them – & are most of them like shady lanes with pretty wooden houses with (generally) very pretty faces at the windows! For another attraction which this place possesses, is the beauty of the women, both of the upper and lower classes. Not that we have seen any one *very* beautiful woman (such as one sometimes sees at home) but that almost every girl you meet is very *pretty*, & very gentle & sweet looking. The young ladies have particularly pleasant unaffected manners too. I tease Alex: & tell him that if he *had* come out without me, I don't know what the consequences would not have been! We were not surprised to hear that when the 15th were stationed in these parts – 17 of them married ladies of the province!! The 22d Regt is stationed here just now[3] – & seems a particularly nice one – there are some very nice married couples among them whom we know, & all the officers seem particularly gentlemanlike & friendly. They have a capital band – & a string band as well as wind instruments.

We happened to arrive here in a very gay week, & so came in for 2 balls – one at Government House,[4] and one given by the 22d. Alexander & I had never been at one together before – & so we had our 1st valse in New Brunswick! We came to the satisfactory conclusion that we had neither of us ever been exactly suited with a partner before, & in fact enjoyed it immensely. He keeps better time, & tires me less than any man I ever danced with. I danced with some of the 22d at their ball—but he wouldn't dance with anybody but me—though there were some wonderful young ladies there, with complexions exactly like wax!!!!!! We came away rather early, & walked back to our hotel which was close to the Mess room—where the ball was held. It seemed so strange—walking in an evening dress with only a white bernous & nothing on my head—so late at night. But it was a mild lovely summer night,—& walking about in my wedding dress with Alexander in his uniform—among the old willows, & picturesque wooden streets, & fire flies—by the light of a good many stars, & very few lamps—it was more like being in a fairy tale, or taking part in an opera than anything else!!

Some people who have a pretty place in the neighborhood asked us to a picnic the other day. It was in one of the lovely pine woods that abound here, & very pretty it was. There were lots of people & it was very jolly.

The ferns, flowers, mosses, & lichens in the woods about here are most beautiful, & it is an utterly new pleasure to me to find such lots of plants I have never seen. In fact the Botany of these parts seems richly luxuriant & to have been very little investigated. I have dried a few things in my blotting books &c. but we have no apparatus with us. However we have ordered 2 boards at the carpenter's for a press, & when we have out a box from home, which we are going to have soon, we shall have some proper paper & portfolio sent—& I hope we shall be able to bring home some specimens of the beautiful things out here. For want of proper means to preserve those we first got—I have been making rough colored sketches of them in a notebook of Alexander's which we have devoted to the purpose; & whenever we meet anybody who seems likely to be knowing on the subject—we ask the names of the flowers. Some have exquisite perfumes—which unhappily one can neither figure nor preserve!— One almost wonders that more plants from this country are not cultivated in England. As whatever can stand these winters would well live with us. We have just heard of some wonderful orchids in a bog 2 or 3 miles away, & I am awfully impatient

to get at them, for vegetation is so rapid here, the flowers are out &
then gone in a day or two. But I don't quite know when my good-
man will be able to take me, for we are in the thick of a more practical collection – namely getting things together to move into the
house which we have taken![5] Can you fancy Alexander at a *sale*,
bidding for pots & pans? Our predecessor's effects were sold just
after our arrival & we attended the auction of his remains 2 hot days
in succession. A. looks quite as dignified & solemn as Alexander the
Great, his manoeuvres (such as bidding high at 1st on principle &c.)
amount to military tactics – & he sees 12 patty pans at 1 cent each
knocked down to him with the eye of a conqueror!! He really
managed splendidly though. We started on the principle of only
bidding for absolute necessaries – & we really got a lot of useful
things wonderfully reasonably considering where we are. Almost
all manufactured articles are dear; but *living* is decidedly cheap. For
a good many things such as house linen, winter furs, &c. we shall
send home. It is really cheaper, & we are going to have a box, *and*
Alex's dear old dog out in a sailing ship before winter. It is so hot
that we even mean to do without blankets till we get them from
England. Those sort of things are both dearer & inferior here. We
came away in such a hurry we did not get many things we might
otherwise have done before our start. I am sending you a small
sketch of our house – & also one from a hasty sketch I made in my
notebook as we came up the river into Fredericton. It was in fact
our 1st view of our new home. They are hardly worth sending, but
the paper wouldn't take color, & also I have got my left hand in a
sling with an inflamed finger, which makes me awkward in drawing & writing. (By the bye Rex thinks you will think this letter is
written by *him*! Our handwritings are very much alike; which we
considered a significant coincidence!) My invalid finger is very
inconvenient at this moment, when I want to be unpacking,
hemming kitchen cloths, &c. &c. &c!!! but it brought me into
acquaintance with the surgeon of the 22d, who is an Aberdeen man
(a Dr. Adams[6] – Rex thinks he was at college with him.) – He is a
botanist, & told us about the orchids. You cannot think how lovely
it is coming up the river from S. John to this place. The coloring is
so exquisite – the sky & clouds are so beautiful – the pine woods

look at times the richest purple in the distance – & the foliage of the white birches – & brushwood – & grass near the shore was of most vivid pale greens when we came up. I suppose in autumn – when the maple trees turn scarlet – it will be lovelier still. People say that whatever you may have heard or read about American woods in autumn – nothing but seeing them can give you an idea of the wonderful brilliancy of their colors. Last night (July. 24) – after a *very* oppressive day a thunderstorm came on. When it does rain here it rains with a will. One looks out of the window, & the water appears to be coming down as if poured out of gigantic buckets. The rain stopped at last – but then we saw 1st the most wonderful sky, & 2dly the finest lightning – I ever beheld. The sky was the most intense deep blue – it is impossible to exaggerate the beauty of the color, & on this about sunset were cumulus clouds of such rosy & golden tints as it is impossible to describe. Behind 2 banks of them there was a sort of golden glare – & Rex & I both thought it was like what one might imagine Sinai to have looked like when the glory of the Lord was like devouring fire on the top of the Mountain. One almost expected to see the tables of the Law appear! After this faded, 2 masses of clouds came together, & then for I should think an hour — the most splendid lightning played between them. We sat watching it for long. The sheet lightning was almost incessant, & the forked ran splendid amongst it. It was rather funny to see the calm uninterested countenance of a man over the way – who was looking out of *his* window. He could see nothing of course. *We* were looking over his head & over his house! I must tell you about *our* house. You will, I think, be amused at its *palatial* appearance. It *is* much larger than necessary, though Rex justly says I always give it a more magnificent appearance on paper than it really possesses. It *has* however – 21 rooms in it!!!!!! though they are not very large ones. We *could* keep a hotel – or invite my 7 brothers & sisters to visit us! One room now goes by the name of my youngest brother, who is a great chum of ours & was a most discreet "gooseberry picker" before we were married!! – & we talk of giving *Trot* (the dog) a bedroom-sitting room (& he *might* have a dressing room!) to himself when he arrives. Don't think us quite mad! We had much humbler intentions but it fell out thus: when we arrived we were told we should have to wait a long time for a house as none was vacant. Of course hotel life is expensive, & it was desirable to get one as soon as possible. The 2d day—Rex discovered this one—which was in an awful state of disrepair, but was being put in order by the landlord—a scotch Professor at the College here. The Principal in fact.[7] He has let us have it for 10 months (that is till next May.) for £25—& as we should probably have had to pay quite as much for a smaller house, Rex took it, & we are only furnishing just what we want. It has many great advantages. It is in the best situation we could have chosen. There is a well of good water, & from unperfect drainage the water up in the town is far from wholesome sometimes.[8] We have very nice neighbors (a Professor Campbell & his family).[9] We are close to the Cathedral.[10] We are not overlooked, & have a lovely lookout over the river—with a ferry boat

just opposite to our front door.[11] There is ample space for a good garden, & our landlord is building us a huge sort of barn[12] —which I fancy is to embrace coach house—stables &c. & which (as we possess no equipage) I think will have to be devoted to the *pig* we purpose to keep; & who will consequently have as much spare space as ourselves!! Fancy Alexander coming in yesterday & announcing to me his intention (please the pigs!) of fattening a porker for Xmas!!! One of the 22d— a newly married man who was at the *sale* with us—has told him that a young pig may be bought for 1/2 a dollar, & live on the household refuse till Xmas—& then either be killed or sold. As we neither of us like pork—I think *our* "little pig will go to market"—!— Most opportunely in turning out his (very untidy!) drawers yesterday, he found a 1/2 dollar which had been there since he was in China.[13] So we may look upon the pig as purchased—so to speak. I think our only misfortune has been the loss of my sewing machine—which rather goes to my heart—as it was a neat little hand lock one which I bought to make my trousseau with. It was lost in some of our endless *moves*—& we fear has been stolen. But we have not quite given up hope of seeing it again.[14] I never had one before, but now I shall groan over every duster I hem without it!!—

[*The sketch (including key) is from a missing letter.*]

In the little sketch of the house. A. B. are the windows of our dining room towards which we have got a table—2 chairs—& an impromptu sideboard made of packing cases!! It looks out on the river. E. & F. are the windows of our bedroom—a charming room with a blue & white paper (our landlord allowed us to choose the papers) & *such* a view. Rex kept me awake from 3 A.M. till we got up this morning in raptures with the lovely lights upon the river &c. & with the novel satisfaction of using a telescope in bed. We ex-

20

amined a tug steamer & a man in a canoe. (We think of keeping a canoe ourselves.) C. is the bay window of our drawing room. D. of an unfurnished room like it. We have hired a harmonium for the old boy to play upon, & when the books get up, & some water colors of mine on the walls &c. &c. it will be a very pretty room. I wish you could see us in it. Alex: is going to add a line. I hope I have not wearied you with this long letter. Your son is the kindest & best of dear boys, as I need not tell *you*! & I promise you that please GOD – I will do my best to make him happy. I hope we may meet someday & I am always dear Mrs. Ewing your affate daughter in law

Juliana Horatia Ewing.

LETTER

3

29 July. 1867. Fredericton.

My dearest Mother.

I can only write a very short epistle this time – we are so very busy getting into our house: but I shall write (& send the list for the parcel) by the Quebec route which you will get in a day or 2.[1] I wish you (oh *how* I wish!) you cld come in at this moment. You would laugh. We have moved in in spite of the carpenters – I have got a *gal* in spite of the fates – & the dismal prognostications of lady friends – & am sitting in our drawing room – heaped pellmell with books &c. &c. & a pale ale bottle & glasses – Rex, I, & our landlord Dr. Jack having been partaking of a friendly glass to relieve our feelings after a hot morning's work. The front door is wide open – do. this door – ditto the windows – carpenters & painters in-side & out. I have just been into the kitchen to tell Maggy (my "gal") & another woman – a maltese – who is here washing blankets &c. for me – to roast a bit of mutton for lunch. Meanwhile the Commis-sariat "messenger" has carried off Rex – whither I know not!! We thought it was best to move in as soon as there was space to put up a bed – & the kitchen stove was in its place. So here we are. We *shall be* rather elegant than otherwise when we settle down I think, at present we are rather in the backwood style – & very good fun it is. Till today we have been keeping our hotel rooms – & going up there for late dinner &c. Yesterday morning to our dismay our maltese never appeared – (she had had to go to Govt House we afterwards found) so we lighted our stove & made our own breakfast. Rex professed himself incompetent to cook the chops, so *I* undertook that department – & turned them out very creditable I consider!!! Today my gal has come, & we have moved in altogether, & she & I have been busy this morning putting away clothes &c. &c.... (Must go with the Orderly about some boxes upstairs. Adoo!) I have set him to work – He is Rex's Orderly – an awfully "cute" nice man – one of the 22d. Rex is going off on an expedition into the country on H.M. Service & as he will have a trap, he is going to take me with him. I anticipate it awfully. We are going tomorrow I believe. One of my little fingers has been rather inflamed, (I suppose I hurt it or something.) & Rex got the Regt Surgeon (who attends "*us*" gratis) to look at it. The treatment only amounted to a "poultice" – but I was very glad to see him. For he is an agreeable & clever looking man. A Scotchman – an Aberdeen medical man – the son of another doctor, & so likely to be clever, which is very satisfactory if one *were* seedy. Not that I am the least in want of his talents or Rex either! – Also he is a botanist – & told me something about my flowers. I have had 2 boards made & hope to get some tomorrow.... We have the most charming bedroom. 2 windows looking east to the river – & Rex says the view beats the Lake Hotel at Killarney! He wakes at unearthly hours & lies wrapt in the enjoyment of using a telescope in bed!!!!! He kept us "on the go" from 3.A. M. the 1st morning & indeed it was lovely – the white mists rolling off the river – sunrise behind the pine woods & willows – (we always sleep with both windows wide open – unless it is damp.) & canoes coming down – reminding one of Hiawatha's.

"Like a yellow leaf it floated."

They *do* look just like autumn leaves floating on the water. I don't think Rex will exist long without one. N.B. We think of keeping a *Pig*!!!!! By the bye Rex says since you asked if yr birds might fly over my barn – that I am to tell you that a large barn is rising in the hands of the carpenters just outside. (I don't know what we shall put into it!) – but I wish your birds could fly over it. Did I tell you that here they build houses for the swallows on the roofs of the houses? R. says I must put it into print — I think I must!!! . . .

I have no more time today. With our dear love to all I am

Ever dearest Mum – Your
Most loving daughter
Juliana Horatia Ewing.

. . . Implore the girls to read Lamb's letter to a friend in Sydney aloud. (in the Elia)² We roared over it as R. read it to me before breakfast the other day! It *is* so appropriate to one's feelings!!!!

LETTER
4

1. August 1867 Fredericton. N.B.
REKA DŌM'.

My dearest Father.

I am going to write to you this time, though I won't expect you to send me a long answer. The mail came in yesterday, & all the dear letters were a great treat! – The Mum's seemed to me in rather better force: for which we were awfully glad. I *expect* the Quebec Mail will go today, but we are not so near the P. Office here – & in that department the most blissful 'ignorance on anything remotely connected with its own business – prevails. I strove to send my little MS. last mail by Book Post in vain. You should have seen the man handle it, & poke at it as if he smelt treason – then he gave me a soulpiercing glance of J.P. severity & astutely observed – "There's *writing!*" "Certainly –" I said, in an equally knowing & decisive manner – "It's manuscript — BOOK POST!" But after due consultation with his fat principal,¹ that gentleman from a distant post of

authority shouted with the determination of a policeman in a
pantomime – "No! no! we can't have it! Charge it full – charge it
full –" or words to that effect. The affairs of this public office seem
to be conducted as roman Catholics hope we may be saved – by
"invincible ignorance"!! The fat gentleman certainly would never
have seen the Emperor's new clothes – for anyone less fit for his
situation – it is difficult to imagine.

    11. *August. Sunday.* I have been so utterly busy, dear Pater, that
this letter has been put away, & Rex wrote a mere scrap to the
Mum with my list of commissions. We have had some very rainy
weather – and some *intensely* hot (even Rex allowing that it *was*
overpowering – & like China). Today – a cloudless sky – & brilliant
sun; but a refreshing breeze. And whatever breeze is to be got – we
get – living by the river. We had just got into our house when I
wrote a *letter* last, & today I think may be considered our 1st day
of comfortably "settling" – I hope so. My new *sarvint* has come
today – & you must expect a good many *cook stories*[2] this mail –
as "our talk has been of" *gals* – & cookery for the last few
weeks. . . . *Gals* applied for my situation of as many shapes & sizes
as Monsr. Crépin had tutors,[3] but none of them would *shoot*, &
eventually an old lady friend here recommended a "gal" of 14,
strong & capable &c. She was a small help, & very small help we
found her. I thought I might train her, but she was *very* scatter-
brained, & I doubtless a poor instructor. I instructed her many
times in laying the cloth, but she had a predilection for putting
tumblers & wine glasses as part of the *tea* turnout, which was suggestive of spirits with the tea!! One day before I went out I gave her
a tablecloth to hem. When Rex & I returned we found her in the
drawing room, seated by the writing table hemming one end of the
cloth, whilst a friend worked at the other, who (by the stains
she left on my new linen) was of the "berrying" profession. (A
strawberry gatherer!) Both hems had to be cut off & resewn by one
of the soldiers' wives!!! One day she told me her mother was ill, &
she should leave next day: which she did, & I have not seen her
since!! Since then we have pretty well "done for ourselves" in concert with Rex's most admirable orderly – William. His surname is
Cluloe – & as it is the thing to call him by it, I tried hard to learn his

extraordinary name; but never could remember it. However I found it marked in large letters on his shirt front – so I have only to gaze steadfastly at his chest – & say "Cluloe! will you fetch me a gill of milk?" &c. &c. At this moment the admirable individual is "annexing" (military for *boning*)[4] some of the wood about, & the carpenter's tools & nails, & is knocking up a stand for me, to put one of Rex's chests on – to cover with red moreen for a sideboard!!!! (N.B. It is *Monday* [12 August] now.) Our other "help" was also called off by family illness, & we absolutely had *nobody* but Cluloe. Tell the girls to imagine me gravely making our bed in concert with a tall individual in the uniform of H.M. 22d Regt. I don't think he had been much accustomed to bedmaking, but he has the greatest dislike to being supposed incapable of anything. He used to watch me beating the pillows on my side, & beat his accordingly in the utmost silence & gravity. Once when Rex came in & caught us at it, the ghost of a smile disturbed his composure. He annexed all he found necessary to the work of the kitchen – he evolved kitchen cloths & washed floors, & wiped wine glasses *somehow*, & one day (alas!) I found him cleaning the plate with knife powder, as I afterwards saw him brush his own trousers with the shoe brush!!!! Poor old Rex used to get wild on my account, & threaten to carry me back to an hotel – but I am awfully glad we held out; it wld have been miserably inconvenient moving again – & my new servant promises very well – & cooks very nicely. *Our* cookery was wonderful!! Truly wonderful! One thing we could all do – Rex, I, Cluloe, & my sarvint, Susan Rose —— cook potatoes. We were really dab hands – & I never tasted better cooked "Murphies." My new help doesn't do them 1/2 so well! – Tell Dot that I *did* make 6 pots of raspberry jam though, by the Domestic Economy[5] receipt – & it was 1st rate!!! But Rex refused to allow me to stand over the stove in this hot weather, so latterly – I have had to cook in the pantry, & keep Cluloe running backwards & forwards to the stove. Thus: "Cluloe!" "Yes 'M." "Mr. Ewing does not like me to be near the stove (the principle of obeying orders quite comprehended by C.!!) — please boil this egg hard, & you can put down the meat." Our common incompetency was delicious – (Cluloe with the stove!) C. with a very grave face would say "About how long should the joint roast, or the beans boil M'm?" & either I made a happy guess, or retired to look it up in the Cookery Book – (as M.M.[6] taught Spanish – with the English Gil Blas in the next room!!) Dinner hour was literally when "wittles was up." Through all our troubles (& our neighbours are little better off.) the comfort decent knives & silver have been you cannot think! – It has really given a decent *appearance* & a comfortable *feel* to our table, & "Domestic Economy" – tell the Mum – has been invaluable!!! My new servant has lived in good places, & promises to be very comfortable in every way, so we are in smooth water again. Last Thursday we went to dine at Government House – the 1st time. About 22 people, & as we were in the very worst of our difficulties — a capital dinner was an absolute treat. I told an officer I sat near that I heard my coming sarvint was a good cook (we were telling each other cook stories) but he shook his head & said "The *General* has a good cook – *but nobody else.*" It was a *dullish* party – & poor old Rex was rather *ennuyé*. As it happened *I* enjoyed myself – for the General[7] introduced me to the Bishop, & to my considerable astonishment the old gentleman took me in to dinner. Why on earth I was given to him, we could not make out – as he was 2d swell to the Governor, & sat opposite to him in the middle of the table: but I enjoyed it uncommonly, for he is very clever, & awfully amusing, & told me the funniest anecdotes. He has been away till now: but next day *he* & Mrs. Medley called on us – & we like them both extremely [Plate 9].[8] Mrs. M. told us some clergyman had been raving in their house about the Mum's writings, & had said that whole pieces were taken out of Aunt Judy's Magazine into American newspapers – sometimes without an acknowledgement. When he went away the little Bishop looked at me in his pointblank way & said very kindly after his rather awkward fashion – "If you would like to see Maryland Church[9] – I will drive you there. Not tomorrow. Saturday is a busy day with me. But next week." Isn't it kind? So I expect we shall probably get to see some of the country in very good company. Yesterday he preached both A.M. & P.M. & I really doubt if any of our english swells beat him on the whole. The learning, the logic, the irrepressible irony at times, the intense simplicity, & the exquisite touches of pathos – I hardly think Oxon – Vaughan – Ebor[10] – or anybody could excel. He preached A. M. on the "whole creation groaning &c." & brought out a forcible & (to me) new idea. That if we had been alive in any of the 'periods' of great 'disturbance' of the physical world (the glacial – or volcanic &c. &c.) our faith would probably have failed to foresee the physical beauty & order that would come out of it all. The rocks on the sunny hillside – the waters in their own places – the flowers &c. &c. – & that although the divisions of the Church of Christ – the distractions & confusions & inconsistencies which make Xtianity seem almost useless – the darkness of dispensations & all the disturbance of the moral world – make one inclined to give up hope – we were to draw comfort from Creation. He had been charmingly sarcastic on the hastiness & almost invariable erroneousness of man's very self-satisfied judgements of Providence in all times – but there was a sort of earnest authority that was very impressive, as he admonished us that since GOD had loved His lower Creation so well as to bring such beautiful order out of such ghastly confusion – He *would* bring out of all the moral disorder & disturbance a new heaven & a new earth for those whom Jesus died to redeem. A paragraph towards the end nearly upset me, coming when one had been on the stretch so long. He gave a practical turn, & speaking of the love of Christ – "A love such as no earthly friend can feel for us – suffering as no earthly friend ever suffered for one – that intercession as no earthly friend *can* plead – a Home at last – such as none who love us can provide here, however they may wish & try." He uses very simple forcible language – has a voice as soft – though not quite as feminine – as Vaughan's – & it is as clear as a bell – He hardly ever lifts his eyes, & uses no action whatever – his premises & deductions – his biting bits of sarcasm – & his touches of pathos go down the Cathedral without the slightest assistance from "delivery" — but they are just the reverse of the style of sermon which old Goulburn calls "like the arrow shot at a venture that hit King Ahab, with the difference that they seldom hit anybody in particular."[11] When he is most severe, he looks so awfully innocent (the old beggar!!) It makes one inclined to laugh, when one perceives how he is mentally wielding the flagellum!!! P. M. He preached on Rizpah the daughter of Aiah & the execution of Saul's sons. It was *cleverer* than the other. One of the ablest bits of biblical criticism

one ever heard. Rex said the *composition* seemed to him so perfect.
It really is a wonderful piece of good fortune to be under him. He
has been out 22 years (or more – I forget) & he 'trots about – turns up
at the 7.30.A.M. daily service & trottles into the Cathedral with a
pastoral staff *much* bigger than himself.[12] *Endless* people have called
on us, & some of them are very jolly. Tell Regie I have got a "relic"
for him, which I will send him. It is a bit of lichen from the name-
less grave of one of the 1st settlers here. In old Judge Parker's
garden (a very pretty place with a lovely peep of the river through
trees like an italian lake) — in a field are the graves of the 1st
settlers. On one are some rudely cut initials, the last being B. "The
ancestor of all the Barkers" said the old lady (Mrs. P.)[13] As I stooped
over the graves I annexed a piece of lichen much as R. will remember annexing horsehair from Barnvelt's Chair!!!!![14] It was really an
affecting sight amid the prosperity to which this lovely spot has
attained. One imagines how beautiful it must have looked to their
eyes as a spot to 'settle' in. No stone had any mark but that one, &
ladyfern grew amongst them. Tell the Mum that the book which
Rex gave me for my birthday gift is a *delightful* one of Asa Gray's
with awfully good figures.[15] We have made out a great many both
of the ferns & flowers (R. has – chiefly) & we have a good many in
press – & today I am going to try & get some paper to "fix" them in.
The old boy went to a sale on my birthday too – & the next thing I
heard of him was Cluloe arriving with all Bach's fugues in 2 vols.
which he had bought for a dollar ($4/2) "the lot." — as a birthday
present to himself!!! (He is playing away at this moment.) We have
hired a very nice harmonium & he is going in for his things – now
we have ceased to be our own cook & man-of-all-work. He has
been distractingly busy, for all the flour was bad[16] – & the Contractor's bread uneatable – & the men had to live on biscuit yesterday, & there was only a limited supply of that. He was expecting
flour from New York, but it has been kept out by fogs. On Saturday
we were down between 10 & 11 P.M. to the wharf to meet the night
steamer & quickly discover if there were any decent flour aboard,
as Rex wld have given any price for it. Amusingly enough "well met
by moonlight" we fell in with the flour contractor – *on the same er-
rand.* We found several barrels, & it was awfully amusing to see the

old party fumble out the plug of wood – & Rex dipping his nose & moustaches in to test the new arrival!!!!!! By the bye I made an allusion to my unfortunate sewing machine – which must have been puzzling without further explanation. Alas! alas! it is lost! The difficulty of keeping our baggage together during our incessant moves has been great. We had 2 lists & looked very sharp up to this point, & Rex thinks he could swear he saw it in our 1st hotel *here*.[17] But we could only get a most cramped & confined room – & so a lot of things were stored away in a sort of lumber room off the bar. It was not till days afterwards that Rex discovered that odd men who came in late had been put to sleep in this room – (It was a very busy time.) He got our things away at once, but when we came to move to the other hotel, the sewing machine was nowhere to be found – & we cannot hear of it. It is really a severe disappointment to me – I have so many bits of finishing sewing – mere tacking together – for which it would have been invaluable. But it is no good fretting about it – though I have felt it awfully. It has certainly been ill fated!! – It is *just* within the bounds of possibility it *might* turn up yet – but it is very unlikely I fear. Both the Bishop & others have warned us to get everything we can get in England – (of clothing &c.) as everything is dear & bad here. Rex's love & he is much obliged for your letter. He has been awfully busy as I said. This morning he was off before 6.A.M. & came back in time to go with me to the early service. He has been tearing up & down in the heat all day lately, & it has worried me so he should be so uncomfortable at home – though I believe he doesn't mind much except on my account. Now however we are really in bliss & comfort comparatively. Rex says *I* am looking better than he ever saw me, & indeed I am very well & jolly thank GOD. I have no time to send sketches this mail. I hope I may *next* – & some for Dina – & some photo.s for the Mum. The scrap I send is from our dining room window & the Man is a portrait. He dresses in white, wears a quilted hat. "John Fredericton" (as we call him) told me some awfully amusing "experiences" – One (only I cannot properly remember it) of the exquisitely impertinent queries put to him by a Yankee on board a steamer. The Yankee had been looking fixedly at him, & at last coming up said – "I wish for *in*—formation." "Indeed," said the

Bishop. (Yankee) "What's the *sentiment* of your dress now?" (B.) "It's the ordinary costume of a Bishop." "Are you a Catholic?" (The Bishop says he was disposed to say Yes.) "Are you a *Shaker*?" "No, Sir." The Captain interfered & endeavoured to show the gentleman that he had no right to intrude his enquiries, but he was not to be baffled. "Is he a *Methodist* – or is he *Missionary*. I want to know what he is." At last after being quieted on this head he began again "Where are you going now?" on which J.F. says he thought it time to say "If you will attend to your business, Sir, I will take care of mine" – & cut short the dialogue.... Ever my dearest Father Your loving daughter J.H. Ewing

Now I have time I am going to work on Reka Dom.

LETTER

5

17. Aug. 1867.
Reka Dōm'. Fredericton. N.B.

My darling Mum.

I will begin a letter in good time. Thank you and Dot 1000 times for yours, which were most welcome.... I *am* so pleased you accept & like the little Idyll. You are so right to *remind me* of the great blessing & advantages attending what in some respects was a hard wrench... the going so far away from Home. By this time I hardly need reminding of it. In *Mid Atlantic* – I fear one's cowardly soul would accept 4 walls & the prospect of Dog Leg Lane[1] for ever with thankfulness, if one had the fatal power of choosing one's fate. But I do think I have been pretty good – & very little homesick – for such a novice in furrin parts as I am! And oh! *how* fortunate I am to have begun my experiences here. It is so lovely, so healthy, & has such innumerable attractions, comforts, & advantages. I am quite afraid of not appreciating it while I have it – & am thankful to be reminded! From the way I felt the heat at 1st I have some idea what it would be to live in a very overpowering climate where from hour to hour life was harassed by thinking of the weather, & struggling to keep at an average temperature. Here – (though we have oppressive days – & today is one.) the nights are generally cool, noxious beasts comparatively few, & plenty of cool days & fine breezes when one can do anything. As to the winter – they say it is charming. One only wants plenty of wraps & fuel to *take care.* Butter is ^d8 – & meat less a pound, which goes far to make up for manufactures being rather dear. Now I must tell you all our news. 1st about the Episcopal Family!!! You know they have been away for 5 weeks, & we met them 1st at Govt House. Since then they have certainly done their best to make up for lost time, in the way of kindness – & it is not the least of the many blessings of my Home here, to have such very kind people about one as our neighbors in general are – & such unusually good, intellectual, & friendly friends as the Medleys. He is quite a curiosity. Oh! such a funny little man! Very clever, and nearly as funny as Oxon, & such a green old age! He was a friend of John Newman & associated with him in working at the Lives of the Fathers[2] &c. & Newman's secession was a great grief to him. He is awfully fond of music & composes chants &c. He seems a fluent Hebrew Scholar, & is certainly as I told you one of the ablest preachers I ever heard. He has been very near to going Home to this Council that is to be held at Lambeth[3] – only he could not make out that the subjects of discussion had been settled – so he was not *certain* that it wld come to much – & had Confirmations here, & did not like to bring Mrs. M. back in winter – for she is as bad a sailor as I am. Or – you might have seen them, & heard of us!! They are *great* admirers of yours. Especially they are devoted to the Parables.[4] Mrs. M. told me today they owed *you* so much, she was delighted to do anything for your daughter – So you see, dear Mum, you have, so to speak, provided me a motherly friend in these distant parts. She is almost as great a character as he is – & as nice – & in a way as clever. She is a great gardener & a botanist – & lithographs a little – & seems generally clever – & well educated. But besides — she has *nursed* in English & foreign hospitals for 20 years, though I do not *think* she has ever belonged to any order of Sisters. She horrified the natives here by administering chloroform on her own responsibility when she 1st came – but now she says the doctors ask her to come & give it for them during operations &c. &c. She nursed in the King's Cross Hospital in London – the Hotel de Dieu in Paris – & somewhere else abroad – I have forgotten where. She considers herself a good ladies' doctor – & is amusingly "professional." She has looked at my finger – (which is getting all right – only the nail is coming off WE think!) requested me to call her in whenever I feel at all seedy; & announced her intention of keeping a motherly eye over me during the winter, as she knows the peculiarities of the climate – & what one may safely do – or not do. I tell you this, dear old Mater, since between *Rex* & *her* – I think you will feel comfortable as to my being well looked after – & you see she has been 4 winters here, & knows all the peculiar effects of the climate &c. &c. Wet feet are *the* things to be avoided, I fancy. They are going away again on a confirmation tour directly, but meanwhile we see them constantly, they ask us in perpetually to wittles of some kind, & send us vegetables & flowers. I need hardly say that Rex & Episcopus himself are pretty inseparable at "the instrument" – & that Rex is appointed supplementary organist – & has joined the choir. (I am awfully glad he should – though I feel rather lonely without him in Church, having gone with my 'Usband so long!) He is going to play at the Anniversary Festival next Sunday – & the choir generally are quite as much edified & charmed to see the author of "Jerusalem" & quite as much astonished to find (& still a little sceptical!) that Argyll & the Isles was not the composer——as if we all were living in a small english watering place.[5] This you would anticipate – but you will hardly expect to hear that the Bishop evolved in his little head & propounded to me the proposal – that if I would teach him German this winter he would teach me Hebrew. So Rex & I are to swop our united German – for Hebrew – & we have got Arnold's 1st book[6] from the B. today – & he begins his German when he returns from his Confirmation Tour!!! He buys books, evidently with an *appetite*, & will lend us *any!!!* So we are well off to an extent that seems marvellous & is truly delightful! We have free access to the Provincial Library[7] (as military people.) We have subscribed $2/2 to the Cathedral Library (an *annual* subscription!)[8] This is an admirable theological

& grave Library. *All* Jeremy Taylor – & almost every ordinary theological reference book – besides Greek & Hebrew grammars & lexicons. I am absolutely the only member at this present time. "Privileges" are certainly not quite fully appreciated here as yet!! At the present moment – I have all "Nature & Art" (for the water color lessons)[9] & Rex has Blunt's "Undesigned Coincidences"[10] from the Bishop – I have Harding's Lessons on Art[11] & a book on Color from the Provincial & Alex: Knox from the Cathedral – Libraries. We only want a modern foreign Library to be perfect so as to get at Schiller – or Faust for the Bishop – As it is, we mean to put him through Grimm!!!!! I have promised Mrs. Medley one of your photo.s. Will you please send me one for her? – I think one of the new ones wld be jolly. If your box hasn't started — I wonder whether you wld give them the big Parables?[12] Do just as you think well – dear Mum, but I am sure they would really prize it – & they are so *very* kind to us. Mrs. M. got out the "Bit of Bread" the other day, & told me she had been showing it to the doctors here, and meant to hold a young ladies' class in the winter to read it – & was anticipating their *horror* – as people are a little Yankeefied in their ideas of delicacy. But she considers it will be much for their instruction & improvement![13] –

My Sarvint goes on very well; & for these parts I think we are very fortunate – We hear of a parson only 7 miles into the country who can't get a servant except with the stipulation that she "takes her meals with the family." But then *Bears* are to be seen within that distance – so what can you expect?!!!! Our "Sarah" cooks very nicely – though she is a very poor housemaid – but she is civil & willing – & I think honest & steady – & not extravagant. We breakfast at 8.30 if we go to "Matins" – about 9 if we don't. Lunch at one – & dine about 6.

I am very busy just now upon an interior of the Cathedral – at which I work while Rex practises. I have got some good hints from Harding's book about drawing the arches &c. I get dreadfully grieved at my stupidity over the colouring about here. I do wish I were a better artist!!! & Rex thinks I have gone *back* rather than *forward*. However I have got at some good books here, and I mean to work hard this winter indoors. I think my *interior* looks wonderfully promising so far.

. . . By the bye I am going to save seed of all the wild flowers I can, & shall send it Home. So have a nice sunny bit got ready to sow them in!!! You know what lives here will live with you & some of the flowers are truly lovely. Spotted yellow lilies & *splendid* Michaelmas Daisies grow wild. And a lovely white flower *something* like a white foxglove—(*Chelone glabra!*)—which I hope will seed like a foxglove & so be easily grown. Beautiful spiraeas too, & oh! the pitcher plants grow here, but we have not seen them. One plant held 4 or 5 *quarts* of water they tell us.

. . . As it is possible the box may even yet not have started . . . I send a few other notes. Chiefly of things *left behind*. My child knife will do capitally for butter. Thank dear father, he gave us the *gravy spoon*. What he *took back* were 2 tablespoons he had thought of giving us. The silver *ladles* are most useful for the sugar. *Better* than *tongs*, as the sugar is all *crushed* here. We are going to be photoed soon. I hope you are pretty well. We are both very well & happy thank GOD. Ever dearest Mum

Your most loving daughter
J. H. E.

LETTER

6

Fredericton.
11 Sunday a. Trinity. [1 September] 1867

My dearest Dot.

. . . You can't think how kind people are here to us in the matter of vegetables. We buy nothing now but potatoes—& we have almost more beans, cucumbers, vegetable marrows (or *squashes* as they call them!) &c. &c. than we can eat. The other half of our semidetached house, is tenanted by Professor Campbell & Mrs. C. & their young family. They are quite young people & she seems to be a favorite with everybody – *On dit* that he occasionally exceeds, it is very sad if it is so! – She is very pretty, though fragile looking, & looks like a little nun or pre-raphaelite picture. She looks such a quaint little image in her black dress with her baby

in scarlet over her shoulder, standing under the willows & looking out over the river.[1] (I beg Dina to excuse the in- adequate representation of the baby!!) She sends us lots of vege- tables, & her "young barbarians" play perpetually under our win- dows & by the river. To see the little fat girl of about 3 fetch  water from the spring by the river, washing out the cup with a knowing fling, & tasting it with the air of a connoisseur is a sight! – Children here seem to spend a most blissful dirt pie sort of exis- tence, & as people keep very few servants in comparison to what they wld in England – the bairns naturally have to look a good deal after themselves. The Medleys kept us going with vegetables too when they were here. They are away now I am sorry to say – the Bishop having taken a german grammar of mine with him, & left us Arnold's 1st Hebrew book. He flourished the grammar before Mrs. M.'s nose – & said "If my company is not so charming as usual my dear, you will know the reason." I also lent them Eleanor's *tea maker*, for an episcopal tour in these parts is not attended with all the comforts of civilization. I was afraid when *she* went that my poor table would have no more bouquets, but just when her last nosegay was finished in spite of all my nursing — a new acquain- tance (a Mrs. Inches)[2] whom I have only seen once – sent me a beauty – with an intimation that if I would like some house plants she can give me some nice ones!! I have had a flower stand put up (a shelf fixed on to the middle window of the bay –) but have not yet bought any. We went to bid the Medleys goodbye before they left – & after we left them met them again at the P. office (for it was Mail Day.) In the few seconds of this last meeting – Mrs. M. promised me enough compost to pot my hyacinths — & the Bishop trotted after us to shout that he took in the Saturday Review & we should see it regularly!! *I* told the Mum I think how well the Festival went off. Rex has played again today & they put on 'Jerusalem' – but he took it off – as he wants them to learn it the right way 1st.[3] There was a pretty introit by the Bishop, & a *lovely* anthem of Elvey's[4] – which Rex really plays to perfection. He had practice yesterday – there is a splendid passage on "Open Ye the gates that the righteous nation which keepeth the truth may enter in." Then a lovely tenor solo – "Thou will keep him in perfect peace &c." Did I ever tell you about the parsons here? Long before we knew them, we were greatly taken with one man (very like White of Masbro!)[5] he seemed so awfully good & earnest. He is so. However – he has a charming voice – a tenor – & it has a tone somehow that seems *good* & pleasant & like himself. He sang this "Thou wilt keep &c." & it was charming & seemed to *suit* so awfully well. The other (Mr. Coster) is also the Army Chaplain – not quite so *saintly* – but a nice man, with a really fine bass voice. I teach in his school. He is Oxford M.A., has a cast in one eye from a gunshot, has a pretty lively wife who flirts freely with the General – & he is they say as good a canoe paddler as an indian.[6] Mr. Pearson is a S. Augustine's man – & his wife is considered by Mrs. Medley as the model of parson's wives. She is not pretty, & I shld think never flirted with anybody – not even with Mr. P.!![7] One of their children (a damsel of about 12) I have rather fallen in love with. She reminds me so of *you* in old days. N.B. Rex is growing his beard, & kissing him is at present very much like kissing a scrubbing brush!! He flatters himself he has safely passed the stage in which it looks like *neglect* – & that the embryo beard is obvious! If I had one *I* shld grow it too for the winter!!! Last Friday we were asked to Govt House for a picnic – We went at 3.P.M. & after we had been in the room a few minutes "his Excellency"[8] sent for Rex – & when he reappeared it was simply to make his Ex.'s apologies for not being ready. Getting ready in his Ex.'s case I must tell you means irreproachable get up. *Mauve trousers* – white waistcoat – dyed moustaches & (on dit) rouged cheeks. He seems a plucky, cleverish sort of man, who fills the place very well, but quaint old buck sort of old bachelor. Well,

36

we went across the river & by water up the Nashwaak *Cis* (i.e. *Little Nashwaak*) & landed at a very pretty spot where we ate a swell luncheon off such lovely old China – I wonder he had the heart to risk it at a picnic! The A.D.C. lent Rex his own boat that R. might row me there, (boating is one of R.'s accomplishments I find.) but he told us we must take the Attorney General,[9] & as he freely confessed that he was a very disagreeable man I told him I must have a good "wrap" as a set off – So I got a buffalo robe to keep me warm – & sat like a Queen in the Stern – & R. took one oar & the A.G. the other & away we went. Mr. Coster paddled Mrs. Clerke (A.D.C.'s wife) in his canoe – she paddling with him (she is a dear little thing – I am awfully fond of her) she being the swell lady. There were lots of other canoes & a few boats. Well, the old A.G. could no more row than I could! Rex says that for the benefit of the initiated I am incidentally to mention that he made his 1st stroke with his hands as far apart upon the oar as they could go, & really I got very nervous that we should be capsized into the river – At last R. contrived civilly to get the oar from him, & pulled there & back by himself. The A.G. (like other govt swells here.) is not much of a gentleman. He is very well off however – & has some swell daughters who dress in the most astounding way! But he seems not highly respected – & Capt. Clerke told me afterwards that at the picnic he had seen him go up several times with his plate – & say "For a lady." & having got a tit bit – retire & eat it & return to do the same thing. If you could see the solemn – rather ill tempered looking middle aged man – the story seems ludicrous!! ... Coming back down the Cis it was lovely — 1/2 dark – & the canoes gliding past among the shadows – The Cis was very narrow & required some steering. I got some new water lilies. When we got into the big river again – the wind was very high & it was nearly dark – & the waves were quite wonderful. Rex pulled home splendidly – but the canoes found it tiresome work. Little Mrs. C. had had to paddle her hardest with Mr. Coster & got in very hot & tired. We went back to Govt House where there was tea & a dance & supper. But R. & I had only thick boots, so we did not dance – & left in good time. We walked home, & went to bed. About 1/2 past one I was woke by Rex asking me if I were well – or if anything was the matter. I was turning round again (& hearing nothing myself) when Rex exclaimed—"it's the *fire bell!*"—& was out of bed like a shot. I must tell you that the day the Medleys left, the Bishop told us that he had told his next door neighbor where the Church plate &c. was in case of a fire–& what he specially wished to be saved–adding that the man had looked at a long box & said "Is this valuable?" "*Very,*" said the Bishop. "What is it?" "*Music.*" On which, as the Bishop said, he didn't seem to see it. Rex said, "Well if there's a fire–*I* must save the music." Well–when I went to the back room & saw the blaze in the sky–it seemed to me to come from the Medley's as I told Rex. "Then I must save the anthems!" said Rex in a thunderous voice (it was almost amusing) & off he went. We couldn't find matches, so he dressed in the dark–& in the dark I was left. I could hear the peculiar *roar* of the fire, & see the flames rising up through the open window. I got awfully lonely, so I woke "Sarah" with much difficulty, & got a light & told her to make fire & get tea ready for Rex when he returned, & went back to the window to watch. It was a strange sight–I almost mean to try a sketch from memory— This gives a rough idea. A. is the

blaze of distant fire. B. the river, a queer opaque sky blue. C. a pale greenish Aurora Borealis. D. line of town along the river illumined by the reflected flames–night dark, but stars. Time went on–the fire got larger & no Rex returned. At last I got so nervous I wrapped up–left the house–took my maid with me & we went off to find the fire–& *Rex!!* When we got to the Cathedral & Bishopscote,[10] happily it was not there, so on we went. (Fire is very illusive at night, & I may as well say, it was *in the position* of the Bishop's place, only about 1/4 of a mile or more farther up the town.) I had dressed on the top of my night dress & had to stop en route to tie up my stockings with p. handkerchiefs! As we got nearer we seemed to be going into the blaze of falling sparks – & at last we found it. We had passed the place an hour or so before! It was a square called Phoenix square, & how many times it has risen from

its own ashes I know not, but the other half of the square was burnt down just before we came, & when Sarah & I reached the spot – not one stone was left upon another (or rather not one *plank* for it was wood of course) But a large building at the corner – a brick house – offices – which had held out some time was in full blaze. It was a wonderful sight. The flames poured out of the windows & *licked* round the walls reminding one of the fire that *licked* up the water in the trench round Elijah's sacrifice. It's quite hopeless to attempt to give you an idea of it – It looked very like all pictures of great fires in the 'Illustrated.' Rex was with the other officers – keeping an eye on the fuel yard which was near & from which soldiers were employed in sweeping away the burning embers as they fell. It was most providential that the wind set over the river instead of over the city. Otherwise – being a dry night – high wind – & the fire engines about as available as a boy's squirt — probably 2/3 of the town would have gone.[11] There was something rather comical in meeting our friends again in all phases of demi-

39

toilette. Capt. Irvine said "We hardly expected to meet again so soon." I found there a deaf gentleman we had met at Gvt House & who like other deaf people is apt to speak almost in a whisper. Amid the din of the fire he poured a remark into my ear which after much repeating I discovered to be that "we should all require a 2d supper after this." We waited till the walls of the brick house came down, & then came home. No lives were lost except of some horses. An almost comical element (as one didn't suffer oneself) was to see the spectators who kept getting the falling sparks into their eyes & going about with pocket handkerchiefs to their faces. Also a small boy who laid a complaint (to Major Graham) against the soldiers who were protecting the rescued property–because they wouldn't give him some small article that belonged to him. The disgusting part is that these fires are said to be almost always the work of incendiaries! You will wonder how R. & I are getting on with Hebrew. Working from Arnold is a very different thing to puzzling at it as we have done hitherto–& *so far* "points"[12] really seem to be a help, though confusing from their numbers & variety. We are getting up the dead languages together. R. 'rubbing up'. He goes to his office with a latin book in his pocket, & we do Greek & Hebrew together at Home.

I wonder what you have done about our parcel. . . . it is within the bounds of possibility it has not yet got off. *If so* here are a few final orders! Mrs. Bryce has an admirable pattern she once gave me–but I don't know where it is—for a little sort of invalid flannel jacket to sit up in bed with. It is a wonderfully simple affair made from an oblong bit of colored flannel. Now & then if I am rather tired, or seedy you know–I takes my breakfast in bed–& a dressing gown is such a *lumbering* thing to throw on for this. If Mrs. B. will give that pattern–I know 'Mary' will cut it out for me–& Mrs. Johnson might make it–of *blue* flannel. Also I want a little *nasturtium* & *sweet william* seed (the latter from the Mum's bank if possible!)–some *foxglove* seed–& if you could root up a few *wild anemone tubers* & some wild hyacinth bulbs. One or two *bulbs* I think I would like. I shall get a few here–they are dearer than with you though & just one or two from *Home* would be jolly. A few crocuses, & perhaps 3 hyacinths. We mean to have a garden next year – & fancy! – I hear that *Cardinal Lobelias* (what old Brewin has – the crimson ones) grow wild in the Province!!! What *can* Brewin mean by saying they won't stand the winter in England! I mean to cultivate the wild plants as much as possible.... We are invited to another picnic for tomorrow by the 22d. Alas! that I can't chaperone "my sisters"—I will set some of the officers on the hunt for monograms if I can find one *shootable* for a flirtation! The enclosed sketch is for her. I will send her & the Mum some more soon – Mrs. Inches has just sent me a "cherry pie"[13] and an ivy leaved geranium! – Last night I found my maid sitting on an inverted candlebox with a *sojer!!!* However I allow followers in moderation!!!!!!! She is rather a character. I warned her the other day to put no *onions* into anything for us – as Mr. E. detested them. Afterward she told me "that dish was *spiled* for want of onions." "Well you must not put them in" I said. "Mr. Ewing can't endure them." "Well" she observed confidentially, "He's *very quiet so far*, & we won't rouse him up for sake of an onion or two!"

By the bye I wish Sarah for my sake would send me a few *cooking notes* – A simple soup or two – & the secret of *ungreasy* gravies (both for roasts & for hashes) & any receipts she may think well. A beef tea one. Also if Mrs. Crisp could be adjured to give you her exact & infallible receipt for *stay:washing*, for my benefit in an alien land far removed from her invaluable services!!!! ...

I *must* stop – Adieu darling – With dear love to all – Boys specially included.

Your Everloving Sister
J.H. Ewing

... N.B. Tell the Mum Mr. Coster says we shall be very *warm* in our house – he knows it of old – the most comfortable house in Fredericton!

There's balm for a Mubber's heart.

...

LETTER

7

[9 September 1867]

My dearest old Mum.

I wish you could come in this moment! I have got a nice wood fire in my grate, (for it is a *coolish* morning. One of those clear, fresh, sunny mornings that I fancy we shall have pretty consistently through the Autumn) & Rex is gone off to his office – and I am alone in my glory. I am afraid I shall hardly have time this mail, but I must make you a sketch of my room! – "Sarah" has a great admiration for my table of little things (of which she always leaves the dusting to me!) She says "Mrs. Coster" (her former mistress) "had a great many little things too – not so many as *you* Ma'am – but then she was burnt out 3 times[1] – but any little things she *did* save, she was very choice of. She saved one plate out of her dessert service." The coolness with which people regard being "burnt out" here, is amazing!! The day of the fire, Sarah was telling me all sorts of "burning out" anecdotes. Some people seem to lie under a sort of evil spell as regards it. "The fire hunts him everywhere." There is a certain man she told me of, & wherever he settles fire follows him!! One could make a splendid Salamander story from it! – in the Edgar Poe style! One comical idea one can quite understand – viz. that as much is broken as burnt in these fires often. Sarah told me of one in which in his anxiety to save — a man flung a fine mirror out of the window into the street to *save it from the flames*. Of course it smashed to shivers!!

Talking of stories, if I only caught the full facts of his history, I think I shall send A.J.M. a short paper on a Fredericton Dog. Did I ever tell you of him? Bless his nose! He has the loveliest face I ever saw I think, *in any Xtian*. He knows us quite well when we go up the High Street where he lives. When he gets 2 Cents (=1^{d}) given him – he takes it in his mouth to the nearest *store* & buys himself biscuits. I have seen him do it. If you only give him *one* cent he is dissatisfied & tries to get the 2d. The Bishop told me he used to come to Church with his master at one time, he would come, & behaved very well——*till* the Offertory. Then he rose & *walked after the alms-collectors* waggling his tail as the money chinked in, because he wanted his $^d_1$ for his biscuits!!! He is a large dog–part S. Bernard & has magnificent eyes. But (my Poor!) they shaved him this summer like a poodle!– There is a bear in the officers' quarters here–he belongs to the regiment– I have patted him, but he catches at one's clothes. To see him *patting* at my skirts with his paw was delicious–but I don't like his *head*–he looks very sly! The Dr.Adams (regt surgeon) I spoke of is an author it seems. There was a splendid review in the "Saturday" of his book "The Naturalist in India."[2] He seems a very nice man–& his wife[3] has now let us have the "Revue des deux mondes"–so we are pretty well off for literature. We also know a Professor Bailey[4] at the College here– His father was a friend of Harvey's, but he did not seem to rise to much interest about poor H.[5] He is a delicate looking man–& we have not made much of him yet. I fancy he is a good botanist. We got on very well with our Hebrew, though (tell Dot) the *WOWLS* (as poor dear Wolff[6] called them) are maddening!!! I suppose our parcel *has* started–but still ask the girls to look in an S.P.C.K. list for a Hebrew Bible & see if it is not pretty cheap to subscribers. If the parcel has *not* started, I should like a german bible to be got there (it only costs $^s_2$ /-). I would like to give it to the Bishop as a little return for their kindness. Also has Dot remembered to put up Elisabeth Ellacombe's braided garibaldi that she gave me? It would be useful for autumn evenings at home. My old *white cloak* with the black velvet binding did not come either–& it is a sort of thing that wld be awfully useful for common next summer. People wear white cloaks & jackets of every shape & material. Also if it has not started, Miss Thompson[7] might be asked with my love, if she would give me (if she has any to spare) one or two of her *immortelles* flowers–to put in my room in winter. I would be glad of a few of the common yellow ones tell the girls. The winter is so long & I dread the loss of the flowers for six months or more! ... I have got you a dial & mean to make the sketch, & send it herewith.[8] It is in the garden of a funny little old lady here–a *Mrs. Shore.*[9] She is very *tiny* & very old – She goes to the 7.30 service like clockwork – has a garden – paints *life size portraits in oils*!!! & complains that "between housekeeping, literature, & the fine arts" – she never has time for anything!!!!!!!! As Rex says, she is like a little creature of a *beetle* tribe – (more like a devil's wheelbarrow than anything!!!!!) She has a delicate throat & wears a band of velvet on it. She says

she has tried many things & she *seems* to have tried a *stretching* process, for her neck is about 3 times as long as anybody else's!!...N.B. The little old lady has this moment walked in!! I hid

her portrait rapidly. Rex & I are asked there on Wednesday evening. The "Mistress of the Rolls" as we call her (she being wife to the Master of the Rolls & decidedly *judicial* herself –) has offered me any amount of motherly advice & doctoring if I need it – & any amount of either *physic* or *jam*, for my throat. Mrs. Pearson also is going to give me a lesson on N. Brunswick housekeeping & how to pickle my eggs (I expect she & my Sarai will *clash!!!!!!*) – so I am well looked to!! & *I* have undertaken to give *motherly* advice &c. to a young lady in the choir with a charming *alto* but a delicate throat, who won't take care of herself – so you see we are very charitable to each other! – I have been making up my month's accounts – & I think living here is very satisfactory. Some things are dear – (wine & beer *very*; we shld save greatly by taking the pledge!!) & some *bad* – (*tea* dreadful!) but meat is ^{d}5 a lb., butter – ^{d}8 1/2, salmon – ^{d}6 – of course there is much expense in *setting up*, but as far as our living goes, I think we may get on *quite well* on our present income & shall be *most comfortable* if the scheme[10] brings us good. It certainly is about as good a place for a *start* pecuniarily as one could have found. Our meat & fish in August only came to 1.15.6½ — & our bread to ^{s}10/- & butter, cheese, eggs & bacon together to a little over $^S11$ /- vegetables to $^S5$ /-! (but the latter were given to us so much!) This will give you some idea – for you know we are both good "knives & forks" & have meat 3 times a day. We have just started a paraffin lamp. It works capitally – but I wish you could have seen our 1st attempt to light it! Rex is as awkward at such things as I am – It flared up – it smoked the glass – if we turned it down it went on burning below in an alarming manner. Rex walked helplessly from one room to another with it – Every moment we expected it to *explode* – the more we *blew*, the higher it flamed & when we got it out, R. uttered devout thanksgivings. I really could only yell with laughing. Rex's best love dear Mum & mine to all. Ever yr most loving

J. H. E.

Always say how you are please.

I am as jolly & happy as possible. My house is delightful. The landlord is going to put up a hall stove for us.

LETTER
8

Fredericton. 21. Sep. 1867.

My dearest Mother –

The room being rather warm (with a fire!) & having been very busy all day sketching &c. &c. & having just done my Hebrew Lesson in a sleepyish sort of manner — I have turned lazy about working at Mrs. Overtheway[1] tonight, & am going to get on with my letter instead. Rex is mouthing Hebrew gutturals at my elbow, so don't be astonished if I introduce the "*yatz yoty yomah*" &c. that sound in my ears! I must tell you we have actually despatched a small parcel to Ecclesfield – though as Miss Grundy (Dr. Adams'

45

sister in law) who has taken it goes in a sailing vessel – it will not reach you for an indefinite period – probably a fortnight or so after you get this. . . . We wish the little mementos were of more value – but they come with our dear love – & we both kissed the parcel!! We crossed early one day by the ferry & went to the indian settlement[2] – where we bought a small & simple basket of a *squaw* which she had just made – & which shows their work & will hold a few of your odds & ends dear Mum: for you haven't a work basket. We have sent Dina a Tennyson as promised, & one also for *Dot* – as I think she will like to have In Memoriam & *everything* he has written in a handy volume.[3] Tell her I also have sent the *earrings* for her wear. She forbid me to do so – but I make a compromise: if ever I bore my ears – or have daughters who bore their ears – I will have them back – till then she may as well enjoy them, & failing the above conditions I devise them to her – her heirs – & consignees!!!!!!!!!!! They are much too *delicate* & lovely for hair pins – being old Chester's wedding gift I couldn't *exchange* them for anything – & at

Wigwam of the Micmacs of Algonquin [near Dartmouth, N.S.],
21 June 1867.

present they do nobody any good & as we *may* be burnt out – they are safer with her!! – We send Maggie a little card case of indian work – & Reggie a cigar case of ditto – & a piece of canoe birch bark for the museum. I saw some *pipes*, but all the indian things are very dear – & the pipes particularly so – but we hope some day to be able to enrich his collection with one. I think he will like the case. It is genuine work – in figures which are awfully like the people! – I fear poor Charlie will hardly know what to do with a *tiny* canoe of the same work – as he has no "best box," but somebody must take care of it for him till he sets up a knickknack table, or he must sell it! These three things are worked by Huron Indians in stained moose hair. The Melicetes who are *here*, work in basket work & in *colored beads* – I got 2 strips of *their* colored bead work & Sarah & I "ran up" 2 red velvet bags & trimmed them with these strips for tobacco bags for Brownie & Steenie. I thought you would like to see the different kinds of work. The *Mic Macs* work in stained porcupine – but I have not sent any of their work. They are only very little things – but they come from *us*! – We have had so much to do I have got on very badly with my botanizing but I have sent one or two ferns for you – N.B. Rex wrote your *museum text* outside in Hebrew – not quite so

47

well as he *can* write it, but *all* was done in *one day* to be ready for Miss G. or everything might have been nicer. I have also sent one or two flowers for Stephen—but none of the most beautiful I think. We were *late* for flowers. Also a few ferns for Miss Thompson with my love. The tobacco bags were done in a great hurry, but the girls will improve them I daresay. Being so hurried too, I was not able to name most of the ferns & flowers—but I will send them when I can. Tell Steenie the Impatiens Fulva is a wonderful flower. When you touch (almost when you *shake* with approaching) the seed vessels, they burst & curl up like springs—& fling the seed away.... I mean to *try* to preserve seed. The *Chelone Glabra* as pressed by me gives no idea of the beautiful dead white flower something like a foxglove only more *compact*. I have told you what the parcel contains that you may not expect greater things than will appear from our little Xmas Box!— We have sent the dear Govr nothing—but he & you are one—so he must share the workbasket!!!! We are all becoming curious to know who is to be our new Governor—as General Doyle goes to Nova Scotia next month. He has been very popular—& I fancy will be welcome at Halifax. It has been a lovely day today! We have had rather cold weather—& began to feel as if winter were setting in—but today has been *lovely* & we have enjoyed it. Rex has been with me all day!—(bless his nose!) though when I speak of his being with me—I speak of his bodily presence only. In spirit he is with the conjugations Kal—Hiphil—&c. &c. He has bought us Gesenius' Grammar[4] & a very fine one it seems. Tell dear Pater that if he could be with us now, his customary ingenuity in tracing Hebrew lineage (at least on the mother's side!) would not be much taxed to discover a Jew in his son-in-law. What between his beard, & mumbling over Genesis—he will look a Hebrew of the Hebrews shortly I am convinced!— He lives with Gesenius & if he doesn't take it to bed, it is not that he leaves Hebrew in the drawing room— He undresses to the tune of the latest exercise, & puts me through the imperfect & perfect of קְטֹל before we get up o'mornings!!!! (He has just discovered that Eden was about the same latitude as Fredericton!!) There is always Morning Prayers & Holy Communion here on Saints' Days—& today being S. Matthew we went to the II. service. After Church a 12.30 lunch & then we went a little way up the road, & I did a sepia sketch of "our street" [Plate 7] – Rex sitting by me & groaning Hebrew. It was gloriously sunny – & such a lovely sky, & such an exquisitely calm river with white sailed boats on it. I have enjoyed it awfully. We sat till near 4. & then the ladies gradually assembled & they & Rex went off to choir practise. I came in towards the end – & then R. & I went up the town & paid 2 calls (both *out* happily.) – then on to the officers' square, being band afternoon – where we got tea & chatted with different people – & heard a *glorious* selection from Faust beautifully played – (It included that *march* you are so fond of.) I walked about with R. who explained all the scenes as the music went on — (& *sang aloud* to the principal airs!!!!) He says it's bed time so I must stop. Much learning is fast making him mad I tell him. His head is that *crammed* with Hebrew – he hardly knows when you speak to him – & as to paint on his coats (as Mrs. Nickleby wld say) he rubs against our newly painted door –

[AE's Continuation]

Monday. 23d.

Dearest Mum. It is mail day, and I (in my quality of a domestic tyrant) have peremptorily *ordered* Jowie to allow me to finish this, and not to attempt to write another word herself. She has a shoulder a little stiff; – (some accidental muscular strain, as she is otherwise *perfectly* well) – but I have ordered her *absolute* rest – and she is "playing" with a rare fern. . . .

Today we are getting the first breath of the cool weather. The wind has gone round to the North, and is blowing strong. It is not really cold, only it is cool; and divinely bright and clear. The maples are rapidly turning to the colour of flame, and stand in the woods like burning trees. We can see, already, that nothing we have heard about the loveliness of the autumn woods has sufficed to prepare us for the reality.

The lines have fallen to us in pleasant places! When I think that if I had my deserts I should not escape whipping, it does overwhelm me to have *such* a wife, in *such* a lovely land, with *such* an organ to play on Sundays.

49

Jow is going to add one word – (chiefly to prove that she could write quite well, if I would let her.) So with my best love to all at Home. I am

Ever your affct son in law.

A Ewing

[JHE's Postscript]

P.S. & N.B. Though he talks bosh about his "deserts" he is (excepting for domestic tyranny as exemplified in the present instance – & for breaking of tumblers & sugar-pots (since Hebrew set in!)) the *very* best & dearest Boy that ever was. (He won't let me have "more ink" – but the trodden worm will turn as I believe Mrs. Gamp remarked!) He is quite perfect, so it's no use particularizing!! Signed on oath – J. H. E.

. . .

LETTER
9

Sep. 29. 1867

My dearest Dot.

I cannot thank you & dear Maggie & Dina & everybody who has been helping with our *packidge* sufficiently. We really are truly sorry to have given all the trouble I know it must have been. For I know, though you are very glad to do it for us – that you are all just as busy as usual – Even if we *are* in N. America & want clothes! . . . I had meant to do without a new dress, but I think perhaps I should not have managed so well as I thought – when I came to think of six months' winter – My brown rep. would hardly have lasted with *comfort* till June. As it is I shall use the new one for Sundays &c. – wear my old linsey for very common occasions – & the rep will be jolly in Autumn & Spring again – & my black silk will not get so much wear. *Many thanks.* Rex looks forward to his rough socks. (Tell Dina I had never heard of her *silk* performances! What a luxury! She should have knitted a pair for the Sultan.) Tell the dear Mum Mrs. Medley's name was *Hudson*. They are to return we hope next week. There has been a most extraordinary affair in connection with them. About *3* weeks or less ago – one day at afternoon service (*week day*) when we came to the All conditions of men prayer – at the pause for sick & afflicted &c. Mr. Pearson stopped a most unusual length of time – & at last seemed quite over- whelmed – & got through with great difficulty. We were all very curious to know what had happened – & to our great distress found that he had received a telegram – announcing the death of a son of the Bishop – suddenly – in England.[1] This son is a devoted clergy- man – musician – amateur architect &c. & we knew the blow would be overwhelming. Rex & I wrote letters of sympathy to them both – The Costers went into mourning – The poor old B. we heard was much broken down but went on with his Confirmations &c. bravely. Rex played the Dead March & other appropriate music on Sunday. His own Church out here (of which he is Vicar & which he built himself &c.) was draped in black – his funeral sermon preached to a weeping congregation[2] – obituary notice of his life &c. &c. &c. & my Sarah who knew him received 'such a turn' when I told her as she has hardly recovered!!! Imagine this mail bringing the news that it was all a *hum*! He is alive!! But the extraordinary part is that *he* has given some mysterious hints of his belief that it was done on purpose – for monetary ends!! He had fortunately written to his wife[3] who was in another part of England to warn her against believing such a report, & she got his letter just as her brother in law Sir James Carter[4] was coming to break the bad news to her. *A* man known here only by name wrote to Sir J.C. & to Ed. Medley's money agent out here who telegraphed to Mr. P. *The* party gives his name as Broughton & his address as the Carlton Club – & more is not known. Mrs. Coster reappeared today in colors. And the local paper has just published an obituary notice of his life & death – 3 days after he has been discovered to be alive – (which gives you some idea of the Press in these parts!)[5] Isn't it extraordinary? Aunt Jane[6] will possibly hear of it if she has kept up her intimacy with the Carters. The 1st Lady Carter was an old friend of hers. She died out here – & he married a Miss

Coster—sister to our *bass* parson.[7] We dined at the Campbells last night (next door) Rather a swell party & very pleasant. The night before we had tea with the Pearsons. His little daughter (12.) who reminds me of you—played *very* nicely on a sort of harmonium—Rex accompanying her on the violincello (Mr. P.'s). I played chess with Mr. P.—& as it was something like playing with old White in his most superlunary mood, of course I checkmated him!... Yesterday was a *lovely* day, & R. & I went over by the ferry & I had a jolly hour or two of sketching, he grubbing Hebrew as usual.[8]

Fredericton. from the Nashwaak. Sept. 27. 1867

The trees are just beginning to look *lovely*. If fine on Monday I mean to go & sketch in the College Grove[9] where they are splendid. Rex goes everywhere with me—bless him!—& is as good as gold!! I am now working steadily—by little bits at Reka Dom—& hope to send it shortly. Good night for tonight darling! How stupidly I have written on this sheet!—

Monday. I have not very much time today—as it is a busyish day although there are no *clubs!!*[10] I make up my accounts—& count the clothes for the wash (& as it is the end of the month—I am making up my monthly accounts too!) & I have been showing the orderly where to stow R.'s clothes—for Sarah—good woman!—has *no* genius for *folding* & is as untidy as any other irish woman. I trust they will now be kept in a more *orderly* fashion!! Also a *pile* of the

dear boy's shirts want mending at the buttonholes which he rents &
tears like any rhinoceros, & I wish my fingers were as clever as
yours at it!! To crown all he is going to make me Commissariat
Clerk for a day or two he says—as *his* quarterly accounts &c. &c. are
on hand—& *such* a fat book (like a register book) has arrived I
am so much pleased everybody likes the Idyll—even old Brownie.
Tell the dear Mum it was very good of her to be so scrupulous, but I
was sorry she had not altered the *groundsel* mistake (& yet I think
she *did* introduce the meal cake which mends matters.)[11] We
meant to correct that before it left—for Rex told me it was wrong
but he forgot to alter it. We wrote against time for that mail. The P.
Office waited 10 minutes & it literally was finished in that scramble—without time to read it over: for a lady *called* in the very midst
of our work, when every moment was precious!—It hardly *does*
seem worthwhile to *send* the no.s— I didn't think it cost so much. I
think we must get them here.[12] Tell the Mum, I have fallen head
over ears in love with another dog. Oh! bless his nose! (Rex says he
is jealous). His name is Hector. He is a *white* pure bulldog. His face
is more *broad* & round—& delicious & ferociously goodnatured—&
affectionately ogreish—than you can imagine. The moment I saw
him I hugged him & kissed his benevolence bump, & he didn't even
gowly powl. He belongs to one of the 22d, one I don't know, but I
have warned Rex that if a mild flirtation would procure me a

HECTOR!

photogram of Hector—I won't promise to refrain!!!!! I send the
Mum a colored swallow's house. The Hebrew inscription is my
writing from R.'s dictation. It is "The swallow hath found a nest."

But I think I will write "the swallow hath found an *house*." on a separate bit – to paste under it. The sky is the sky I saw it against. Rex insisted on having my 1st sketch for himself, but I *cut off* a bit of

the sky & drew the house afresh for the Mum. . . . I was dreaming so hard of being at Home last night. That we were at home on leave – & while we were there the indian things arrived – & Pater *would* open the parcel & lost the labels – & there was nothing for Charles – & Regie's cigar case was broken. Not an omen I trust! – Tell the Mum & Miss T. that the fern *without any fruit* – rather large

 (I forget if Miss T. has one – Think *not*) is *Osmunda Clayteniana* I find. The one with two fronds, one with fruit & one without, the fruitful one long stalked is I think *Aspidium Thelypteris*. Another *delicate* one covering the page – with fruit round the edge of the pinnae is I think *Aspidium Noveboracense*. My plan for fern drawing is most successful. I hope really

54

to make a valuable little set. R. is charmed with it. (Which perhaps doesn't prove much. Only he is very critical of my drawings!) The first lovely *delicate* one is I suspect a Botrychium—but I have not yet discovered. We are most comfortable & jolly & well—thank GOD. I am *not* homesick only at times—it would be just *perfection* if one could have you into one's house & show everything & talk over everything. But it's a pretty clear proof of what he makes himself to me—that he *does* supply the place of *so much* that I have had so long—& am parted from just now. Love to Everybody. And once more unspeakable thanks for all your trouble . . . . Thank Sarai immensely for the pudding & good Juno & Harriet for *their* work. We were both *so* pleased!!— *Many* thanks for the receipts—too. We are just making *plum* jam tell the Mum! I wish she could taste it! Sarah goes on most comfortably and really seems awfully fond of us. She says I am the best mistress she ever had—*but one!* As to the Commissary—"He's rale fine looking—& I don't wonder you've a concate of him—but you look real funny beside him—like a bit of a girl!!!!" From which you may perceive she is candid in her expressions—with a dash of irish compliment. But she seems genuinely happy, & is a good soul, and not extravagant. N.B. The present orderly is devoted to me—& *his* politeness is almost too much for me! Yr ever loving

JOW.

The drawings are for the Mum. More another time—& the names of the flowers. I have been *Clerk* this morning. We dine at the A.D.C.'s tonight.

. . .

The white flower is locally called "Pigeon Berry." *Covers* yards like wild anemone. All the berries from the one flower. . . .

5. Oct. 1867. Fredericton.
New Brunswick.

My dearest Mother.

We have been very gay since I wrote last. We had a pleasant dinner party at the A.D.C.'s—where we met the Colonel of the 22d[1] who has been on leave in England, & has just returned. He is the ugliest old bachelor I think that I ever saw. Quite grotesque. No I can't do him. He is all hair too—so unlike an officer! The night before last the General asked us to dinner to meet whom do you think?—Miss Sulivan! Who is staying at Govt House. However she did not arrive that day as was expected. It was a very pleasant dinner party— I went in with a Capt. Holyoake—a very nice amusing little man—very doggy, & horsey, who drives a tandem about here. The next night (yesterday) we were to go to a ball there at Gt House—but poor Rex who has had a dreadful eye—nominally 2 bad *styes*, but more like an abscess on the lower lid—was *too* unpresentable and couldn't go. He insisted on my going without him, so I went in the strength of my *matronhood*—but I didn't 1/2 enjoy it without him—& we had been looking forward to a valse together! Miss Sulivan was there all right—& I like her immensely. It was almost like seeing a bit of home to chat to her. It was a very pretty ball indeed. I danced with Capt. H. & he has promised to get me a photogram of Hector!— Miss Sulivan was very swell in white with pink satin stripes, & danced a lot, and seemed very jolly. *Sunday.* Today the General has goodnaturedly asked us to go up after evening church & dine there, so we are going. Miss Sulivan goes tomorrow. I wanted to have sent some larger sketches, & some autumn leaves by her to you, but as I have got no varnish to do the latter with, I fear I may not get them off. I shall try. On Tuesday next we dine with the Powys's (22d people & very nice.) & the following Monday – a ball given by the 22d. After which I suppose we shall be a bit quiet – only Dr. Ward[2] talked to me at Govt House of a musical party, & the Medley's are going to drive us to the consecration of a little Mission Church – "in the Bush" so to speak. They have come back, & very glad we were to see them . . . . The Woods now are *lovely*! – The Autumn tints are beyond describing or coloring – One day I began a sketch, but it is most unsatisfactory – & now it is rainy, & I am so afraid of getting no more opportunity. A tree stands off against a grey woody background

like this & it is brilliant yellow & crimson. Sometimes a whole tree is canary color, and another near it one uniform rich deep red, another like bronze – & so on. They are not all so by any means of course, but in the "College Grove" as it is called (which is something like a beautiful bit of english *pasture*, & *park*, & *wood* scenery) — are the loveliest varieties of colour. Tell the girls I mean to get & send a lot if possible, varnished so that they will keep, & I would like them to make a device of them for the Xmas Church Decorations. They use them here for that purpose. I mean too, to varnish a lot to dress my own dinner table in winter. I have been copying my sketch of the cathedral for you, & one I did on the other side of the river. I must try & send you an autumn tint one too. I have found another dial – but it has no motto. It is in the Barrack Square.[3] But there do

seem to *be* dials in this part of the world, which is a great point – & I keep an eye open as you know. Capt. Patton sent me 2 woodcocks & a wild duck the other day – so we have had a fine feast. This month we lay in our winter stores – Firkins of butter – barrels of potatoes, eggs for 3 or 4 months &c. &c. &c. Provisioning against the siege of winter which "shuts up" the river till April or May. In winter, by the bye, letters are rather more *uncertain* affairs than now – so never be *frightened* if mine miss – & you don't hear. We have had your little lithograph of Ecclesfield framed in butternut wood, & it hangs above *the* table. On this [the left] side Eleanor's ink

stand – book & envelope case – Mrs. I.J.'s workbox. Japanese lady's shoe. paper case I gave to R. at Sevenoaks. Teacher's prayer book. Thermometer – compass – Mrs. Bryce's pug penwiper &c. &c. &c. On this [the right] side – A. Regie's chinese wood box. B. Aunt Anne's work basket. C. Japanese candlestick. D. & E. Photos of self & Rex. F. Chinese child's shoes brought by Rex from some rebel village into which they went. AB's bible[4] – Eleanor's letter weights &c. Jack Clough's workbox – China dog – old japan box of mine. Japanese bronze – little Chinese boxes &c. – in the middle my despatch box – Your portrait given by Brownie – rulers – & the blotting book F. Smith gave me –

Monday. We had a very pleasant evening yesterday. After evening service Mrs. Clerke, Miss Sulivan & I drove up with the General in his close carriage – Capt. Clerke bringing Rex & the other gentlemen – a Colonel Peters – Capt. Hipsley & Mr. Mundy, & Miss Rainsford[5] – we had a swell little dinner – & a very pleasant evening. I am sitting at home this morning every minute expecting Miss S. to look at our diggings before she goes. We walked home last night – a fine moonlit night: but it is beginning to feel decidedly cold! – Miss S. won't be home till Xmas, but the Clerkes are going home for a bit, so I will send the leaves &c. &c. by them. We were a very merry pleasant party last night. The General is very pleasant & chatty & hospitable, the Clerkes are a particularly nice young couple – he is quite a model A.D.C. Miss Rainsford is a character. She is young (not *very* – but a young lady) always laughing & poking fun at everybody, & apparently very popular with gentlemen – but she is also sort of amateur – soeur de charité-to-the-higher-classes here. That's to say, if she hears of anybody ill, she thinks nothing of taking herself off to them – & night-nursing – & working like a trooper if *anybody* wants *anything.* She seems popularly known to everybody as "Sally" & called upon when wanted!! She seems to have a sort of prophet's chamber in the Clerke's house – who are very fond of her. Col. Peters is her cousin, & seems to have somewhat similar characteristics. He is about 35 & awfully full of chaff, but he won't marry because he devotes himself to keeping his mother & sisters. He is a high Churchman & fond of music. He told Rex he had once heard the Hallelujah Chorus here & when it began he drew in his breath & being too much entranced to breathe nearly died of the excitement. He said "What *must* it be" when a great number of really fine voices sang it! – Capt. Hipseley is jolly & amusing – & Mr. Mundy very nice. Altogether we were a very pleasant party. Miss S. has just been & gone. It is almost like touching a link with you & having to drop it again. Seeing someone who has been at Ecclesfield so lately, it feels as if one ought somehow to see one of you! I am so glad she has been; – for your sake too, dear Mum. You will like hearing of this nice home of ours & of *us* & our wigwam from her – now she has seen all with her own bodily eyes!! I cannot write you a long letter this time – You see I have been so busy. But this will just tell you we are well & flourishing.... With Rex's best love & my own

Ever dearest Mum Your ever loving daughter

Juliana Horatia Ewing

We are both very well thank GOD.

Capt. Clerke is going to lend me a grammar of the Melicete language!

I have got the book. It is not a grammar but a book of prayers.[6] Awfully curious – & clever old Rex had said the other day it sounded to him to have an affinity to Hebrew – which proves curiously to be the case! –

LETTER
II

Oct. 15. 1867.

My darling Dot.

... I can only write a scrap today. I am wildly busy copying sketches & varnishing leaves to send you. Capt. Clerke the A.D.C. & his wife are going to England & will take them for me.... Thank the dear heads *gratefully* for the teapot, & the Mum for her little sketch. I do so love her little sketches – & any she or anybody will ever scratch me down of Home bits will be thankfully received. Especially if a written notice of the *coloring* is appended. N.B. You & Dina *must* go on with your drawing. You cannot *think* the pleasure it is to me – And how people who can't sketch at all do *groan* about it. *Rex* is going to learn this winter!!! He has been working at *Ruskin* & sat down the other day & did really a splendid hasty copy of a thing from Harding's book in pen & ink. My mind is much "exercised" just now on the subject of *curtains*. I hear that stuff is nearly *double* the English price here – & am almost disposed to get you to send them out to me per "Lampedo," a ship which comes soon. I shall decide before next mail. I mean to have plain heavy red curtains in my drawing room I think – that I can make at home – for the winter. I mean to put the pole right across the bow – & have a curtain on each side – to draw & meet in the middle. They will look artistic & pretty in the daytime I think – & I don't

think it will matter shutting out the bow on cold nights. The room is *ample* big! & it will be easy & economical. I wonder whether you are using Miss Jones' *grey* curtains at home? – I know the Mum used periodically to put them up in Regie's room, who as regularly had them taken down. Perhaps now Regie is away they *are* established. But if they are still lying by I am tempted to ask if (supposing I have curtains out) whether they could be spared me for my dining room which is papered with grey. I would gladly give a 2d hand price for them – especially in concert with the old white muslin (Miss Jones) ones which are somewhere in the nursery cupboards! –

I am sending a book of Autumn Leaves to the Mum – & a few for Mrs. Bryce – & for Aunt Mary. Also some bits of bead work for Mrs. Aveling – & Annie Bonar – which might be sent to Howard St. for an opportunity.[1] I am so sorry for this dull letter in answer to yr jolly ones – but the Clerkes go on Friday – & tomorrow we spend the morning at Hebrew with the Bishop – & the evening there too with a choir meeting. Last night we were at a 22d Ball. A very jolly & very pretty one. Being a fine frosty moonlit night we walked there & back – Dancing with Hector's master he said "if you're *that* spooney on him you shall have his photo." I owned to the soft impeachment[2] & "lives in 'opes of seeing" it. It is not esteemed a *pleasing* likeness as a  bone was held before him to keep him quiet – which led to his been *took* with his mouth wide open. As his usual expression is a *close shut* smile I fear it hardly will be as like as could be wished. R. wants me to go to see some athletics of the 22d this P. M. So Adooo! . . . I sat with Mrs. *Shore* (the M. of the Rolls is another party) among the turbans last night for a bit – "Do you find the days long enough my dear?" "Not 1/2!" I said, "but they say the winter *is* long." "You will never find it long enough my dear!!" Literature & the fine arts! Morning prayers – Evening outs – housekeeping – & life size portraits in oils. She's a wonderful party.

Goodbye You beloved old thing. Our dearest love. Your own loving old JOW.

[AE's Postscript]

My dear Love to all and sundry; but I have not the time to *write* today. Yr Afft REX.

LETTER
12

Oct. 21. 1867. Fredericton.

My dearest Dina.

. . . Many thanks darling, for all your amusing letters. I am so sorry I gave Dot such a dull letter by the last mail, but I *was* so busy & tired out, & had been doing my best to write poor dear Mrs. A. an amusing & illustrated one. I will just tell you about the things I got off. I am sorry to say only 2 sketches, but I mean to send some more before Xmas. If you girls or any of you care for them – I will send one each – if not the Mum may have all. I send her especially the large one of the Cathedral – & I think she will want one of the autumn tints when I send them [Plates 4–5] – the others are to be divided – If I don't put the names – eldest choose first. That is if you care for them. How I wish they were not so wretchedly inferior! But you know I draw *pretty faithfully* – & sketches of these parts are not so common in England. We send the Mum a book of autumn leaves (everybody says they are not nearly so bright this year as usual — but you remember how bright the fires always were till one came to the sitting room window!!!) The little sketch outside is from Nature.... The shop where I wanted to get the indian things for Mrs. A. had sent its stock to the S. John Exhibition[1] – so I must take another opportunity. Let someone tell her this please. I send a little cross of leaves such as they make here for Aunt Horatia in case she shld be near you – to hang up in her room as a Xmas decoration – & a few leaves in a book for Aunt Mary – & a small do. for *M.M.* with my love. I send between 3 & 4 dozen varnished leaves to make a couple of devices for the Church, & a few for Masbro' if Maggie thinks the Whites would care to have them. The season really has been bad for them – or I might have sent better, & I was hurried. They will either make Xs or might be

 put so round sort of white shields with illuminated texts. I thought of one over the Prayer Desk & one the Pulpit — with perhaps "From

the rising of the sun until the going down thereof My Name shall be great" – & "Glad tidings of great joy to you & all people" – or something similar – I think there are plenty of leaves, but if not, sooner than make them *poor* – take the Masbro' ones. I return 2 books that don't belong to me – & send a few seeds (none of them of very pretty plants) to be sown on the island & about the moat.[2] Pray *look* at the Asclepias seed. It is a great big handsome leaved plant with a dull looking bunch of flowers, which when you look into them are (like London Pride) very pretty. It was the 1st flower Rex thoroughly *attacked* in the botanical line. He worked & worked at it – pulled it to pieces & found it out on purely scientific principles. We have watched its great pods for some time & at last got a ripe one. Isn't it *lovely*? – Alas! Frost slew the Impatiens – before I got the seed. Put the Asclepias near the moat or in the shrubberies – the Yellow Spirea is a tall but handsome yellow thing. I am just about to lay out my garden, & long for Charlie. Mrs. Medley is a splendid gardener, better than Thompson is I think – which is something. By the bye I was told the other day that as a girl she was engaged to an officer who was killed – & then she devoted herself to nursing – till she married the Bishop. She is a dear old thing & very amusing & as lively as 10 larks. We had such fun the other day. We were at a Choir Evening there when the Bishop told me that the Governor was going to hold a farewell Levée[3] the next day & that married ladies were to go – & that Mrs. M. didn't want to – & he wanted her to be persuaded. Next morning about 9 I went up there to ask her advice as to my own costume – being by no means ready for a Levée I thought. We had no end of chaff. It was laid out that I had only one silk which being black was complimentary to the departing Ex: but unsuited to the occasion. At intervals the Bishop kept putting in his oar "Take the Hebrew Bible under yr arm" "*Do* be a sensible woman, & rise above these vanities" &c. &c. Tell Dot that her *grey skirt* once more came in useful – Having been my "going away" dress it has now graced a N.B. Levée!! I wore it & my white bernous. Rex was in full fig & cocked hat – the Bishop in Doctor's gown & hood (I *settled* his hood for him, & he & Rex just corrected a chant before starting). Mrs. M. turned out in Bishop's purple – & away we went. We ladies were all round the room – the fattest & vulgarest of little Mayors[4] read a farewell address – the General read another – there was no end of handshaking – & we parted in much good humor. It was a comical affair – but more sincere than most farewells I should fancy, for Gen. Doyle is deservedly popular, & there seems a terrible chance of a local man being appointed of low birth – a Wesleyan & very bigoted – undependable – narrow – obnoxious to the R.C. population beyond anything – in consequence of his making sensational statements at protestant meetings – which he couldn't substantiate & wouldn't withdraw, till the R.C. Bishop forced him into an apology.[5] People seem in a dreadful fright about it, & everybody *longs* for a man from England, but I fear there is no hope. Meanwhile Col. Harding is temporary

64

Governor.[6] We went at 9.o'clock to see the General & his party off by the boat. It was one of the loveliest mornings I ever saw – Such bright lights on the morning mists and the autumn trees! We went on board to bid the Clerkes goodbye, & then the steamer went off with a salute of guns, & ladies' pocket handkerchiefs, & gentlemen's hats. About the curtains I can do nothing this mail. There seems a doubt whether we may not move into other rooms (of the house) for the winter. I was up at one of the 22d people's – on Saturday getting some 2d hand things that belonged to Capt. Gilling who was "burnt out" – & is now on leave. We have got a butler's tray – a table – some wine glasses &c. & (if they fit,) some curtains for our bedroom. This A. M. the bishop has been. I am reading Hebrew & German. Mrs. M. – the dear Soul – has told me to send her my bulbs for the winter & she will pot them for me. They are such a good, funny, quaint looking pair! – We are now deep in consultations for Xmas decorations. He does look so quaint in his great winter coat! – Fancy Rex taking to drawing! – He sat down in the wood by me the other day when I was sketching & did 2 sketches with a stumpy old blue pencil – *entirely by himself* – I think I am  very generous to spare the enclosed one for the Mum. *He* thinks it is not fit to send, but considering the difficulty of the subject, & that he had not the least help (I was sketching quite another subject) I think it is worthy of a Household Album. He has done a much better one from the window – & in fact I think quite inherits his Mother-in-law's *touch* with the pencil. My great desire just now is to learn to *spin*. My maid is a good spinster & it is just possible she may get a wheel belonging to her mother into the house & teach me!! As to getting her to *sew*, her sewing is too atrocious even for me to endure so I mend R.'s things & my own, myself. We are truly comfortable with her, & when I see other ladies in the thick of such troubles as we have *passed through*, I feel very thankful. Especially as she seems so fond of us – it is quite pleasant. She is desperate untidy as a housemaid—but one can't have everything. She says she won't leave me this winter, which is a great comfort to me. By the bye do *impress well* on the dear Mum to sit as easy as she can to the arrival of the mails in winter. It sometimes makes between a week's difference & a fortnight. I am most anxious she shld understand this—or she will have no end of worry. She knows now *I* am not apt to *fail* in writing—& if we were both *non inventus* the Medleys would write. No news is emphatically good news from us—but the winter mails are apt to be uncertain. Sometimes in December—very quick fair passages—but quite uncertain. We have had some cold weather & lately a glorious "S. Luke's Little Summer"— The brisk weather makes me feel very jolly, & I don't dread the winter one bit. Mrs. M. is going to lend me a large screen for one of the rooms, & she & the Bishop keep a watchful eye over our proceedings. Today His Reverence told me never to go long without food in winter. . . . N.B. I am much fatter than I was—& R. is always teasing me & saying I shall be just like Mrs. Wake. (He is not a *skeleton* himself!!! as how he *busts*, some of his underclothes do testify!!!!!!) Tell the Mum I lent them "These Three"[7] & they were *charmed*. Mrs. M. thinks it, as I do—one of the best things she has ever done. They had the Brownies[8] at the same time—& have said nothing about *it*. So it is not mere compliment. I am slowly working at Reka Dom. Then I am going to do a child's tale about the "Cat washing the dishes"— By the bye, please ask Mother what is the origin of calling that play of sunlight on the nursery wall "the Cat &c." Was it *she* or the Nurses who used to tell *us* the name—& is it an old idea—or the Mum's invention.[9] Please let me know this. . . . I have begun to make a collection of dog's photographs. And please sometime *Trot* must be taken in Sheffield for us. I have got *Jim*, Rough,[10] Jack's old dog, & am expecting *Hector* daily. Any contributions thankfully received. . . . I had a jolly drive with the Medleys the other day. We got out & went across country a bit—over hedges & ditches & I sketched a little at intervals. Once I said—"I really hope we may be here another summer that I may get some of these *trees* done"—& the B. groaned "Don't *talk* of another summer! You must stay here forever!"—— R. is still at the organ—& the Bishop bristles with new chants which R. throws an eye over. R. is at work on a Xmas anthem. Words my choosing –

Recitative & bass solo – "And Balaam said — I shall see Him but not now – I shall behold him but not nigh." Alto solo – "There shall come a Star out of Jacob." Chorus – "A star out of Jacob." [Alto solo –] "& a Sceptre shall rise out of Israel." Chorus – "And a Sceptre out of Israel." Quartet – "Thy throne O GOD is forever & ever. A sceptre of Righteous-ness is the Sceptre of Thy Kingdom." Final chorus not decided on. I must stop – ADieu – Dear Love to all

Ever your most loving sister J. H. E.

R.'s best love.

LETTER

13

"Hector" – property of Mr. Parry 1/22 Regt from a photogram
in the possession of Mr. Alexander Ewing.
Fredericton N.B. Oct. 1867

19 Sunday. Trinity. [27 October] 1867.

My dearest Mother –

It is libellous of the dear old thing's mouth – & of him generally!
Imagine his dear *pink* mouth & nose! – Mr. Parry & Capt. Patton

called the other day with the photo. & a charming one it is. Hector called also & I kissed his pink nose & round head. We are *so* grateful to you for loving poor old Trotus. Rex *groans* after him occasionally, but I do think this winter would have been his death. And it is delicious to hear of him with his nose close to the hospitable Yorkshire bars – & to think of you kissing him, and bringing us to his remembrance. Poor old dear! – Give him kisses from us both please! – and say – "*Who* bit the strap of his master's armchair?" — in his ear!!

I was *especially* glad to hear viâ U.S., as the Halifax mail was delayed – having to put back into Liverpool for a storm we hear – so there were no English letters till Saturday morning, & last time we had them on Wednesday. But the season of uncertain mails is beginning, & though we *may* hear very regularly, one must be prepared for any amount of *possible* delay. We were rather surprised not to get a "bill of lading" from the agent at Liverpool who sent our boxes – & unfortunately we cannot quite decipher even the name of the ship. In replying to this, just give it & all particulars (name of agent at Liverpool & date of sailing) please. Don't *bother* about it, as by the time you get this, we shall probably be rejoicing in our things, but *on the chance* of any untoward delay, we may as well have all the facts. Meanwhile I shan't *freeze*. I have got Maggie's old linsey to scrub about in – & my own brown rep which is warm – & no end of good flannel petticoats – & some jerseys & warmish stockings & the sealskin cap – & good velveteen jacket (it *has* been a treasure. I wear it regularly now with much comfort) & the thick black one I bought at Sevenoaks – & a monkey muff. I can keep warm till the things arrive & we pile our bed with cloaks &c. &c. As to Rexie, he has some flannel shirts &c. & some thickish merino stockings which are new & warm. (N.B. I *wldnt* let him wear them in the summer. I made him wear his old & *holy* ones, & these (after presenting the worst of them to our milkman (!!!)) I am mending up for next summer!!!!! There's economy for you!) He bought his predecessor's military coat – a large thing frogged & braided, & trimmed with black astracan – & his fur gloves – & he will get his astracan cap here. We have just had a bit of such glorious weather, & I even hope we may yet have a bit more. Frosts at night & a good deal of cold – but during the *sunny* part of the day, the most divine clearness & warmth – so that for 3 days we have *sat out* sketching at *noon* – when we had to have a fire in our bedroom at *night*. On Friday Rex came home early & we took *our* things (he has a big note book like mine, & sketches vigorously!) & set off up one of the "back streets" as we call them – (they are really more like broad lanes) & he took to a distant view of the college grove with a foreground of willows (I would proudly send it if I could spare it – which I *won't*!!!) I made a tolerably successful water color of the broad street with its quaint wooden houses, & one of the huge magnificent *pines* that remain here & there in the town — trees of "the old forest" as people say. Id est – the remains of that part of the universal forest that was "cleared" for Fredericton to stand upon. I was rather proud of the pine when it was still in pencil – (though I said to R. "if only *the Mum* could have a go at these trees!") I had hardly time to do it quite so thoroughly in colors, for Rex *wldnt* let me outstay the sun! – Sarah beheld the sketch yesterday & observed "Now that *is* really good. It's not in the power of mortal hands to do more!" Before, in looking at my sketches she came to the complimentary conclusion – "But you've a *great head*, & there's no two ways about that!"!!!!!!! . . . I wonder if I send it per next mail whether you would have room for a *very* short Xmas sort of prose idyll suggested to me by a scene I saw when we were hunting for a sketch the other day.[1] If I *can* jot it down – I don't suppose it would be more than 2 or 3 pages. If A.J.M. declines! send it to Miss Yonge.[2] (*Try next door!*) I don't think it will be well to begin afresh with *Mrs. O.* without going straight forward till it is finished off. I am working steadily at it. *Monday Evening.* I was interrupted by the arrival of the Medleys, to fetch us up to "Bishopscote" to tea. His little Reverence carefully examined me as to whether I had on proper *wraps*, & expressed his opinion that I ought to "stuff with meat" — !!! & asked me to make him a sketch of the Cathedral. He has chosen the one he wants – an autumn tinted one. I am only too glad to be able to do *anything* for them – They are so kind. Talking of curtains the other day – Mrs. M. was showing me how they have sort of quilted curtains, made of old blankets covered, – put close upon the windows instead of shutters – a luxury in which we don't indulge here – & forthwith gave me what she calls "an old blanket to tear up –" but till the box arrives we have it on our bed!! They went off on another Episcopal tour this morning, & have left us the use of their carriage for a week!! Fancy my joy! Today we crossed by a ferry, & drove for several miles northward through the forest. There was a good deal of *sameness*, but some lovely bits, & I got a new & lovely lycopodium, & two fresh water algae – one I think what I sent before, & the other common looking. I have just laid them out, but wish I cld find something better. A jolly Catrochosperme or something. I suspect the intense heat dries up the streams in summer – there are so few. There seem lots of diatomaceae only I know *nuffin* about 'em. This is from memory a sort of

sketch of the "clearings" we have passed through today. They begin by setting fire to the underwood, which clears the way to the felling of the trees. The result is, that a "cleared" place like this is covered with *bleached* & *charred* stumps of pines, & many of the pines lie full length – being I suppose too much burnt to be worth removal. The distance today was a lovely blue. This melts into the nearer belts of rich evergreen firs, spruces, hemlocks &c. & against these the white & blackened pines stand out in ghostly relief on the clearings, & perhaps close by is a new pine wood settler's house – the tree in all its stages poor thing! – I have put our *carridge* on the road, & you may fancy Darby & Joan jogging along, surrounded by scraps of fern, moss, &c. picked up en route, notebooks in hand – old Jacob the Bishop's man driving, & old *Bruce* the Bishop's dog running (bless his nose!) by the side....

Certainly this lovely bit of autumn weather is a charming "let down gently" before the winter. When we were out at about 11.30 the other day – I can only describe it by saying that the air felt as it sometimes feels in England *very early* on a fine beautiful morning. The lights were misty & tender in the quaint quiet streets, & there was a silent sunshine over everything that was lovely, & just a touch of invigorating frost in the air. I expect to see many amusing scenes by the riverside in winter. Our bedroom & dining room you know face the river – & the horse ferry is just opposite to our door – From 7.30 to 9.30 about – A.M. – the market carts with vegetables, butter, poultry, potatoes &c. &c. are coming over from "the other side." One characteristic of this place is the way the weaker sex drives itself about. From the Misses Simonds & their Mamma (our very nice neighbors who have a place further up the river)[3] to farmeresses & their daughters – *shanderydans*[4] of all shapes & sizes driven by women – go about all day long. You may meet Mrs. Simonds, driving any number of her numerous young people into town – & it looks so funny to see her matronly, quiet face in its close bonnet – over a big horse's nose – & we have seen pretty little Bessie Simonds driving 4 or 5 of her father's workmen into town early in the morning. Again old Simonds (Ex. officer & very goodlooking & gentlemanlike) has passed us with the early worm – driving his own *truck* to town, 2 or 3 of his daughters having

taken the opportunity to come down upon it! Excuse the horses! You know I am not equal to them. Now in the morning it is 8 o'clock or more before the mist has cleared off the river – & then there is a fine hoar frost on the ground & the ferryman wears a cap like an esquimaux & the carts that come over have fur rugs, & the

"Begining to feel cool!
"Xmas is coming!"—

farmeresses are all in *boas* & most of their husbands in fur caps—&
long boots. Bed time!— I must say good night for tonight dear
Mum. *Tuesday*. I am all my lone—for I have let my maid go to see
her Aunt who is ill . . . —I have just answered the door bell—to find
a fat old lady from "the other side" who wants to know if I want any
"hog's fat" or any butter. I have declined both!!! Sometimes it is
very amusing. Imagine a ring before breakfast into which Rex
rapidly investigates. (For like all the masters of households I have
ever known or heard of, he is always impatient to know who is—or
has been—to the front or back doors!!)— Voice from the road. "Do
you want a quarter of beef?" Head of household of 3 persons.
"No—we don't." I suppose though, before long we shall be storing
our cellar with more than one quarter of beef, & 2 or 3 sheep for the
winter siege!!— If I send it at all my tale shall come by the Halifax
Mail without fail. It will be called "The two Xmas Trees"—I *think*.
The Algae are different to the other I sent. I think I shall take them
to Prof. Bailey's tonight—we spend the evening there. Goodbye
dearest Mum. With Dear love to all. Your loving ones J. H. E. &
A.E.

. . .

LETTER
14

Oct. 29. 1867. Fredericton.

My dearest Dot.

... I *must* have a little feminine sympathy over my domestic concerns! & tell you what I have been doing. Sometimes I really long for a good quiet – feminine chat with you!! How we *should* gossip if you *could* fly over for an hour or two! – I must tell you some of the 22d – the Gillings – were burnt out before they went to England, & what they saved was left in the hands of Mrs. Tyacke to "dispose of." So I went up – & have invested £5.8.4 very satisfactorily I think. Item. 1 *carpet* for our dining room in very fair order – a formal pattern by no means ugly – for $10 – that is about £2.1.8. cheap enough! – then 12/6 for a butler's tray of butternut wood, which is quite an ornament to our dining room – and about 12/9 for a butternut wood sidetable for the dining room – & I got 2 remnant chintz curtains for 3/4 which we have made up for our bedroom, & as the paper is blue & white, & the chintz red rosebuds on a white ground – the effect is decidedly good!! 2 lovely little glass dessert dishes for 3/9 – (ground glass) & for ^d9 (clever me!!) I purchased a little old glass sugar basin – that has been smashed to smithereens – but *well rivetted* & beautifully *cut* all over. For "thinks I to myself" – I have no sugar basin but the one belonging to my tea set – which is both ugly & broken. Now when the dear Heads' teapot comes – & I have my Estcourt cream jug – I shall fill my glass basin with loaf sugar – & the rivets will never show! & broken glass lasts long!!!!! For you see in time we must return some of the endless hospitality we have received, & Rex says I may do so *as* I like, & I think tea & supper will shoot our means & constitootions. We dine off the thick white pottery of the Province ourselves – but I felt a longing for something rather better in the way of what Mr. Darling would call *desert* dishes. Well!!! Once upon a time when

Mr. Manners Sutton was Governor[1] – he had a lovely set of china – breakfast, dinner, dessert &c. &c. all complete. *Something like our* dessert service at home – only I think handsomer, flowers in the centre of the plates & a broad buff coloured border with *lots of gold*!! – At his sale it was distributed among lots of people & eventually the Tyackes found themselves in possession of 12 plates – & 11 dessert dishes. Of course they had more dishes than they could use! – But "on dit" that an auctioneer in the town had got some of the plates years ago – & *might* not have sold them. I went to the auctioneer & found he had 12 plates – a good many *chipped* but no cracks or breakages. We have bought the 12 for $4

i.e. $16/8 — & 5 dishes for $5. i.e. £1.0.10 (2 of the dishes being broken at the *edge*) so we have got this set — 12 plates – 3 high – & two low dishes – for £1.17.6. which I don't think would be a bad bargain in England!! — A ring! If that is the carriage I must stop.

It is! – How provoking!! He is about 1/4 of an hour too early. ADoo darling – Yr lovingest – Judy

LETTER
15

[from AE]

Fredericton, 4th November. 1867.

Dearest Mum

I have only very little time to write a line this mail, for I have been acting as Secretary to Jow, who was anxious to send her Christmas story by this mail. It is splendid! I have no doubt you will think so too. It is, in many respects, the best thing she has done.

I have little to say. We are almost incredibly happy – (only I *did* think I *should* make her happy) – and we get fonder of each other every hour, I think. That is "good news" for a mother, I know. Jow is very flourishing— You have never seen her so well, and she gets (for *her*) so much "filled out" that I tell her—(N'en dites mot!) that she will be a little round thing like Mrs. Wake before she gets back to you. We have, indeed, been placed in a delightful place—out of England, I hardly know any place so desirable—and, in some few respects, it is even better than England.

Our house is going to be very warm—at present, we cannot always *bear* the drawing room fire at night—it *does* throw out *such* a heat, and we have got our *hall stove* now "fixed"—and many people here never use any other fire *but* their hallstove, as it warms the whole house (we are told—we have not yet lighted it.)

The Medleys are very "tribey" and like ourselves—and Mrs. Medley is like a Mother and Sister combined to Jow—while Episcopus—a brother:composer—he is a great delight to me. . . .
Ever your afft soninlaw

AE.

[JHE's Postscript]

Dearest Mum. I send the M.S. by this mail to Bell,[1] to save a day in case you have given him instructions to print. This is in case you can put it in—but it has run beyond my expectations, & I fear will be 9 pages if not 10!!! It is dreadfully late I know, but not a word of it was written last mail— I saw the house on one of the sweet days we were out sketching—and it is so appropriate to Xmas it seems a pity to miss it. Please don't let Bell put a great *Fredericton* in caps. after my initials. The Bishop's initial being J. it looked exactly as if it were his signature.[2] He might just as well put *Ecclesfield* after yours. Please tell Dot I have discovered with horror that one of the earrings is left behind— I will send it by one of the 22nd whom I know. We *are* well & happy thank God! as the dear old boy says. No time for more— Always yr loving—

J.H. Ewing.

Waiting for the Ferry, 5 November 1867

LETTER
16

Nov. 12. 1867.

My dearest Dot.

I am grieved when I think how you must have been fidgetting about the earring. Though I am almost astonished at your *dreaming* of its having been "abstracted." One odd earring – from a parcel sealed & in the keeping of a known "party." I hope nothing – or very little was said to the Grundys – for it wld fidget them, & it was a real kindness in her to take it, for I barely knew her. It was densely stupid of me to have sent it alone, but in a little heap as it lay, I suppose I concluded that the 2 were together – & everything was got & sent in such a hurry. When I got to Halifax I found that the voyage had upset things a good deal – the powder puff was all over the dressing case – I put everything straight & wrapped all the jewellery in bits of tissue paper – so when I go into the case for my lockets &c. I don't really *see* what is there or not. If it had not been that I was *hunting* for a brooch, I shld not have

76

found it the other day. I hope you will get it all safe – & very soon: for I have sent it by a Mr. Tatham of the 22d who goes home by this mail – He is a pleasant good fellow. Very young, & rather in the boys' style – fair &c. – but with a *firmer* look rather, & somewhat grave like Steenie. *Why* we know not – for he is obviously a gentle-man – but he was *in the ranks.* He rose, & is now Lieutenant. I *suspect* him of a penchant for Miss Grundy. They looked very pen-sive just before she left, sitting on 2 chairs listening to the band – & when she was gone & he got me tea – we began with the choir (he is in the S. Anne's Choir here)[1] – & gradually arrived at the conclusion that the winter was very dull here for a *lonely* fellow. Of course if a man takes his home about with him it is different &c. &c. The next thing I hear is that he has got a 4 months leave to England which may get extended to six. Just time to do it nicely – & I shall not be surprised if Miss G. returns as Mrs. Tatham. He will post the earring to you – & he will also post to Mrs. Aveling some little indian things for her & Annie Bonar with our love.

I say this 1st as I am so sorry my carelessness has bothered you. Now I am sorry to say that last mail brought us the news that Rex's Mother is dead. He is very good about it, & though he is sad, he only says *I* am now literally Everything he has. We expect *partic-ulars* next mail. The poor old lady has been so many years an invalid you see, that in some respects it is almost a matter of thankfulness. For years & years – before her husband's death – a mysterious sort of nervous affliction, with periodical fits neither epilepsy nor pure hysteria, has been on her. Her husband had every possible advice & no one could do anything, & it has gradually been wearing her down. On the 17th Octr she was more well and cheerful than she had been for years, & before dinner went upstairs to her room, & not coming down, someone went to her & found her "reclining on the bed" – dead – without any sign of pain or struggle. They call the immediate cause of death – apoplexy. Rex says she was the sweetest tempered person he ever knew – & she seems to have been so good – & had so many troubles that there *is* nothing to regret, & there seems nothing for *me* to fret about except for his sake. But somehow it feels sad – I would have liked her to have *seen* her son happy with me. 14 years without her husband – & the same

blow that took him, to exile her only child from her![2] It seems a
hard life, & to have *seen* him happy before her death, & heard from
me that I appreciated their troubles & would do all that lay with
me so far as I could to make the rest of life smooth to him—would
have been a comfort one fancies. It is a great comfort to me to
think that I *did* write her as nice a letter as I could, & sent her a
sketch of our house—& a view on the river—& told her I would do
my best to make him happy. Perhaps it *did* please her a bit—& she
felt—"Nunc Dimittis &c—"!— Mr. James McCombie wrote—& sent
very kind messages to me. She had sent my letter to them all—&
they seem to have liked it. She is buried with the rest of his people
in the churchyard of an old country church that was once the
Cathedral Church of Aberdeen. I am going to get Mr. J. McC. to
send me a photo. of it.... It is Sunday [10 November], & I am
rather sleepy!!— On Sundays we don't dine till after 8— A. M. service is at 11— At 2.30 I go to school. Then I come back, & sometimes
bring Mrs. Coster with me, & we have afternoon tea à la Ecclesfield. Then Evensong at 6.30—& then we dine! We have had a taste
of winter, but it has receded for a while. On the 6th the 1st snow
fell— On Thursday night it went down to 16 Fahrt & on Friday
night to 14. There were great fears that the river would close at
once, and there was good skating up the Nashwaak. It was most
curious to see wood boats &c. trying to get down to S. John before
it was too late—ploughing through the ice. However a warm wind
came—the ice has disappeared & we have been living in fogs so
thick you couldn't see more than 2 or 3 yards ahead. I fancy we
may have open weather for another fortnight now. *Tuesday* [12
November]. Thank you darling, for the list of our things. We quite
long for the boxes. I am so glad of the *shawl*. For the Cathedral—or
any house one may be calling at—are apt to be hot—& one can't
"throw off" jackets—but a Himalayan shawl would make a serious
difference. The thing I fear you have forgotten, as it is not down,
the Negretti & Zambra thermometer for Rex. He wanted to test
this climate *accurately*. Common thermometers vary so, & people's
accounts are so vague & exaggerated. However, if it is omitted—
never mind. You have had such lots to remember! If the Editor
A.J.M. accepts my Xmas story—I think Bell will owe me nearly

£10 – which is about the amount you have *paid* of our things. Now a good bit of Mrs. O. is *ready* & I mean to finish it off as steadily as is consistent with doing my best – & also Rex has a gun & some things at Aldershot which are to be sold, so that very shortly we shall have some money of our own *in England*. . . . I made up my mind on 1st commencing to regulate our *living* if possible, by the table for an income of £250 in "Domestic Economy."[3] (Tell the Mum that noble work is invaluable, though what a moral mollycoddle that domestic medical man who compiled it must be!!!!) As our income is £300 it "leaves a margin" as Dickens' young man said[4] – and (as we have paid on the nail for our tables, chairs, carpets, beds &c. &c. &c.) "*no doubt you need it*"!!!! We have not been frozen, though it has been so cold. All the great coats, tschoga – chinese dressing gown &c. of the establishment have been heaped on our bed, & though we shall feel truly grateful, for a style of bed clothes more equable in distribution, & less liable to slide gracefully on to the floor in the night watches – we do very well. Today it is pouring cats & dogs so no fear of a frost again at present. That 1st night, though we had a fire in our bedroom, my sponge was frozen in the morning! It was only a wood fire however, & in the bitter weather we mean to burn coal which is *much hotter*. All our fires burn well & are very warming, & Rex has ordered double windows for our drawing room, as the landlord don't seem disposed to fork them out, they never having been used to this room before. Everybody says the houses here are only *too* warm in the winter. I went out on the coldest day for a walk & enjoyed it very much. People say the winters here are not nearly so cold as they used to be. One reason for which I long for the boxes is to see what my new dress is like. It seems so provoking to have to buy a new warm black dress – & as yet I have not done it, but am wearing Maggie's old dark linsey o'mornings & black silk on Sunday. If by any chance my new dress is an iron grey or any very dark color I might make it do. People are very kind. I had to make myself a black bonnet – so I got 1/2 yard of crape – & my last year's black shape, and was setting to work when Mrs. Coster (wife of the Rev. *Bass*) came in, & being a dab hand – took it out of my fingers & with some black ribbon & 1/8 worth of black flowers has manufactured the prettiest little affair!! With my silk – &

79

velveteen jacket & monkey muff – my Sunday turnout is swell rather than otherwise. The Chauncey's (22d people – she an awfully pretty irish bride) asked us to dinner last night – but of course we didn't go. We did go to the meeting of the glee society at the Coster's – a quiet evening for practise. You may imagine how I hear Rex's praises sung!!! Though the organist is well, the Bishop still holds him fast to one service, & at the other he sings in the choir. He is just copying out his part songs for production at the glee meetings: and his new Introit is to be practised at the next choir practise. "They that trust in the Lord &c." . . . Thank the Mum so much for the *dear* little drawing – it is in my Bible now. I enjoy the bits of home so much. I know that view from her window so well too. I am amused at her taking poor Dina's sketch & will send her some contributions to the New Album soon. I think she will be pleased with the 2 colored ones, but when I send others for you girls, she is not to be "*mean*" tell her!!!!!!!! Rex is going hard at drawing – & I wish you could see the naked Elm he has done branch by branch from our window – à la Ruskin. He reads "Modern Painters" to me at night, & is *that* severe upon unfaithfulness to Nature, that a lithographed willow (I strongly suspect by Harding) on the Medley's screen is an offence to him. Yesterday P.M. after service we went a walk, but as we went we saw an exquisite sunset sky developing itself. "Is there a window in the house we could sketch it from?" I asked. "To be sure!" shouted Rex "Come along!" & off we set, & *ran* home as hard as we could pelt – snatched up our books & pencils – & cut up the 2 flights of stairs into the garret. As Rex was in his uniform & long boots, & as I, by his orders, clenched my fists, & bent my elbows in approved "runner's" style, we must have been rather a public scandal, flying past the houses of respectable residents! By the bye, I have a fact "for a mother's ear" – viz that the Church being cold on one of these weekday services, Rex persuaded me to go home – so as the clergy came in – I went out! – Tonight we go to the Bishop's for Hebrew. Tell the Mum I will send some Reka Dom by next mail *if possible*. After R.D. there will be the Captain's return, & the Conclusion. If I can, it wld be advisable to go straight ahead now I think. . . .

Our dear love to the dear Mum—the only Mum between us now!—& to dear Father. Thank him much for his letter—& with best love to Dina & Maggie & everybody. I am always my darling duck

Your most loving sister
Judy.

. . .

LETTER
17

Nov 18. 1867.
Fredericton N.B.

My dearest Mum.

I shall not be able to send "Reka Dom'" by this mail, but I do hope to send it by next—(the Quebec.) I think this *may* be in time for January. I would have had it ready if I could—but I could not. A good deal that I had done seemed to me longwinded & unsatisfactory, & I have been cropping & improving it. I hope now it will prove "up to sample." My old man won't let me overwork, & neither he nor I like to send anything too hastily done. I think I told you that I think the latter no.s of A.J.M. very good. There is a nice variety in them. The idyll illustration was *nice*, but not one of Pasquier's *hits* I think. I think if ever it comes in with other stories in a volume, it would be almost worthwhile to have the ghost bird on the Pinetop done by Wolff.[1] Pasquier's *might* be 2 "converted" sailors drawing a moral in the British Workman. I do hope you may have liked the Xmas story. The house that inspired it—had really 2 Fir Trees in front. We saw it on that exquisitely clear day of which I told you—that felt like early morning. I daresay I seem very mean to

(This street is really much broader.)

you, not to send you more little sketches. But I have been so busy with Reka Dom, &c. &c. I mean as a Xmas offering to send you some little sketches of winter scenes &c. for the Album. I want to send some to the girls too – but I fear – you dear old lady – you will grab them all. But you must not. Winter is with us now I think – though no *great* cold yet – & the river is still just open I am thankful to say – for our things have not yet arrived, & we do hope they may do so before the river closes – (We *can* get them by land, but it is more troublesome –) We think they are pretty sure to come this week – The Calista Haws must be daily expected now. We have got the name all right now you see – & everything is in proper train for the boxes' coming straight forward. We have seen several sleighs already, & the jingling of the bells is becoming almost as familiar as the clang of the cowbells. You may imagine us now in our winter habits, & soon I hope in our winter clothes! I do not have the drawing room fire lighted now till after lunch. 1. The dining room table is more convenient for *work* & especially drawing, which one must chiefly do in the morning, as it gets dark so soon. 2. it is an east aspect, & looks out on the road & river – & is cheerful. 3. Rex is often away – & 4. I have made a rule to go out myself the 1st thing after breakfast. Going out in winter is so *troublesome* here, from the amount of dressing required, that one is apt to shirk it. Then the mornings are lovely often & P. M. it clouds over. The last 2 mornings I have walked with Rex to his office – It has been cold, but I do not mind it. Today there is a good deal of snow on the ground, & it has been rather amusing. It has not been worth getting a winter petticoat till I saw what came from home. (I shall wear the scarlet one.) and I have not got my winter shoes – so I was rather in straits as to how to hap myself up! – To crown all Mrs. Coster is ill – so my going to school was imperative. I wish you could have seen me!! The result was splendid!! & you may believe that under Rex's auspices I wasn't allowed to go out without more than due protection. Imagine me in 2 pairs of stockings of my own – Then boots – then a large pair of knitted stockings of Rex's over the boots & all – *then* goloshes!!!! I did protest against the heel of the stocking sticking out thus – & we got it stuffed in — 2 flannel petticoats – & my crimson baize one on top – which without a crinoline was *just* long enough, especially as no one could suspect one of a desire to display one's *ancles* in the circumstances! Regie's fur cap – with a shetland veil over nose & mouth – & my "cloud" 3 times round my neck. I *was* warm!!! For it is not so very cold, & being a lovely clear day I enjoyed it & *ran* a good deal for mere amusement. You

shld see the children now the winter is beginning – They tumble about in the snow like Newfoundland Dogs! I made a little sketch of the young Campbells next door with their sled the other day. I hope to send you it among my "scenes." Monday. 18. Nov. My dearest Mother you won't get much more epistle today! 1. I have been trotting about all this morning to Mrs. Medley's &c. &c. to see different kinds of winter leg & foot gear, and 2dly – the ice field on the river is so lovely with all its exquisite snow forms – that Rex & I are given up to drawing. *He* is making accurate studies of the foreground groups, *through a telescope!!!!!!!* After much consideration the telescope has been "fixed" thus – The window opened, & an old blue bandbox inserted – with holes cut through which the telescope passes "en position." The rest of the open space is filled up with Balzac's novels & clothes that want mending taken (without leave) from my big workbasket!!!!! He has really

made some lovely bits in pencil, & the shapes of these snowcovered blocks of ice *are* lovely. I must go & go on with mine – which is the more difficult task of making a large sketch of the whole field of ice. I have been out all the morning and quite enjoy it. Mrs. Medley has lent me a scarlet petticoat, & 2 pairs of *very* warm stockings till my things come. We are going to move into a back bedroom for the winter – that has double windows, & the stove pipe passing through it. Also we have made a splendid discovery. We have 2 *landings* – one a little one shut in with 4 doors opening on to it on which is the "dumb stove" as it is called. Well: this little landing is as warm as a little hothouse o'mornings & we have made it our bathroom! Sarah moves the bath there & shuts all the doors – & it is luxurious!! – The sun did look so lovely rising over the frozen river this morning. In fact our "views" remind me of my dim recollection of the beautiful plates in Kane's Arctic Explorations,[2] more than anything. Rex laughs at the Nickleby style of my letters – & foozling enough they are!! But I have so many things of such incongruous kinds to tell you, & such lots of other things to do. Tomorrow morning the Bishop is coming to read Hebrew & German & to stay to lunch. We are reading Genesis. He reads in German & we in Hebrew – so we can neither of us laugh at each other. I don't think we have stumbled at any Hebrew word – more than he did over the pronunciation of *Zwischen!!!!!* My love to all enquiring friends. I do mean to write to a few people soon!!! I am very much grieved my silver bracelet has never turned up. It is most extraordinary! I can't think how I *can* have lost it! – I am getting so terribly *Nickle-bean* it is time I stopped!! – Yesterday in Church we prayed for the 1st time for the New Dominion Parliament now in Session.[3] The Bishop (who has been preaching successive Sundays on *the Senses*) wound up the series last night, by preaching on "Common Sense." A great deal of it was admirable. My mind is chaotically divided between the considerations of – how to clothe my feet for the winter – what to have for luncheon tomorrow – how to represent an icefield in proper proportion – whether I can make a jacket & 2 gaiters out of an old greatcoat of Rex's – & how to compose my mind to Reka Dom!!!! And Mrs. Campbell because I have not got 1/2 a dozen bairns to mend for – swears I *can* have nothing to do & may come & sit with her while she darns stockings & makes winter overshoes for the little ones. She is a dear little thing, but I *have* plenty to do all the same!! Ever with our dear love Yr loving daughter

J.H. Ewing.

[AE's Note]

My love too, dearest Mum; to you and all the rest. AE.

LETTER
18

Fredericton. Advent Sunday.
[1 December] 1867.

My dearest Mother.

"A merry Xmas and a happy New Year" to all of you – We do wish it you with our dear love, and all our hearts. I cannot write much this time, for I am going to make a vigorous effort to finish tomorrow morning, the drawings that I have begun for you. I have had, somehow, so much to do in a small way that I have not got on so fast with them as I wished. The sketch of our drawing room is for *you* – for *the* book. N.B. The carpet really is dark green with narrow yellow stripes, & the screen is covered with pictures. Several of the "dry stores" (i.e. drapers' shops) are having cheap sales – & at one of these I bought the green cloth for our little square table for 1 dollar & 50 cents. = 6/3 – a nice little black and green thing – & now this table is devoted to the *tea tray* – for which there is as much difficulty in finding a place as ever there was at home. But already the little table begins to get covered up, & has to be "cleared" for tea!! As I came from school today, I met one of the "Express" carts going into "Orr's" (the Fredericton "Mitchell") full of boxes – Mrs. Coster's imagination (she was with me) stretched so far as to make her believe that she caught sight of our name on one of the boxes! I didn't see that, but I have hopes that the Xmas boxes may arrive tomorrow morning. Rex must be at his office till lunch – but he so much desires to have a hand in the unpacking that I mean resolutely to leave them for him, even if they arrive early. The weather has been very good to us! It has been quite mild, & yesterday the ice fairly broke up & away from the banks, & sailed in huge masses past our windows. It was most curious to see a *path* that had been marked by fir branches, to show the best *crossing place* – & which had originally been opposite to the Medley's house move slowly past our windows. Oh! there has been *such* mud! Such *ploughing* through earth saturated with melted snow & rain. Yesterday at noon it was 43° — and now behold the marvellous variations of the climate! – this morning at about 9 it was 2° – that is a difference of 41 degrees in less than 24 hours. Add to this a strong wind blowing, & a bright sun, & you *may* have some faint idea of how it felt as we went to Church. It is like swallowing very pleasant-tasted – & refreshing *knives*. The mud ridges on the ground have frozen like stone, & it is like walking on rugged rocks. At the same time I think it preferable to snow. There is no fear of getting one's feet *wet*. Early this morning – Clara Coster (she is a jolly nice girl of about 12) arrived with a parcel from Mrs. C. – a quilted jacket, & a pair of Clara's knickerbockers on loan, as she thought I ought not to go out today without the latter articles. Was it not good of her? "Clouds" are a great institution. The knitted veils you put all over yr head, & bring them around yr neck. The cold really is wonderful, & yet it is *splendidly* fine & invigorating, only one cannot do *much* outdoor work. It seems fatiguing. Today has really been cold because of the wind: but they say that generally when the thermometer is very low, there is no wind, & then it is delicious, as it was that lovely day when we were on the ice. Now you see that the boxes could not have arrived at a more appropriate moment. I have not felt a longing for my furs till today, but now I *shall* be glad of them! – I bought some grey yarn the other day, & Sarah is going to knit me a pair of stockings, & I am in daily expectation of a *squaw* to take the length of my foot for a pair of moccasons – for I have decided upon *layers* of stockings crowned with moccasons as my *snow* feet gear – moccasons being *warm* & the cold *does* nip one's toes!! Dearest Mum I must say goodnight. Rex says it is bedtime – & I want to get to my ("that is your"!) drawings in good time tomorrow.

ca. 25 November 1867

[AE's Continuation]

Monday. 2nd Decr 1867

Dearest Mum. Jowie is busy with your drawings, and therefore I add a few words to the preceding pages, instead of her doing so. Your, (and Dot's) letters of the 15th Novr arrived this morning. We, ultimately, got the Bill of Lading all right – it was delayed in consequence of the Consignees of the Vessel being a New York house. The boxes have *not* come: they *are* in St. John – but the roads have been almost impracticable for the last few days. A slight rise of temperature to-day has brought the snow which was anxiously looked for, and now the winter roads will be soon fairly formed, and all wheels discarded until spring –. This will soon make a path for our boxes to come to us quickly. We shall be much rejoiced to get them. We are quite *warm* enough, and all right; but blankets *are* more comfortable in bed than an assemblage of coats, cloaks, &

chogas, surmounted by an eider down quilt. They have a pestilent trick of being uncomfortably rugged and heavy. I sometimes lose my temper at them in the night, and wake Jow by anathematizing them as "loathsome duds"—and declaiming against the "intolerable servitude" under which we are as regards them. So the blankets will be hailed with gladness.

We are glad it pleases you to think of the Medleys. They are, indeed, kind and valuable friends. (I *can* take care of Jow without them—for, after all, I *know* more about her than anyone else—out here, at all events)—but, indeed, everyone is kind and nice. See what a *dea ex machina* Mrs. Coster proves, in the matter of millinery— She made Jow a mourning-bonnet out of a few scraps of stuff, which *looks* quite as if it had cost 5 guineas out of Madame Elise's (or whatever her name is) Boulevard des Italiens, Paris. There has been more discussion, and more ups and downs, as to the description of *chaussure* to be adopted by Mrs. Ewing for the winter than would (almost) have passed a dozen measures thro the local legislature. One (numerous) party recommended "Canadian Over-shoes"—composed of felt for the legs footed with caoutchouc—another section of the community nailed its colours to Wellington Boots *wholly* of India Rubber. Moccasins (now decided upon), I do believe are the best. And Jow and I enjoy the idea of her being a little squaw as to the "tootseys." I am going to have moccasins myself. (You are requested to observe those depicted on the feet of "Old Nokomis") "Old Nokomis", by the way, was a Micmac squaw, the first we saw, when we came to Halifax. I stopped and had a talk with her, and we thought her a dear old thing, and Jow logged down a rough sketch of her as I talked to her. She has on cloth trousers, (you understand) stuffed into the moccasins, and Jow has some thoughts of adopting this garment. (*Not* of wearing the ʰ———in any other sense, bien entendu!)

We (the troops particularly, I mean) are in our winter clothing now, and as soon as Jow's furs come, we must be photographed together.

I enclose (as a *temporary* substitute) *myself* in fur cap—long boots, and coat trimmed with fur, (considered like!), and long fur gloves. (J. is fond of the gloves, because they are like doge's paws!)

Now I am sure I have chattered more nonsense than you will care to read, and as I have to go back to my office for a little, I shall say Good Bye.

With the best Christmas wishes and love to *all* at Home – (more than ever my only Home now) I am

Ever yr afft Son in law
AE.

. . .

N.B. It is awfully nice of you to be so kind to our dear doggie. I often want to kiss his dear black nose! The lock of his hair is highly prized – and sticks behind one of his portraits. Be good enough to give him a kind message.

[JHE's Continuation]

Not as many [drawings] done as I shld like – & one is from the *original* of Mrs. A's sketch – but someone may like it. The 2 of Old Nokomis are for Dot in compliment to her birthday. The drawing room, the other sqaws & all little ones for *you*. The 3 big sketches are for the 3 girls & eldest choose first! – You know I sent you 2 before, & will send some more before very long. You will recognize our house in Our Street. The figure is Rex! – The bay window is our drawing room window. The road goes on to S. John – that is – going *into* the picture [Plates 6–8].

Must stop – Dear Love to all. . . .

Ever your loving daughter.
J. H. E.

LETTER
19

 — *My Moccasins!* —

Dec. 16. 1867

My dearest Mother.

I would have liked to have sent you a good letter – & February's Mrs. Overtheway but I have not been very well, & my old Boy won't let me do anything but nurse when I am *not*! Nothing to mention except for these reasons. A little cold & sore throat. (Don't imagine I'm hiding a quinsy!! I'm *not*!!!) The weather of the last few days has been most unusual even here at this time of year, & coming on so suddenly, many people have felt it a good deal. On Sunday – yesterday – 2 or 3 of the female staff of the Cathedral so to speak were not on duty. Item – Mrs. Medley – Bishopess – invalided. Mrs. Coster – wife of principal bass & herself soprano – invalided. Miss B. Roberts[1] – principal alto – invalided. Mrs. Ewing – wife of honorary organist & leaf-turner-over – invalided. We all seem to be looking up again: today is much milder, & now we shall probably have it so for a time. If I have a *cold* — people come & ask after me in the kindest way! – I have had Mrs. Medley & Mrs. Coster nearly every day though Mrs. M. is up to her eyes in decorations, & Mrs. C. has plenty to do. As no extra flannel came I commissioned Mrs. Coster to get me some in town when she went up, for my out-door knickerbockers, & the next time she appeared she brought – not the flannel – but the knicks, beautifully made up with black scalloped frills & ornamentations![2] – Isn't she a good soul? She said I wasn't very well, (as if *she* was!) & she thought she'd save me the bother of making them. She sent me some splendid Bermuda arrowroot the

Governor had given her. I quite enjoyed exhibiting my things to her & Mrs. Medley, and last night Mrs. C. was very busy looking at all the Gatty photo:s with great interest. . . . I never answered yr remarks about the "Scheme" dear Mum. One always has so much selfish news. We hear *nothing* hardly, here. I suppose men never *do* write to their friends abroad as they should. Rex says he knows he never did when he was at home. But as far as he can hear, the Scheme seems to be in a *disputatious* condition. R. has no doubt that Sir Wm. Power[3] will carry his own way eventually. Meanwhile, I fancy points are disputed, & under discussion. However even if *all* our hopes failed – which is not likely – Rex's next step is not far off, & we really can live here on £300 a year with *comfort*. We pay most things by the month; we are not very likely to be moved till we *better* ourselves, if "we" have then got our majority we can live anywhere. All this is *irrespective* of our "prospex" from the Scheme. Our debts are very small, & our furniture (paid for) will sell up for a nice little sum when we move. So you may imagine we don't feel very anxious. What I think we would both like wld be enough for a quiet little home at Home when we are *older*. Whilst one is young, going about is both pleasant & a great advantage, *especially* to *any one who writes*. And as when "we" are higher up in the service there are such things as retiring pensions & as we have abilities to – perhaps add some other vocation to this — we feel very thankful & contented with our lot! – There!!! Another thing you mentioned was my urging Rex to write. But about this I do not *want* to urge him unless he feels a "call" thereto. I don't think any good comes of writing below one's best because one has a relation who will get it into print, & it *would* be 2d rate, if it wasn't done spontaneously. And the few pounds from Bell wouldn't repay this to my mind. I want him in time to send you some good translations – because *they* are not the worse for being done by an effort, — He translates well – & I think A.J.M. is greatly enlivened & varied by an occasional introduction of this element. (Vide. Macé – & the spanish tales.)[4] At present he is working *hard* at Hebrew & his own turkish grammar. He wants to go well in for eastern languages – & has (no fixed) some idea of utilizing this not *very* common acquirement eventually. I will send Mrs. O. without fail by Portland, which will I think be in time. I hope it will be good. I have ideas of 2 other short stories (irrespective of Mrs. O.) The story of a *Screen*,[5] & another – When these are finished we may think of a volume I think. . . .

He says I must stop – & there is a caller I fancy too. ADieu my own Mum with our dear love.

Yr Ever loving daughter
J.H. Ewing.

Dear Love & 100000 Xmas wishes to all.

LETTER
20

Fredericton. N.B. 22d Dec. 1867.

My dearest Mother.

. . . Many thanks for A.J.M. for Dec. I think now you hardly need send it, as we mean to get it ourselves. It is a good No. I have known better for the letterpress but the illustrations are capital. All 3 good. Lewis Carroll ought to be pleased with his. . . . Did I ever tell you that Mrs. Medley prefers the *Emblems* to anything in the Maga.s? Next to that I think, she likes the Scaramouches which she is always alluding to.[1] (She was a confirmed pickle & tomboy in her youth – grew up a beauty, a rider, skater &c. before the 20 years in hospital. She mayn't skate here as she is Bishopess, but I think she regrets the fact! I told you how she bolted over the churchyard gate one day?) . . . I am awfully glad *my* contribution improves on acquaintance, & that Bell liked it. I should be *very* glad, please, always to hear any criticisms adverse or favorable that anybody happens to make on my things. It helps one. . . . We have just come back from Evening Church – where Rex's Anthem has been a thorough success. It went *capitally*. Old Coster's beautiful bass came out awfully well in the Recitative & Solo & altogether it was beautiful. The music altogether "went" thoroughly well tonight. The girls

93

will know the satisfaction of such occasions. We had a Xmas Carol the last thing. "Jesus is born in Bethlehem – Sing & be glad Jerusalem." & it went splendidly. (By the bye the choir should have the S.P.C.K. collection of carols.) On the 19th the Bishop's birthday, we had a choir practice & supper at his house – when R's Anthem &c. &c. were practised. On these occasions I always take work. Nobody else does, but as I am privileged so to do – I do: for I cannot stand sitting idle all the evening. There is a very nice young sort of Squire here – a Mr. Rowen whose young wife is a soprano – & he dutifully trots after her to musical parties &c. He & I chaff a good deal. I tell him he should bring work, & he threatens to bring moccassins (which he makes himself) but he doesn't. So when my musical husband & his musical wife are fairly at work – & I am sewing – he looks comically at me & says "You've got the advantage of me again –" & I say "Where are yr moccassins?" They made Rex propose the Bishop's health the other night which he did remarkably neatly, & his speech was considered pithy!!! It was very gratifying to my wifely feelings to hear the Bishop's reply, I can tell you!!!!!

Xmas Eve. N.B. The mail has passed out of Cunard's hands, & is now under another Company – They only mean to charge £18 instead of £25 for passengers – & henceforward *their day* for letters leaving here is to be Friday instead of Monday[2] – So I expect you will get my next letter as soon if not sooner than this. So as we are very busy – I shall say no more than our dear dear love & Xmas wishes. You know how we must think of you & Home! Rex played "Xtians Awake" after Church last Sunday that I might not be without it. It was his own thought. He has given me a *dear* little drawing room clock as a Xmas Box – & I have shod *his* feet in slippers.

I have had a jolly sleigh drive today. We are well & happy.

Ever your dear & loving
A.J.H.E!!

Best of love to all –

Please thank Mrs. Wake most gratefully for the pink flannel jacket.

LETTER
21

The Revd—Tippet, & Alex: Ewing Esqr. (honorary organist.) as they
appeared at the Consecration of a Mission Church in the Diocese
of Fredericton. New Brunswick. JAN. 2. 1868
  "O'er (trackless wilds–pathless fields–boundless wastes–I can't
remember which!!!!!) of snow." [1]

[ca. 5 January 1868]

My darling Mum.

   ... I have seen Bombastes for the 7th time. The 22nd have had
some private theatricals–(last Friday) & very good fun they were.
The man who acted Bombastes has such a prominent nose as
[would be] a fortune to an actor, & he was *capitally* got up. Tell
the boys he sang "Kafoozlum," & I laughed as much as ever. There
were several other comic songs in the regular style, but when they

don't *quite* make you roar, they are dreary things. Kafoozleum was
very well done, but the others, not so good as the Boys – and there
was nothing equal to Betsy Waring, The Twins & some of the boys'
best. They say only one of the fellows had acted before, but they all
did capitally – & they had learned their parts *thoroughly* which was
the great thing. The comic man was not as good as Stephen – Bombastes was very well done, & I laughed very much, though I don't
care for burlesques: but their "ladies" were made up splendidly.
One of them was awfully pretty – & Distaffina was very good. The
pretty one in the farce "Done on both sides" was as pretty a girl as
you could wish to see – but when she spoke in a deep bass voice, &
with masculine abruptness it was awfully funny.[2] Mrs. Rowen (the
Soprano whose husband isn't musical) called in the morning &
offered to take us in her sleigh, so we went with them. Theirs is
what I think the nicest (though not the most swell) kind of sleigh. It
is in fact a big box full of buffalo skins on runners. In it we ladies lie
down & are buried & tucked up in buffalo skins & then away we
go – the bells ringing – over the snow – as hard as you please. I &
Mrs. R. were on one side, Rex & Miss Wright (the pretty sister) on
the other. We were all well *buried* by Mr. R. – he & the man on the
box. It was a *lovely* night. Moonlight, starlight – clear & still: & except for a "nip" in the air, you could not imagine how low the thermometer really was. The other day we were out walking, & I was
saying how "mild" it was & R. said "Do you know what it is? 25."
Which is what you in England have been so "took aback" by its
going down to – in the *night* – in London. I was in the town the other
day when it was at Zero in the street & I felt *quite warm*. I was
wrapped up to the eyes it is true, & walking; but the great thing
is – if it is *still* – the clearness, & the powerful sun make it *very* jolly:
but if the least breeze gets up – you feel it then. We had a nice walk
yesterday on the river. The "fields of snow" here are very beautiful.
The shadows on the snow are really almost as blue as the sky – &
when the sun shines & it is a nice quiet day, it is glorious. But I must
tell you. As we were coming back Mr. Barker called us into his
house – Mr. Barker is a young farmer here, son to a man who raised
a company of fencibles in the american troubles — & grandson to
the old settler Barker who is buried in the garden of the Master of

the Rolls, & from whose grave I took the lichen for Regie. Mr. B. & R. have always been friends & Mr. B. always asks very politely after *me*. Rex had been talking to him about the old times here – & about the *ring* that was found near Fort Nashwaak – & of which I promised to get Regie an impression. We can now give him any amount, for Mr. B. has presented the ring to Rex!!! I don't think it is gold – but it is curious – & certainly *old* – & very probably *did* belong to the Recollet "Father Simon" who brought his troops of indians (Milicetes) from his Mission to help to defend Fort Nashwaak against the English.[3] The ring was dug up near the fort – where arrow heads – pikes – balls & other relics have been found. Mr. Barker is very nice – & they were awfully civil – When they saw us going up the road – they lighted the fire in their best room – & Barker laid wait for our return. Through them we hope to see all the "remains" of the old times here of which traces exist – & I hope to pick up something to add to the Reginald Collection. I will send a sketch of the ring. . . . You must know that about 17 miles from here in the parish of Douglas – (Mr. Dowling – incumbent.)[4] the people have built a little Church with their own hands – the bishop's son designing it: & Rex & I were bidden to the Consecration, where R. was requested to act as organist.[5] As I had had a cold – & the drive was long, the frost hard, & the hours of *feeding* uncertain – it was decided I shld not risk it: Mrs. Coster resolved on equal prudence – & came to lunch with me – our husbands being away. When R. came back he gave me a vivid description of the amusement caused by the costumes of himself & one of the clergy with whom he was walking. This parson (Mr. Tippet[6] – a nice old man.) has *scormy*[7] long white hair & whiskers – fiery eyes – & *such* a fur cap & coat as had impressed themselves on my memory when I once saw them. Rex had on the indian *tschoga* (that great brown thing he had at Ecclesfield – like a dressing gown.) *over* his military coat – his long boots – big prayerbook – & the fur cap with ears which I made him. The likenesses are supposed to be good.

You cannot tell, dear Mum, what a relief it is to me – that you have so judiciously deferred Reka Dom. It was really *worrying* me, & I know it was getting longwinded & poor, & I think I can do it better. It will not be delayed long, I hope, but I cannot write under

97

pressure, & it is foolish of me to try it. Now I feel free, & will not neglect it, I assure you! – There will be Reka Dom, the father's story – (short.) & the Conclusion.

I was impelled to do the above (which I see as I sit from the window in the twilight. "Old Sarum" (as Rex calls her) has just brought tea & closed the windows – so it is only just done in time!) but it gives you no idea of the beauty of the river in its white robe – with the snow roads across it. When the river first closes, the *safe* paths across are marked by sticking in little firs. As it finally hardens & snow falls – people mostly stick to these old tracks, & they become regular beaten snowroads with ruts – & wheel tracks – all in white. As the roads are narrow (why – goodness knows! – as all the river is before them) if 2 sleds meet – the one with the lightest load "turns out" – that is turns aside into the drift, to let the other pass. . . . It is hard not to be able to see each other at any moment, & to be "parted" even for a time. But to us all, who all enjoy everything to be seen & heard, & heard of in new places & among other people: the fact that I have to lead a traveller's life gives us certain great pleasures we could not have had if Rex had been a curate at Worksop[8] (we'll say.) & we couldn't even afford a trip to the Continent! Also if I have any gift for writing, it really *ought* to improve under circumstances so much more favorable, than the narrowing influence of a small horizon – such as prevents Miss Yonge from improving as time goes on. I only wish my gift were a little nearer *real* genius!! As it is I do hope to improve gradually: & as I *do* work slowly & conscientiously – I may honestly look forward with satisfaction to the hope of being able to turn a few honest pennies to help us out: & it *is* a satisfaction, & a blessing I am thankful for. I only wish I could please myself better! However small writers are wanted as well as big ones, & there is no reason why donkey carts shouldn't drive even if there *are* coaches on the road!! I am *very* glad the Xmas Trees are liked. Rex said from the 1st it was one of my best. His advice & criticism *are* great helps to me. He doesn't *expect* me to follow his advice, so I am not hampered, but his suggestions are often of great value to me & he is perfectly candid, & I don't think at all influenced by my being his wife. It was kind of Bell to pay at once. I hope Dot will have all the rest we owe – soon. But Rex has not heard yet from Aldershot about the sale of his things, & I *hoped* Mrs. O. wld have been to hand sooner. . . . They say we are not likely to have it so cold again this winter! It has been the coldest December for 19 years, Mr. Barker says. We are very jolly & happy. Rex will add a line. With our dear love to all – & all our hearts' best wishes for the New Year & the years to come. Your everloving daughter

J. H. E.

LETTER
22

[missing sketch]

Fredericton. 1 Sunday after Epiphany.
[12 January] 1868.

My dearest Dot –

The above is not an egyptian mummy or an esquimaux squaw – but myself returning from a musical event at the Coster's – "hauled" – as it is technically termed – on a sled over the snow in the exquisite – day clear – moonlight. Mrs. Coster had been afraid I wouldn't come – it being rather windy, & their street *ojously* cold, so she begged me to try the sled – & George Coster duly brought it down – I wrapped up & put Rex's indian coat on the top, & squatted on the sled. It goes so easily that it is really no effort to the "hauler" – Coming back – George – & Frank Robb (his cousin)[1] took me – & wouldn't let Rex have any hand in it, as I was to be "raced" home. We went like the wind, & it was delicious, though rather "*narvious*" as you expect to be over every moment! – The moonlight nights here are really wonderful. Like daylight for clearness, & if the night is still – to be out is delightful. It is fine, but very cold today. In fact the steady severity of the winter so far is quite unusual. Dr. Jack has put an outer door on to our house – which adds greatly to the warmth & our comfort: & very jolly & comfortable we are. The 22d are under orders to move in the Spring, and the 74th (Highlanders) are coming.[2] Rex was with them in Ireland last year. I do not think we have any news. The alto who was laid up with a throat at the beginning of this severe weather (Emily Roberts by name.) is far from well yet: & as I thought she was rather moped at home, & as she is very much devoted to us, I asked her down to spend the day here. Rex read the Xmas no. of Dickens' affair "No Thoroughfare"[3] aloud, & I got through a power of needlework. I want my maiden underclothes to last till summer, amongst other reasons because the washing is rough work in winter & the clothes get a bad color &c. &c. so I have "topped" a *shime* most successfully under the influence of Dickens & W. Collins, & felt quite like *Mrs. Johnson*. Tell her I thought of her as I did it, & told Rex I felt as if I were sitting with Kezia "topping" for one of the young ladies!!! Also I am at work on Reka Dom. There has also been one Hebrew Lesson I think since I wrote. Also we have exchanged our very insane orderly for another, who seems to work better with "Old Sarum." "Owen" was getting *too* cracky, poor man! – & neglecting his work, & when Rex was not in the house, I felt rather nervous as to what turn his eccentricity might take! — We are going to dine at the Graham's on Thursday, & 2 more musical evenings are laid out, & then *we* mean to give one. Before that, my child's party will probably come off – if I can drill some of the Costers & Wards into charades. I wish you could see – or I could draw – some of these moonlight nights. The two old willows opposite, *paint* such exquisite – sharp – black shadows of branches on the snow—that they look not like shadows of their branches —but like roots ramifying from the bottom of the tree trunk.

The other night we looked out, & saw that the moon was shining on the snow, looking exactly as if the river had opened, & there were a water surface. This was because the intense frost had crusted, & glazed the snow on the river so that it reflected. Meanwhile a high wind was blowing what *loose* snow there was in white wreaths hither & thither. The indians, by the bye, call February "the Moon in which there is crust on the snow." One really hardly knows what snow *is* in England. It is so dry here it is like dust, & is blown about like dust in the streets. It takes a considerable time to melt when you get it into the house, & of course does not wet your feet or clothes out of doors, unless it is thawing. We keep little brooms in the halls here to brush the snow from our feet & clothes when we come into a house. November is called "the moon in which the frostfish comes"—by which I suppose are meant the *cusk* (as they call them here.)[4] a very nice fish we get when the river closes. The men cut holes in the ice & get them out. I do not know the process though I have seen them in the distance, I suppose the fish come to the hole attracted by the light; but I don't know. Rex says they had them in the north of China. The wind is very high tonight, so on *prevention* grounds (for I have no cold whatever) I have let Rex go to church alone this evening. It is *very* severe today—so it is best not to tempt a night wind & the possibility of draughts in Church. Rex couldn't be spared to the organ this morning, the choir being rather deficient. The principal tenor, ditto soprano, & ditto alto being laid up with the cold, & one of the basses away. There goes the Parker's close sleigh I think! It is such a wonderful ancient affair. I have had some comfortable drives in it though – They have been very kind in taking me to Church &c. &c.

I have great joy & comfort in my warm things, & am grateful to you again & again. But one or two things that are not right – I think I had better mention for future benefit. N.B. my size in gloves is 6 1/4. You have sent the coloured ones right, & all the white ones a size too large! – But the fact most to be regretted, I fancied I had dwelt upon very powerfully. The size of the sheets. They are awfully *skimpy* – & I am sure our bed is as small as 2 people can well sleep in. I fancied I had said a good deal about it, for the 2 pairs of sheets of Rex's that we have are so splendidly large, & it is *such* a comfort (especially as Rex can't abide the *feel* of blanket.) – that I wouldn't have *saved* a quarter of a yard in them for anything! I hope the other pair may be larger. *Never mind* deary about it, only I mention it as a warning. I know you have tried to save our purse, but *plenty* of unbleached cotton would be more comfy than paucity of a genteeler material! – The blankets are glorious, & in this weather they are the great thing. The pillowcases are roomy & capital too. As we may someday be so "situated" as to have a single bed spare room – the sheets won't be wasted. Even if they are too small to use with comfort now. We have 2 pairs of large linen ones of R.'s you know: and by & by we shall be able to afford some more. Perhaps I ought to have measured these, but I knew that full size for the best bedroom or the Mum's room would be *ample* for us. One thing I have been busy with is stopping out draughts – & one dodge I have learnt here – I mention for the benefit of the french and best bedrooms & Dina's ditto, & all other draughty doors. Get some old *drugget* or any old stuff strong enough, & some *ropes* (box cords) –put the cord into strips of the stuff, as if you were going to *pipe* with it–baste it in ⸺; & then *tack* it round the door so that the round of rope covers the place where the draught pours in. If you do the bottom of *your* door so–it will be better than any *mat*.

 The rope side downwards of course, & by tack I mean nail with tacks. . . . Rex is now as happy in his moccasins as I am in mine. He is a good old Boy, & sticks to his Hebrew & his wifie's apron string like an old dear as he is: & as most of the ladies here are widowed for a fortnight or so at a time when their men go off into the woods; & as my neighbor Mrs. Campbell has just got back *her* husband after a moose expedition in acute rheumatism, I feel very thankful my old man likes his ain fireside–though if his breech-loader had been here instead of at Aldershot, he might have been tempted away with the other fellows, as he is fond of shooting. As it is I think he is safely tied to Gesenius–pro tem.

He very likely will add a bit, & I must stop for the present. That dear girl Clara Coster worked me an awfully jolly set of toilette things–pincushion & mats in red braid &c. this Xmas. As she hates work it was a great compliment & she wld let no one else touch it. Miss Jacob[5] too–a member of the choir–has knitted me a "Sontag"[6] to wear under my outdoor things.

What a conglomeration of small facts this letter is! Good night my darling old thing– With dear love to all, the blessed old doges included

Your ever loving sister
Juliana Horatia Ewing

Many many happy returns of yr birthday when it comes–Beloved.

Whenever we meet a dog we 'peak' to him. Whenever we see one we pat him, & when we hear one *bouf* we see what's the matter. This P.M. we heard one *boufing* & out rushed Rex–& in he came Doge & all. Such a dear large smooth black one!! I got him bones,

& he followed me about the house – & was very loth to go when Rex put him out at last to find his master. My special love to the dear Mum, & say I have some more drawings in process. When anyone writes to Aunt Mary, let them give our love, & say that I am going to write to her very soon, but I want to send a contribution to *her* Album when I do.

Rex's P.S.

My dear Dot. Jow thinks I never thanked the Mum for Trotus's hair; but I surely did, as I was *so* thankful to get it. Please to bless his dear nose for me, and to give my special love to *every* one. Jow says I am a particularly good boy this morning – I have had a *deal* of writing for the post, and shall now ask you to let me stop.

Yrs afftly
Rex.

LETTER
23

[AE's Letter]

[n.d.]

Dearest Mum,

I wanted to have written a *long* letter to you this time, as I have not written to you for several mails – but a "concatenation of cir-cumstances" prevents my doing so. I was *compelled* to "waste" all my morning on my *public* duties – and I have to copy out the parts of one of my part songs for a Musical evening to-night.

I am happy to say, to-day, of Jowie, that "elle *crève* de Santé!"; she has been, off and on, *somewhat* coldey of late; it has happened to be the severest winter for 19 years, the old residents say. To quote a passage from a letter I am sending to Mrs. Aveling, "She is *learning* to take a *little* ordinary care of herself, and not to sacrifice herself *entirely* to other people, and to a mistaken conception of duty, (as she used to do before she was mine.); but I kick up such a shindy when *anything*, however trifling, is the matter with her, that she finds it *best* to take some care of herself." The weather, when not at its severest, is most lovely. The snow is like marble, the sky is of a bright glowing blue such as I have never seen elsewhere. And the air is *health* & *life*; so long as the wind doesn't blow hard – *when* it does, one knows what "cold weather" really means.

Jowie, then, was a little below the ordinary mark for a short space in December – having gone out one awful day, and having been the worse for it. But truly I have never seen her more *brilliant* than she is now again. . . . I am glad you came round to my opinion that the 3 Xmas trees was good. It is on *a small scale*, but highly finished of its class. Pardon a longer letter to-day, and with my dear Love to all At Home I am

Ever yr affectionate
AE

P.S. The two creatures selling baskets (in your last batch of pictures but one), are *squaws* – not children as you thought . . . .

LETTER

24

Jan. 26. 1868

My dearest Mother.

. . . I must tell you about the sleigh drive. It was given by Col. Harding (who is the temporary Governor as well –) The etiquette of such affairs is – that the leader drives wherever he likes & the other sleighs must go after him. (They say Gen. Doyle used to go into the most *owdacious* places to try & upset the tandems!) The young men ask the young ladies to drive with them as they wld ask them to dance, & we old couples go Darby & Joan together. Rex got a nice little sleigh with buffalo robes in it – & the horse went capitally. I wrapped up to the eyes (2 jerseys & knitted waist *under* my dress – 2 knitted things above – warmest jacket furs

& shawl – gloves covered with lined "mitts" – bags with one place for the thumb – & muff – a cloud over my face & a hot bottle to my feet!!!) We met before the House of Assembly[1] – & kept driving round & round in circles till all assembled (about 26 sleighs) Then – bells ringing – red tassels waving – away we went. The Col. took us in & out about the town, but no really nasty places – & then into the barrack yard where the soldiers cheered – & his horses got so unmanageable that he & his young lady nearly came to grief – then out into the open country. I do not think I ever saw anything much prettier than the line of jingling sleighs – flying over the snow roads – with the pure fields of snow on all sides broken by the dark firs & country homesteads. Once we went up a narrow hill – meet to be drawn by Doré (or rather Doré *might* give one a faint idea of its beauty) snow pure white before us & under our feet & great dark firs on each side almost touching over our heads. —————And————one mayn't sketch!!! —

You may imagine my feelings. We stopped at a country inn where lunch was prepared – Sandwiches & hot spiced negus, & very jolly we were. Rex's *tschoga*, which he wore over his coat, exciting considerable admiration! – In the sketch of this you will see my back – & the lady by me is Mrs. Graham, Major G.'s wife (with

HOT NEGUS AT SPRING HILL. (N. Brunswick)

whom we came out from Home −) When we came out a big deaf &
dumb man standing by the road laughed one of those *animal* grins
one is so familiar with in "dummy" (& he was not unlike him) &
pointed to the grey sky. Sure enough the snow came long before
we got home − but nothing to confuse the way or hurt anybody. We
returned a different way to that we came. We crossed the river
(vide *Maggie's* letter − the horses flying up a steep little bank awfully
prettily.) & drove along, & then crossed back again when we got
opposite the town, vide one of *your* scraps: then some more in &
out, & then home, as warm as a toast! I *did* enjoy it! & we did so

long for some of the brothers & sisters! I don't think *you* would
have so much appreciated it − dearest Mum, as you wld have been
nervous about the horses. Only a spill in the soft snow is nothing: &
it doesn't *wet* you here, you know. There is another drive the day
after tomorrow but I fear I shan't go − having got a boil on my hip!!²
On dit that boils are "about" & that it shows a healthy season!! so
one must be content − but I am sorry just to miss this one. Only
probably there will be some more yet. On the appearance of my un-
romantic ailment − Rex ordered in bottled porter as the appropriate remedy for me. So tell Charlie it forms an excuse for the
glass,³ & Jow & her black bottle are in company as usual!!! I
am quite well otherwise. . . . Do you know we mean to "flit" this

May! – It will be a grief to part with the lovely views from this dear old Reka Dom – but it is *too* huge & too cold in winter – & burns enough fuel to——well, as one of Rex's men said—"It wld take a Major General's allowances Sir." We have burnt so much more than our allowance *this* winter that we want if we are here next to try & *save* the extra wood to be square again. Also Dr. Jack now wants £40 – which doesn't *shoot* our purse. We have our eye on a comfortable little house close by with garden – & 8 rooms in it – & they say well built & convenient. It is much cheaper—the furniture we have wld *amply* furnish it – & I much prefer a rather less charming house, & a little ready money in the summer to go about & see this lovely country while we are here – as we don't know how soon we may leave it forever. And last summer we went nowhere. We shld have 2 sitting rooms – 2 bedrooms & dressing do & 2 attics, & a nice kitchen. However it is not settled. I have no time to send the scraps *this* mail dear Mum – & I don't like to keep our nice old Orderly from his tea. He is a good old soul – a widower with young bairns; & does all we want without complaints, compliments, or Spanish – which is a great comfort!!!! Old Sarum sticks by me & is going to teach me clear starching & pastry – at both of which she is a good hand. She says my boil is sure to heal rapidly because I'm "good natur'd," & she had a brother who was very selfish & an uncommon nasty temper & his flesh never *would* heal!!!!!!!!!!!!!!!

> Goodbye darling old Mum Your
> ever loving children   AJHE

LETTER

25

Feb. 3. 1868.

My darling old Mum –

... I am so infinitely obliged to you dear Mum for yr wisdom in Reka Dom, & very thankful for the criticisms, to which I shall attend. I mean to *compress* it very much. I will keep the river part–though that is really the shadow of some of my best writing I think in the *dutch* tale describing that scene at Topsham.[1] I wrote a good bit last night, & was much wishing for the returned M.S. But the sight of the proof will help me more than anything. I lose all judgement of my own work in M.S. I feel as if it must be as laborious to read, as it has been to write. Whereas in print it comes freshly on me, & I can criticise it more fairly. It will not be *very* long when all is done, I think, & I am so anxious to make it good. I hope it will be satisfactory. If you fidget yourself at every little cold I get I shall be obliged not to tell you. But I *do* tell you, (down to a boil!) trusting that when we say it is nothing you won't fidget, & will remember that by the time *you* hear of it–I am probably perfectly well. I have really fared much better than most of my neighbours in misfortune. Both the soprano & her tenor husband are very shaky still. It has been a most severe winter, but now our house is so warm we hardly know a cold day from a hot one. And the weather is very pleasant just now. I am looking forward to some more drives. It seemed provoking to be kept in by a boil, but it doesn't do to risk getting the frost into a wound. Mrs. Medley cut her toe the other day & has got the frost into it & has been uncomfortable. However she is out today. Mrs. Coster *is* a dear soul–& he is an awfully nice fellow (the good bass.) When these people here *are* nice & not Yankee–there is a modesty & simplicity about some of them that is very taking. The eldest lad who is about 16 or 17 is just of his father's type too. He is *very* goodlooking–has *remarkably* nice manners, a sort of quiet dignity which really proceeds I believe from his never thinking of himself for a moment. And from dragging me on a sled to buying fish at the door for his mother he will do anything he is wanted to do. Clara too I am particularly fond of– They are so un:Young Englandish & jolly. Mrs. C. married at 18–& is very pretty still. But she is far from strong. We have made the happy discovery that she is susceptible of mesmerism from Rex–& he can take away her neuralgic headaches. We have given notice to flit!!!!! & have taken the little house–& already I feel fond of it. It is only about £24 a year which as rents are rising, is good. It has drawing & dining rooms–frostproof cellar and kitchen– 2 bedrooms & a dressing room & corresponding attics above *that* – a nice garden – a yard – wood shed & stable. We think we shall be able to make it a little gem!! It is detached – is next to a brick house (good in event of fire!!)² has trees near it – & is back to back with the Costers.³ I don't think I shall write any more tonight. Good night, my dear Mum. Monday. The Bishop has been with us for our Hebrew this morning. Mrs. Medley took me a jolly drive on Saturday & I *drove* to Church both times yesterday with the Master of the Rolls & his lady! – It was a *lovely* day, & *so* mild. Today it is very fine but cold again. But I don't feel it now at all. We shall move into our house if all be well on May. 1. I like it *very* much, & it is close by. Near the Cathedral – Medleys – &c. &c. Rex was at a Masonic Lodge the other night – several of the 22d being initiated – so I had the pleasure of rubbing up & putting on his "jewels.". . . Rex's dear love & mine & we are ever dearest Mum Your

loving children A.J.H.E.

Imperfect remembrance of our new house!

LETTER
26

Feb. 3. 1868

My dearest Dot.

... While I am on the practical tack–allow me to enter on the subject of *paraffin!!*[1] ... Everybody uses it here, & we burn it regularly, & though our lamp is a little *aukard* at times– A gallon of paraffin costs us about $^S1/10^d$ and lasts us about a month–in midwinter. Supplying our drawing room lamp and a small lamp not much used in the kitchen, for Sarah prefers tallow dips to go about with. Our Lamp–white–with glass bowl & white china shade– cost about $^S10/$- I think. We really do not suffer from smell a bit. It does not smell when burning, but if the least drop is spilt it does. If the lamp is *well-wiped–the wick regularly cut*–& the globe well  filled with oil: it works like blazes. You mightn't like it in the drawing room but I do think a small lamp for the hall would be a great saving of candles! It gives a splendid light with the white shade. But then it mustn't be snatched up, & run about with!– This is only a suggestion. I have just accomplished a sketch from the window here of the field of snow on the river–& wretched as it looks by the original–we are pleased with it, & think it will look well when we have left it: & will be refreshing to look at in the summer. Rex has got a pair of snow-shoes–& a pair are ordered for me! Peter Poultice[2]–our Indian brother–guffawed loudly at the idea of my having them, & says *She*'ll make *them* (i.e. his Sqaw.) You shld have seen Rexie wading about on the deep snow of our garden the  other night. The Costers, Sarah & I watching· him. Everybody said we should tumble down at 1st & Rex said he must have out the Orderly to pick him up. "Hartney!" "Yessir!" "Be

ready in the garden to pick me up when I fall." "Yessir." The above is a very poor representation of the incident, for he managed very well, & didn't fall, & marked with one eye–& looked as "Captain"ish & dignified as usual!!!!...

Ever your most loving old sister J. H. E.

LETTER
27

Septuagesima. [9 February] 1868
Fredericton.

My dearest Aunt Mary.[1]

The...sketch is to celebrate & notify to you the fact that I took my first walk upon *snowshoes* yesterday, and got along very well and didn't tumble *once!!!!!!* — I am the more proud as I was always awkward to a degree on *skates* & feel glad that snowshoes suit my *constitootion* better. They were made by an indian here, & are dear little things. It is not at all difficult and very good fun. Some things about the winter here are very charming. The sleigh-

drives for one. The individual who gives the sleigh drive, (the other day it was His Excellency the Govr!) goes first, & wherever *he* goes all the other sleighs must follow. We hired a jolly little sleigh for the occasion. The horse went capitally and it was great fun. There were about 26 sleighs, with red plumes & jingling bells to the horses, & I never enjoyed anything much more. Creeping over the snow between dark pine trees that nearly met over our heads, or flying full speed across the river—which is now a level plain of snow with roads marked by fir trees stuck into the ice—it was charming. One only regrets that it is impossible to sketch! — We spent our Xmas Day with the Bishop, & they were very kind. The Cathedral was very well decorated, & of course we "pricked" our own house with firs. It seems so odd to see no *holly*! It has been the most severe winter known for 18 years or so—but we are none the worse for it, thank GOD,—& there really has been some glorious weather. It is so clear, & dry, that you do not feel the cold unless there is a wind blowing. And the beauty of the moonlight nights just now, with the clear air & gleaming snow, you cannot imagine. Then too, the sun is now getting great power, & when it is out, & the sky blue, & the lovely snow *crunching* under yr feet, with all the exquisite lights & shadows, & a bit of misty blue distance, I long to plant a campstool in one of the drifts, & try to scratch down some remembrance of a scene I shall never see again after we leave

Canada. And now one begins to look forward to summer. I long to be at my garden! Your seeds are most acceptable, & they will not know themselves in this quick growing climate. For in the short summer we have—everything grows & rushes into flower & fruit at tropical pace. We are going to leave this big house in May. It is *too* big, & consequently expensive. We have got a jolly little house near here—with a nice garden, & everything we want—at a moderate rent. Everybody moves about here in May. It is quite funny but it seems the fashion—& we are going to do it too!!!— We have been rather gay lately—and another ball (at Govt House) is yet before us. The people are very kind and hospitable. . . .

Ever your loving niece. J. H. E.

—Rex's love.

Crossing a fence in Snowshoes. N.B.

LETTER
28

Fredericton. Feb. 24. 1868.

My darling old Dot.

As you are probably very busy, you will excuse the fact that I can only write a scrap this time. We have been living in a perfect Carnival the last day or two. Last Wednesday was the Govr's ball (which I enjoyed immensely – though Col. Peters danced me off my feet to that extent – I have been more or less stiff about the muscles ever since!) I had arranged *my* party for Saturday, thinking that thus it would be clear of being the "next day" to any of the pending festivities – so that no one wld be tired, & yet get in before Lent – But early on Friday morning – Mr. Seeley (22d) began to run about the town showering invitations to a bachelor's ball *that night* – and upon him followed Capt. Holyoake who after sitting up all night writing invitations flew wildly about in a sleigh bidding us to a sleighing party at Gvt House. As it happened they were 2 of the jolliest affairs of the season, but we didn't go to either – & I think I should have been knocked up if we had. Then came Mrs. Ewing's musical evening! & it has been a *success* if everybody is to be believed! Rex wrote out programmes on pink paper – & they were scented in my best box!!!! We enclose one. The music went *very well* – & (though I says it as shouldn't, having set everything on table from the salt cellars to the centre piece my-self!!!) the supper was rather above the average Fredericton supper both in appearance & *wittles*. Rex will tell you about the music. We were about 25 or more, in all. We had some very pretty girls, & 3 of the fellows in their Mess jackets &c. – & the room looked very well. The home *immortelles* were most useful as I trimmed the candle-sticks &c. &c. with Lycopodiums & immortelles. We had a catastro-phe in the fact that the "help" I got in to "char" got in some liquor to help her – & was dismissed by Rex at an early stage of the pro-ceedings after balancing my china plates in a miraculous way on the fender – happily without breaking them! —

A caller!!! —— & now I have no more time, for we are going to a ball at the Graham's tonight – & I have some work to do at my "things." Then I suppose we shall be quiet till Easter. It is still bitterly cold – but we are very well & jolly, & there is very *fine* weather off & on, & we have had one attempt at a thaw – which has frozen up again. The illustration is Rex surrounded by his lady per-formers!!! Our dear love to all. I am so glad you & Dina have had some good balls this winter. I wish I could get hold of you for all these. ADoo

Your ever loving Judy.

[AE's Postscript]

Dearest Dot. Jow has thrown on my shoulders more, in the way of description, than I can possibly accomplish to-day; but I enclose a programme of the music on Saturday night, and *would* enlarge on the subject of it, but that there really is no time left. I am very sorry I have so long neglected to send the music which you have twice asked for, but as soon as the Carnival gaieties are over, which must be two days hence, I will try to set to work at that, and at other things which are waiting. Meantime, with my love to everyone at Home, (not forgetting the beloved doges). Believe me

Yours evr afft   A. Ewing.

LETTER
29

COASTING.

March. 3. 1868.
Fredericton N.B.

My darling Mum

You will wonder what *this* is! It is *the* sport of the winter; though we have not been indulging much in it. It is "Coasting."[1] Imagine a very long–very steep hill–something like Sheffield Hill–but I think steeper–with snow in deepish drifts on each side thereof. A party of ladies & gentlemen assemble at the top with *troboggans*– ▰▰▰▰ sleds on runners–common wooden things–about 2 foot or less wide–with iron rings where I have put the dots. On to the top of this squeeze 3 or 4 people as tight as they can pack, the ladies crosslegged, & the gentlemen as most convenient. Somebody kneels the last, & steers with his or her feet if necessary. Attentive friends give the machine a push, and away it goes down the frozen hill–at the pace of an express train–more or less rapid according to the steepness of the hill. When one is off another starts, & they go in close succession, the big sleds varied by small single ones manned by one or more boys of the cad order!! The rings are to hold by to keep yourself from being thrown off in the wonderful bumps that occur where the road is uneven. The sleds sometimes jump 2 or 3 feet in the air. We were out walking the other day & we came upon the Graham's party, & took a coast. Rex's sled went down splendidly— Mine ("Worms for bait" was its name.) came to grief— The rope got under the sled & over we went—about 1/2 way down. Fortunately we ran into the drift, which is like tumbling into a featherbed, but I twisted my right arm rather, & feeling also rather *narvious*—I took no more coasts!!!!!!!! It is rather alarming when you are not used to it—though mere children think nothing of it here— The pace is *tremendous*, & you are simply in the very smallest possible compass on a bare bit of wood half the size of a chair seat, going express pace—about 60 miles an hour. They say it is delicious. I really haven't enjoyed it yet—my experiences being limited & not successful. This was the packing of "Worms for Bait." 1. Miss Bessy

Roberts. 2. Mrs. Ewing. 3. Mr. Edge (22d). 4. Miss Sophy Graham. Mr. Edge's legs packed us in. Sophy steered. There were some other wonderful spills, but nobody hurt. It is the funniest thing to see them coming down that you can imagine. I don't think I shall ever take *much* to it, but probably shall have another try. Snowshoeing I do thoroughly enjoy. The other day we had a glorious walk again. The sky was the deepest, purest blue you ever saw in summer— The snow had a splendid crust—it was exquisite!!! There is such a sense of freedom in wandering over tracts of

untrodden snow feet deep with impunity – a summer sun & ~~dead~~ living! deep unfathomable blue above – & everywhere pure sparkling white beneath your feet. Look at the picter – & I fancy you giving a *shriek* & saying "Why there's a Dog!" —— "Hector" the beloved bulldog, is at this moment *flopping* his tail by the stove. His master has gone to England to fetch a wife, & has left him to me till his return in June! – He is, I do think, the best behaved, & most affectionate *hanimil* I ever knew. Though his hair comes off as much as dear old Trot's did, & I am never decent now!! Another peculiarity is – when he hears kissing he thinks *he* ought to have a share, & if Rex so much as kisses his wife, Hector comes ramping & sprawling & rubbing his great pink nose in our faces, to get us apart & absorb all the attention himself. I have no time for much this intermediate mail dear Mum: being rather in domestic difficulties again – as I have had to dismiss Sarah, to my infinite regret. I kept her as long as it was possible, but her friend & her husband[2] between them seem to have taught her a taste for the *bottle*, & in a wooden house often left in her sole charge – this peculiarity was not to be endured. I passed it over once or twice, & have done conscientiously all I could think of to get her to reform, but we are too near grog shops of the lowest kind – & she can't resist invitation & temptation – I have been really *grieved at heart* about her, as well as sorry to lose a good servant; but I have engaged one who will in some respects be superior I think, at the same wages. At present we are — a maid – & + the orderly, & takes our meals with our kind neighbors the Campbells. We have a bedroom which opens into their house – & so we go in & out!! Hector went *once* – had an awful brush with the

-Cats

Bats &

Rats—

—tell Ruffles—& now we leave him at home. He is just having his dinner before the Orderly takes this. The night before last was the coldest there has yet been. Wonderfully so! But it can't last long now—& I declare it is much better than extreme heat. I have really enjoyed the winter much. We are *so* charmed with the flowers! Fancy *flowers*!! It seems so odd to us. Poor darling Mum, not to be able to enjoy the fine weather. But you will have a daughter with a carriage soon!![3]—— Our birds fly most lovingly over yr barn & thank you for all the news. Dear love to the Dot & all. I will write to Dina & Brownie. I have a drawing class of young ladies twice a week—& one of them has been copying one of yours. They excite unbounded admiration.

Please send the italian recipe for the *macaroni*. . . .

LETTER
30

Fredericton. March. 7. 1868

It is so impossible – dearest Mother – to give you any idea of these snow scenes! They look so *dreary* in pencil – or put down any way as *I* can do them, they *can* give you no idea of a fine winter's day such as Thursday last – when the Rowens took us out for a drive, & when I made a note of the above sketch. This great white ridge on the left – *dazzlingly* white in the sun – stood off against a pure blue sky. The effect is curious – The contrast is so intense & unmodified, it is more like some effect of Art than of Nature – at least to English eyes. On the bank I beg you to observe the *rampacks*.[1] Rampacks are the bare, gaunt, (& often black & charred) stems of trees left on a clearing. That by the path is also a rampack. To the right you will see a wonderfully tall tree. I must give you a sketch of *him*. I got a mere note, but mean really to take his picter in summer. We started directly after lunch, & drove about till evening, stopping at one house where we got gingerbread nuts & cherry brandy. (all but poor Rex, who was holding the horses outside! –) Mr. Rowen has the patience of——a fellow artist – in stopping for "views." Their dog Tim came with us. Hector the beloved was left at home. That lovely animal lies near me, getting occasionally too hot by the fire for his own comfort, it being a mild evening. He is a splendid watchdog, & is just gowly powling at some passing footstep. The Rowens are very nice people. He was in the 63d but sold out &

settled here. They are a young couple (married about a year) & her sister–an awfully pretty girl–is staying with them. Mrs. R. has a fine voice, & is in the choir. Both of them draw a little, & are anxious to get it up. I have started drawing classes on Tuesday & Thursday mornings–for *Ruskin practice* &c.–to get up our sketching before summer. Two Miss Roberts & Mrs. R. are members, & Clara Coster is to come when she is better–but she has been ill–poor child. Your sketches & etchings are duly exhibited, & hugely admired as they deserve to be– Mary Roberts has been copying your pencil sketch of Ecclesfield–& Bessy & I–an etching of Turner's in the "Modern Painters," which we got from the Library. Mr. Roberts is a schoolmaster here. He has several daughters more or less grown-up–& nice warm hearted intelligent girls, tremendously devoted to us.[2] Mr. R. is a *bass*, & his daughters *sopranos & alto* in the choir– Mamma is rather a caution, but a good old soul. They are not "*quite quite*" (as Miss Noaille used to say) but short of aristocracy–are well educated–& the daughters refined nice girls, especially the eldest–Bessy. They have started Hebrew under Rex's superintendence! They are wonderfully pleased to be helped a bit about drawing &c. &c. & have fairly bullied me into promising that some day they shall hold a Bee here, to do some of my sewing as a return compliment!! My new sarvint is a coloured girl. Not very deeply so–but unmistakable. A *pretty* specimen though. *Very* well mannered, a very nice cook–& with powers of cleaning & dusting which satisfactorily exceed old Sarum's. I hope we shall get along very comfortably. She can make soap & candles, an astounding fact to *your* minds I dare say–but we makes our hard & soft soaps, & our *taller dips* on this side of the water!!! Name —*Hetty!!!* . . . She got her feet wet coming here though, & has been "badly" all today. I administered hot brandy & water & ginger ("& if you *had* a little *red pepper* in the house Mum!" suggested the old orderly!!!) & she has slept about 10 hours–& seems pretty nearly well. I had more difficulty to get her to swallow the potation than I should have had with my late *coooook*!!!!!! *Pray* never do anything but *smile* at my cook stories. Sarvints are not of a high type here–but it sounds so much worse to tell than it really is– People all suffer alike, & help & lend to each other–& if you are well, it is

no more than a joke. I daresay if one were in shaky health, it would be a serious trial. But you can always shut up your house & go into one of the hotels for a bit, at the worst. In fact as some British Lions threaten to go to their clubs on the occasion of any domestic discomfort—Rex (who only growls for *my* sake!) has got a trick of saying–"I can't stand this any longer!" (time of endurance say a couple of hours!!!!!!!!)—"We'll go into the 'Barker House' tomorrow." The Barker House is the hotel where we 1st stayed–& where I lost my poor dear sewing machine. And when I hear the famous threat now, I fear I only irreverently *bust* out laughing!!!!!
Sunday [8 March]. Whilst we were without a sarvint (2 or 3 days.) we took our meals with our neighbours the Campbells. A bedroom of ours opens into his dressing room, & we used to go through & take our wittles. *Once* I took Hector. But about the middle of tea–when 2 plates of bones had been put out for him & the cats; & *he* had eaten *both*—I caught sight of the *backs* of the 2 ladies–& in 2 seconds one was on his back & the other scratching his poor dear nose!– Rex rushed to the fray & found cats, plates, & bull

doges mixed together in wild confusion. (i.e. a *heap* in a corner, consisting of these ingredients.) He is a wonderful dog about *music*. He howls as I never heard one howl when Rex is playing– He goes up & down–& seems really to be *singing* to the best of his ability. He sleeps a good deal with us, & is in every respect as exigeant a bedfellow as Trotus, only *heavier*, & with a wonderful knack of planting his paw on your eyeball when he changes his position!!!!!
He is just *boufing* & barking at the avalanches of snow that keep shooting off the roof with a roar like thunder. For we are in the

middle of a thaw: & after being about 35° *below* zero last Monday morning—today it is 50° *above*, & the ice is beginning to thaw upon the river. However I fancy it will all harden up again. A priest was ordained today, & there were 2 awful avalanches during Service— Such a noise it does make! The musical abilities of our clergy were brought into effective use today. For they & the Bishop *sang* their own lines of the Veni Creator—the choir singing the alternate ones. The effect was really most impressive. Coster's fine bass, Mr. Pearson's sweet tenor &c.—& the Bishop's hearty voice support alternate lines with ample power—& it was very pretty. The men's voices as they all stood round the new Priest, & then the response of the choir. It was to a simple old Psalm tune. *Monday* [9 March]. We closed the Carnival with a famous ball at Major Graham's. We both danced "no end" & enjoyed ourselves greatly. Tell the girls I had worn my wedding dress everywhere & at so many balls till it was beginning to look sadly dirty, for alas!—the rooms here knock up one's clothes. So I took counsel of Mrs. Coster—& we decided on trimming it with something. I had a workwoman in for a couple of days (cost 1/1^d per diem & her wittles!!!!!!) & put white tarlatan bouillons³ on the bottom looped with black velvet, & a white tulle berthe trimmed with black lace & black velvet. (I had both the lace & the tulle in my possession!) I had my white roses & scarlet velvet in my hair, & scarlet velvet in my locket. The turnout was very successful I think, & has quite *brightened up* my dress, at a small expense. I mean soon to send you a list of one or two things I want from home, as—if there is no earlier opportunity—Capt. Parry (Hector's Master) is coming out with his bride in June. Our new house *will* be very cosy dear Mum I think, & a great improvement in many ways—though it has not this lovely river view. I am looking forward to my garden, which has one "fixture" a crab tree that blossoms beautifully!!!!— "Hetty" goes on capitally. Whilst old Sarum in her soberest moments never had the kitchen in any but an irish stew, Hetty at this moment (midday) is knitting for her own benefit with everything "cleaned up" & all her work done till this evening—our lunch being cold. I am in *hopes* she is able to work, for she has lots of time & it wld be a great comfort to me. . . . Ever darling Mum with love to all. Your loving children.

AJHE.

LETTER
31

13. March. 1868. The loose sketch is for the Mum.

My dearest Dot

Experience of imported Hibernians in this country has brought us to the following domestic conclusion.

"No Irish need apply."

—which, by the bye, would be rather a good refrain for a comic song – if Brownie wanted a subject any time. I could furnish a few leading facts! – then *craters* would rhyme with *taters* – *whiskey* with *frisky* – and *lend* (what doesn't belong to you) with *friend*. My darkie gets on capitally, & keeps her kitchen charmingly clean. It is a very great comfort. The irish lady whose picter I send you—was a hasty study from one who applied on behalf of her daughter (*not* the one Rex found making herself at home in the absence of Hetty in the kitchen—& after expostulation gently removed by the shoulders—she shouting "Be'*ave* yourself! Be'ave yourself!" as she retired—or was assisted out of the house!!) They *are* a queer lot!— Most of the very raggedest & queerest—perfectly honest I believe, & one may almost say—*none* of them speaking the truth if it can "convaniently" be avoided!! I think our pertinacious visitor must have been a hanger on of Sarum's—who didn't know of her departure. My drawing class is most popular, & we are wonderfully industrious! It is forming a splendid "nuncleus" for the sketching picnics in summer. And summer really begins to look near. It is *very* mild today, & the sleds are coming backwards & forwards across the river with wood as hard as ever they can work, (this being the way in which the wood for next winter's use is got over from the forests. It comes *direct*, & much more easily on the ice.) For now it is becoming a question how long the river will be safe. It is really rather exciting to hear all the ups & downs, & hopes, & fears, & prognostications about Spring. Whether there will be an *ice freshet* this year for one thing. I only hope there may— We should have such a good view of it. An ice freshet is when the ice having been very thick breaks up & bursts out with awful force—sometimes carrying away houses &c. &c. (one barn went down the river one year & some 'cute parties put out in a boat & grappled it—& landed it!!!!...) We should be quite safe here. Everybody's weather prophecies seem to have gone wrong this year, it has been so exceptional, & we have come to the conclusion (as somebody wittily remarked.) "Take the opinion of the oldest inhabitant, & make up your mind for the reverse." We were at the Bishop's for practice last night—& some nice things were practised— Amongst others an introit of Rex's— Before we left there was a sort of "meeting" held by the gentlemen—with speechifying to the little Bishop—who stood stiff & attentive—we ladies thronging round to listen—on the subject of starting a big Choral Society in the place.[1] In the course of an elaborate speech Mr. Roberts alluded to their having secured "a professional gentle-

126

man (the Bandmaster 22d) – & the Prince of Amateurs." – I couldn't help thinking of Sleona!!!!![2] I believe the Society is likely to *go* – I expect it will give Rexie a lot of trouble – but he will enjoy it I suppose. He is in the middle of his Easter Anthem now. We have Morning Prayer at 9. during Lent every day. So we breakfast at 8.30 & go – & then Rex goes on to his work. There are P. M. prayers every day but one also. In the evening with a sermon on Wednesdays. About 30 or 40 (there have been 47) come in the morning, which is good I think. . . .

Your own loving — Judy.

LETTER
32

Fredericton. March 22. 1868

My dearest Mum.

At last – your dear letters arrived!! We began to think that this time the mail really must have gone to the bottom, however she came in all square, & we got our letters last night – a week later than even the usual winter delivery. We have not yet heard what detained her, though there was an idea, that she had got among the ice. The intermediate letter came really about 1/2 way this time, & broke *my* gap beautifully. I say mine – for alas! – this mail has been less kind to the poor Medleys. By the previous regular mail Mrs. M. heard that her mother was ill, she heard nothing by New York, & hoped that "no news &c." – but that & the other proverbs as to ill news coming apace have proved as false this time as proverbs do occasionally prove – After a sickening suspense of 6 weeks – she has heard the worst – Her mother is dead. You may guess that *I* have felt for her, as people living here *with* all their own belongings close at hand hardly can. Morning & afternoon at the Cathedral services she has looked so "screwed up" – & so sick at heart – & *grey* — that really I think even this is better than longer suspense. Her mother seems to have been a very superior person – & she was greatly devoted to her. The Bishop had been telling her this week that she should go home for a visit this summer – & she said it had comforted her more than anything. Dear darling old Mum, I did feel so thankful to have such nice comfortable happy letters from Home, & so so sorry for her! One cannot help feeling what the distance is in such a case – though at the same time that is not the truest way to look at it. If it is GOD's will that such things shld be – the actual distance makes little matter. Rex was no more able to reach his Father's deathbed in time than his Mother's – as I thought this morning – though the old gentleman died at his country place – & Rex was only a few miles off in Aberdeen. The old lady must have been really *old*, for Mrs. M. is middle aged, so in a way it is not otherwise than natural, & she could hardly have hoped that she wld survive a severe attack of pleurisy. Only people never can be *prepared* for what is so unwelcome. One can only submit, I believe; as she is well able to do; but she probably will suffer considerable physical prostration after all the suspense. Rex's Easter Anthem being complete, & approved, was to have been practised at the choir meeting at the Bishop's on Thursday. But in the circumstances – the practice is to be held at our house instead, so my housekeeping energies will be put in force for a party of 30 or so – & Mrs. Campbell will have to lend me her chairs again!!!! Our big rooms have considerable convenience in an emergency of this kind. I hope the Anthem will be very successful – it begins with a bass recitative solo. "Very early in the morning on the 1st day of the week they came into the Sepulchre." (trio of women's voices) "They have taken away the Lord – & we know not where they have laid Him." (Alto solo. Angel.) "Why seek ye the living among the dead? He is not here –" (Chorus) "*He is not here*– He is risen" (Chorus) "*He is risen.*" It ends with a full chorale – "Christ is risen from the dead, & become the 1st fruit of them that slept – Alleluia – Amen." The Choral Society seems going on. Father McDevitt has given his support on behalf of the R.C.s[1] & now the "Denominations" are to be tried. For it is to be a common ground affair in a public hall, independent of creed or class. Rexie has got some *lovely* songs lately. A lot of Franz's & of Schumann's. The way those men "marry music" to Heine's "immortal verse" is wonderful! *You* really would enjoy

128

the exquisite delicacy with which some of Heine's gems are set. He is altogether inexcusable in his behaviour to Dot about the music he was to copy. I hope he will do it soon, but Hebrew really swallows him up, & when the Choral So. gets afloat I don't know what will happen.... I see that "Ancient & Modern" wants additional hymns,[2] & I want him to send some. But he is afraid they will be too late. He is a bad boy in that respect, that he is rather deficient in the bump of *hope*–& always elects to think that things have gone to smash–& that it is "too late"–& "no use" &c. &c. which is a pity as it much oftener turns out that one can do things than that one can't!! All which he will read in this 'ere letter, & I hope profit by; but bless his nose!–he is playing a fairy like thing of Schumann's with a fairy touch that "covers a multitude of sins"–!!!!!!! & utterly absorbed therein. Bessy Roberts sings his "Teach me"[3] *very* prettily, by the bye. I heard her the other day. N.B. He has every reason to be jealous of the attention of the Master of the Rolls. He is a white haired tall fine old gentleman, & he & I carry on a courtly flirtation together!– He takes me to Church on wet Sundays–& today he presented me with a lovely red rose!!!! after morning service. And a red rose–in all the desolation of a fresh snow storm–is not to be despised. People are very kind. I was walking to Church when we met Dr. Ward going off on a professional drive. He turned out his man, took me into the sleigh & drove me to the Cathedral before proceeding on his way that I might not have to wade through the snow. Old Mrs. Shore (the Fine Arts old lady with the dial in her garden.) says (she comes regularly to the daily services with small regard to weather) that she thinks Providence always sends somebody to help her home. In this weather she needs someone, & Rex occasionally tenders his arm! *I* begin to think the same–for though I have often expected to be kept at home unless I could get a lift—I generally *do* get one!– We suppose this *will* be our last storm for the winter, but it is past prophesying this year. But you need not *shiver* on our behalf– Your house I suspect isn't half as warm even as ours! & I have done a good deal in the way of *airing* the house lately, for the heat begins to feel *stuffy*, in a way suggestive of spring. Tell Dot that the *ancles* are *quite* equal to snowshoeing, which is a 1000 times easier

129

than skating—though Capt. Patton *did* yell with laughing so loud that I told him he could have been heard at S. John—the first time he saw me on them about 1/4 of a mile off—and could give no further account of himself than that "Mrs. Ewing on snow-shoes"——"wading up a bank" was too many for his feelings. But I believe that my "carriage" is rather graceful than other-wise on them! Rex says I go like a *squaw* which is really a com-pliment—though the gait is more peculiar, than absolutely beau-tiful. A sort of upright, easy, swing—of a walk!!!!! *Monday* [23 March]. The Master of the Rolls took me to Evening Church & brought me back!— Bessy Roberts came back & dined with us—& we had Goose & fried Roly Poly!!!!!! That's our latest news. I wish you could dine with me on a roast goose day my dear old Mum!!! Poor Mrs. Medley was at church this morning— The dear, obsti-nate little Bishop—who goes at a thing like a highminded Bull, has made up his mind that it is too much for me to undertake the choir tea; & that he will "send round a messenger" (in his little despotic way!) to tell the people whom I have invited, not to come till after tea. Rex has had two interviews with him on the subject, & has finally handed him over to me. *I* had ditto ditto this morning & re-spectfully stuck to my guns—& so it is to be—unless he issues an episcopal mad bull to the contrary!!!! Having been a nursing sister for 20 years poor Mrs. M. does not take easily to "parties"— They generally knock her up, I believe, & so the Bishop, who knows *nothing* about it, thinks a plain choir tea is the most awful under-taking. He says it takes 3 women & Mrs. Medley. I thinks to myself "they're not Yorkshire women then!"— Hetty takes it perfectly easy, & as it simply consists in tea, bread & butter, & cake—all on table like a social tea—with 2 trays—Dot will believe it won't break *my* back!!!! Moreover the choir includes several people to whom I am glad of the opportunity of being hospitable—such as our ex-cellent friends the Pearsons &c. &c. And of course when once in our *small* house no such opportunities can occur. I hear that Mrs. Clerke is not coming out till May or June. I quite stick to my de-cision about the black lace— It will be unspeakably useful. It would make my black silk swell—or my old white silk—& when the said white silk is dyed blue—it will be pretty on *that*. N.B. I wld rather have a *goodish flounce* than a less good skirt I think. But I think if Dot wld drop a line & ask Kate Fisher, she wld know about it, & where best to get it. Also please *N.B.* I will have 4 *good* pairs of white kids instead of 6 cheap – I have come to the conclusion that I can't afford cheap gloves, especially out here where if they *do* split – or all the thumbs are too tight – & the fingers too loose & they won't fasten – or wld fasten over both hands – & otherwise become useless sooner than one expects – one can't send in to Sheffield & get 1/6 worth more of rat skin!⁴ to supply their place!!! Dot will remember that at some shop in Sheffield we once got some *nice* ball gloves for 2/- & something. I have got a capital chloroform mixture for cleaning them – & if they are good they will clean nicely – Of the colored gloves sent me at Xmas – 1st the black & white pair – all the sewing split at once – fastenings came off – *one* of the thumbs too tight – &c. The other day I just tried the double buttoned pair on – to which I had been looking forward for summer – they fit – but not one of the 4 buttons will meet! Now anyone who knows my wrists must know that gloves that will come on to my broad hands & not button round my small wrists, *must* be badly made! En revanche the good pair I bought in *Dublin* a year ago – & have worn ever since I wear still – both fastenings good – perfect fits—6 1/4 – & will mend & last me long enough yet. They were ˢ3/- I think. I almost think if you could ask Mrs. Cobbe kindly to get me a pair & send them per post to you I will have a pair of *grey* single buttoned 6 1/4 ones, stitched with black & white – or black. . . . Do I *persecute* you all dear old homepeople with my little *wants?* . . . I hope to send the whole of Reka Dom by next mail, as it is nearly done, & I hope really it will do. I think you might really venture to begin it when you get it, for I will work steadily at the rest – & it certainly is time Mrs. O. worked herself off the Maga. The account of the Reading Room is really *delightful. I am* so glad! Has our Library been incorporated with it – or not? – It is a most admirable thing I am sure, & the people *ought* to be grateful to the Govr for taking it up. I only feel it is a shame for us to take the Guardian which wld otherwise be so nice for them, but if you like to let them have it for a day or 2 *first* pray do. We don't mind getting it late. We are thankful for small mercies in the newspaper line here! It goes on from us into the town, & thence to an old gentleman at a farm in the country.[5] Anything within the current year is "news" – & beyond it may be regarded as history!!! ...

Old Hector is getting frightfully fat – bless him! – he gets so much to eat. . . . Pray thank Aunt Fanny 1000 times for the lace. It is lovely. I will write to her soon.

Our best & dear love to all. I am very well & happy & so is my dear old man. (He is just coming in – cocked hat, sword & all!)

Always dear darling old Mum

Your loving children   AJHE

N.B. I also very much want some *embroidery cotton white* six knots *fine*, & six rather coarser – ordinary thickish size.

[AE's Postscript]

Our dearest Mum. It seems long since I sent one of my Postscripts, and to-day there is not time left, for I have had to attend (officially) the Prorogation of Parliament, which came off to-day, and have only this moment returned. Spring is coming to us rapidly. The thermometer goes down to +20° or so of nights, and rises to +40° or more in the afternoons. The sun is getting powerful and melts the snow rapidly. Jow is very flourishing, and has been, on the whole, very free from throats.   AE

LETTER

33

31. March. 1868.

My dearest Mum.

. . . I don't think you would think we shall have summer before you, if you could see the river – still a highway of ice & snow – &c.

&c.! But when it does come I expect it will be a roaster—& I am getting all my most gossamer clothing together. Mrs. Coster (good soul!) came down the other day to look over my things & put the workwoman into the way of doing them up—& I think I shall get

her help over my bonnet. *I* mean to use Aunt Fanny's lovely bit of work in a bonnet, tell Maggie. I am going to make a bonnet of blue crape & put the white lace on it, & put white lace edging to my *strings*. Tell the girls I don't  know if they ever mean to go in for *walking skirts*, but if they could get a good pattern of a gored walking skirt—they wld find it very economical—& for young slight people they look very nice out of doors I think. You can take the *best breadths* of a nearly worn out dress & make it— I have made one of my old black & grey spotted dress—to go botanizing in—& a pretty new one—of the spare bit of

grey alpacca that belonged to my dress—a wonderfully small bit! There is no holding up—& they wld be very useful to go about the village &c.— By next *regular* mail (arriving a day or two after this) I shall send the final order of where my things are to go to. I have heard nothing of Mrs. Clerke—but Mrs. Coster has some things coming out by a 22d lady—& they may come with these. *N.B.* While Mrs. Batty is over about Maggie's things, will some one  charitably tell her—that I have not got *one* high dress that fits me decently. Some are miles too large, others too small. The black silk was fearfully *ripped*, but I think that was owing more to the way the *brace* trimmings are put on than anything. Would Dot ask her if she would be so very kind as to cut me out 2 patterns in calico or firm paper. 1. a high waist pattern as good a cut as she can— 2. a low waist do. like my wedding dress which fits well. Tell her there simply is not a dressmaker here I *dare* trust with a new waist—& I have an unmade high dress & a black silk low—I want to have done—& I have no one high dress well cut enough to copy. I shld really be *awfully* grateful if she wld! —the patterns not to be made up or only *tacked* together. . . .

I think now I may *promise* to send Reka Dom by the Halifax mail. If Pasquier illustrates – may he be asked to take as *characteristic* subject as he can.[1] Not one that wld fit any other story. In all descriptive art one must choose the *characteristic* points – not those in which all characters are alike – & I hope you will like it. All your letters are delightful – & it is so thankworthy to have such good news.

We get on jollily, & now the weather is comparatively mild.

Mrs. Shore (the dial lady) is as lively as ever. We have a little joke every day almost after Morning Prayer. I say "Mrs. Shore – allow me to be your particular Providence" & she says "My dear – I was looking for you –" & I give her my arm to take her home over the slippery ice.

It is nearly church time & I must go or Rex won't wait – he plays at *both* the daily services. More next mail——

Your ever loving daughter
with dear love to all—

J. H. E.

LETTER
34

April. 4. 1868

My dearest Mum –

I hoped to have sent you the whole of Reka Dom this mail. But a most unexpected fall of snow has made the travelling so insecure that it is considered a risk to wait till Monday & I must send off what I can today. It is so nearly done that I am not now afraid to send off the 1st part (which will be more than you will want for May.) & you may rely on the rest by next mail; & the remainder of Mrs. O. as rapidly as possible. It has certainly given me a wonderful amount of bother this time, & I was disappointed in the feel-

ing that Rex did not think it quite up to my other things. But today
in reading it all, & a lot that he had not seen before – I heard him
laughing over it by himself – & he thinks it now – one of my best – so
I am in great spirits – & mean to finish it with a flourish if possible –
I have cut & carved & clipped till I lost all sense of what was fit
to remain, & Rex has insisted on a good deal being replaced.
I miss poor old Fisher[1] awfully – especially with so few books of reference as I have. Please to look at a place where the bibliomaniac
refers to people who don't know an Elzevir &c. &c. I wanted a good
typical sort of comparison. As I first hastily wrote it I put down
"who does not know pigskin from calf—" but I really want to express a man who was ignorant of the difference between certain
editions – or books & others which to a real collector were price-
less.[2] If you can improve the sentence, please do. I shld think about
8 sheets more will complete the story. There are about 5, I think,
written, which I have not sent.

We find now that the lady who was to have brought out the
things for Mrs. Coster & myself is coming out too soon to do so, &
Mrs. Coster's sister is not coming at all. So we must hope in Mrs.
Clerke. But I am in no violent hurry for the black lace, as with my
done up wedding dress, & the evening toilette I am getting out of
my old white grenadine I shall survive Easter festivities. Fancy
everybody's astonishment when spring really seemed to be here
– that on Thursday evening in a few hours, came a fall of snow
that has wrapped everything up again. Wonderfully deep. Rex was
at the Roberts' & came home about 1/2 past 12 – I went up to bed – &
Rex let Hector out at the front door – where unhappily Mr. Far-
quharson was passing in his sleigh with a big black Newfoundland at
his back – Out flew Hector – & at it they went – Rex rushed to the
rescue – & at last tore the black dog off Hector who however kept
tight hold of his adversary's leg – so Rex handed the black dog to his
master & at last got Hector off. I heard the moans & struggles upstairs & thought the poor old Bull *Doge* was killed at last. I got R.'s
hunting whip & fled to join the melée in slippers & demi toilette! — If you *could* have seen us all in the snow!!! Poor old
Hector bled awfully, & has had a face swollen up like a prize-

fighter's ever since – but is better now, bless him, & as patient & loving as possible. It is not very cold, in spite of this return of winter, & it is probable that the river *will* open soon – but all prognostications seem at fault. We are very jolly & well & happy dear Mum – & seem always busy somehow. The Choral Society is a-float[3] – Rex is accompanist & is at a meeting at this moment! – ... It was a *lovely* morning this morning! So clear & delicious! – I hope you are pretty well darling Mum. With dear love from Rexie & myself & Bulldoge! to all — Ever your most loving daughter

J.H. Ewing.

. . .

If there is time I *wld* like *proofs* of the Reka Dom for *June*.

LETTER
35

Easter Tuesday. [14 April] 1868.

My dearest Dot.

I was casting about for something to head my letter with, & "the Miss Fishers" occurred to me. . . . I really think I must tell about them, & about some of the other people here, for there is no special *news*. Mr. Charles Fisher–father to the above[1]– is a high ministerial swell (not of aristocratic origin) He was one of the delegates to England, whither Mrs. F. accompanied him, greatly I shld imagine to the amusement of the swells they visited – & she is now Lady Oracle in these parts on the domestic life of Dukes & Duchesses. She is *very* odd, though a good natured soul I think – Ill-natured reasons are given for her peculiarities, but very likely quite without foundation. Drinking is so common here, that the next difficult thing to escaping the habit, must be to escape the imputation. Mr. C.F. is a silent man, who wears an ordinary chimney pot & cloth coat in winter when everybody else is covered with fur to keep from being frost bitten. He is at present in Ottawa I believe. There are 3 young ladies. The 2 above – & a younger one "finishing" in the States. No caricature *could* caricature their costume! They look as if they had been covered with sticky stuff & then rolled in the Houndsditch box to bring away what they could.[2] They are generally covered with small *bells* which jingle as they go – & come off at balls, & are scrambled for by the officers! – Strangely enough they are very quiet nice mannered girls, with soft voices – very pleasant to talk to – & seemingly very amiable with not *very much* in them. They are the incarnation of *peplum* in sashes, petticoats, & every kind of clothing. The eldest is very plain, poor girl, & looks *awful* in her finery; the other is very pretty, & does her best to spoil herself. They do their hair in private. No one is ever allowed to see it prepared – & they say that as their great object is to be quite unlike other people, if anybody shld ever imitate their style, they wld give it up at once. Unfortunately for them, no one seems likely to do so. The Prince of Wales was supposed to have been rather smitten with the younger.[3] They are in the choir, & as I said, are really very nice, little as they look it [Plate 11]. Dear little Mrs. Shore

I told you about. We have been so grieved the last week as she has been very ill. On Good Friday she was given up, but with some difficulty the Bishop obtained leave to see her, they told him it was no use as she was unconscious &c. However she revived when he went in, & he bathed her face with eau-de-cologne & she revived – & he sent Mrs. Medley to her, who has been nursing her since, & she is now recovering. Today – *much* better. Mr. & Mrs. Saunders her nephew & niece are a very wooden couple externally. Mrs. S. sat in her bonnet waiting for the death so to speak – & Mr. S. in a funereal manner below told callers that there was no hope. He went in the other morning & observed sepulchrally that there was *a change*. The little old lady said quietly "Yes – for the better!" Mrs. Campbell my neighbor is her great niece. She is a pretty little creature, with a wonderful capacity for taking everything perfectly *placidly* in this world. She is very nice & kind. Mr. – or Professor Campbell – is a very youthful looking professor – a relative of the Manners Suttons. Their bairns are jolly little things. With Mrs. Shore lives a Miss Garrison.[4] This girl's father is an American storekeeper, I believe. Also he is a "nothing particular" in the religious line & her mother is a very textified Baptist. She had been educated & was musical, & came off with the independence of Yankees to earn her living here by teaching. Govt House at that time was full of young men – among them a Mr. Skene – (Zoe's brother) – she is pretty – dresses well & is rather *mannierés*. – Mr. S. went to the hotel where she was & told her he had come to have lessons in singing – However after some little fuss she firmly refused to let him come, & finally went & told Mrs. Medley about it. *They* took her up – & Mrs. Shore seeing her there took a liking to her & offered her a home. So she is Mrs. Shore's companion & also gives lessons. She is a ladylike pretty girl, & the old lady takes her everywhere – to balls &c. &c. rather to the scandal of some of the élite. Her name is Harriet Martineau Garrison – (American! n'est ce pas?) She was baptised here – never having been so. *She* is in the choir. The Roberts I have described. Ditto the Costers & Pearsons. Mrs. Robb[5] – a widow sister of Mrs. Coster's – large – handsome – & hesitating – devoted – & *touchy* – an alto – who *can't* sing fast, (or won't!)

& drags all the part songs with her own peculiar swing. *Mr. Carman*[6] – in a Govt office – a *wonderful* old young beau . . . – slim & active – dark beard & iron hair – irreproachable in get up – a 2d wife & young family—&—about 8 years older than the Governor (or more!) with his first family married & settled. Mrs. Carman – nice but perpetually laid up with snowblindness &c. Mr. C. excellent churchman. Ditto Mr. Bliss his brother in law – a widower in mitigated affliction . . . with 7 young children & his eye on Mary Roberts!!![7] — Miss Jacobs – a factotum of the Cathedral – & devoted to us, particularly to Rex. Her father Dr. J.[8] was head of the college here – but his sons were awfully spoilt & extravagant & took to drinking – & matters altogether got so bad, that this sister went off to earn her own living by teaching, & eventually Dr. J. gave up & retired to a farm in the country. Miss J. (who is a *very* strictly religious person & awfully sensitive) has felt it all dreadfully, she got her brothers sometimes out of prison – then nursed them on their deathbeds – & finally settled here & teaches a small school. Her mother was a frail english lady, & Miss J. used to send her delicacies & things till she died. Then the father sent word to her to come, & *bring a coffin.* She got a coffin & made her dreary pilgrimage into the country, & when she got there, her father *would* bury her mother *in the garden!* Can you imagine the feelings of a high church, sensitive single lady? Poor Miss Jacob! She now waits on here as long as her father lives. When he dies she will get her mother's body & have it laid in consecrated ground – & then go to England & join a sisterhood. She is awfully excitable, poor old thing, & great fun sometimes. Rex is teaching her school to sing – He goes every week. She has a voice like an old tea kettle herself – We let her have the Guardians – & she sends them on to Dr. Jacob. She knitted me a sort of violet winter waistcoat – & gave me winter mittens; but though she is awfully poor, she is so sensitive, it is hardly possible to do anything to help her. She did accept some fresh eggs from me the other day though. She illuminates (feebly, but to the satisfaction of Fredericton) in order to have money for the Offertory. Judge Parker the Master of the Rolls I have described – the Mistress of the Rolls also. The single daughter[9] who lives with them is also a great friend of ours, & has now joined my drawing class. Not *very* young, & *exactly* like a good young lady of the Miss Edgeworth age & school. Her large eyelids always down. She *glances*, & *trips*, & seems to apologise for existence albeit of a very firm temper really, with strong theological views, & an immovable objection to face east at the Creed. (Though I *fancy* this is rather in deference to her Mother.) She is very good & active & very intelligent, though a leetle tiresome at times. Dr. Ward–medical man–English– His first wife was a sister of Mr. Coster's–& since we came he married a Miss Street–principal soprano. . . . He seems an intelligent man, & is very musical. They are great friends of ours, & have nice little children–his family by the first wife.[10] The Streets, an old lady–2 single sons & a delicate daughter–are nice people too, cousins of the architect.[11] Old Mrs. S. is very feeble & frail, but a regular old *lady*. The Simonds I have described I think. He is an officer "settled" here, has a countless family of *blooming* daughters all as pretty as flowers, & he looking like their brother. A *very* goodlooking slight–dark eyed, bearded young man–& he drives down a waggon load of these pretty girls to church, or to the band & it is a wonderfully gay looking turn out. They are regular settlers–*very* simple habits–flavored with english memories & good taste. The girls make their clothes, & drive carts or carriages–or walk or skate as need requires. I hope all this won't bore you, deary– I thought you might like to feel to know our neighbors. N.B. Please in MSS. I sent alter the name of old Mr. Brooke wherever it occurs from John to James. Please don't forget!!!![12]

My bonnet is quite a success I think. It is delicate blue crape–with Aunt Fanny's bit of white lace on it & white cluny lace all round the front & back & down the strings. I *had* the lace–& the strings are the strings of my fur cap–which I couldn't wear when in black–so I only had to buy the crape & shape which cost about $2/8!!! I took it to Mrs. Coster's to make it there, but she did it almost entirely. However *I* have made another bonnet even more successful! Bessy Roberts has hitherto had the knack of wearing the most awfully unbecoming, overfashionable, homemade bonnets, to Rex's agony, who has rather a weakness for her, & also sits opposite to her in the choir. I found her compiling *such* an affair – for Easter! – & as she was not well I picked up what materials I could, took them home, got a shape like my own – & the result is considered a work of art!! It is grey crape, trimmed with silk blende lace, with little pink asters in front, & pink strings to tie behind. I also insisted on her wearing a black silk dress & velvet jacket with it, & the effect was remarkable! —

We are going tonight to another musical meeting at either the Wards or Costers. The Choral So. goes on – at the last meeting Hector went with Rex, & in the middle of the discussions jumped on to the table. Hence he is now called the President! I must go to my Hebrew, as the Bishop comes tomorrow.

. . . It has been *awfully* cold. Today is milder, & we suppose summer *will* come! Though as someone remarked, it is hardly worth the while of the ice to move now, it will be wanted again so soon!! Yr ever loving Judy.

LETTER

36

April. 17. 1868. Fredericton.

My dearest Mum.

. . . We are now on the eve of our "flit." I am doing bits of packing by degrees – that I may not have an overpowering "bust" of it at once. I packed the books yesterday & have packed another large box of knickknacks &c. The weather has delightfully changed, & we think it is hardly likely that there will be another freeze-up now. A few days ago it was bitter beyond description; but today it is quite warm — nearly 60° Fahr — & universal *sludge*. I have been rather shut up for a day or two – from having cut one of my goloshes, & being unable to get another pair of my size in Fredericton! – & successive wet feet don't *shoot* the *constitootion*. At last, however, I have found a pair, although the other stores freely assured me that they were "out" of the size – & not only in Fredericton but goloshes of that size could not even be procured in S. John!!!!

We have now got together our few indian things for Maggie & they shall come by the earliest opportunity, together with the Tennysons which I shld have sent by Capt. Parry; only Fredericton was "out" of Tennyson as of nearly everything else. In the bit before the river opens, you have to take what you can get, & do without what you can't!!! The sqaw has been making the blotting case – & Peter brought it today – & I am very much pleased with it, & hope Maggie will like it. I would *like* to have got an envelope case & a canoe, but they are so difficult to pack, & it wld be so aggravating to have them broken so we got a few *flat* things. The blotting case, & moccasins – & a cigar case for Frank – & a tiny pair of snowshoes. The blotting case is a good specimen, as it is made of the lovely birch bark; & they were all got direct from Indians we know. A sqaw with a sad face of rather a high type called to beg the other day – She could hardly speak English. She said "Sister, me no ate today." – So I gave her some bread & butter, which she gave at once to the boy with her, and went away.

We have had some splendid Auroras lately. They are not *rosy* here, but very beautiful otherwise – & very capricious in shape – Long, grand tongues of light shooting up into the sky. But I cannot

sketch it! And I suppose there are finer ones in Arctic regions; but these are finer than any I have seen in England. The Bishop is going Home in the summer for a month or two. Mrs. Medley was to have gone with him, but she is not going now. She says she cannot bear it, as her mother's welcome is gone. She is much better, poor dear, than she was. I wish you could see the little Bishop whilst he is in England. Your magnolia sketch was delicious, dear Mum, as all your bits are. *I* shall have a "household album" of *your* productions in time!!!! Rex's Hebrew studies continue to flavour his daily life with occasional orientalisms!! Today at dinner he burnt his mouth awfully with hot cheese macaroni. He did *not* swear in English, but being much exasperated with his mouth gaping & steaming — to my infinite amusement he gave vent to the expletive Abel-meholah (that is — as it should be said — *Ah*bel me holah)....

We are beginning now to talk of "May flower expeditions" — I think I shall give one to a few select friends. I had thought of a child's one, but a nice old schoolmistress here gives one children's one, & I think one raid of the united juvenile population on the poor lovely flowers is enough. The May flower is a lovely waxlike ground creeper with an exquisite perfume — It is the 1st flower — & is to be found before the snow has left the woods. When we find some — the Mum may expect a specimen. Mrs. Shore is getting on bravely, bless the little old lady! —— I am now busy doing up Rex's summer military cap — & various 2s & 3s of my own — With drawing, & Hebrew, & packing, & Passion Week & Easter — I have been busyish just lately.... And I have got my own hat to trim, & I wanted to write some other letters. Hector is *dear* & well — & sends his love to Grandma' Gage. If I go up to bed a good bit before Rex — up comes the old beast & without the remotest heed to my injunctions springs on to bed, *pushes* me a oneside till he has got the place he wants — buries his head in my neck to keep his nose warm — & composes himself with a satisfied *grunt* to sleep. But when he hears Rex's boots on the stairs he cocks one ear — & sits up — knowing that his ejection is nigh!! — Goodnight darling Mum. Our dear love to you & Father & all — Your devoted daughter

JHE.

Mrs. Clerke after all is not coming till June. Then she only comes to Halifax. Now if Capt. Parry does not get extension of leave, he is coming *here* in June — & that would be a good time to have our things out I think. I will accept Maggie's dress with pleasure, at the price she puts on it. It is simply impossible to get waists decently made here. Oh! how I wish I had a good "fit" anywhere in England. But I am very tidily off for clothes for the present. I have one good ball dress in my wedding dress, & another, tell Dot I am very proud of. It is the skirt of my old white grenadine – *turned* & gored to be long. Of what came out of the gores I have had a sort of swiss belt waist made & trimmed with the blue & white lace that was on the dress before. Above this comes a white puffed chemisette trimmed ditto — & I wear Aunt Fanny's sash – It makes a very pretty ball dress – After the Queen's birthday there probably won't be many

balls. I am *very* happy & well dear dear old Mum. The old dragon is *such* a dragon!!! "How are you this morning? — What are you *swallowing* about? – Is your throat wrong? – Are you *sure* –? Does your face ache? – Did you get your feet wet yesterday? What were you doing whilst I was at the office? Tired? Oh! of course that means you're not well. Of course you won't think of going to Church!" &c. &c. &c. &c. He is really *awful*.

There are about 100 members of the Choral So. now, & he says *I* am to be an Alto!!!!!!!!!!!!! I mean to stand with my *hearing ear* to Bessy Roberts tell Charlie – & sing after her!!!!!

Rex's P.S. The child is really very well and flourishing; and it is a great pleasure to think that there is now a prospect of some summer weather; though, at the same time, I consider that I require to keep a watchful eye over her at *all* times. But she *is not* quite so heedless as she once was, for I have *bullied* her into taking a *little* care of herself now & then.

I think, if you people at home were to see her now, you would look twice at her before you quite decided whether you knew her. The delicious winter of this place, (for it was delicious, after the very first severe bite of it was past, which took us somewhat by surprise, before we had quite made our preparations to meet it) really did her a great deal of good; She has "put on flesh," and has not the overstrained, *maladive* look which was so habitual to her in old days.

I *do* try, as well as I can, to make her life happy; I am sure you will not blame me for being sometimes a little over careful.

I should think you will like Reka Dom, when you see it completed; and agree with me in thinking it, in many respects, her best attempt, as yet.

With my dear love to all

Your afft ever
Rex.

. . .

LETTER
37

27. April. 1868.

Darling Mum.

The 2d steamer of the season came up today. The river is almost clear– The ice went out with ignominious quietness, & we can only console ourself for not having seen an ice freshet (or even heard the roar which usually accompanies the river's breaking) by the reflection that *some* people in exposed situations, must be very thankful that it has gone out & done no damage. The river is higher than we have ever seen it, & will be yet higher, I suppose, & whilst it is so the weather is cold – The extreme changes are very curious here. About a week ago, there was a very hot day. (Rex laughs at my "Hot" days – but both the Bishop & I felt quite knocked over with the heat – & having been out a good deal – I got a regular bad headache at night.) The roads were dry – This fierce sun beat upon your head, & on the winter clothes one has not yet thrown off, & I found myself slinking to the shady side of the street & longing to be *cool*!! In less than 2 days down went the thermometer – round went the wind – & we had one of our heaviest falls of snow!! The snow is nearly gone again, but the winds are very cold, & will continue so till the river subsides. Then we shall burst into full summer heat at one blow, & happily – summer clothes also. But one dare not unrobe yet in spite of odd warm days. You will hardly wonder that 2 or 3 of us have had colds at this juncture – Miss Roberts – Mrs. Ewing – Mrs. Coster &c. &c.!!!! Mine is nearly gone again, & it has not touched my throat. It has been awkward as we were just in the thick of flitting – but old Rexie has worked like a trooper (assisted by Hector!) & tomorrow I hope to be able to go out. Bessy & Mary have been here today helping to pack – & we have moved everything almost – but our beds! – My mind is quite absorbed with the thought of my garden. I do look forward to it with such pleasure! &

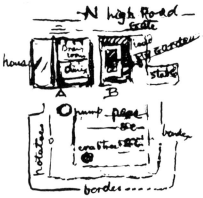

it more than compensates for losing this pretty airy drawing room. I have a tiny flower garden shut in with palings – But here is a plan of the place. The square A is the house. B is *my* garden – a border & one oblong bed!! About the size of 3/4ths of our old garden outside the kitchen windows. Beyond this is the kitchen garden with a well *convanient*. Which I have mentally planned− planted−watered−& reaped!!!!!! It has one crab-tree!− it is a very cosy little place−& when you think that we get it for less than £25 a year, it seems very cheap does it not?−

Poor dear little Mrs. Shore was buried on the day of the snow-storm.[1] Such a wild day. I was not able to go to her funeral for which I was sorry. The choir went in black & sat in their places− Rex went−& played the Dead March−& went on to the cemetery. I went to see her after she was dead. It was a lovely little face. It is to me *very* comforting to see how faces that have been marred by the sting &c. of life−& disfigured by the odds & ends of mortality−(queer caps−& wigs−& wrappings−mannerisms & traces of illness &c.!)−become beautiful in the peace of death without becoming unrecognisable. Don't you know?− I saw so clearly what a pretty girl Mrs. Shore must have been−& it makes one understand how *hereafter* one may be beautiful−& *yet* recognised. There were lovely flowers in the room−& a saucer of *salt* on her breast. I fancy she must have been laid out by an irish nurse. We all feel very much for poor Miss Garrison. She has lost a happy home. She will remain here a bit−& Rex will give her some lessons on the organ, as she wants to get an organist's place. She's a nice, gentle, pretty thing to have such a rough life battle to fight.

. . . The mail is rather late this time, but we hope to get it to-morrow. I do so wonder if Maggie & Frank are married yet![2]− Oh! if they may be as happy as we are!! But no one *could* be such a dear (in my humble judgement!!!) as that old Himage a grubbing away at his Hebrew on the other side of the table, & *fidgetting* (like a fidgetty old male animal as he is−) for me to stop this, for fear I should be *tired*!!! I must stop−if only to please him−bless him−though I am not the least bit tired, & have no reason to be. Mrs. Coster has given me such a nice pat of musk.

. . . We had a very successful first meeting of the Choral Society[3]−& I am entered as an alto!!! Rex has done it that I may not be left alone on the meeting nights−for strangers are not admitted−only *performers*. I hope I may be able to do my parts!!!!! I chaperoned a lot of young ladies (the Misses Fisher among them. Mrs. F. called in the afternoon to ask me.) & though it was my headache night – & I could hardly hold up my head I enjoyed it very much. Dr. Dow (the little fat Yankee dentist who drives about in a sulky.)[4] made a very *galant* speech on behalf of the ladies *not* being charged with fees &c. — I saw him spinning along on his sulky against a snow storm the other day – looking so funny!

Rex's dear love & mine – to all – I must write to the dear old Guv soon I think. My love to him & to everybody – Ever your loving daughter.

Juliana Horatia Ewing.

LETTER
38

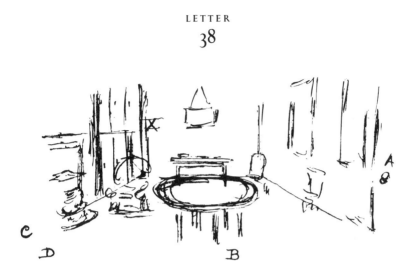

Fredericton. 4 May. 1868.

A quite out of proportion attempt to give you an idea of our little
dining room, dearest Mum–but it may show you how our
furniture is disposed in it.[1] It is a wee room after our big ones–but
so sunny & bright & snug!– X is a fine cupboard–a *fixture*–which
holds my stores–the house linen–the spare glass & china–& also
acts as our wine cellar!!!! A. is a door leading into the kitchen department–at B. stands our own little chiffonier sideboard with 2
drawers & 2 shelves chiefly devoted to drawings & drawing mate-
rials. D. is another door. At C. stands the butternut butler's tray.
We do not regret our move one bit– We are so much more snug
–& it is so *much* easier to keep things tidy & comfortable when
they are a little within compass–& when one can go to one's dress
closet without being frozen! I have been very busy making Rexie a
nice little dressing room of the little room next to mine. He is
awfully pleased with it–bless him!– I had a shelf put into a box &
have made him a dressing table–& clothes cupboard thereof–& he
is supposed now to enjoy every luxury down to a large stock of
shaving papers & an apparatus to hold the loose letters &c. he pulls

149

out of his pockets. The contents of *his* travelling bag (the Wakes') adorn the dressing table – & he is very fine in the pincushion & toilette mats department. He is very good, & keeps it very tidy. With this mail I hope comes the end of Reka Dom. It seems absurd I shld have anything to do to it, as it was finished save for writing out & corrections last mail – but you don't know what *moving* out – & *moving* in is! The mere item of getting your *blinds* to fit windows of a totally different size is absorbing to mind & body! – & then my cold kept me hors de combat a day or two. We are delighted with our little nest – & we like this quaint quiet street with the elms down it so well, we hardly regret even the river! – We bought the hall stove awfully cheap – & it is a little *wunner* to "go" — We shall save to such an extent in fuel, as I hope will compensate for the huge consumption of *Reka Dom*. . . . It is Sunday [3 May] – & has been a wonderfully fine bright warm day. The music has gone very fairly, & the Bishop preached an excellent sermon. In the evening a wonderful looking little whippersnapper "stood up for to read" —the 2d lesson. A whiskerless boy with a curious preraphaelite face – *fuzzy* hair – & a strong suspicion of darkie blood somewhere in the genealogy. One felt strongly inclined to laugh at him in his starched little surplice, looking much like a youthful edition of Disraeli in a starched nightdress. But by the time he had got well into the 2d chapter of Romans, it was apparent he read as if he understood what S. Paul meant. And when he had given his fuzzy wig a little expressive shake over the 2 last verses – & reached – "whose praise is not of *men* but of GOD" – I felt inclined to give an audible "hear – hear – " —

. . . I have been busy teaching Hartney to blow the bellows of the organ (It is Monday [4 May] now.) He is the 4th orderly I have instructed in that art – so I shall send *this* off today & Reka Dom by the 2d post tomorrow. There is always a supplementary mail on Tuesday which gets to Halifax in time if the roads are good – & they seem to be so now. . . .

> Our dear love to all
> Always dearest Mum —
> Your most loving daughter
> Juliana Horatia Ewing.

Rex's P.S.

Not only do *I* not "regret" our move, but I have never felt *so* comfortable in my life as in this little house; I am sure we have every cause to be most thankful that we have come to it.

Early summer is with us now, though there was ice and snow only a week ago; there is no spring here. (Somehow, my P.S.s always seem to take a meteorological turn – like any old sailor's diary, which is sure to begin, every day, with "Wind E. & by N. (or whatever it may be)." Jow has had a cold, but it is gone now. It happened just at the time of moving, but *we* ([JHE's hand] i.e. Rex did) took all the brunt off her. I have begun regular organ practice to-day, now that "weather permits" – for during the winter it is too cold to play in the church on week days. If all is well, and I can go on regularly for six months I ought to be beginning to play better at the end of that time. People here think I "play" well already; but that is because there is not anybody else who can play quite as well. *I*, however, know my own weakness on the instrument, and have now an opportunity of getting a little stronger. "Ars longa" &c. – especially pedal playing. Goodbye, our dear Mum; of course I join in happy wishes to the couple who caught the infection from us on the 1st of June. Qu'ils soient heureuses.

AE

. . .

LETTER
39

May 12. 1868

My dearest Mum.

We are so glad you like Mrs. O. And as it *is* to be a month later, I have all the more time to get well forward with it, which is perhaps as well, since settling in the new house & getting the garden afloat takes up a good deal of my time.

I am so sorry you have had influenza— It is so wretched & uncomfortable. I hope you are all right now. How *can* you say your writing is bad? When one thinks of that poor lefthand writing, it is so delightful to see your *own*—& so much clearer than most people's.[1]

You *shall* have some photos of Rex. We have been talking of being taken so long—& really do mean to, though there is no very good man here.

Think of the doges of Ecclesfield coming in with wounds to be washed. The blessed old Hector is behaving rather better in that line. He is such a good humored old soul really. As to kissing his nose—if once you saw it *wouldn't* you kiss it! It gets bright pink when he is excited, & is so sweet & soft. He was left at home the other day with the word of command "*Goodbye* Hector" which he quite understands—but he had his own ideas as to where we were going—& when we came out of church we found him waiting at the porch—& when he found that he was right & we *were* there—he capered & bounded & flew about like a mad thing. Now he comes regularly & waits outside as good as gold.

... *I* have a wonderful lot of gardening on my shoulders..., for we have no *gardener*—only get a soldier to work in the kitchen garden—so I have had to make my plan & arrange my crops for the kitchen garden as well as look after my own—& I feel quite like M.M.!! We have really 2 *charming* bits—a little hot—sunny—good

soil—vegetable plot—& quite away from this—by the house, my
flower garden. Two round beds & 4 borders, with a high fence & 2
little gates. I have nearly got this tidy. The last occupant had never
used it. It is a *great* enjoyment to me & does me awful good I think
by keeping me out of doors. Rexie has given me a dear little set of
tools—french ones, like children's toys, but quite enough for me.
They form the subject of one of the little *rhymes* that Hector & I
make together, & that I croon to the bull doge to his great satisfaction.

"The little Missus with the little spade
2 little beds in the little garden has made.
The Bull doge watches (for he can't work.)
How she turns up the earth with her little fork.
Then she takes up the little hoe
And into the weeds does bravely go.
At last with the smallest of little rakes,
Quite smooth & tidy the beds she makes."

Another that was made in bed on the occasion of one of his
raids on my invalid breakfast was—

"'Tis the voice of the Bull doge I hear him complain
You have fed me but lately; I must grub again.
As a pauper for pudding—so he for his meat—
Gapes his jaws, & there's nothing a bull doge can't eat."[2]

We sing these little songs together—& then I let him look in the
glass where he gowlypowls & barks dreadfully at the rival *doge*.
Please tell Dot that as I am going to have Maggie's pink & white
dress, & as the black lace is so expensive I will defer the latter for
the present— It would be worth giving a fair price for I think, but I
do not need it at present now—& there is no great gaiety going on.
Any time that Maggie or any one had the opportunity of incidentally enquiring what the price of a *flounce* (instead of a skirt) would
be—I wld just like to know. I am *so* sorry that the dear Vergiss mein
nichts were dried up when they arrived. Thank you all the same for
the dear thought. The flowers that come in letters are in *capital*

condition & the sweet ones smell. Send me just *a few* seeds of Brompton or Emperor stocks, & I will sow them & keep them in pots in the winter. *Seeds* are really a boon.

I have not much time today dear Mum. The paperer being in the house &c. Our dear love Ever your loving daughter J. H. E.

. . .

LETTER
40

18 May. 1868.

My dearest Dot.

The intermediate letters have just come, & are very welcome. I have not time to say much today, we have been so busy with house & garden &c. Tonight we are going to dine at Govt House, & I am a little bothered as to what to wear in my hair. I think if there had been time – I would have asked Maggie when in Paris to get me one or two good flowers – a white one of some kind & a blue of some kind (convolvulus?) & one or two scarlet geraniums. Bad flowers are so horrible, & when one goes on wearing a white silk encore & encore – a slight change in head gear is desirable. . . . I am awfully busy with my garden, & people are very kind in giving me things. Tomorrow we go to lunch at the Rowans, & I aim to ransack *his* garden! I do think the exchange of herbaceous perennials is one of the joys of life. You can hardly think how delicious it feels to *garden* after 6 months of frost & snow. Imagine my feelings when Mrs. Medley found a bed of seedling bee larkspurs in her garden – & gave me at least 2 dozen!!! I have got a whole row of them along a border, next to which, I *think* I shall have mignonette & scarlet geraniums alternately. It is rather odd after writing Reka Dom, that I should fall heir to a garden in which almost the only "fixture" is a south border of lilies of the valley![1] After herculean exertions our rooms are papered, & the house *almost* tidy. (N.B. I am becoming a "lean Betty" of old maidishness, & watch the mud which "Boy & Bulldog" bring in to my drawing room carpet with discontented eyes!) I want you please to get me a paper of *chicory seed* & send it out by next mail. I can't get it here, & it is said to be a good winter vegetable (see the yellow 1/- book!) Another thing you can hardly understand is how utterly weary & sick one becomes of winter food. Meat (never very good) frozen up & "thawed out" again – is not at its best – potatoes, carrots & beetroot till you are slightly tired of those excellent vegetables – & of neither seeing nor tasting green. Now the seedling lettuces rejoice our eyes, & as to the lobsters which are very good & very cheap here – they are a charming change from 1/2 frozen meat. Send me also a pinch of foxglove seed please. . . . The bulldoge won't let me write – I've been washing my head, & am sitting on the floor in my red dressing gown – & he dotes on a bright colour, & always wants to lie on it. We have been having a good deal of rain, & the river has risen wonderfully. I must add to my list of friends our new neighbors, or rather Overtheways. Two very old ladies who were among the first settlers.[2] (The Loyalists came here & "settled" Fredericton in 17 —— alas! I forget. 88 I think.)[3] There was one old wooden Church "in those days" – & terrible battles about pews which were put up to auction in the Church – 8 "principal residents" insisting on having pews of double size. The parson lived on the other side of the river, & one day he came over in a birch bark canoe – & went back the same way, & was heard of no more! "Miss Bailey" remembers that on June 1, being the King's birthday, they fired cannon over the river to raise the body, but it was not found for 8 days.[4] When the Bishop came people went once to church on Sundays, & in the afternoon paid visits & played cards. You may imagine the storm created by his insisting on free seats![5] One man went about with a horsewhip for a long time threatening to flog him. He excommunicated Mr. W. Odell for fighting a duel. I mean he simply refused to admit him to the Holy Communion.[6] I have been to see the old ladies twice. The bulldoge is behaving awfully. I can't keep him quiet!

Dear love to all.

LETTER
41

27 May. 1868.

My dearest old Mater.

...I am getting our house quite spick & span. The only draw-back is that none of you can see it. If only you could go over *our* house...I think you would think that in our humble way we have got it very nice. The garden too, is getting to look *like* a garden—to our old orderly's great pride who elaborately "ex-plained"...to me yesterday–that for a long time past it had never been seen in such order & condition. The dirt & untidyness of New Brunswickers combined with the prevalence of the *irish* element in servants & workmen, is enough to cure an untidy party like myself–& I have "set my face as a flint" against one "irish corner" inside or out. It is slow work, for *every* corner was an irish corner when we came; & though the *owner* of the house lived in it (a lady, in the choir &c.) the only drain on the place was stopped up (in fact she did not know of its existence.) & the slops were poured down a sink & dribbled out in front of the dining room windows on the exact principle of sinks in houses in Ecclesfield streets. I had felt very fidgetty about it, but of course poor Rex–as he said –couldn't go & talk to a young lady about *drains*, & I am so hor-ribly weakminded, I knew I couldn't be *firm*. Especially as I did not know the ways of the country in reference to drainage. So I got Mrs. Medley to call with me. Miss Partelow[1] was very fair & kind, though... she "didn't feel it herself"–& it is to be put right–please the carpenter[2]–& when he has not better jobs on hand! Meanwhile I never allow a drop of anything to go down the sink–so we do well enough & Rex has had *lime* liberally applied in all directions, & we have got a fire in the kitchen garden consuming all our refuse. Old rags, boots, trees, & rubbish of all sorts accumulated on the prem-ises. Our good old orderly is irish & never takes up anything

156

clean, nor lays down anything straight if he can avoid it – But happily the gardener is an "Essex calf," with a silent tongue & a straight eye, & a nimble hand. After the long spell of *dry* weather – we have now had such a ceaseless rain for many days that it is becoming serious. Every morning a change is expected & every day the same steady downpour comes drearily on. It has rotted some of my seeds I fear, but it has "settled" the transplanted things nicely – so I hope when the burst of overpowering heat which is pretty sure to follow this arrives – everything will progress with rapid strides.

Monday [1 June]. Rex has to go down to S. John tomorrow on Govt business, & I think I shall go with him. It will be a little change — & it *may* be fine! Also I shall call on Zebbi Cox (Symonds that was.) I have not seen her since I was at Simonides when they were in the height of their little affair – & Mrs. S. seemed perfectly blind – wonderful to say – & I think rather set out Major C. toward *me* if anything! – He was a pleasant man with a lovely mop of fair hair on his head – who gave us tea & delicious brown bread & butter at Hurst Castle.[3] She has expressed a wish to see me – & I shall be very glad to see her.

The blessed old Hector has had another awful fight – & his head is like a large discolored dumpling!! He *snoogles* up against my knees to be petted – & drinks warm tea, & naps on his dressing gown, & is as well as can be expected.

S. John. Wednesday [3 June]. We came up here yesterday, & I am enjoying it very much. S. John is a *seaport* you know, so one gets a whiff of sea breeze. I looked in vain here for seaweeds last summer, but there wld be more chance at Carleton, the little bathing place near, & if by any chance I should be there this summer I will have a good hunt. The river looked very pretty as we came up, for all the country is flooded with the freshet, & looked quite different to what we saw when we went from S. John to Fredericton last year. We got in very quickly – between 5 & 6 hours – & I enjoyed it very much though the *screw* even on fresh water makes me a little squeamish. I met Zebbi & Major Cox in the town, & had a long chat & she is coming to see me this morning & we shall probably go there this evening. She is looking very little altered & very sweet, & he is looking very well too. As far as I could make out one of the sisters (*not* Julie) is ill if not dying, & she is much cut up, & says it will upset Simonides so dreadfully. Do you know about it? The only sisters *I* knew were Julie & Zebbi. She has 4 children, one 6 years old. It seems so strange! It seems so short a time since that we were at Simonides' garden picnic together! Rex found a letter here from Mr. Monk (Comm:Officer here, & an old Australian acquaintance) asking us to spend the evening there, so we went. He is a very curious man. I had heard about him before. He is one of the *preaching* military men – but a really unaffectedly *good* man Rex says – & decidedly interesting. The 60th rifles[4] are here now, & there are several street preachers among *them*, & one of them (a brother of the Lt. Warren who is on the Jerusalem Exploration business)[5] was there, & another "light" from the 4th. There was a good deal of edifying allusion, but no extempore prayer as we had expected. The Monks were married just after us. I like her, & we got on *very* well, though she is more *pugnaciously* edifying than her husband. Very stout, blooming, handsomely dressed, fine lockets &c. – & the house spick & span with really expensive handsome furniture, beautiful plate & everything as dainty, as if they were settled in England for life instead of being wandering military folk at a colonial "station." She told us that they had asked the Lord to provide them with a servant, & that He had done so – & that she was a very good one – capital cook &c. &c.!!!! She is rather overflowing with such information & sly hits at roman catholics; but he is much less *obtrusive*. He has what I must think a *saving* sense of humor, which helps to guide his taste in the display of his convictions. Lt. Warren who came in late for tea from holding a meeting, observed how curious it felt to see in all the english papers "At the late execution at ＿＿＿＿＿＿＿ (I have forgotten where) Capt. (– forgotten whom!) preached the Gospel assisted by Lt. Warren, both rifles, & a pious costermonger." Mrs. Monk (who has *not* a strong sense of humor I think) fired up, & said "I suppose that was sarcasm from the Pall Mall. *Like it!*" Mr. W. (who evidently saw nothing but what was highly complimentary) said "Oh no, I believe it was copied from the Record. He *was* a costermonger." But Monk's melancholy eyes twinkled, & he fairly guffawed. There is to be a Bible & Prayer Meeting at their house at 3 P. M. to which we are invited, but I think shall not go. Of course we wld have no objection to join Mr. Monk's family worship, but Rex is well known, & his connection with the Cathedral &c., & the Bishop has such uphill work in this place – that we think it unadvisable to create a gossip by joining a rather anti-Church demonstration. From them we heard that Zebbi was to be there. I had no idea she was in that line. It is so jolly that the Parrys will bring our things: & further on, the Bishop will be coming out. What I most want is *Maggie's dress,* & *Mrs. Batty's patterns,* & those will come I suppose. Also the *crowquill steel pens.* Would you ask Dot if by any chance my *old (tweed)* cloak is not given away. It probably *is,* but if not I would like it, & one of the old hoods which were extant in nursery cupboards! There come very sudden showers here sometimes, & I mean presently to get myself a proper waterproof cloak with sleeves & hood – but I do not want to get anything I can help just yet. When we *are* rich, I shall certainly get a sewing machine again, & I almost think a *hand* one still. I dislike *foot work.* I had no one to teach me at Ecclesfield, & now I am surrounded with them. . . . I hope my gloves will come by Parry, & perhaps an artificial flower or two. Am I to have Maggie's apple blossom with the dress? I will gladly take it. I suppose she & Frank are enjoying their tour now. It will be very charming I should think.[6]

Our dearest love to all. Don't forget to drink our health on the 1st of June! –

> Ever & always dearest Mum
> Your loving daughter
> Judy

Zebbi has been & we go to tea there tonight at 7. I am enjoying myself *greatly.*

LETTER
42

[1 June 1868]
Fredericton, N.B.

My dearest Father.

. . . We go on as usual. Well & happy thank GOD. We had a little trip to S. John the other day. Rex had to go on business & took me with him. It is a steam down this lovely river of from 6 to 8 hours. The country is very beautiful, & as from the freshet the land is flooded, many bits were very weird & queer looking–Old barns standing in the water &c. But I remember I told the Mum of this. We went to tea with Zebbi Cox & her husband, & she had engaged a blower–& got leave to take Rex into one of the churches that she might hear him play the organ. I sent the *proof* from S. John & Rex said it was a great comfort to be able to post it at book post rates without a struggle. The postmaster here won't believe in it & always charges us as for letters which comes in expensive! Rex wrote to the Postmaster General, & got a letter saying it was to be as we thought & he sent it to the Head man here, but he takes no notice, & so we go on as before. I meant to have sent the *finale* of Reka Dom which is done, as is also a bit of the next story, but it is not copied out, & I think I shall hardly bother with it today.

It is our Wedding Day–& I was bent upon a John Gilpin outing somewhere, but we can't manage it. 1st Rex had to play at the Cathedral service, which was not till 11. today. He has a great deal of business on hand—& it is very rainy & mail day!! So after lunch I am going to help him to tune the organ for *his* pleasure, & then he is going to take me to the Nursery Gardens, & give me some plants for the garden for *mine*.

I have been very busy furnishing our spare room as a *working room*. To *draw*–sort specimens &c. in–for our drawing room being so tiny, one cannot do much in it, & keep it nice at the same time.

The spare room has a dark blue paper – & 2 windows – one looking over the "college grove" (a lovely wood in autumn!) & almost into the Coster's garden —the other looking into my flower garden. As we do not wish to go to the expense of *buying* furniture – we are *making* it! On Saturday, Rex being out, Hetty & I borrowed the tools of some carpenters who had gone to their dinners & we sawed & nailed & fitted, & we have rigged up a large table to draw at – & the wood work of a *divan*, for which we are now going to make matrass & cushions filled with straw, & covered with *turkey red*. The windows will have dark green curtains to keep out the sun when it is *too* hot, & we mean to adorn the walls with Arabic & Hebrew inscriptions. It will be a wonderful combination of colours!!!! But there are 2 dear sunny windows that will *keep* my poor plants this next winter I hope. It is really *much* more comfortable than our other house, & so much more easy to keep nice – & so much less expensive! – Hetty continues to do very well. Please do not have *Fredericton* put after my name in A.J.M. any more – at least not in the magazine itself. It looks comical I think – especially out here, where people don't think much of crossing the Atlantic. . . . I begin to look forward to the time when you & the dear Mum will have "settled" all the Birds of the Nest – & will keep your carriage & begin to enjoy the evening of life in comfort. Rex promised me this morning *a silver ring* in 24 years more!!! Our dear love & I am always

Your loving daughter
J.H. Ewing.

43

[From AE]

Fredericton. 1st June 1868

Dearest Mum

This day twelvemonths I told the assembled company that I could hold out no hope to any of the bachelors that, in "following my example", they would acquire "such a treasure" as I had; for that there was only one such, and I had got her. I think it 365 times more strongly to-day. *You* know her, (you suppose) pretty well – *very* well; but – as a daughter. It has been given to *me* to know her as a wife. I only wish I could be a little bit more worthy of her, and make her a more adequate husband. But she is so good that she is happy with me, and I try to be a good boy to her. We have had a happy year, and, in fact, every week seems to bring us some new source of happiness. What pleases us both most, just now – is that she has a garden, and I have an organ – and I am *going* to have the Choir handed over to my tender mercies altogether during the Bishop's absence in England.

We are just going now to have a good tuning at the organ; Jow will hold down the keys, while I hammer the pipes.

We wish you, with our Dearest Love, many happy returns of your Birthday, and we hope before many anniversaries of it come round that we may be present at one, though, of course, we *know* nothing as to this.

And *I* am ever yr afft soninlaw.

A. Ewing.

[JHE's Postscript]

My dear love, & many many many happy returns of your birthday dear dear Mum. The old Boy says *much much* too much about me. Who could help being pretty good to such a dear loving old soul? Indeed we do hope to see you before *very* long, but we have such a nice home here–& such abundance of blessings that one hardly dares to wish. We mean to order a pair of *tiny* snowshoes (what will go in a letter.) for a birthday present for you. ADieu J. H. E.

LETTER

44

Rex on the "Nashwaak Cis"—waiting for his wife!–
8. June 1868. *N.B. To the right—a Kingfisher on a branch.*

8 June. 1868. Fredericton.

My dearest Mother –

Does the above give you the faintest idea of what it is to paddle up & down these lovely rivers with their smaller tributaries & winding creeks – on a still, sunny afternoon? It really is the most fascinating amusement we have tried yet. Mr. Bliss took us out the other day – it being the 1st time either of us was in a canoe & Rex took one of the paddles, & got on so well [and was so charmed] with it – that we are going to set up our own canoe. Peter is building it – & I hope soon to send you a sketch of him 'paddling his own canoe.' – Of us – I may say – for I tried a paddle today – & mean to have a little one of my own to give *my* valuable assistance in helping the canoe along. Next month when Rex can get away – we think of going up the river to "Grand Falls" (the next thing to Niagara – they say.) by steamer, taking our canoe with us – & then paddling ourselves home with the stream. About 80 miles. Of course we should do it by bits – sleeping at stopping places. One art Rex has not yet acquired, & it *looks* awful! A sort of juggler's trick – that of *carrying* his canoe. Imagine taking hold of the side of a canoe that would hold six people, throwing it up, & overturning it neatly on your head – without injuring either your own skull or the canoe's bottom –

When accomplished the result is thus

. . . Your snow shoes are ordered with our canoe! And also a "pipe of peace" to add to Maggie's collection – I hope to send them by the Bishop in July.

I am longing for letters. Of course I was prepared to get none by the intermediate mail but now that the Halifax mail has had to put back to Liverpool – it seems a very long wait! – We shall probably get the ones viâ New York quite as soon if not sooner than those written by the mail before. This canoeing is really a source of great pleasure to us, & will more than double the enjoyment of summer to me. You see, having no carriage – nor unlimited means to hire *conveyances* – we get about *very* little – & in a lovely country which one may leave any day never to return – it seems a pity. Now with a canoe, Rex can "pull" me to a 100 places where a short walk from the shore will give me sketching, botanizing – & all I want! – Moreover the summer heat at times oppresses my head – & then to get on the water gives a cool breeze – & *freshens one up* in a way that made me think of what it must be to people in India to get to "the hills." I have never wished for some of you more than on this lovely river – gliding about close to the water (you sit on the very bottom of the canoe.) – all the trees just bursting into green, & the water reflecting everything exquisitely – kingfishers – & all kinds of birds flitting about & singing unfamiliar songs. Boblinks going "twit twit" – little yellow birds – king birds – crows & the robin:thrushes everywhere – I landed today at one place – & went into a wood to try & get flowers. I only got one good one – but it was very lovely! Two crows were making wild cries for the loss of one of their young ones which some boys had taken – & as I went on I heard the queer chirrup (like a bird's note.) of Ajidomo the Squirrel! & he ran across my path, & into a hollow tree. It is a much smaller squirrel than ours – about the size of a water rat – & beautifully striped. The  flower was a little pinkish bell on a pretty stalk & leaves of an orchidaceous appearance.

We have joined an archery club – Not that *I* shall become a toxopholite – I have irons enough in the fire! But it will be sociable & pleasant – & Rex will do the archery for me. I certainly *do* wish I were a better hand at drawing. One does see lovely bits!! –

The only drawback to the paddling is that the beloved Hector cannot go with us. He would endanger the safety of the canoe — One has to sit very still! —

My garden gets on very jollily. At a sale on Saturday I bought some plants rather cheap. One silver geranium I gave less than $^S1/-$ for, & I have got a dozen cuttings from it already besides the mother plant. It was a great straggling thing & I got it to cut up. The season is still very backward — & we have a great deal of rain — & some really cold days. Before the sun comes out — we breakfast with a fire — & I put on my warmest winter jacket to go out in. When the sun once shines it is so powerful — that one can hardly walk about with comfort. But I have enjoyed the Spring thoroughly — I much prefer it to plunging into boiling heat at once. Mrs. Medley has been very ill, but is nearly all right again. The Bishop has gone to Halifax. We are greatly looking forward to hear of Maggie & Frank & how the wedding went off. We had a bottle of champagne in honor of our own wedding day — I hope you remembered us. Today is the day we sailed from Liverpool! I do thank GOD for all the happiness I have had in this "strange land." It is bedtime dearest Mum — Ever your loving daughter J.H. Ewing.

LETTER

45

16. June. 1868.

My dearest Mum.

We sent off the first part of "Kerguelen's Land" yesterday to Mr. Monk at S. John that he might post it per "book post" which *works* there. Today we hear that he is coming off to Fredericton, & so will probably miss his letters — & *so* you may not get the MSS. — unless his junior officer has orders to open his letters. We are very sorry, but we could not foresee this.

Rex is so much pleased with the story that I am quite in spirits about it, & hope you may think as favorably. He thinks if you read this end bit before you get the rest you will never like it, & yet I am very anxious to take the *chance* of the 1st part's having gone, as I want a proof,—so if you do not get the 1st part please put this by till you do, & don't read it.

Would it be possible for Wolff to illustrate it?[1] — If he knows the breeding islands of the Albatross he would make a lovely thing of it. This is the last *story*. There will only be a *conclusion* now. I have got my "information" from Rex, & "Homes without Hands."[2]——The only point I am in doubt about is whether the parent birds would have remained on the island as *long*— I mean for *months*. Do you know any naturalist who would tell you this? When they are not breeding they seem to have no home, as they follow ships for weeks.

How we miss Harvey & his fidus Achates—poor old Fisher! — I so often want things "looked up" — & we do lack books here! —

I am wild with mosquito bites today–& it is so hot that we & Hector lie about panting & rather irritable with darkened rooms!!!

We have got a jolly canoe. Rex was out in it at 6.A.M. this morning–& I did a good stroke of gardening before breakfast.

I do hope you are better dear Mum—

Your most loving daughter

J. H. E.

LETTER

46

S. Peter. June. 29. 1868

My dearest Mum—

I was very sorry to write such a scrap by the last mail!— Not that there was any news if I had had time for a longer letter. We have a small item now in the fact that Mr. Strickland (Com:Chief at Halifax & C.B.)[1] has [come]—inspected—& gone—& that all has gone off very satisfactorily. Two [weeks] ago he "relieved" that Mr. Routh you may remember about at Halifax—& the Commissariat gossip ever since has run upon his strictness &c. He is rather a tiger in the Department—but it only seems to be that he is merciless if anybody's duty is neglected or improperly done. A few weeks ago we heard that he had put one of the officers at Halifax (an older man than Rex & of higher rank—the one who met *us* at Halifax) in arrest—!! & was sweeping away like a dozen new brooms—not to say birch rods. As it happens Rex had never seen or served him. He says that ever since he heard Strickland was coming he has made the lives of his subs. a burden to them by holding up S. as a Bogy—painting pictures of himself in arrest, & all the contractors—storekeepers—sergeants &c. &c. swept out with the besom of destruction. Matters being in apple pie order at last—R. relaxed a little, & poor old Hudson (one of his men) finding him in a milder frame, related how he had saved all his spare money to educate his son—who is now a rising lawyer in the States. It is really interesting for he is quite a common man. Well, on Friday morning I made my Boy "parade" before me to see that his hair was brushed & his white uniform clean, & he went off to meet the Chief, whilst Hetty & I devoted our minds to the consideration of tea. Mr. S. went over everything, & then made Rex a little speech to the effect that everything was all square—that he had not known him before—but now on any emergency he *should* know what he had to expect, &c. which was very gratifying. Quite "unbeknownst"—Mrs. Strickland turned up with him, & they spent the evening with us. She is a curious party, *fade*, & fine ladyish, though good natured. She is well known in the "Department"—I believe!! We got on splendidly.

Old Strickland was awfully civil to me – has begged some of my sketches, & my receipt for scalloped lobster!!! & asked if I would go & stay with them at Halifax. *That* I hope will fall through, as I couldn't leave Rex, & indeed he says he wouldn't let me go. Tea was very successful. He ate some of nearly *everything* I think, & vowed that he meant to have lobsters cooked in this way for himself – on which she replied that she knew nothing about cooking – & didn't see the fun of paying a cook & cooking yrself – & they were very amusing on the subject. Mrs. Brooke – the scotch *meeneester's* wife – had sent me some asparagus – & I had got our 1st cucumber & we had beefsteaks & salad – & fresh & scalloped lobsters, cakes &c. & the Chief took tea – & iced sherry – & beef & lobster – & asparagus – & cucumber – & cakes – & salad – & talked *incessantly* through it all!!! After tea he & Rex went to look for Hector who had strayed away, & Mrs. S. & I went round the garden & chatted – When the men returned Mr. S. & Rex sat on the door step – & we sat on chairs outside – & Mr. S. smoked – & quaffed cold whiskey & water – & told me he was a Roman Catholic – & gave me a full sketch of his career. His whole mind is full of the Scheme, & I never heard so much *shop* talked before. He is really sure to be a Comptroller – having enormous influence in the Dep. & being very distinguished – for service in New Zealand &c. But he is anxious about it – for his wife hates Halifax & they feel unsettled. We walked to the inn with them when they left – & I had his arm & his confidence the whole way! Then he took her in & walked back with us – & still "Department! Department!" till my head reeled with Department. But his *abandon* of frankness is very taking & was complimentary – for he said "Lor! I haven't talked so much about this to anyone but you for I don't know when. I don't like the officers I have at Halifax, I can't talk to them &c. &c." He is at any rate without any "official reserve." Of course *I* scrupulously kept to *his* interest in the Scheme, but he said once, " A great many junior officers look very hopelessly on it, & think they will be knocked here & there, & forced to take things they don't like, & so on. But *I* have great hopes of it, & I believe men in your husband's position will find themselves better off than they think. And I don't speak without book either. I have reason for what I say." He repeated something of the kind to Rex, who said *he* had always taken a hopeful view of the Scheme, & they both agreed that those who held the other view knew nothing about it! Indeed he really seems to think exactly as Rex always has talked about it. He is a great ally of Sir W. Power – you understand. He gave me the whole history of why & wherefore he had arrested the officer above alluded to. Bad meat (carrion he called it!!) was being issued to the troops, he kicked up no end of a dust, & the officer wouldn't obey him. Hinc Illae &c. Imagine *me* on the arm of a huge stout man puffing his cigar & strolling up the street behind Rex, & Mrs. S. doing the elegant in front of us. "The moral" of the anecdote with him was "Good gracious! If such iniquities are to be winked at in the Department how can the Com. be respected. How can *I* be respected as a Commissariat officer? How can *you* be respected as the lady of a Commissariat officer? I was rather startled to find the bad rations brought so forcibly home to *me!!!* You will believe that (whereas – whatever I have been doing & thinking during the day I almost invariably dream of Ecclesfield –) for once I dreamed solely of Department! I thought we were ordered to Halifax – & that Dot told me on the Governor's authority that living was exactly 4 times as dear as in Fredericton. I was hearing from Rex's Sergeant Dwyer a full account of Strickland's opinions as to the efficiency of the station when Rex woke me – ! It was nearly six, & a lovely morning, & he was almost dressed, going to inspect the rations, which he does from time to time – I got him something to eat & then went out myself, & sketched till 8 – Then we had breakfast, & then went to the boat to see the Stricklands off, & got back for Church. They were as jolly as ever, & she has offered her own & her maid's services to shop for me &c. &c. To our great satisfaction he has promised not to move us from here at present. (There was a rumour we were to be sent to Halifax) He was charmed with Fredericton, & is coming back to see us in the Autumn when the leaves are in full glory. I don't think I told you that about a week since we had Mr. & Mrs. Monk in the same way for tea &c. They were *particularly* pleasant, & she was not at all "improving" this time. They were very genial, & praised our little drawing room so – They are very much interested in the botany of the place, & they were in such raptures with your seaweed book, that I think they will *collect* for me when they have the chance. Everybody admires that book wonderfully. Someday you must give me a zoophyte one please. I do prize all your dear handiwork![2] We have got the illumination framed in an Oxford frame[3] to stand on the table. The Stricklands admired it much. I borrowed a June A.J.M. and think it an *excellent* no.... I wish it had been convenient to get in more of Reka Dom. I thought 13½ were to go in.[4] I wonder whether the whole of Mrs. O. can be got in by December?– I think I ought to get a Xmas book out, if *possible*. I cannot help having a hope that "Mrs. O." may take. I really *do* think that worse writing & duller stories make their way! Mrs. Medley rushed at me when the June no. came out–about Mrs. O. She had read the other parts long ago–& had never realized that I wrote it. It appears she is a tremendous admirer of it, which astonished me, as she never had said a word about *my* scribblings. (Though a great admirer of *you*) She has borrowed it all for the Bishop to read. I am so glad you & the dear Govr like R.D. & hope you will like "Kerguelen's Land." N.B. I shall put a *note* on the subject of the said island, & its being a great breeding place for the Albatross. Do the girls like R.D.?– Thank you *very* much for the Elia. The Parrys have not arrived yet. How we shall ever part with Hector I know not!–

The weather is very lovely, & we are very happy. I spent the rest of my day on Saturday after Church in the yard & garden. I am firmly resolved against any untidy *back premises* & I made our old irish (dis:):Orderly quite irate by insisting on the yard being weeded. "*If* you wish Mum–I'll do it–but it's no manner of use &c. &c."—— As it was he overlooked so many little corners, that in the evening Hetty & I set to work, & weeded, & raked, & moved logs, & swept up rubbish till nearly dark. The result is pleasant to the eyes! Moreover I dug up a sunny corner of the yard, & laid down wooden borders, & have made Hetty a flower bed under the kitchen windows. She is fond of it, & I hope it will interest her in helping me to keep the place decent. Then I took my old man "round the grounds" for an evening stroll, & he was as pleased as Punch with his Judy–though–bless his nose!–he would be pleased if I put the furniture in the kitchen garden, & laid the drawing room down in potatoes – I believe!!!! He likes to see me paddle about my gardens, though he is not *much* more use himself in that – department – than our old boys at home. I often think our *hands* are a curious fact. His so rough & strong looking you would think him a born carpenter, & very ill adapted to the execution of fine arts. Mine *look* very like harp playing or anything elegant – & not useful. Whereas on most fine evenings his fingers are bringing the tenderest tones & most exquisite renderings of Mendelssohn out of the harmonium, & mine are, I flatter myself, not inefficiently carpentering, digging, knocking in nails & taking up twitch grass, whereas they lumber about on the notes like so many logs in a strong current!!! The Bishop's hands are less practical than R.'s & not so skilful in the other line. It is said that he never tried to hammer in a nail but *once*, & then it was a *screw*!!!! I may as well boast of all my performances at once — it is the next thing to showing them to you – (though oh! *what* a difference!!) Rexie struck out the idea of making our spare room into an *eastern* looking sitting room for *use*, it being pretty & sunny &c. It has a dark blue paper – & we could not afford more furniture – so we have made a *divan*. Hetty & I borrowed a carpenter's tools (without leave – he being at dinner!!!) & made it one morning. The plan is

simple. 2 old Commiss: Store Candleboxes with boards nailed on to them. It is in a corner of the room against the wall. Rex got us some straw, & I got some sacking & Hetty made the mattrass (a *huge* bag) which we filled & covered all with turkey red. Cushions for the back

ditto. That is all. The effect is good. Above it on the dark blue wall is a black & white text in arabic characters – It is the common turkish welcome – *Kosh gueldin safa gueldin.* "You have come in peace – Depart in peace." I enlarged it from a turkish book of R.'s. I am now going to do another in compliment to you dear people – to the effect that though mountain does not meet mountain, people who are parted meet again. It is a turkish proverb. Another of my efforts was to nail cedar bark over a box & make a flower stand for the drawing room – rustic – you understand! How we wish *Dina* could come out & pay us a visit!

She would not mind a sailing vessel, which is indeed in some respects more comfortable though not so fast as steam. If somebody wld only give her £10 for her voyage – I wish *we* could! She shld have the turkish room. I have become very much attached to my little nest & garden – It is *very* cosy, & really cool – & in winter will be a Paradise of warmth after the other place. We have been in Fredericton a year today. Our 1st service here was on S. Peter's Day [29 June] 1867. We do thank GOD for the happy time we have had since! – My old man's dear love & mine to all friends. The Vergiss mein nicht from my garden. Hector has kissed it. It is not a wild flower here. Your ever loving daughter

AJHE

All from my garden.

47

July. 7. 1868.

My dearest Dot.

It is so *hot* . . . that one's hands stick to the paper – & one's wits are on the wane – so excuse stupidity. Your letters are always very jolly. . . . Regie's letter was splendid as usual. We roared over it – & the poem excellent. He knows *I* always appreciate his efforts – I shall acknowledge it by an indian pipe of peace as soon as I can afford it, but we are rather short of tin just now, or I would *so* like to send you all souvenirs by the Bishop. But tell Regie to make up his mind whether he will have – a *beaver*, or an *indian* – or a *tortoise* on the front of the bowl of the pipe – so that I may give Peter his orders when the funds admit. I am sending Maggie one with a beaver. We hope she will look favorably on our small offering. I think the pipes are really curious. It is all hand work of course. I am sending 4 Tennysons. I think you want at least that, & it *may* not be possible to send them much oftener. They keep making new regulations. The price of these is raised. They are $^{s}4/2^{d}$ each – & that was a favor because I took 4. Put it to *our account*. At last the Parrys are here – & so are all our things – for which unnumbered thanks. Tell Mother we are so *much* obliged for *Elia* though I would have liked her writing in it. The dress fits me capitally. Ask Maggie what I am to pay for it please. I am *so* glad of it – & only wish she had added the flowers – However I shall probably find *natural* ones to wear with it – or black lace & pink ribbons. . . . I had wanted the foxglove seed from the Mum's corner, but am very glad of it any way, & doubly so of the chicory. My garden is really beginning to look well, & my bushes of cinnamon roses (well watered with house slops) have been *masses* & *wreaths* of bloom – I have got a slight sketch of them. N.B. Let me advise the following recipe. Make Addy put a few forkfuls of manure into an old tub or can & fill up with water. The result is a decoction which you can keep in the stable, & if you put a little of it to a watering can of water & do your flowers that are ready to bloom–asters &c. it does them worlds of good! Roses too it helps awfully. I keep a tub in my barn, & water my garden constantly with it. I sent the Bishop my first dish of *spinach* yesterday & was rather proud. I have peas almost ready–beans in flower–ditto cucumbers–we have had radishes for long. The Mum will envy me when she hears of *tomatoes* planted out in rows.

You can imagine our feelings– Hector is gone!– I cried off & on the whole day he went, & though we don't say much about it now, I don't think we are either of us a bit reconciled to the loss. I never did know a dog like him, or love one so much! He was so good & so awfully knowing. I really wish I could forget him! Rex was as bad as myself on the subject. We see him sometimes, but that is almost worse than nothing!–

This paper is *vile*. And we can't get straw paper here unfortunately. Nothing but thick note paper or this wretched trash. . . . I think I shall send Maggie's indian things &c. to MacKenzie at Liverpool & ask him to forward them: for I shall also send some *plants* in a tin box–in hopes of their surviving. Plant *every scrap* carefully as I shall send nothing but what is worth taking care of. I want to get some *Trilliums*[1] to  you. "Three times Three" as they are called–flowers of this kind–& some fern roots. I will try hard & persuade the Bishop to go to you–& you shall hear next mail. He sails July. 17–I think–so you may calculate when he will be in England. . . .

We have had some very hot days here–but they don't last long together, & the weather is exquisite on the whole. *I* get wild over *my* sketching!! I advise you to try *sepia*, & *sepia* & *blue*—for a time before taking to complete water colors. It is a great thing not to be hampered with choosing colors & the effects are very charming. Ruskin advises it, & Turner stuck to browns for *years*.

Our dear love to all – We are very jolly. Oh! how I wish for you on moonlight nights in the canoe. The other evening we went out before sunset & stayed late – The sunset was wonderful & whilst the crimson was still deluging the sky & river, the moon looked through it like a ghost. We went up the Nashwaak Cis (Little Nashwaak – a tributary of S. John.) & *lay to* close to a large green bullfrog who looked at us, but never moved. A bittern was groaning in the ferns by the bank (masses of Onoclea.) & songbirds were singing everywhere. We came out into the S. John as the moon rose – & finally 2 other canoes joined us & we flew up & down through the water & then lay to & listened to the 22d band through the Mess room windows.

Doesn't it seem funny to you to fancy *me* paddling on a great beautiful river like this? – Rex & I go alone now (I bows – he stern –) & enjoy ourselves amazingly. I am eaten alive with mosquitos – blackflies – & midges – but one may be thankful there are no scorpions — or *sarpints!* —

... N.B. I wrote to Day & Son for very clean copies of the Jan. Feb. & March. 1867. no.s of Nature & Art. Mrs. Medley had lent them to me, & there was a drop of water on the cover of one – & the others looked a little tumbled I thought – & they are *very* particular – So I am anxious to replace them, as I hate obligations of that kind – & I want to get them before she asks for hers back. He has never sent them. Is the firm dissolved? Could you find out? Ask them if Mrs. Ewing has ordered &c. & if they have been sent, & if not wld you try & get them if they are to be got?[2] I should be very grateful. I fear my commissions are a great bore but we are so helpless here. Ever your loving sister   J. H. E.

LETTER

48

July. 18. 1868.

My dearest Mum –

We got your letters on Friday – which was altogether a very pleasant day to us. 1st it was cooler, & I felt quite brisk, after having been rather overdone with heat. 2dly dear old *Hector* spent most of the day with us, & had Welsh rabbit for dinner! – To crown all, it was a very pleasant mail. . . . By this time the Bishop must have come & gone – with you. I hope you have liked him – He is a good soul, & has done a power of work out here. I do so hope the *roots* will survive the journey, dear Mum. I know you will like them. I am afraid you will be disappointed at the size of the snowshoes, but some day I hope to collect you a nice lot of things for your museum – a canoe about a foot long included! I *do* mean to send you by one of the 22d (if I can get him to take it) one of the curious hornets' nests of the country. *Bed time*! Goodnight darling Mum.

July. 20. We had an awfully jolly day yesterday. It was a lovely day, & directly after dinner Rex got a carriage from the livery stables, & took me a lovely drive. First we went to a country house near where Col. Maunsell & his wife[1] are now living– (Very nice people–in the choir too.) We had some tea there, & sketched–& went into the wood–& then Rexie took me a long drive in another direction, & we kept staying to sketch little bits in my notebook–& got an orchis, & enjoyed ourselves greatly. We did not get back till dark. Pray don't worry your dear self about the heat. If I never have a hotter climate to bear in my peregrinations I shall be very well satisfied. It knocks me up a *little* at times–but nothing to speak of–a little headache or giddiness–or prostrated feeling for a day–most people feel it now & then. But *it never lasts long together*, & there is the great comfort. Today–for example–is probably cooler than with you–grey–breezy, & refreshing. The street thermometers register 100 & goodness knows what–but we don't think that really on the hottest day it has gone beyond 96° or 97° in the shade–& July and August are the hottest months. I assure you I *thoroughly enjoy* the climate as a whole–winter–summer–spring & autumn! Rex is very busy–being "Precenter" in the Bishop's absence!! Having the care of the choir–I mean. He wrote a new hymn tune yesterday, which is to be sung on Sunday we hope. In compliment to the day–it is called S. Margaret. He has also written an awfully good (I think!) single chant. The illustration to this epistle represents us on our way to "French Village"[2]– Alas! We did not reach it. We got up soon after 4 & being all ready by six –were on the point of starting, when a tremendous thunderstorm broke, which delayed us till midday. Then we started, but the Costers and Streets having taken a boat instead of canoes, they could not get on fast enough against the current, & through the shallows & rapids–so we stopped 1/2 way & had our dinner on the river's bank. At one place where a strong current was coming over a very shallow place, we had great fun– The fierce struggles against the rapids– *We* got over at last, but Mr. Coster broke one of his oars, & get on the boat could not– So the 2 Street men jumped out into the water, & dragged her over the bar amid shouts of laughter. About Mrs. Overtheway, I should much prefer to print

178

it *alone*. I think the A.J.M. size wld do, & I should like a red glazy cloth binding (like the Elia you sent me–) & some of Pasquier's illustrations, & I mean also to have the hymn tune Rex wrote to the hymn in the beginning of Mrs. O. put in.[3] But I will write to Bell soon about it. I think it ought to come out at Xmas–& in good time. Don't you? Is Bell willing to undertake it?– I will send you the conclusion at once. I have not felt much inspired the last few hot days. It was certainly a pity that 2 such *bites* had to be made of Reka Dom in these 2 no.s.[4]...

My dear love to Father–& tell him the canoes are *much* safer than outriggers–& accidents *very* rare–& we–very careful!–

Our dear dear love
Your everloving daughter
J.H. Ewing.

...

LETTER
49

Hector on a visit to his late Master at Miss's. 17 July, 1868.
N.B. He is allowed to lie on that which is forbidden. Object of his desires — his Aunt Madge's Sofa Blanket—
— as a welsh rabbit is preparing in the Kitchen!—
His little Miss is taking his portrait' — of which he is
perfectly conscious.

July. 27. 1868

My dearest Mater.

The above is a picter of that old darling whom I have not seen since the day he spent with us – though I hear he has had his blessed old tail pinched in a door, & is now I believe out at "the Camp" on musketry practice!!¹ It is such a lovely day! – The extreme heat seems over – for the present at any rate – & we are revelling in some of that exquisite – bright – clear weather which is really characteristic of this climate. I am sitting out in my garden, for it seemed a sin to stay indoors on such a day! . . . I suppose today or tomorrow, all being well, our little Bishop will be with you. I am sure you will like him, though you will probably have a "round" on ecclesiastical matters!! But – if his theology may be judged of from his sermons – he is both sound & moderate, & staunch to the Church of England; though I don't know (I really don't) whether Father will find him quite so strong on the advantages of state protection & authority. I fancy the experience of Colonial Churches is less favorable in this direction than that of the Home Church. I mean to send you a copy of his charge – It really is first rate.² Rex was delighted with it, & so was I.

As to Dr. Marnerais' letter. I send my answer in which Rex agrees with me, & which I think you & dear Pater will think wise. I think too that Bell ought to see it. But what I want you to tell me is – Can an author *prevent* his things being translated? It is no good my making stiff terms, if his asking my leave at all is a mere matter of courtesy. However consider this please, dear Mum. I wish to oblige him – & *don't* want to be grasping. But if he or the publisher are making money by my writings, of course it is but fair I shld have a share. I shld almost think Bell might make some arrangement with Dr. M. & the publisher, so as to authorize him to translate both your things & mine at a fair rate.³ But do as you think best as to this. My letter contains my "sentiments," as well as I can express them, not knowing really what the law is, & whether I have any right to ask what I do.

Our vegetable garden is giving us great comfort just now. We

have lots of peas, beans, &c. &c. & to spare for our friends who have
no gardens: & I really rejoice in the thought of how warm & cosy
we shall be in this little house in the winter! – Our latest news is
the appointment of Judge Wilmot to the Governorship.[4] It is not a
popular appointment with either the "gentility," the Church people, or the R.C.s., but he is a clever man & may do well. He is a
plebeian, & an ex:Church of England man who joined the Wes-
leyans from an "affront" & is the backbone of that interest. A Tee-
totaller also. He is a great gardener – & is even personally like
Quaker Smith – & reminds me of him.

We have really no news otherwise. We are going to an evening
party at the Fishers on Wednesday – a ball I fancy – where Maggie's
dress will be most useful! Did I tell you how I have been reading
your parables to the blind wife of the Scotch minister here? A capital scotchwoman of the strong sensible thoughtful type.[5] She liked
them awfully. Always with dear love

Dearest Mum your loving
daughter JHE.

How are you?

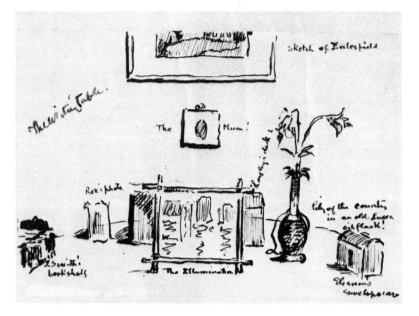

[4 August 1868]

My dearest old Mum

... You are certainly the best of good Mums in the way you take my being so far from home. It is so really good & helps me as well as yourself–for if you fretted & fidgetted I could hardly help worrying too. You do so exactly the right thing in just not fidgeting as to the *when* we shall come home, since in our position no amount of speculating can help one. We may be ordered home any day, or we may not for a year or two longer–or *a dozen things*!! Meanwhile we are really in clover for a foreign station, & putting the hypothesis that we were coming home next week to some employment in England with no more "foreign service" for the rest of our lives–(I sometimes think) we might perhaps a little regret not having seen more of the world at Government expense whilst we were young! But you have been so good about it from the time I went away, when you were the bravest of all! Considering now how the Scheme has been postponed in this unexpected way (& even now really nothing seems to get much hearing but the irish church question!)[1] – we cannot but be so thankful that we did not wait for it – for we have enough which is as good as a feast & as much love as if it were only a dinner of herbs!! As to our future, I really sit very easy. If we had children, one might feel more anxious perhaps, but as it is I really think very little about it. We has what we wants, & we pays our way in the present; & as to what tomorrow will bring forth——the *worst* & *least likely* thing would be for Rex's name to be amongst a certain no. of Com:Officers who will probably be "retired" from the service on 1/2 pay to make way for certain civilians & others to be introduced – (this is a very feminine incorrect way of putting it, but it gives you the main idea as it affects *us*.) Supposing this thunderbolt to have fallen—The sale of our furniture here would pay my home passage & then we are landed with a small life income to start with, & if Rex could not find occupation to bring that up to a comfortable income I think we should have reason to be very much astonished, considering what his abilities are & how he has comported himself since he was thrown on his own resources at 25. Moreover we are both of us able to do something for the exchequer independently of professional income. Well, when you consider that this is the worst we have to fear, & that all reasonable probabilities are in favor of promotion & increased income – we have reason to be very thankful and contented, as we are. I thought you would be pleased to hear how well Rexie and the Bugaboo chief got on – though I was afraid my letter was very long winded! We heard afterwards that Strickland had said at S. John what capital order this station was in. I have done him some sketches, & am going to send them.

 We have had some very cool weather, a good deal of it; & now there seems likely to be a hot phase again. But we have heavy refreshing showers – no lack of water, & no sunstrokes, so we are more fortunate than in some places.

 ... We have got a new occupation just now & one admirably adapted to the hot weather. We are reading french novels together.

183

We have no dictionary alas! & are occasionally stumped by a provincial or technical word–but we call it Nazackth & let it pass–& the process is one of the very few I have known that really *does* combine amusement with instruction, for I am getting up my colloquial french thereby, & we talk of taking to parlez-vousing at meals &c. as I want to learn to speak properly. The only drawback is the difficulty of finding a luxurious & easy position for *both* in which we can read from the same book. The sofa is small for two, & if Rex lies on the floor he cannot find a comfy corner for his head in which he can read without squinting!– Don't be scandalized to hear we are reading Balzac. A good deal of his narration certainly lies in fashionable Parisian society, & is not altogether edifying–but I do not think he makes the border line between right & wrong as hazy as the Miss Braddon school,[2] though he calls a spade a spade. But the charm of him is the brilliant bits of *photography of life!*– We scream with laughing at times–he is so brilliant!– In "Eugenie Grandet" there is *such* an old miserly overreaching wine merchant–a wonderful character!

–My dear Mum–about Dina–It makes me wild to *think* of having her out though I hardly like to say anything about it, now you have only her & Dot at home. But if you *do* think of it, she ought to come out *soon* to see the autumn tints–(also before the equinoctial gales). Everybody says the sailing ships are *more* comfortable than the steamers, and if she is not sick she won't mind the voyage being rather longer. The New Lampedo is a capital ship & capital Capt. they say. It comes direct to S. John where we would meet her–and Mackenzie Smith would make enquiries no doubt both as to ship–Capt.–& when it was coming out. It costs about £10. Of course it would be charming for us to show her the canoeing, the country & all the winter fun–&c. &c. & I am sure *she* would enjoy it. I don't think you need be *much* afraid of her being snapped up–*partis* are not much commoner here than elsewhere, though we have plenty of pretty girls. I think Mrs. Parker will lend me bedroom furniture *if* she comes & I don't think she will mind a small house. I wished I had had her in the canoe yesterday–it was so lovely!– It is Aug. 4. today–& yesterday Rex ordered a bottle of champagne–which as it was one of the hottest & dampest days we

April. 3. 1869

My dearest Mum.

As you perceive "the floods are out" & it is
not supposed that the river can much longer
stand this continued thaw & rain. An ice freshet
is anticipated. I dare not wish it, as it is
uncharitable towards our friend Mr Baker,
(of Nashwaak fort, & the priest's ring – memory)
– whose property gets much damaged on these
occasions: but if it does come – I think the
"John Gilpin" aspiration is permissible –
"may I be there to see!" I fear we hardly shall
see it – being so far from the river. In other
respects our position is a desirable one – when
blocks of ice & masses of escaped water
coming dashing along regardless of expense
Not that much damage is done in Fredericton
I fancy. Isolated farms & barns at points
near the river – sometimes get carried away
or blocked up in a "jam", but it does not
deluge the town much I think. These backstairs

I

2

3

Plate 2. Reka Dom

Plate 3. Queen Street,
Fredericton, ca. 1875

Plate 4. "The Cathedral
from near Beechmount
Fred. Oct. 17. 1867.
St. Luke's little summer!"

Plate 5. "Autumn Tints
near the 'College Grove.'
Fred. Oct. 9. 1867 "

4

5

7

8

Plate 9. The Bishop and Mrs. Medley

Plate 10. Bishopscote

Plate 6. Reka Dom
Drawing Room

Plate 7. "Our Street"

Plate 8. The Basketsellers

Plate 11. The Fisher
Family; Judge Charles
Fisher, Mrs. Fisher,
Frances Fisher and Jane
Fisher

12

Plate 12. Canoe Scene

Plate 13. Portage Crossing

13

Plate 14. Amateur Theatricals

14

15

Plates 15 & 16. Major and Mrs. Ewing and
Hector

16

have had was as beneficial as agreeable! –

I was a good deal puzzled to get your letter by the Halifax mail with viâ New York on it – Are you sure you have got hold of the right days? – The proof has come & I will send it next week if not today. Pray tell us about Dina – It certainly would be a great opportunity for her to see these parts! – Our dear love to all

Your everloving daughter
Judy.

LETTER
51

Aug. 15. 1868.

My dearest old Dot.

... I do wonder so what will be decided about Dina! I have not much hope – but if she may not come this autumn I hope they will let her come out with Capt. Cronk in the spring if we are here. I must say I think it is rather an "opportunity" for some of you to see furrin parts !! How I wld like to see *your* dear old face my darling! But an Atlantic Voyage wld only be to you as it is to me – dire penance I fear. It wld do Dina good I think. However, as I said, I shan't fidget, and *she* needn't – for we are pretty sure to have her *somewhere* to come & see us in our foreign homes. On thy dear face & the others I hope to look when we come home! – I quite *understand* what you say about Matrimony. But I had no end of fears & *dégoûts* & fancies about it while I was "single" – which used to put Rex into a rage *then*, as he never could understand them. They have wonderfully melted away before the facts of a happy marriage – as you will find some day. Of course nothing is perfect – & perhaps the reason of many little disappointments is that one is apt to expect much more from a husband than from any other relation whom Providence has given for one's daily companion. I don't think you would find household affairs much of a bother – unless one was *very* poor with a large family! – What as a *female* one feels most is

185

that (probably) *no man* does quite "understand" all one's little feelings – many little things that a mother or sister *would* — but again I think it is a wholesome tonic not to have one's small *sentiments* too much indulged – when there is real Deep tender love at the bottom – & when it comes from really not comprehending – not from unkindly overlooking – one's *pheelings*. Another thing one does find. Every day *solidifies* one's happiness. I certainly think my honeymoon was the least happy moon of my married life! – I think Maggie is probably not very well, & the awful wear & tear that brides with relations & connexions are subjected too is proverbial. I escaped it!!! Married life is much more like any other homelife than *novels* lead one to suppose! With the indescribable pleasure that circumstances occasionally bring to the front – that the "man" of your household life – is yours especially – that you are his 1st first thought – that you have him to turn to, & a right to the strong arm above anyone else &c. &c. My dear old man & I have had our little troubles like everybody else – (& N.B. he gets a little jealous when I get very sentimental over home letters &c. &c. *I* am *his Everything* – & he prefers almost any country to Gt. Britain – which makes it difficult to him to *understand* that as poor old Eastwood[1] once said "A stone off the Ecclesfield roads &c. &c.!!!!" ———) — but he is *so* good – & so awfully fond of me – & we have lots of occupations, & lots of love – the 2 great things – & so we are the happiest of Darbys & Joans. And this is such a charming station, it would be real *sin* to worry about England – when we shall probably be home again too before so very long –

Now my deary as to what I *want* for the winter. I want nothing. I have heaps of warm things – & 2 swan's down cotton high petticoat waists bran new. My new linsey is perfectly good – I have not done yet with Maggie's & my old black linseys! I mean to take the best parts of the skirts & make a walking dress for outdoor & morning wear. Then I have my brown rep very good yet – & my black silk. I have lots. Now the Mum talks of giving me a present – I gathered in the winter clothes line – But what I want to say is this. I know she can't afford to send me things as she wld like, & I really don't need them; but if now & then she wld like to help me – when anybody is coming out the thing that would be most good to me &

least expense to you–would be occasionally to send me some of *your* & *Dina's* things–(especially Evening do.) that you may happen to be rather tired of at home–or if by chance in any old black silk of the Mum's (or evening silk &c.) there should be good breadths enough to be useful to me– I would gladly pay something for them that wld help towards new things for you all & they would be of course "as good as new" out here. In the present fashion of skirts I take so little you know, that the good breadths from you tall people's dresses would do a good deal for me. Now par exemple–are you tired of that pink silk & net dress of yours? There is a great deal in it–& I think *I* could make a dinner dress of it. If I got a plain or spotted black net dress–I could wear it with my black silk for one "toilette"–& over a pink silk skirt & waist for another. But if Dina does not come, I don't quite know whether the Bishop is coming straight back here. I wish you would ask him if he *can* bring me anything, & if it wld not be best to send me a little box done up separately–merely to be part of his luggage– Now supposing he *can*. *If* you happen to *be* tired of the pink in question (which has seen a good deal of service!) send it to me–& get for me on my account–enough plain black or spotted (better spotted I think.) tulle or net–for a skirt & for me to make a garibaldi of–a fair amount–so that I could make a big sash of black net & pink silk together–& perhaps a *berthe* to the waist. I shall then wear the black net–either above my pink silk as a dinner dress—or above my black as ditto with colored flowers–or with a black net garibaldi above black silk for demi toilette. If you happened to see Mrs. Batty & she had any dodge for making up the skirt prettily have it done to my account– If not send it plain. You must know I am now supposed to be able to wear pink–& my dear old man thinks I can–& does *not* like me in green!– I had had some *thoughts* of a plain net skirt over the black silk not quite meeting in front but fastened with bands & bows of white satin ribbon–& a little white on the waist to correspond–

but the simpler the better. They have some fashion now of *puffed* sort of skirts looped up in odd ways. If Mrs. Batty could make me a black net or tulle (whichever is most economical – *wear* as well as *price* considered) in any way of this kind – to go simply over black or color – I could do the waists here. I say all this just to show that little accommodations of this kind with things of yours, such as we should be sure to accomplish if I were at home, would be a great help now & then – but I have abundance of warm & comfortable clothing – only I take a little more pains now for my dear old boy's sake, with the *smart* things. It is very good of you to *give* me Maggie's dress. It will be so useful – & *just* prevents my having to get one. I must not linger long, for my old man will be waiting for me with the canoe. He sends his best love, & was awfully glad to hear all the good news of last mail. He is so busy – bless him! – teaching the choir – & the school children practising – Govt Accounts – & paddling his wifey about the river. We "play" like a couple of children sometimes by the river on these lovely afternoons. He cares for nothing unless I am there.

I meant to have written to the dear Mum but do not know if I shall have time. What I wanted to say was in reference to the climate. Rex said long ago he wld be sure to frighten you as the dear old man is very strong on the subject. But you have no idea how charming the winter is – all said & done. The figures on the thermometer are very alarming – but you never have beheld or felt – what it is to walk over a glittering plain—of pure, dry, exquisite snow – under a sun as hot & a sky as pure, deep, & unclouded a blue as if you were in Italy. There *are* bitter days when the wind takes your breath, & freezes your nose & fingers – but ladies can simply stay indoors – where the heat would make you stare!!! The Bishop has knocked about in these winters for 27 or 29 years – going long day's journeys of 50 miles in sleighs or ricketty stages – & yet with all the hard work of a Colonial Bishop's life – you see him as active & lively as a man of between 60 & 70 can well be. As to the overshoe story – I think he has confounded me with Bessy Roberts who has a knack of forgetting her goloshes & leaving them in Church, especially when she has got a "throat" – to his great disgust. I never wear winter overshoes – always moccasons. The warmest & most comfortable of footgear! – & Rex would turn Fredericton upside down with indignation if *I* ran any risks from forgotten overshoes &c.!!! As to the fatigue of walking on snowshoes – *I* don't think it fatiguing – It is charming – Moreover you *needn't* walk on them! It is an amusement, like skating – & is quite optional. I much prefer them to skates – & think it the greatest fun possible. It is a swinging – rather dignified gait – & you get over a wonderful lot of ground with little trouble. It is a little troublesome to remember all one's wraps when one goes out in winter – but what is it? – 3 minutes more time to spend in dressing & undressing perhaps! – I *wish* the Mum *could* realize what the climate really is. *For life* – it *is* trying to delicate women. Years of extreme changes seem to affect the feminine constitution as a rule, in the *long run.* But people live here to great ages – & the mortality among regiments stationed here is *exceptionally low.* And it is so magnificently dry & bracing – & there are so few days & nights when you can't be out in the year, that I cannot fancy its being otherwise than a boon to *anybody* for a time. Just now it is splendidly fine. *Such* a sun! – such a sky! – such breezes – & cool nights – it is lovely. With melons, & squash, & tomatoes ripening in your garden. . . . Finally, tell the Mum above all not to fidget about our £.S.D. matters. We are perfectly comfortable. Of course it was a little expensive starting – & the remains of some old matters at home not quite cleared off that came on poor old Rex – we have been anxious to clear off whilst in this cheap living place. I just allude to this to show you that when we have no extras – but only to *live on* our income – we should be *perfectly comfortable* if the Scheme hangs fire till Michaelmas 10 years. I made up my mind (knowing that we had furniture to buy &c. &c. &c. &c.) that we would live at the rate of £250 a year as set forth in Domestic Economy. We have full £300. Whilst Sarah was with me – I did not always manage it. *Now* we live if anything on *less.* Moreover on that scale £31 is allowed for "rent & taxes". We pay only £25. Our *living, washing,* & *wages* only cost between £2 & £3 a week —& we have meat 3 times a day —a small bill of *good wine* (paid monthly) from the "Mess" (22d) – beer in barrel as at home – & everything we want. I have my dripping "clarified" to help out with cakes & pastry – & we get 2 lbs of delicious butter per week–which I *make do.* Just now the "feed" is beginning to be very good, as *birds* of all kinds are coming into season– We have vegetable marrows–tomatoes–& lots of all kinds of vegetables, besides supplying many of our neighbours. Tell the Mum we have *abundance* & live in the utmost comfort, & have champagne whenever there is an excuse for it! Rex ordered a bottle on my birthday–& if the Mum will get quite well–we will have 2. . . . Mrs. Parry & I have great fun over our domestic concerns. She thinks me a great hand I believe!!!!!! & has now got Domestic Economy–& started her accounts on my principle!!!!!!!!!!– Tell the Mum housekeeping is only *amusement* to me. Our income is *more than ample* here. It is a splendid place for that. We *could not* live in London on 1/2 as much again with *comfort* & the feeling of being like other people. Here we are rather wealthy & swell than otherwise. Rexie never complains of anything–& lets me do it all my own way–& says he & I live on less than he could manage to live on alone!!!! ——

I must stop darling–

Your everloving old
Judy———

. . .

LETTER

52

The Nonconformist Skyrockets !!

Aug. 23. 1868.

My dearest old Mum.

I do not feel as if I had half answered my splendid budget of letters in the one I wrote to the dear old D.O. The various bits of good news have come back to me over & over again with pleasure. Mrs. Medley shared in my enjoyment of the account of the Bishop's visit – for (by some odd mischance) *his* letter has not reached her, & she eagerly listened to all my news. What news it was! I think you may tell *me* all the good old man said of my Rex – It won't feed *my* vanity —but I *do* hear his praises liberally sung here, & it was very good of you to tell me so much. And though no one can know better – or so well – as I, that I *am* fortunate in so good a husband, it is certainly very gratifying that "Fredericton" shld congratulate you on your son-in-law – for the Medleys are rather severe critics, if anything. Rex *is* a good good boy, & I think we get happier every day; & he seems to get fonder & fonder of his "Wifum", & we are altogether so blest, & so comfortable; & when to this is added good news, & never failing remembrance & love from Home—I am afraid of not being thankful enough. Dot was saying in one of her letters that one felt almost "afraid" in thinking of the calamities that overwhelm some families—ours being so blest. *We* sometimes say these things to each other, & come to the conclusion that GOD sometimes disciplines by happiness as well as by trouble, & that we ought only to doubly try to be good!— Besides though *I* have lived in sunshine all my life—my poor old boy has had plenty of trouble; & you can guess & know what happiness it is to me, to see him looking so much younger, brighter, & happier than he used to look, that it is outwardly & visibly evident that matrimony suits him. And while I am saying all this, dear Mum, I want to impress upon you what I said something of to Dot, that you are not for one instant to dream that we are at all pinched in money matters—or comforts of any kind. Our love in a cottage is of a very substantial sort.... I get along very well with my housekeeping—& keep accurate accounts. We never keep more than a few shillings in the house, as Rex keeps our money at the office, which is satisfactory in reference to fire—& thieves!— He pays all the bills, & housekeeping books from his office, which I feel doubly satisfactory, as there are some New York housebreakers afloat. I keep all the bills paid & unpaid, & take the latter to him for payment, & he always "lines my purse" whenever he finds it empty, as he never likes me to be without cash. With this I pay my "Weekly Bills"—which include the various things we buy at the door & pay on the spot for; & get anything I want. We do a good deal of door traffic in this part of the world. Butter—eggs—& often meat in large quantities &c. &c. The farmer people bring round farm produce—and our only fishmongers & poulterers are itinerant. We get capital fish, lobsters, &c. from an amusing irishman—a very honest soul. The best feeding part of the year is just coming on—at least in *my* eyes—for now we begin to have birds of all kinds—plentiful & cheap. They are *very* good, & the meat here is never *first* class. We freeze the birds up for winter consumption too. I got a capital pair of ducks for about ^S3/- the other day, & am looking forward to my Michael-mas goose!! Then come the partridges which are delicious here. Wild fowl &c. & abundant turkies. I hope you will take *my* word for what this place – climate &c. is – deary Mum. I only know if you were here *at any part of the Year*, you would draw comparisons most unfavorable to dear old Ecclesfield! We have been out canoeing this afternoon – & oh! how lovely it has been. I always have my sketchbag notebook &c. with me – & often a book as well – (Carlyle's French Revolution just now) & so we float along – & sometimes stop to catch a bit of color & effect – when I wash out my paintbrushes over the side of the canoe – there is a remarkably luxurious feeling – a sort of dignity too – in having the whole river to wash out yr brushes in! – My old man takes with him a certain little music book which I have made for him – in which *he* does exercises in harmony whilst I sketch. Hebrew is in abeyance just now – he eats, drinks, sleeps, talks, & *thinks* music! . . . Rex is now studying harmony *hard*, & he is teaching *me*! I shall never do any-thing with it, but I feel it gives me a so much more reasonable *com-prehension* of music that I hear, that I know in some degree what the want of proper knowledge must be to anyone who has a com-posing power in him. I hope *Rex's* present work may eventually lead to his doing something good in the composition line. . . . *Sunday. 23. Aug.* We have just come back from Evening Services, & have had tea, & strolled round "our grounds" in the moonlight – in the kitchen garden where the "Squash" whose strong shoots & tendrils, & splendidly formal handsome leaves seem resolutely determined to outgrow everything, are creeping on like a tide! – They always suggest Andersen to me. *White snails* could live so splendidly under the leaves — & really *they* do look as if they would eventually overgrow the world![1] – It is sometimes very jolly in the moonlight in the kitchen garden – we sometimes wander about & "pretend" to be lovers, & that there is a terrible duenna in the person of a harmless old lady next door who may hear & betray us!!! Sometimes we do a little astronomy — I wish you could have seen me in my dressing gown, standing on a kitchen chair late one night, when Rex had called me downstairs again – balancing his big telescope on the top of a fence, & being *very* stupid at catching sight of Saturn's ring!!!

On another occasion when our present Governor had a great Wesleyan entertainment in his grounds (present–"*Our Mr. Poonshon*"–really!) we sat together on top of our *pump* & enjoyed the nonconformist fireworks gratis!!!!² Of course the fire balloon went up when we were *not* looking!– We have been rather gay lately. You knew we went to see Tom Thumb & party. I do consider it a most curious & interesting sight. Tom himself *is* slightly disproportioned, & seems dull, but all the others seem intelligent above the average. Tom Thumb looks really tall & large by the side of the others. His wife is smaller, with fine eyes–a large forehead, & a *remarkably* pleasing expression & manner. Commodore Nutt (smaller still) is in complete proportion, & fair & good looking, beats the drum *splendidly* (no one appreciated it–but Rex clapped him) & acts comic characters awfully well–& apparently much to his own enjoyment. Minnie Warren–the tiniest–is just like one of those wax dolls with big foreheads–& has a pensive melancholy air that is awfully touching. When the man who "showed them off"–dilated on their being intelligent &c. & not stupid as dwarfs are supposed to be, & made a progidy of her, & got children onto the stage to measure her height (one of *4 years old* was about her height)–it made one *creep* for her–& feel such a big brute!! She looked so grave, took hold of the ones next to her with her little hands, put the rest in their places, & then stood still & sad whilst the man showed her off—& then she kissed the children very prettily before they went back into the audience. She is 23 I think, & I remember hearing before that she feels so terribly being so small, & won't marry little Nutt. Now they say she is going to marry him. He is awfully funny, & acted an irishman capitally. It is a strange sight certainly!³–

We had a very pleasant picnic the other day–went up the river in canoes &c. & tomorrow we are to have another. The Parrys are going with us in our canoe. Yesterday the Governor gave a lunch and croquet party, & very jolly it was. Rex had to leave in the middle of it to hold his "Church practice"–but he came back for me, & we had great fun altogether. The grounds are charming. My dear old man is playing some of Haydn's Seasons in the most distracting way–& whistling the melody. Miss Bailey (the very old lady opposite) says she "doesn't think Mr. Ewing *can* eat any meals, for when he is not out he is playing"!!!! Have I told you of her & Mrs. Emmerson – 2 old sisters, 93 – the oldest – some of the 1st settlers – loyalists. The Bishop used to go there every Sunday afternoon, & as he came away he was generally drawn by sounds of music to *our* side of the street also! – I accuse Rex of flirting with Miss B. through his dressing room window!! I have hardly answered any of your letter, but I must stop – & tomorrow we have our hands full. Saint's Day Service – Mail – Picnic – &c. &c. &c.!!! Goodnight you dear one – and – all! (dogs included!!) *How* we delighted in those verses! & pictured the golden dog & the benevolent Bishop. You can now fancy *him* patiently suffering *Hector's* advances during the Hebrew Lessons!! That blessed dog is now a sort of common property between us & the Parrys – We ask for him now & then & he comes to see us, & is fully as fond of us as of them I think. I went in this afternoon after school & found Capt. Parry had just washed him with Naldine's soap!!!

. . .

Your ever loving dau.

J. H. E.

LETTER

53

Aug. 29. 1868.

My dearest Mum.

To my horror (& it is Saturday!) I find both paper & ink pretty well exhausted. However I have "tilted" the ink pot, & found a scrap! Your jolly letters came in this P. M. How thankful I am that my letters *have* somewhat counteracted the Bishop's vivid descriptions of the climate! In this glorious autumn weather it does indeed seem a "need not" for you to be distressing yourself as you sit in the fogs of dear old Yorkshire – about us in our bright, clear atmosphere. I can *understand* the Bishop's feelings. I would not like to

195

live here for nearly 30 years as he has (though the involuntary testimony of his vigour is pretty strong!) but an undercurrent of
homesickness I suspect influences the testimony of anyone so far
from Old England – He gets weary of the place & people at times, &
amid mental cravings & bodily fatigue of long diocesan journeys,
no wonder he wearies of a climate *in the extremes of which* you have
to fight with Nature; combined with a population on the whole so
far below an english diocese in general education & cultivation.
And then he is not a young man – & was "riz" in the 'warm mois-
ture' of Devonshire. Meanwhile, for a short sojourn – with no
necessity for 50 miles' journey in sleighs & suchlike fatiguing expeditions – we are simply unspeakably fortunate in the climate. I hope
I told you that snowshoeing is an *amusement*, like *skating*, & that
there is no more necessity for me to snowshoe on this river, than
there ever was for me to skate on the dam!! I thoroughly enjoy it.
People make parties to snowshoe & awful fun it is – Why *we picnic*
in the winters here which is more than you do at home! Picnic in
the woods & hot spiced claret supersedes champagne cup!! – And
sometimes girls meet & make *snowhouses* inside which you are as
warm as an Esquimaux. I talked of having one last winter to sketch
from, & this one perhaps I shall! – But the proof of the pudding
&c. – We 'have our health' thank GOD – & as long as we have that, it
doesn't much matter whether we are quartered at Nova Zembla or
the Torrid Zone! – How good you all are in sending me things!!
But I fear you have been bothering yourselves about it. I am so
much pleased! I am sure I shall like whatever Frank has sent me,
though I am not told what it is. It is very good of him to think of
sending me anything! And I am awfully obliged to dear Maggie for
the bonnet. I am almost sorry *her* views did not prevail about the
color, as my winter dress is violet & my present bonnet blue. But
blue is always pretty & becoming to *us*, & I quite look forward to my
'english bonnet' (this = *quite* as much as "my new bonnet from Paris"
at home!!) And what shall I say to you for sending me the swan's
down!!! Do you know I have often thought of that swan's down,
but I fancied it was destroyed years back. I am very glad you sent
it unmade – I shall make something awfully jolly of it *I* know –
probably trim some velvet affair for winter evening musical parties.

Oh how snug I shall be! & what a swell!! Only I feel ashamed to take it. It should have been made up for you!! But you are all sending me just the things I want. I was wishing the other day I had some little *fichu* or thing to wear with white muslin–or with black silk skirt & plain white garibaldi–to *vary* my demi:toilettes. You *can't* buy these things readymade here–& one hesitates about buying yards of silk or velvet & trying to *devise* one! Whereupon Dina sends me what I am sure I shall be able to use either with or without alteration. Thank her 1000 times if she is with you. *If!!!* How I wonder whether she is even now on her way to me! I don't at all think you *will* send her, joyful as I shld be to see her. But I feel it is not fair to ask you to spare her–though perhaps if the Scheme leaves us here–next summer you may!– I had no idea the Bishop wld return so soon. I hope you will not *bother about* my last com-missions. *There is nothing of any importance.* I can get an umbrella here. I am in no present need of boots. Any chance six months hence will be time enough for that. So pray don't bother the B. or worry yourselves with any late parcels to catch him. He is very 'par-ticular'! & not fond of commissions. But you will judge & decide all this yourselves with him. Only the umbrella &c. &c. are *not neces-saries.* He offered once of his own self to get me a waterproof cloak if I would commission him, therefore I think perhaps he *would* bring *that* himself if he knew what it was. We have not been well up to his movements–Mrs. Medley's letter having miscarried. Thank dear old D.O. *much* for the pincushion which will be very wel-come. You are all very good. I am *so* glad some more beeveed[1] books are coming. I show my *one* to everybody! All my visitors admire it!–and you are considered a wonderful Mum–as you are. Mrs. Parry looked at your photo. the other day, & said how hand-some you must have been—which as it is that photo. you hated so (the colored copy that Blessed Brownie gave me) is gratifying, for I don't think it's a flattering likeness! I am very busy helping the Parrys to "settle" in their new house–though we don't do much more than measure carpets–gossip over past, present, & future *sales*–& drink afternoon tea!!! They are very jolly. He is par-ticularly nice, so awfully good tempered, & pleasant. We hope the 22d won't leave before us, but I fear they won't stay much longer.

(However if your best friend *will* die, it is some consolation to be remembered in his will; & if the 22d *does* go, they will all 'sell up', & we shall probably get one or two things we want in the house line cheap!!) I should be sorry they hurried away for that though!! for we want very little. We are *very* comfortable now. We seem so thoroughly *settled*–the worry & expense of furnishing over & paid for–the house & belongings so well within limits– Hetty & I get on so well together & she is tidy & careful, & our housekeeping costing less instead of more than it did. I dwell on this dear Mum, that you may fully realize us as we are–looking forward to the winter in a cosy, well built little house, with goood stoves, double windows &c. &c. *Such* a different state of things to last winter, & this one will probably be less cold. I have been very busy preserving vegetables fruit &c. to vary our winter fare. Fancy me going out into my own garden & picking 7 or 8 cucumbers at a time to preserve in salt!! I am *drying up* bilberries on shelves to make pies of in winter, & Hetty knows how to dry up our delicious vegetable marrows for the same purpose. I have been preserving melons too. So if Dina *does* come she won't complain of our winter feed!– We have a good frostproof cellar, & shall store our potatoes, carrots &c.–Our little garden has really borne abundantly. We have bought no potatoes & have had–marrows, cucumbers, beans, peas, french beans, haricots blancs, carrots, turnips, spinach, salads, parsnips, cabbages &c. &c. &c. *in abundance*. I hope to give the Parrys plenty, as they have no garden now. It is bedtime so I must stop. Hector is on a visit to us & on the sofa at this moment. He sends his deepest gowly powl to Trotus the beloved!– I send the end of Mrs. Overtheway. You must have long since got my letter about my book. I hope you approve my ideas? I have begun a short story for you—*Boneless* by name!![2] A sort of companion to the Brownies. Thank Dot *very* much for paying Cockayne. I am *awfully* sorry he has had to wait, as it is *agin* my principles–but it seemed foolish to spend money in these expensive P.O. orders to send cash home, when there soon wld be some at home. It is best to use my money, & Rex refunds to me when I want. Goodnight to you all, dear people!

198

Monday. 31. Such a lovely day! As Mrs. Medley said to me this morning as we came out of Church, "It is a *splendid* climate! We have so few dull days. So many clear bright ones!" Did I tell you of our latest picnic? No. It was the jolliest we have had I think. We took the Parrys in our canoe. I had a little funked it, it was so hot, & I sometimes get a headache from the sun, & when we paddle against stream & wind I can't use an umbrella – & we had a good many miles to go about midday. But we found an old "puggeree" (or white turban) of Rex's of Constantinople days,[3] & fastened it on my hat – & it answered *perfectly*. We had a charming day. I did a little sketching, & we came home by moonlight – 14 canoes lashed together. We were in the middle so Rex & Capt. P. were idle except that Rex 'conducted' the singing with a paddle! – We had a good

many comic songs though none equal to Ecclesfield efforts! – & some part singing. The most interesting to me was a song sung by Gabriel the Indian[4] – a curious wild, monotonous, plaintive affair, but wonderfully in keeping with the motion of the canoes & the plash of the water in the moonlight. Mrs. Graham has just called with an invitation to another picnic on Wednesday – to be followed by a dance – which will be good fun I expect. There is *some* scheme news, but you probably know it. Matters really *are* going forward now, & the new regime is to be tried *at once* in Ireland & one other place – & to be gradually extended to foreign stations. We ought to hear something to our advantage soon! Dina asked me to say what she should work for me to send by the Bishop. I think she is sending me more than enough – but if she *does* do me anything I should like a pair of *cuffs* for winter made exactly like the charming white & purple ones Dot made me – only of *plain violet*. I am so sorry I did not know sooner that the Bishop's luggage was coming

by the Lampedo–as I wld have sent my commissions earlier. (2
interruptions!–one of Hector fighting with a little sandy dog who
visits us often–another which wld look strange to you. A squaw
puts her head in at the window–"Sister!"–so I go out to her, & she
says "Sister, my baby very ill. Give me 2 or 3 cents" which I do–&
also read the order on a chemist which Mrs. Campbell has given
her, & teach her to say the man's name.) You will understand that if
you trace that, it will bother the Bishop. You need not send
anything by him, but use your own discretion. If he comes to you
you will easily know. Perhaps if he *does* come to you–he would *not*
mind a new umbrella for me being fastened up with his own– But
you will see– I *can* get one here, you know, quite well. Rex's birthday is *Jan.* 3. I feel that *none* of my commissions can have reached
you in time, which I am very sorry for, but as I only knew that the
Bishop was coming back in October or thereabouts, I did not think
of writing directly after his departure. However *your* dear things
will come, & I can really get things here. Don't suppose we are perfectly hopeless!! only some things *are* better & cheaper in England.
I do wish I had known of his Lampedo parcel (but if Mrs. M. knew,
she did not tell me)–for it seems so unbusinesslike–& must have
bothered you, & he is in a great fidget already I fancy, because some
other people haven't sent their commissions. If he comes to you &
is willing to bring me a parcel, well & good–if not never mind.
I *can* get–

 Curtains

 Umbrella–& even waterproof cloak here–& there is going to
be a sale in Oct of a very well furnished house near here, where I
probably could get curtains. Above all dearest Mum–never distress
yourself with fancying that we are really *short of* or *in want of* anything. We are most comfortable in every way. I know it must have
been nice to see a daughter in her own house, & it is *such* a pleasure
to me to think of dear Maggie in so comfortable & nice a home of
her own. I hope before very long please GOD *we* shall see it, & that
you will see me "in my own house." If we do not move next Spring,
I really must have Dina out that you may see me by proxy. I wish
she could have seen our winter, but I have left it entirely to you.

200

Last night we had Choral Service. Rex played—& *splendidly*. It was a thorough success. He really *is* improving the choir, & they respond to his efforts. I forgot all about what you said in re. Kerguelen's Land— I mean your criticism. I enclose a paragraph which you might insert I think somewhere where the mother bird first takes an interest in watching the men on the island. Do as you think well— I think it *would* be better. I hope the book will be nice. And that you will agree with my choice of *size* &c. You told me so little, I didn't know *for certain* whether Bell was willing or no. Nor whether it would lessen expense to keep the A.J.M. size. I think it is a nice size. I think I must stop. Our dear love to all. Ever dearest Mum Your most loving Judy.

Did I ever thank you for the seeds? I am so much obliged.

I am going to set up a fresh water aquarium.

LETTER

54

Sep. 7. 1868—

My dearest Mum.

... About my book, dear Mum, *I* never counted. I took the Govr's report for granted, though I was rather astonished at the quantity. I think the plan you mention very good, except—what do you think? the *price* seems to me a good deal. I cannot help fancying it wld do better selling at ^{S}3/6. Ask Bell to consider. The designs *are* paid for as Maga. illustrations—those linen backs are not an expensive kind—the amount of matter is small—& look at the children's books that Routledge publishes. But I will leave this with you & him, only tell him just what struck me. He perhaps knows best—but I think that with not quite such a good paper &c. it wld sell better at a smaller price than ^{S}5/- However I am quite willing to leave this to him, only I want him to know that it strikes us both as a good deal as children's books go.[1] I hope he has gone on with it – I am so very anxious it shld hit the Xmas Market. We had a nice dance last night (Monday) & are having rather a gay week. Tomorrow Mrs. Medley takes me out into the country to see a new window in a church that has been put up. On Thursday another ball. On Saturday we go to Heron Lake.[2] We had a most amusing interview yesterday with Buckmaster & Co.[3] i.e. the head of that eminent tailor's firm, who is making a tour of Canada to get orders. He is Rex's tailor, & very thankful we were that he arrived, for R. was in sore need of some things, & I grudged his getting them of the wretched tailors here. The old fellow was such a regular *specimen* of the army tailor — He said at once to R. "We met last in the Crimea Sir, I think," & made all the professional observations on the alteration in him, & on their both being "a trifle wider round the *chest* than you was, Sir!!!!" — It was awful fun to hear him discussing one officer after another – "You remember the Rouths Sir?" (great Commt family) "They always did justice to their clothes – fine figure Sir W. Routh – but they all dressed well. Those trousers you have on Sir – made *here* Sir? (a *very* old pair that I have patched & mended – & N.B. – R. had just come in from organ playing – with I think no braces – & a good deal of Hector's hair on his coat.) – I met Mr. Batsford just now Sir. We made for him years ago, Sir. He *had* on clothes, Sir – (measuring rapidly) they looked – (continuing to measure) as if they had been made by a blacksmith Sir."!!! I went to the hotel with Rex to see the patterns & choose a suit of *dittos* for him – & R. had *my* measure taken for a jacket – in case I shld want one on some future occasion – as tailors make jackets so much better than dressmakers. . . . I have a good many household matters to see to this morning so I must stop dear Mum. Our dear love to the Govr & Dot & All – Ever your loving

Judy

. . .

LETTER

55

14 Sepr 1868.

My dearest old Mum.

. . . You will be amused to hear *how* your letters arrived. The mail was very late – It was put off & off – & at last announced for Saty afternoon – Then a "report" said it wld not be delivered till Monday. I *insisted* on working it out to the fountain-head, & finally learnt that the mail wld be up at Saty *night* – & if we liked to go at 11.p.m. we could get them; if not we must wait till Monday. I went to bed at my usual time, being a little done up that night. I soon slept off my slight headache – & then I lived in a kind of 1/2 awake dream – whilst Rex in uniform was going in and out after the mail. In the middle of the night he threw your letters on to my bed – & began to cut open the proof parcel with quite the Governor's air – you know! – I read your letters & part of the Maga. & dozed off again – & then he just *tried* some music we had sent for – & so we went on in a dreamy way through the night. I think I never enjoyed the mail more – In the morning when I thought all was over – the sergeant arrived with a letter from Dina – an awfully jolly one — So altogether I was rich in last mail!! . . . I *quite* understand about Dina dear Mum. I know the Winchester trip &c. *must* have been expensive[1] – Perhaps some future time it may be managed. I hope you don't think I meant in any way to dispute your judgement dear Mum – only in case it could *otherwise* be managed hereafter, I wanted just to clear away any ideas that might arise from our being as a family so little accustomed to moving about. I *do* wish (merely in reference to myself) that you could realize the climate as it is! – We are having splendid weather just now. We had a charming paddle yesterday – & landed on an island to sketch & get river sand for my aquarium – A 100 yards or so away 3 herons sat on a strip of sand – & wild ducks swam almost within reach of us. But I must try a sketch some time. *How* I wish I could wield a pencil as you do. I do

203

get so aggravated with myself!— Dear Mrs. Coster has come back from a trip at the seaside & brought one or 2 weeds – but they are *nought* I fear. If we are here another summer – I think we shall try & get a peep of the sea. I am going for a day or 2 to stay with a country parson & his wife at a "Mission" in the hilly country here. He is a very good little man – & she[2] a little pattern – of dutch descent – the image of M.M. only *as* quiet as M.M. is excitable – but with all M.M.'s energy. They have very little – & he serves 3 parishes (one 25 miles from his house). They have papered their own rooms (she can do *anything* useful) & the house is a little gem. He is a S. Augustine's man – name – *Dowling*! – The little church in the forest – is beautiful – so simple but so nice.... No Scheme news this mail. By a new arrangement which forbids our getting our wine from the "Mess" we get £10 "compensation" — which will *more* than "compensate" *us* – which is so far satisfactory. We are very jolly. I am put into the choir now!!!! Boy says I must come out – in a very *marital* tone – so goodbye dear Mum – Our dear love Your loving dau:

J. H. E.

LETTER
56

18. Sepr. 1868.

My dearest Dot

I think you will appreciate the "situation" recorded above![1] – I was in Rex's office this morning & as we came out into the Square we found the Bear at breakfast as you see. I made a sketch of the queer pair of friends in R.'s notebook, & only wished I had been a Landseer. It was a very pretty group, under the old willow tree. It is very funny, the bear used to hate dogs – they bullied him – But he has "taken up" one or two black Newfoundland pups who live on the happiest terms with him. As they are about his own colour we conclude he takes them for bear's cubs or at any rate for distant relations. (I suspect the Mum will want *this* sketch! If she does I will do her another, if you want this for yr scrapbook) Our gaieties are not *quite* over. We had another dance at the Graham's last night – a very jolly one. We walked there & back. Mr. Ewing, the Parrys & I have never got off to Heron Lake yet – the last day we settled for – it was too cold. It *was* cold! & last night a frost has burnt my Squash (my poor grand luxuriant squash in all its pride – a squash rampant!) – my cucumbers – & my tomatoes – Rex & I dragged in the fuschias last night after we came from the ball, so they are saved. Today has been an exquisite day. One of our real autumn days. With a sky of solid turquoise blue – the Cathedral standing against it – like pictures of Milan Cathedral against the typical italian sky (in which Ruskin does *not* believe!) I have been busy getting in the cucumbers – squash – tomatoes &c. to keep for winter. It is grievous, really, how soon things are cut off. The cucumber & squash vines in *flower* still – & bearing abundantly – but hey presto! – gardening is over for another 8 or 9 months! We shall have plenty of splendid weather yet – but no *security* from nightfrosts. The maples are beginning to burn. It is curious to see a whole pale green tree with *one* single spray which has just 'turned' — the most vivid crimson in the sunshine that you can picture. We were out in the Grove today, & saw one like this. The "Grove" is a lovely wooded place with some flat land, like part of an english park. *This* is a great attraction – but it is a jolly place, & we are rather frequenting it just now. I am going to *try* & study the trees in it this autumn. Rex lies under one of them & reads meanwhile. It is really – exquisitely, peacefully, lovely today, a sort of day when being out in a certain kind of country stroll, makes one feel rather a "good child." Don't you know? This bit has a very english – homelook too. Except for the flaming bits that look like the angel's sword waving above the trees of Eden, & for the black cicalas hopping & whirring in the grass, & the tiny Adjidomo running along the fence. You know that these squirrels are only about the

size of *rats* & have a handsomely *shaded tail?* . . . Please tell the Mum that I corrected & sent off the proofs by the Quebec Mail, & 2 days after they had stamped & passed it, the post people here sent it back to Rex's office saying they hadn't sent it after all, as they had no instructions about the Book Post. R. kicked up an awful row, & I hope we have got the regulations understood at last, but let Bell just be told to send nothing with any writing on it. (this had "an uncorrected copy. please take care of this &c.") It is very fortunate it was not the Halifax Mail– As it is, it won't make a difference of more than a day or two I think. I wrote to Bell, & the *letter* went. . . .

Saturday [19 September]. Today has been even lovelier than yesterday–so bright & beautiful. Warmer, too– I wonder whether you will have a very cold winter after your hot summer.

The enclosed woodcuts are for the Mum, if she likes them–for you if she doesn't. The sled on which the man is driving is just what they use here for loads of wood &c. It is a working sled you know–not properly a driving sleigh. The stumps of the felled trees too are very characteristic. Oxen too are used for ploughing & "hauling" in the country here–

. . . We have no special news. We are very happy & jolly. Rex's best love (He is at the "'armony" as usual!) & very dear love as well to all–

Always darling your loving old
Ham.

Fancy me in the choir as an alto. Some altos have left & they are 'short' in that line. How I wish I had a little more musical genius! However I hope I may get to sing mezzo soprano in time– I *have* a few *low* notes. Though I can't get *up* a bit, as you know!– Rex's own particular practice which he holds once a week, (besides conducting the usual weekly practice) for the choir, is a splendid affair. He does teach music so well. The people are awfully pleased with it– There are 36 "parts" to copy every week!!!!! I hear you are getting on awfully well with the choir— I fancy myself coming through the little door into *the* choir with Rex!!– Ah!——One will thank GOD that day! Meanwhile we are *so* happy, & I hope you can realize our home to some extent–as we can remember Ecclesfield. I am busy right now with many little household preparations for winter. . . . I am going to have all our winter clothes got ready–light summer things put away–when our annual pest of flies has quite disappeared to have all the rooms cleaned – wash the pictures &c. &c. (you don't know what the common housefly can be!!!) —have the fernbox removed, & the winter stoves put up – take in my winter flowers & make shelves ready for them —choose the happy moment when our clever gardener is neither "on guard" nor "in the guard room" (for drinking) to have both gardens well dug up & dressed for next year. Hang up the cabbages & store the potatoes, squash, turnips, carrots, cucumbers &c. &c. &c. in the cellar. You can imagine the comfort it is to me to have a house in which these matters are "within compass" – & where I haven't to make Arctic Explorations into the store closet. ... Goodbye darling. The country women are just beginning to come to early market in *furs*! Tell Dina Rex wld be very grateful for the baccy pouch, only he doesn't smoke now! – However if it is done we will find a use for it! – The Lampedo has arrived, though we haven't got our things yet. She made a splendid passage this time.

ADieu. J. H. E.

. . .

LETTER

57

[The following fragment belongs to a lost letter, perhaps the one written to Maggie and referred to in Letter 58, ca. 2 October 1868.]

To begin!!!
The sketch at the top of this is from a place in the Province where I was the other day. I went to stay with the Dowlings (a S. Augustine parson who has a "mission" here about 12 miles up the river –) Mrs. D. is of dutch descent, a capital little woman, very like M.M., with all her energy & more ballast – very *quiet* too, & self possessed. Fat, fair, splendid dark hair & grey eyes. *Tidiness* its very

self. Of course their income is *very* small. Something from the Church Society[1] here, & part of the weekly offertory at his 3 Churches. (Some of the offerings towards his support are given in *kind*. As he drives to the various parts of his mission, one will say "A bag of oats, for you, Parson."—or a sack of potatoes or something in the farm produce line) But they manage *very* well. They have no children, so it is all the easier to keep up their speckless, methodical neatness. They papered their own rooms themselves, & the little parsonage is awfully pretty. The Church near them is a lovely little building—wooden—but most correct with beautiful altar cloths & very nice & awfully clean & neat. Ed. Medley designed it. Another of Mr. D.'s churches is 25 miles from his house!! I mean to go there with him in the winter. I think I will tell the Mum about my visit to Prince William,[2] so you will read it— The parson there has another mission at Maguadavie[3] where his people are building a church with their own hands by gratuitous labor. It also is from one of Edward Medley's designs. They want some of the accessories very much—Communion Vessels especially. Mr. D. told me, saying he thought perhaps the Ecclesfield Mission Army[4] might think of devoting their collections to this if they had not any fixed object. You might tell the Mum please, but I fancy they have an adopted son somewhere in *barbarous parts* to which the money goes. I think of saving my tenths myself for the Maguadavie Affair; if when the Bishop returns he confirms Mr. D.'s account, which was most interesting. A Belgian set—in very good taste—of Paten, Chalice, & a glass vessel instead of flagon would only cost £5.5.0 & would be sufficient for the small Church. Mr. D. has a similar one at one of his Churches. The English sets are dearer. You know I still keep a 10th of all my earnings for such purposes, & as I shall get a good haul presently, I think I could soon save it up. We have been hampered at the outset with expenses not likely to recur: but when fully settled, Rex & I both purpose to take a definite sum off our income for charity. It is to my mind the only satisfactory way. I shall be very glad if we can manage this—& really it is the Churches & Ministers who want support here. There is *no pauperism* such as we have in England; & again there is as little real *wealth*, that there are few people who can give a 5 or 10 pounds with the ease that so many people can in Gt. Britain.

My dear old thing–how *well* I know what you say about the truth of the Mum's sayings of the soothing effects of Nature!! I used to feel it about gardening also so much. Visions of 3 yellow, 3 white, & 3 purple crocuses blooming in one pot *beguile* the mind from less happy fancies–perhaps too the *largeness* & *universality* of Nature disperse the selfishness of personal cares & worries. Then I think the smell of *earth* & *plants* has a physical anodyne about it somehow!– One cannot explain it.

LETTER

58

[ca. 2 October 1868]

My dearest Mum.

. . . I have partly told Maggie about my visit to the Dowlings. Mrs. D. drove me there (12 miles in a one 'oss shay.) As we crossed the ferry a lad was selling oranges on it (à la the gallery of a theatre) & 2 men in a large wagon behind us–told him to "give those girls one apiece" & he "would pay"!!! I wonder what you would have thought of one place we crossed–where a bridge *should* have been & where we went sideways down a very sharp incline & then rattled over a few logs!! But Mrs. D. drives like a New Brunswick girl–which means contempt of ruts, logs, holes, stones, & ups & downs of all kinds!! It was a lovely afternoon, & the country cer-tainly looked exquisite–such peeps of the river, with the mud islands–such bends–& folds of wooden points in their autumn coloring! I enjoyed it *very* much. The next day–breakfast at 8–& then Mr. D. heard that a neighboring parson had lost his child & wanted Mr. D. to bury it. A neighbor in this case meant a Mr. Hannington[1]–16 miles away at "Prince William"– It rained, but I wanted to see the country–so we ate a good breakfast–wrapped up to the nose–& took to the *one oss shay* once more. Mr. D. & I alone. When we got to a ferry by which we were to cross the river, we found that our horse had cast a shoe, & cut his foot – so we had to turn aside to the nearest blacksmith's. He had no shoe ready, so we had to wait – I took refuge in a small shop – & tried to sketch the cart & oxen of a gentleman who was purchasing, & prognosticating

bad weather inside. In due time he & his oxen lumbered off – & the horse was shod, & we proceeded also. The Hannington's was another mission parsonage – but Mrs. H. is a bluenose – not a dutchwoman – & it was not so good a specimen as the Dowling's for neatness. Then this bairn was their first – & it was dead. *I* did not see her – We had a funereal dinner – a turkey split-eagled & lots of squash – cooked & served by such a dark lady as you could not in most Huxleyan moments picture – She was like a *very* plain chimpanzee with 2 teeth like tusks of whitest ivory sticking over her lip. When I 1st saw her she was cleaning the knives & cooking in a broad straw hat. She afterwards brought the spread eagle & squash to table, & I tried to be philosophical – & ate as much as I could! – When she went in to look at the bairn in its coffin – there was no mistake though! – Man & monkey are far apart "for a' that & a' that." But she was a wonderful creature! – Funerals here are very solemn affairs – We had such processions to see the poor wee waxen corpse – such arrivals of feminine friends, such perfect self possession & "cap-

abilities" on their parts, such sympathetic solemnity & utter awkwardness among the male mourners who gradually thronged the passage, such unnatural repression mixed with conscious dignity in the boy mourners whose hats were carried off by a capable female to be banded with white tarlatan, & whose fingers were encased in white gloves which fitted the occasion but not them—(a country urchin gazing at the inch & a quarter of white glove beyond each finger tip was really a picture!) In the midst of it all the mother-in-law announced to the other ladies that Mrs. Hannington was so terribly grieved at having no photo. or memorial of any kind of the poor bairn—which gave *me* something to do, for I slipped into the room where the coffin was, & made a sketch of the poor little face in its coffin & with flowers at its feet— It was not unlike—though it looked *dead*, & I wrote under it—"but the Spirit unto GOD who gave it." & sent it to her. She was very much pleased I believe. Then they shut the coffin up, after an active lady had taken in all the boys in turn, who came out shuffling their feet, & sucking their fingers, & looking as if they had been saying their Catechisms! & so the little funeral set off in the rain, & as it wound up the hill we could hear the poor mother break out into moans & cries upstairs. As soon as it was over we packed up again—had some hot brandy & water & drove home— We had a longish wait at the ferry & it was dark long before we got back. The next day was lovely. I went out sketching, & the D.s came & sat in the wood with me, & I felt horribly lonely without my old man. I got very *bad* by evening—& was settling a very homesick & lovesick Pickwick to some sewing, when I caught sight of 2 figures in homespun at the gate. I leave you to imagine my feelings! They were Rex & Mr. Bliss who had paddled up the river, left the canoe at "indian village" & walked on—night gear under their arm. We had a jolly tea & evening chiefly spent in talking of old Wolff—about whom Mr. Dowling is most curious. . . . Next day it poured again—but Rex was obliged to be at home for choir practice, so off we set again—in the canoe this time—& Rex & Mr. B. paddled me home. We were none the worse & it was very good fun.

I am so very sorry to have missed the Quebec Mail this time. By the bye I shld have added that Rex & Mr. B. brought the English Mail with them. So I had all my delightful letters as well as Rex!—

212

The intermediate ones came with the others–you must have posted them too late. You must excuse my bad writing dear Mum, as I have an invalid 1st finger. It is inflamed from some reason–so I don't use it much.

I have not half said how delighted I am with the zoophyte book– It is really beautiful, & you don't know how we prize it! – By the bye–some other occasion of sending out–I know Mrs. Medley would prize a book of that kind awfully if you liked to make her one. She admires mine so much. Thank dear Dot so much for her letter. Tell her I would not *for worlds* have her send me the pink silk– I am only so glad she is using it. I only meant that sometimes being so much smaller–I might perhaps make some use of the best parts of things she & Dina had *done with*. But I really don't want anything at present. I quite understand about the Bishop's "small parcel"– I can get cloak & umbrella here quite well– I have bought my drawing room winter curtains, & though not expensive I think they will be warm & pretty. They are to be made of dark green baize with a gold yellow braid all round (Our carpet you know is green with yellow stripes.) They will cost be-tween $30/- & £2 & Hetty & I shall make them–& put them up. Baize is much thicker than unlined mo-reen–& will keep out the cold winds well I think. I have found a very  pretty cheap wall paper at a *stationers* in the town, & (not to be behind the bluenoses) we are going to paper our dining room ourselves. When it is done I will tell you–(& you may tell Hannah Harper!!!) Today (Oct. 2.) has been a gloriously fine day, but we have had so much rain that much steady sketching of these glorious tints has been impossible. I am contenting myself with pencil sketches, & notes for future colouring. But I long for *your* hands among the trees. Tell Dot & Dina–if only they will get up their pencil drawing a bit–I will in time send them copies of the colour lessons in my splendid book with instructions what to do– I think they will be astonished at the good they will get. We hear from Mr.

Strickland that the Scheme is to be applied to New Brunswick in a few months – so whatever is coming will probably come soon. I hope we may not be just moved to S. John or something of that kind, but so long as the station is healthy, & we are together, it wld be sin to complain. Certainly Rex has a friend in Strickland, which is well as *he* will probably be made Comptroller in Canada. So far so good – you see dear Mum. Our dear love – to all. Your very happy & loving children.

AJHE

P.S. Saturday [3 October]. Finger better.

LETTER

59

[October 1868]

My dearest Aunt Horatia[1] –

Would that I could depict some of the autumn tints which for about a fortnight make these woods like glowing gardens! This bit I saw today. One burning crimson maple in a nook of firs–with amber colored foreground of frostbitten ferns. I don't know if I will color it. It is so difficult to give any idea of the tints. I cannot say how long I have been intending to write to you; but I suppose you hear all our news from home–& I don't want to give you the right to pull my nose for old news!! Still I think you will like to hear from *me* how we get on, & it would take "a long pull" as well as a strong pull to tweak even my nose across the Atlantic!! We are a very good Darby & Joan, as I daresay you know; & we are *very* comfortable here, & have hardly anything to wish for, except to be a *little* bit nearer a good many dear old faces! Whenever I come across any R.C.s & any facts connected with your Church[2] I always think of you. Now imagine me calling at the Priests' House[3] here on my own hook, & making acquaintance with "Father Magua-davie" as we call him. (His real name being McDevitt! but Mac-guadavie is the name of a settlement near here, colloquially pronounced Maccadavy.) I did! The reason was I had an irish sar-vint who took to drink & other enormities & even after she left, I felt anxious to do what I could for her: & as she pretended to have been to Father M. &c. &c. I went after him to find out about her. We know him now & he is a very nice man, I think; with a taste for gardening & farming; writes a fine foreign looking hand–works his people–& is generally respected. There seem to be 2 others here–commonplace looking men of a very typical kind; one a nar-row looking irishman, & the other fat & round. The Church is a wooden building–not very ecclesiastical looking, with pews, organ gallery, & an immense amount of stove pipe inside. There are fine brick priests' House & Nunnery with Schools. At S. John, on the contrary, where *we* have only wood, there is a beautiful R.C. Cathé-dral.[4] We went there once to service. It is very plain, but fine stone, & very good music. A very nice building indeed. The indians up the

215

river about 12 miles from here have a village with a Church, an R.C. settlement.⁵ Almost all Christian indians belong to your Church. Some of the Jesuit Missions to them were splendid in self denial & devotion; but they (races) are dying out. It is a grievous pity, as they are a fine people. I want to try & find out what their rosaries are made of, & if I can get you one, I will. But they are not always very communicative. We call them, & they call us, "sister" & "brother." I wld like to get you some religious relic of them.The Roman Catholic Missions to them have been very interesting, but (here at any rate) they don't seem able to rescue them from debasing with drink & from slow & sure decay. The women & children die so— I suspect that the 1/2 civilization is worse for them physically than mere savagery. In wigwams in the forest the women & children had plenty of open air life— But now they shut themselves up, basket & beadworking & close filthy huts, which must be awfully bad for them. A baby slung up in a tree, & a mother sitting outside the wigwam, had a much better chance.

. . . I wish I could send you a hamper of kittens across the Atlantic. No less than 2 cats have taken into their heads to make a Nursery under our barn, where we can't get at the kittens till they are so old & lively we haven't the (want of) heart to kill them. Then the Mammas introduce them to society & all the available plates & dishes through our kitchen door!! To see them lying all round the stove is wonderful!— It is beginning to get cold now—& we begin to think of furs & flannels. Our present house is very cosy though, even if we have (which is hardly likely,) as cold a winter as the last. Rex's love & mine & I am always dearest

Aunt Horatia   Your loving niece   Juliana Horatia Ewing

LETTER
60

Oct. 12. 1868

My dearest Dot.

The paper is up!!! I leave you to imagine my feelings. I told you how Mrs. Medley & I had felt ourselves cut out by "Bluenoses" when we found that Mrs. Dowling & Miss Parker could *paper* & we could not! Whereupon (having found a cheap paper in a stationer's shop where Rex was music hunting) I determined to paper our dining room – & as Mrs. D. was on a visit to Mrs. M. I called to draw out a few incidental instructions in the course of conversation!! I found Mrs. M. had been before me & had papered a closet!!! The 2 ladies announced their intention of calling in to see how I got on – & after Church on Friday morning, having borrowed steps of Mrs. Lee, & an old whitewash brush of Mrs. Coster, & having *cut* a good many rolls of paper overnight – I donned my old blue print, & sent for the Orderly to take out the picture nails. He began – "When the man that's going to paper comes Ma'am" — & I felt *very* proud to shut him up with "*I'm* the man that's going to paper, Hartney" (in the parliamentary sense of man!!) Just then the bell rang & he came back with a very solemn face – "It's the Bishop's Lady, Mum!!" — leaving her at the door. However the B.'s Lady & Mrs. Dowling ended by working with me till lunch – which though it diminishes my credit – decidedly accelerated the work. They were awfully good, & we got fully half done. Next day Mrs. Dowling & Miss Jacobs came & helped me – & late on Saturday evening I finished it off myself. I think it looks quite as well as the other papers; & indeed it is not a difficult art when the rooms are low. I got rather giddy with perpetually standing on the steps by Saty night. The others chaffed me greatly & we had a good deal of fun over it. "Now little woman! Up the steps! – or – on to the mantelpiece – or – stand on the stove!"[1] — When all was done Hetty turned the carpet – which is universally supposed to have made it look as good as new, & I have cleaned the old oil painting – you know – which is our chief dining room ornament – & I have made some furniture paste, & polished our sideboard today, & Hetty must do the table shortly & I have come round our landlady to repaint the windows – & I have today stained the strip of bare board by the carpet – dark à la the dining room at home – & we are getting generally "redd up"! & at present I am slightly in disgrace with my Ogre on the general idea of having done too much – (Not that I am *the least* the worse!) What do people do with a large property & 10 children to look after!! What I find to do in our extensive domain is amazing! You must expect nothing but cook stories. My *very particular* preserved cucumber has failed: chiefly owing I think to Hetty having heard from her mother that cabbage wld do as well as vine leaves for coloring it, & consequently neglecting my orders as to the vineleaves, & the whole affair went into a hideous jelly smelling strongly of boiled greens!! Did I tell you I had been car-

pentering again? We are rather short of chairs, & I have been manu-
facturing a bedroom seat covered with pink & part of my old white
muslin—to match the toilette table— I am also going to cover a box
to match—& white valances for the bed are nearly finished made of
an old white petticoat & trimmed with black braid!— I got George
Coster to put me up a shelf for my flowers in the drawing
room—which I have today stained dark & it looks very well with a
red lily & some ferns on it. To reward him I gave a tea party last
Wednesday & had him & his flame Sophy Butler & her sisters (Mrs.
Graham's children) & Clara Coster & 2 others. I think I must have
them again on All Hallow's Eve. By the bye a characteristic trait of
these Transatlanticans is that on All Hallow's Eve—they go round
stealing cabbages—by way of improving on our Old World notions
of pulling our own cabbages to tell our fortunes by.[2] I tell you my
own chit chat—but we have a piece of news in the town unfortunately. The 1st murder old Mr. Brooke can remember here & *his*
knowledge of Fton dates back 25 years. A girl here, the daughter of
a butcher, has been "walking with" one of the 22d, a smart young
fellow. Her parents & her brother were against it & wanted her to
accept the offers of a young civilian, Shaunessy by name. She would
not—& the other evening Shaunessy & her brother (a lad of 18) saw
her walking with the soldier, & they fell upon him & cut his head
open. He lived a few hours, but insensible, I fancy. At 2 this
morning the brother was taken—S. having been captured—& they
were brought up before the Mayor today. The soldiers have been
rioting rather: they are naturally so enraged, & there is generally a
certain amount of 'feeling' between the Civil & Military inhabitants. And yet with all this the prisoners were brought from the
prison & back *walking*. (we have only 2 police I believe) Rex & I
waited about to see them. It was awfully primitive. The Court was
held in a little white wooden house. Imagine the trial conducted in
Miss Hawksley's bedroom—a crowd round the door—indescribable
squeeze within. We watched the red arm of one soldier who held
himself up by putting his arm out of the upper window. People
came & went, but he never moved—& when the red arm went—we
knew the prisoners were coming. The brother walked 1st with no
one but the Mayor— I began to draw the Mayor but I can't— He is

as fat as Jepson – shorter & not so good looking – but a clever spirity little man. Except today – in Church – & at the Swearing in of the Governor I never saw him without a Meerschaum as big almost as himself in his mouth. The brother has always been a 'bad lot' – a slight – vicious looking little fellow – the other a fine big young man of 23. The brother did the jaunty, the other looked very sad. Oh! it is certainly a terrible sight – No 2 men ever more richly deserved hanging – they bruised & beat their poor victim horribly: but it must be awful in full youth & strength to walk through the familiar streets, & see familiar faces as dead men. It seems doubtful however if the brother won't get off; for the sister either can't or won't swear positively to him, & she is the only witness. She came last, a *very* sweet looking, ladylike girl, – not 15!! The Supreme Court sits very soon – So the trial will soon take place.

It's almost a shame to tell you this doleful news, but naturally it is the prevailing topic just now. Of course one thought of John Newton³ – as the prisoners passed! & one ought to feel awfully thankful that one's temptations are cast in so much smaller ways, & one's troubles also. We pity the poor girl dreadfully – Her people are very violent, & are said to be fearfully enraged with her: & she is so very interesting looking. . . .⁴

About Mrs. Overtheway. I quite understand as to the price, & leave it in Bell's hands. I suppose I shall not get *proofs* of the end? I hope you at home will kindly look them sharply over by my M.S. . . .

It is very kind of the Mum to have tried to get the Bp to take my cloak &c.: but if he can't – don't let her fidget – for as I think I well impressed on her – I *can* get them here and don't want him to be bothered. He wrote Rex a dear little note last mail – signing himself his *affate* friend & *pupil.*

An invitation has just come from Gvt House. Mrs. Wilmot's At Home with Music. . . . The next time you write a *short* letter & don't want to weigh the envelope with correspondence — put in a pair of white kids for me. 6 1/4. They will come by post. I have persuaded Mrs. Graham to have some theatricals this winter I think, but she wants me to arrange them. Could you send me an old copy of Family Jars? – & can you recommend any? – If you have a 20 minutes with a Tiger I shld like it.[5] ADoo my darling – With our dear love

Your ever loving sister Judy.

Our old Orderly has taken his discharge & like all soldiers is as proud as a peacock of his plain clothes – though they put 10 years on his head. He & Hetty have had rather a "difference" as to her not keeping the looking glass where he can give himself continual glances!! (He is 60 & odd – I *fancy*!)

. . .

LETTER

61

20. Oct. 1868.

My darling Mum.

Your Donkey goes to our heart, & we wish you & him all prosperity together. He must be a dear beast – & I quite sympathize with you.[1] Here there is but one donkey in the place – & he is quite alien in ass's skin! A little boy drives him in a sulky & he is immensely admired – though quite a common specimen!

. . . It is so good of you to have sent Rexie a *tie* – He is so much pleased![2] – I have told Hector of that blessed Rough & his exploits, & asked him when *he* will get a green card of commendation. Never I fear! I just heard Rex informing him that his "Grandma' Gage" had got a donkey!!!

I don't suppose Mackenzie will be able to get a parcel sent to us till Spring. And it wld be best to wait – as the river will close so soon now. Then it will be very nice, & I should think he *could* find someone going to S. John – who would take a parcel. . . .

I hope you will not have to be disappointed over Boneless. "Boneless," you know, was an old name for some kind of Bogy in our grandmother's days. It is alluded to in some old writers. I meant to use it something as I used the Brownies. Boneless was to haunt a youth without much backbone in his character. I was afraid it was a little like the Kettle Family.[3] But I shall see. I made a very good beginning–but have *stuck* at present. It *is* so pleasant to me to hear how you & Father like Mrs. O. I heard from Bell this morning, & *he* launches out in its praise–Yorkshire as he is!! I mean to get to work on *something* soon. Pray let Bell know that it was not *my* fault that the proof did not come with the letter. I took it to the post myself the very 1st mail after it arrived; it was duly stamped & put with the others–& then they took it out again –stamped as it was–& sent it back to R.'s office 2 days after the mail had left. He was *furious*! But you can't do anything with ignorance & incompetency in office–specially in Post Office!! . . . I *am* so glad the Albatross is good. I wish the Oct. No. Of A.J.M. had come!–

I have enlisted Col. Peters to seaweed hunt for me, & I hope he will. Mrs. Coster will be charmed to hear of your laying out hers. I wish she were stronger. By the bye we have a wonderful local *quack* who is doctoring 1/2 Fredericton. He professes to go into a clairvoyant sleep, & in that condition speak with oracular wisdom on your condition (with the additional condition of a $5/-$ fee) He certainly told Mrs. Coster some things–it did seem marvellous how he could have got at: & seems a *wonderfully clever* charlatan–if no more. I wish you wld send a bit of your *hair*, & let us hear what he says!!!! for he professes to do it so: I know you like Quacks. . . .

Our very dear love– My Boy gets nicer, & kinder, & better, & more perfect every day!!!!!!!!! So what he will be by the time we are an old couple there's no saying. We are awfully happy–& so *much* more comfortable in our house than at the beginning of last winter that it is delightful.

Goodbye. Always your most loving
daughter   J. H. E.

Best love to the Boys always & to *dear* old Dot. I hope the 2 illustrations to be cut out of Mrs. O. won't be nice ones! Not the 2 girls in the ghost tale–nor yet the looking glass scene.[4]

LETTER

62

Fredericton. 26. Oct. 1868.

My darling Dot.

... No news with us. My winter curtains are up–& most of my labors in the house successfully over. When I have got my winter clothes–& Rex's in trim–I shall return (as dear little Mrs. Shore wld have said) to "literature & the Fine Arts." The other day Mrs. (Capt.) Carey asked my advice on the subject of furs–which ended in my going there to lunch–& cut her out a cap & tippet on the pattern of mine from a beaver skin she has. Capt. Patton was there– He is a curious fellow–he & I have been rather good friends from the 1st–& he has a "gift" on matters of dress. He & I cut it out between us & I sewed it up. It is most successful. I am going back when I have time to do the cap. And then I have to remake Rexie's military one. I wanted him to have a *swell* fur cap this year–but at the last moment the old boy refused; but wanted *me* to have the skin he rejected for a fur bonnet, after 1000 economical reasons for not indulging himself!!! I need hardly say I did not agree to *this*!– Oh! I *have* had one labor of woe–the discovery of *moths* in Rexie's winter clothes. Happily the mischief is not great, & *most* happily my furs have escaped. But I sat in dust & ashes, picking the grubs out one by one, & thinking, if I had had these regularly shaken once a fortnight through the summer this wld not have been!!!! However the only thing *much* hurt is the tschoga: & my furs are *the* great escape!!–as also the put away winter blankets which seem quite free. If I *had* had Dina this autumn, I'm afraid I shld have worked her hard–in small household matters! I have been very busy with my bulbs– Rex has given me a jolly lot from England *per* the Bishop. I hope they will be very nice in our snug little house.

Tell the Mum I am delighted with Wolff's illustration—Rex is less so—but he thinks nothing good enough for Kerguelen's Land!! Pasquier is good too. In the *men* at least— His women are *not* pretty— Of course Wolff's will be the frontispiece?[1] I suppose the book will be "out" soon. It is very encouraging that everybody likes Mrs. O. so much. Even the reticent old Liz—who never threw me a crumb of encouragement over it—says the last no. is "quite charming"—& wants me to start on something else. I am sorry I couldn't have a proof of the latter part—for one or two trifles. I don't know *why* the printers have taken the trouble to remove the capital R from the last word in the book. I piqued myself on ending with the name of the whole thing: after all the scattered notes, I wished to end on the tonic—so to speak—with "Mrs. O —'s Remembrances." But it was not so written in Maunder!!! Did the Mum ever get that bit I sent her to put in in compliance with her feeling about the bird understanding the men &c.? I think it *would* have been an improvement.[2]

Tuesday. 27. We had a wedding this morning at 8. A. M. & there is to be another on Thursday at the same hour. People can be married here at any time of day, & the evening is a favorite time. These weddings are early however, that the happy couples may get off by the morning boat. The bridegroom was ordained on Sunday. It was rather a pathetic affair. 3 brothers here were all "engaged" together. A parson to Bessy Simonds (*their* wedding on Thursday) the other two to two sisters—daughters of an *awful* fat old pig here.[3] She is

tremenjous. Rex says he wishes she would leave the town, as he feels it is not big enough to hold himself & her. No there is no describing her absence of neck—her superabundance of chins & her general resemblance to a prize pig. The worst is she is not good humoured & jovial in proportion—being of a calvinistic turn. She told the Bishop once that she had "examined the Prayerbook critically – historically – & accurately – & had found it full of errors".... We don't know them, but the girls seem nice I think. Well – one of the girls young man has collapsed in consumption – & there have been some heartbreaking scenes, poor thing. The old pig had set her face (cheek I shld say) against the match – but she took her daughter to bid him goodbye when the doctor pronounced his doom. He went to his home in the country a short time since, & it is said that today he is dying. The pig attended the wedding in her full suit of black with white gloves – & looked so exactly like a fat nurse attending a baby's funeral that it quite overcame me, & I laughed disgracefully. She remained fat & impassive till her daughter promised to "love honor & obey," when she burst into tears. Poor Julia sat by her mother with a face of utter misery – & never shed a tear. *On dit* that the old lady only rates at her when she frets, but her new brother-in-law has announced his intention of taking her home & devoting himself to comforting her. I devoutly hope they have taken her with them to her lover's where they are going this morning. It was a glorious morning. Keen white frost – but sunny & splendidly clear. Air like quinine. *This* is the weather that really makes the healthiness of this climate. It was a funny wedding from nobody being in white! The bride was in a very pretty short walking dress – jacket – hat & feather – all of one shade of grey, & the 2 bridesmaids seemed to have simply put on their Sunday-go-to-meeting clothes. The first part of the service was at the chancel steps – & then the old Bishop took up the 1st verse of the Psalm to the Vth tone – & then we (the choir & organ) the 2d – & so on. The effect was admirable as the procession passed up to the altar rails. We sang the Voice that breathed &c. also, & of course Rex played the Wedding March. We were glad it was a nice wedding for their sakes – but we remembered with the fat boy that we "know'd a nicerer."!!!![4] – Bessy Simonds is rather a pet of ours – & I mean to go to *her* wedding – in grey rep – white burnous & gloves &c. & Rex to sport his new tie for the first time.

Impress on the Mum with my dear love that now I never know whether it is a cold day or not till I go out. If only I can keep us from sliding into the most unhealthy habit of the place – of keeping our house at enervating degrees of stove heat I shall be thankful. Of cold in the house there is no fear! Today is *lovely* – I am sitting in our sunny little dining room – getting awfully hot near the stove – with the windows open & the clear air and sunshine coming in on a heliotrope in flower which I have had given to me. My old Boy at his office. We certainly get happier & happier. I am more & more convinced that the 1st year is much the *least* happy. We get so to know each other's little ways with time. At first when any gloomy fit came over him – or he spoke sharply from being very much in earnest – I used to fancy he was put out with me & get into the downs. But now if he is worried about anything – I know it is not with *me*, & we call him the "Bungle Bear" (Steenie's old phantom!) & say that I am the little black dog that plays with the Bear!!! – And he *is* so good. He dandifies himself because I like it – & keeps his music tidy for the same reason; & as his sole earthly object & desire is for me to be happy it wld be very odd if I were not!!! No Scheme news that we have heard. Monk writing on business the other day from Halifax incidentally alluded to the fact that "the Chief" (Strickland) "has such a high opinion of you." Which is satisfactory, though I don't believe anybody but *me* can properly know what an old dear he is!! He has just written an 8 part song on Too Late – which I think you will like. The women sing the foolish virgins' part – & the men the "Too late ye cannot enter now &c." A much better idea it strikes me than the old one of making it a *Solo*, though I know it *was* sung as such. Are you sick of hearing my old man's praises? My dear love to all. . . .

> Ever your most loving sister
> Judy.

. . .

LETTER
63

All Hallow's Eve. 1868
Fredericton.

My dearest Mum.

...Tell the girls I am proud of having just made myself a walking dress & petticoat out of the best parts of those 2 old linseys of Maggie's & mine. I have really got skirt, petticoat & new garibaldi – & trimmed them with black patent velvet – & it has made me a capital everyday costume for walking, & trotting about the house.

I am going to have the Butler girls & some others to tea & *nut burning* tonight. I shall think of our evenings with Hannie 'Awthorn! Ask Dina if she remembers the porridge she & I made together? – & how when we opened the door at midnight – a *cat* came in!!!![1]

Bessy Simond's wedding went off very well. She looked awfully pretty, but I do not at all appreciate the fashion of not having the sisters for bridesmaids – & she has got such a lot of nice & very pretty sisters – it was quite a loss in an artistic point of view. The effect of the chanted Psalm is certainly *remarkably* pretty. I think Rexie's chant must have sounded very well at Maggie's Wedding. We went down to the boat as before – to see the happy couple off – & made her change garters with her bridesmaid – who was greatly elated to hear how very successful the Spell had been in the case of *my* chief bridesmaid![2] Fredericton has gone mad on weddings this week – I told you of *the* monthly nurse of the place having been married, & the reason she gave for having waited so long? That her mother advised her at least to wait till 40 – since if you got a *good* man he was worth waiting for – & if not, you wld have the less of him? The soldiers seem to have taken a fit of marrying all the old women in the place! –

It is a glorious day today – but it keeps quite frosty & keen – It seem hardly likely to go back now I think. I fancy we are fairly into winter, though unusually early. Our cottage is certainly most comfortable – & it *is* a blessing to be able to be warm whenever you like –

… By the bye, I was assured most positively by both Parrys the other day that if you put *whole peppers* in with your camphor into camphor bags – they prevent the camphor from evaporating – Or at least *very* much delay the process!!!! What do you say? –

Rexie has written a 4 part song to the first few words in the Night Thoughts which I think is one of his best efforts. From "Tired Nature's &c." – to "lights on lids unsullied by a tear." Ending again with the words "Tired Nature's sweet restorer Balmy Sleep."[3] I must send it to you.

Boneless has "stuck" just now. But I am actually working on something else, which – if it succeeds – I rather hope to send you by next mail for the Jany No: if accepted.[4]

Boy says I must "get ready" as he wants me to go out with him. So Adieu for the present – Ever your loving daughter Judy.

The Bishop brought us such a lovely Cromolithograph from Home as a present. I suspect from the style it is a thing of Fredk Tayler's. It is 2 dogs finding a fox. An awfully pretty thing.[5]

Oh! I am so grieved & horrified to hear that Cantuar is said to be dead. I fear it *is* true. Those poor poor girls! They have had sad sorrow lately indeed! And really it seems hardly possible to over-estimate his loss to the Church just now. Will Ebor succeed him?[6] I cannot say how sorry I am – & how grieved you will be, dear Mum. There will be a good deal of sympathy on this side the Atlantic for his loss. He seems to have impressed the American Bishops so very favorably. I did not tell you one feature of my All Hallow's tea party – After the girls had pulled cabbages in the garden – & burnt nuts &c. &c. – we took to telling fortunes with the kings & queens – & Hector had his fortune told (the Parrys were with us) each card being named after one of 4 favorite dishes of his, & the object being to see which he wld have 1st &c. You never saw any-thing more comical than the way he put his paws on the table & *snuffed* the cards. But as we say a dozen times in a week, he knows every word you say to him!

I *must* tell you, dear Mum, what Mrs. Medley said to me this evening as we came out of Church. She said "It's an odd place to be-gin in about it, but I *must* thank you for the end of Mrs. Over-theway. The pathos of those old Albatrosses![7] The Bishop & I cried over them, & I suppose it's the highest compliment we can pay you to say it is equal to anything of your mother's – & that you're a worthy daughter of your mother." Wasn't that a splendid bit of praise to hear, all these miles away from one's dear old wonderful old Mum?

As you may gather from this, it is Sunday, & All Saints. All Saints is generally such a fine day – but today though it has suddenly turned mild, all is rain & slosh.

We had very nice services. I thought so of poor old Eastwood & his birthday – & of Harvey & old Fisher – & Wolff – & so many more! & now Cantuar is with them! ——

Goodbye my dearest Mother, Our
dear love to you all.

LETTER

64

All Saints 1868.

My dearest Aunt Mary.

Many thanks for the little note I got from Ecclesfield, to which I do not think I have responded yet. But no doubt you get the pith of our communications with Home from the admirable Dot.

I fancy I could have made a not unpleasant 4th when you, & the other Aunt, & dear old Dina were together! If one *could – could could* annihilate space sometimes for an hour or two, & "drop in" upon one or two people one thinks of——————Well! *I* should then indeed have far away too large a share of earthly happiness. For except for just this one fact of separation, my lot is so very very sunny, that I only fear not being thankful enough – or rather not being *in any degree* properly grateful. Thrown so utterly as I am on my dear husband – if he had been less kind, less sympathetic, less fond of me, less one with me in the greatest – & in so many minor interests, how different life wld have been! As it is we dovetail in our "little ways" –, & grow happier every day. And as to being *here*, we have only reason for gratitude – both because it is such an exceptionally nice foreign station, & also because being a cheap & quiet place it has been admirably adapted to our purse, which we have good hopes will be more liberally filled before any further move. For the "Scheme" of which you have heard so often is to be applied to Canada in a few months, when Rex will probably get promotion & more pay. Whether we shall be moved or not – we have no idea. But if we had had to *begin* at some expensive station either in England or abroad, it wld have been much less convenient.

Our little cottage is very comfortable now; & I flatter myself even ornamental. I am getting rather clever at house contrivances I think – & I must say the Colonies is a good school for learning efficiently to practice the Duke's celebrated advice "If you want a thing done – do it yourself!" Now winter is coming on we feel the comfort of a smaller & better built house than we had last year. We are so thoroughly warm & cosy, we really never know whether it is a cold day or not till we get out of doors.

Last night being All Hallow's Eve – I had a party of "young people" – 3 daughters of a Major Graham in the 22d from about 12 to 15 – son & daughter of the military chaplain 17 & 14 – the daughter of our neighbor the Rector, & the daughter of the subdean of the Cathedral. Capt. & Mrs. Parry came too, & the dear Bulldog. I turned them out into the garden to pull cabbages, & then we burnt nuts, ate apples, told fortunes by the cards, & played at "Consequences."[1] They are all nice girlies & fond of fun. You should have seen old Hector the Bulldog when we told *his* fortune! We put the Queens down & named each after 4 favorite dishes of his (for he is somewhat of a gourmand) and went through the whole process to see which dish he wld eat next &c. he putting his paws on the table & snuffing the cards in the most comical way.

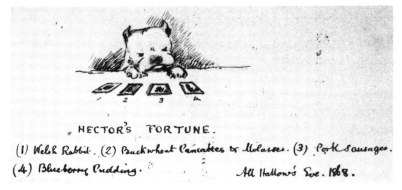

HECTOR'S FORTUNE.

(1) Welsh Rabbit. (2) Buckwheat Pancakes or Molasses. (3) Pork Sausages. (4) Blueberry Pudding.   All Hallows Eve. 1868.

Allow me to offer his portrait to the notice of your Ecclesfield Album.

... Our best love, & the same to B. & all friends

Yr loving niece
J. H. E.

LETTER

65

Nov. 9. 1868.
Fredericton.

My darling Mum.

I am puzzled about the mails. Your letter dated Trafalgar Day which you wrote Oct. 21. on a Wednesday as an experiment (viâ New York) only reached us the *morning* of the day on which we got the Halifax mail in the *afternoon*. But I had already had "intermediate" letters dated Oct 16 written by Maggie at Home. Whatever the day was that *she* wrote on; *that*—I think—is the day to write viâ U.S. by—for I got it so nicely about 1/2 way between the 2 regular mails. Tell me some time how *my* letters arrive please.

...I am so glad you were amused by my account of Prince William dear Mum: & I am *really* obliged to you for not making any use of my letters without my leave— It wld utterly hamper *me* if you did. As to that sketch—I know that the "situation" was a picturesque one–however I may have transmitted it to you: but I wld never dream of printing an account of it. 1.° It would be most obnoxious to the Hanningtons–who would hear of it in an *incredibly* short space of time. 2.° Such "missionary sketches" are a standing joke amongst people here whose daily life is in these sort of places, & I have several times heard it said "that would do to send home for a missionary report." &c. &c. 3.° I *should* be glad if you would just keep the letter–since though I wld not put it in anywhere as it stands I shall probably make use of it eventually to much better effect than if I contributed it as a "sketch of men & manners." Think of this dear Mum whenever anything I describe seems picturesque enough for a "paper," that I have in the long run probably much better use for it than a mere "paper." It was so with the letter I sent home about Topsham years ago. Reka Dom has come out of that–& a dutch tale probably will, yet. Only my Pegasus is rather a slow old 'oss–not as lively as your dear donkey!– I have just come home from a curious & painful phase of life–the Criminal Court. We were going up the town & met Parry who was going into Court to hear the murder trial, so we turned & went with him. The barristers are so terribly 2d rate that it was dreadfully wearying. Once only, one witness was so comically like Sam Weller in the way he nonplussed the prisoner's counsel who was cross examining him in a would be smart manner–the court was in roars of laughter. The men take it very coolly so far. Driscoll especially. I believe he is utterly buoyed up with the belief he will get off. And the people about seem to think they will–though no one has–as it seems–a fraction of a doubt that they did it. If they escape it will just be from want of proof, if the sister refuses her evidence against her brother. It goes on tomorrow morning, but I don't know if I shall go. I don't know if I could stand the scene if they are condemned. And yet I do believe–so far as one can form a judgement about it–that perhaps the only chance of awakening Driscoll to repentance is the terrible reality of Death. The removal of every earthly hope may induce him to turn his face to the Cross! But one thinks of the paintings of the impenitent thief – when one sees the hardened brazen look upon the man's face whom one knows to be guilty. For it is as I said a question of proof – No one requires to be convinced as to their guilt. Driscoll was very well got up today but he has a regular Newgate physiognomy. I wanted to see the sister again – but I don't think I shall go. It seems almost *too* solemn to stare at! –

We are well into winter now – We had several days of bitter cold. Then one lovely fine mild day – & now we have snow & sleds & sleighs &c. It came provokingly in the midst of my gardening which will now have to be deferred till Spring. The day after the mild one – it was colder, with sleet, snow, &c. but as I sat & saw the snow coming I thought "Now or Never" for my earth for bulbs & winter plantings – (For remember when winter once sets in here – & the ground is like iron – there is no getting anything!) So I made Hartney borrow a wheelbarrow & (my Ogre being at his office!!) off we set to the College Grove, got our leaf mould, & came home. I had some difficulty to induce the old irishman to persevere – he thought the gates were locked – we'd as good soil in our garden – & a 1000 other stumbling blocks. Next day the ground was like iron – but my leaf mould was in the house!!! I confess I don't deserve to have been none the worse – but so it was!!!

... Now you darling Mum – You are *not* to fidget when you don't get your letters "regular." If we were in some out of the way place with only ourselves to write, you might. But here – even if we were both ill in bed we have plenty of friends to write to you! Whereas in winter the mails *are* uncertain, write as we will. But I did miss *one* mail once lately I know.

I am getting rather accustomed to working in fur!! I have now made Mrs. Carey a winter cap as well as the cape out of her beaver skin – & am now doing up Rexie's.

We are going to Govt House again on Friday. They are rather dull spreads.

Goodnight dear Mum. Take care of yourself. Oh! it will indeed be a fine day when the cab *does* bring back Darby & Joan! *Such* a happy Darby & Joan! — that — (dissatisfied mortals!) I would

233

like you to see us!! Our house is so cosy–I can't tell you. If Dina were here she would be warm enough!! Ever your loving children

AJHE

Love to the dogs.

66

Monday. 23. Novr. 1868
Fredericton N.B.

My dearest Pater.

You may fancy my feelings when I got no Home letter by the Halifax mail on Saturday! However the English Churchman, A. J. M. & the plays (for which many thanks to our Dot!) relieved me of *anxiety* since I felt sure that you would not have sent off papers &c. but no letter, had anything been amiss. This morning I got letters by U. States, & perhaps the Halifax ones may turn up yet. We take letters now as Mrs. Gamp took her children "as they come & as they go," for of all the official departments of this place the P. Office seems to be managed *worst*, & to the initiated, that is saying a good deal!– And as to understanding it all–it is quite hopeless. It think it is marvellous that both you & we get our letters as well as we do!– And the letters I got this morning by N. York have come very quickly.... Thank you so very much dear Father, for taking such trouble in the correcting of Mrs. O. I wonder if my letter in reference to the last sentence got Home in time for you to alter it. I mean to put Mrs. O—'s *Remembrances* with a capital

R—which the printer so kindly struck out. I think it wld even have been nice to have given it a line to itself, thus.

—"not the least pleasant of

Mrs. O—'s Remembrances

But I will be quite satisfied—however it is. I am longing to see a copy. I hope we shall get one soon! . . . I do long terribly sometimes to see . . . all of you; but this must be "Wann Gott Will"—and I hope I *do* to some extent realize the blessing of hearing such good news of all of you mail after mail—& am thankful for it. I feel as if I never *could* be thankful enough for my *own* happiness & comfort with my dear old Boy. He does get better & kinder & dearer to me every day. He is just now playing away at Spohr's Last Judgement[1] in the loveliest way, in full evening costume—in which he always dresses now for dinner (we dine late in winter)—because he knows I like it. You will be tired of hearing how much more comfortable we are this winter than we were last: but I do want the Mum to realize it. It is a comfort to me that I can't describe. I can always be perfectly warm from top to toe. We have no such thing as a cold passage or room in the house. The hall stove (with dumb stove on the landing) warms all that—& as to the kitchen—it is much warmer than I should like to sit in!! I must write a line to D.O. so with dear love Ever your most loving daughter JHEwing.

23 Nov. 1868. Fredericton.

My dearest Dot.

From the above you will perceive that "fire" is the order of the day with us still— I was 1/2 dozing in the armchair after dinner (about an hour since) & Rex was copying choir music when his sharp ear caught the familiar sounds. As it was a lovely night I turned out with him; more especially as it was near at hand. Mercifully the night is quite still—or much more must have gone. It was a splendid *spectacle*— Deep clear blue sky—crescent moon & bright stars, & the roaring flames going up like some great altar fire surrounded by crowds of devotees!— I don't think it is incendiarism this time, for it is a carpenter's shop & out houses & the words "pipes & shavings" are quite sufficient, the workmen being so reckless. It was in a nest of dwelling houses, but unless the wind rises, these will probably escape.[1]

I have already told you "the result of the trial." The girl's trial has not come on yet. If she ever *is* tried I will let you know! The Bishop told me that Driscoll père positively *did* take the $500 for giving up his son to justice, & threatened if they did not give him the reward he wld go to law for it! One of the papers openly accuses Judge Fisher of having *not* told the truth about the depositions—& everybody feels heartily ashamed of the business. There

LETTER 67 · 23 November 1868

was a report that they wanted to catch young D. again on charge
of another murder–some wretched girl murdered near Govt
House–but I think it must be partly a Cancan–& anyway they are
not likely to catch him, (unless it is made very heavily worth Papa's
while!!!!) I quite acquit old D. of thinking he put his son's neck in
any danger worth naming. He seems to have fully understood his
own plan. He took the reward–got an unscrupulous counsel–
intimidated the only witness–(if not the Judge) & will now
probably flit to the States. He was seen holding his finger up to
threaten the girl whilst she was being examined in open court,
Capt. Chauncy told me. Is it not disgraceful? He & his son have
both been in the habit of keeping people in terror by free use of the
knife. Old D. sold Mr. Rowan an old cow with a calf that did not
belong to her–as being her own once–& when Mr. R. found out
the trick & blew him up–he said "If you say another word about it,
I'll take my knife to you!"–

I *do* sympathize with you over the bedding plants!... You're a
wonderful old thing–with garden & everything on your shoulders!
I hope (it is true I have always hoped!!! Even over Tulipa Gesneria!)
to have some really nice bulbs this year. The house *is* so different.
We used to drag the unhappy pots upstairs with us at night in Reka
Dom, & cover them with dressing gowns & they got frozen after all!
I have got some hyacinths & crocuses brought out in the light
already. I want to have some for Xmas if I can.... Pray "don't
mention" my sending you things. I would only too well like to be
incessantly despatching things & furs! I think I will send your
photo.s next mail. I have got one of "Old Gabe" for you,–carte
size–& I want to send some landscape ones also. It seems very
stupid of me not to have got my story ready yet–but you know how
I *cannot* write "against the grain." It *is* progressing–but slowly. No
Scheme news, except that we hear Sir W. Power has been down to
Aldershot to organise it there, but there are no changes here yet. I
think Strickland wld probably keep us here–or move us to St. John
–but we cannot *guess*–& may well wait thankfully. If Dina does
come to me next year–you shld see if it is possible to get one of
"Cook's tickets".... It would be about 1/4 of the expense I believe.[2]
Goodbye darling– Your ever loving Judy.

. . .

68

Advent Sunday. [29 November] 1868.
Fredericton N.B.

My darling Mum.

"A merry Xmas & a happy New Year" to all of you!–wished from the bottom of our hearts which will be with you & Ecclesfield–though our bodies must stay here! I would so have loved to send a nice Xmas parcel Home to you all!! But if our ship comes home, I hope then I *shall* be able to get one or two things together–Regie's collection not being forgotten!– A small Xmas memorial we enclose in the shape of 2 photos of a beaver's house–& neighborhood! for *you*–"A Beaver's House"–& "Falls near a Beaver's Dam." I send 4 others for Dot–"Old Gabe" (=Gabriel)–"A pile of ice" on the river here–A "Crossing à *Portage* (that is a place where you have to *carry* your canoe) between the Tobique, & the Nepissquit Lakes"–& another little canoe scene, which gives a good idea of the Elms here, & of the scenery of the Nashwaak Cis, where we used to paddle about on summer after-noons [Plates 12–13].

Your Halifax letters never turned up, & I begin to think that they must have been addressed viâ U.S. by mistake–& that those I got a day later, were the ones that should have come by Halifax.

We are fairly into winter now; and I am thankful to say that I still enjoy it, & do not find the cold at all overpowering. There is a fair depth of snow on the ground–& it is hard enough to walk on without sinking much. We have not been on snowshoes yet. I want a new pair of moccasons and cannot get hold of the faithful Peter to make them!– The cold is not extreme yet– It is still consider-ably above Zero in the daytime. It is very pleasant weather, for you are not so *muffled*, & encumbered with coverings as you have to be in the most intense cold. I generally walk with my old Boy to his office in the morning at about 9.30–& when the sun shines on these bright clear mornings it is charming. But I am *very* careful, & wrap up always rather over than under the mark.

I have soaked the photos. rather too hurriedly, for some of them were gummed very tight to their cards; but Dot will excuse it, & can soak them again if needful. We have literally no news – but the good news of being well & happy. For the 2d time the trial of the Driscoll girl for perjury has been postponed. First the Counsel for the Crown was taken unwell!!! Then they got another man, & now they say the papers are mislaid!!!! It seems impossible to draw any other inference than that they are intimidated, & daren't do justice! The other night some of these blackguards took to breaking the sergeant's windows & pelting the *sentry* with bricks. On dit that Col. Harding intimated to the Mayor that he shld give orders to the sentries to load & fire. The little game is now discontinued!! & a reward offered for the offenders. N. Brunswick is not in a highly creditable state just now. There have been some rather disgraceful commercial failures which will make it a very hard winter to many innocent people – & which make *us* thankful we have no money invested here! – One gentleman who has ruined lots of poor single women & people in a "small way" by *his* bankruptcy – was put in honorable captivity in his own house under care of the Sheriff – but (assisted by a friend) he locked the Sheriff up, & bolted. He has since been taken. The Bishop is very full of all this, & a good deal worried, as he has church money invested as well as money of his own, & "confidence" in all kinds of securities is greatly shaken.[1]

I am getting rather anxious for letters from you, though I do not suppose I have any reason for being fidgety. Will you ask Dot to write to Parker & Son & see if he could let me have one of the Diaries (bound up with Church Calendar) such as I have always had——for 1869. It is 2/6.

Our dear love to all. We are rather given up to *novels* just now. If the girls have not read the "Moonstone" (Wilkie Collins) they must.[2] It is splendid – & should be ordered for the Book Club. Another good novel of a different type (very *scotch* but very clever) is "Alec Forbes of Howglen."[3]

Your ever most loving daughter

J. H. E.

69

Tuesday. 8 Dec. 1868.
Fredericton N.B.

My dearest Dot.

... It is almost impossible to keep up to politics *here*. It "sur-prises by himself" nearly as much as it did to Count Smorltork[1] when one sees no papers to speak of– Then we get the principal items of news (such as Disraeli's having resigned) not many hours later than you do, but it is weeks before one gets the particulars, by which time we have had more telegrams, & one feels so confused altogether!! Rex isn't a bit more of a politician than I am, which is rather provoking, as I can't pick his brains, & my own are so ill adapted for politics.... So much more than usual hangs on *this* election. I fear the Reform bill was a good deal too Radical, & not a very good hit of Disraeli's. One really would think that experience on this side of the water would prevent anyone from wanting to ex-tend the franchise more among the uneducated. I can see no con-tingencies in giving the vote to educated women the least com-parable to the danger in increasing the influence of the ignorant mob over the legislature of the country. However it's no good going off! —...

Tell the dear Mum please that I got dissatisfied with my story, & *recast it* & began again–& got on awfully well, & was very well satis-fied with it. But Rex read what was done, & doesn't care for it a bit–in fact quite the reverse, which has rather upset my hopes. However, he says he cannot properly judge till it is finished, so I am going to finish it off, & if he likes it better then, I shall send it next mail. It is a regular child's story–about Toys–not at all senti-mental–in fact meant to be amusing–but as Rex read it with a face for a funeral, I don't know how it will be. I don't somehow think the idea is bad. It is (roughly) this: A pickle of a boy with a very long suffering sister (I hope you won't object to her being called Dot.

You know it's a very common pet name, & it "shooted" so well.) gets all her toys & his own & makes an "Earthquake of Lisbon" in which they are all smashed. From which a friend tells them the story of a dream she is supposed to have had (but I flattered myself the dream was rather neatly done up) of getting into fairyland to the Land of Lost Toys—where she meets all her own old toys that she destroyed in her Youth— Here she is shown in a kind of vision dutch & german people making these toys with much pains & industry, & is given a lot of material & is set to do the like. Failing this she is condemned to suffer what she inflicted on the toys, each one passing its verdict on her. Eventually a doll (*my* Rosa!!!!) that she had treated very well rescues her, & the story reverts to the sister & brother who takes to amusing himself by establishing himself as toy:mender to the establishment, instead of cultivating his bump of destructiveness. I sketch the idea, because (if the present story fails) if you think the *idea* good I would try to recast it again.[2] If I send it as it is, it is pretty sure to come by the Halifax mail next week. I wrote none yesterday because I have had a slight "threatening" of cold &c. & as bad colds, influenzas & so forth have been about[3]—Rex has been a perfect dragon, & wouldn't allow any "mental work"!! The weather has *been* most peculiar. The sun as utterly gone as if it were the foggiest of Novembers in London. Every day looking like a storm of snow—& keeping on a kind of chilly, steadygoing grey winter weather. Last night the barometer fell 3/4 of an inch (72/100) & we had a wild storm of wind & sleet. Today it has been blowing, raining, & sleeting & the storm is evidently not over. Lots of people have been ill, but Rex watches *me* like a dragon—sends me to bed—pours in port wine, won't let me go to church &c. &c. So I keep in our cosy little house & read novels & draw!!! & watch my dear bulbs coming on splendidly. We shall probably have some fine, bright, cold weather after this, & get some snowshoeing.

I do miss poor dear old Fisher so! I very much wanted some *statistics* about toy making. You never read anything about the making of common dutch toys did you? I have hopes yet that Rex will like the story when he sees it finished.

Dear love & thanks to Maggie for her letter. I do so enjoy all the news.

I'm afraid this is a very dull letter. Poor Capt. Cookesley (1/22d) has shot through his hand in the woods–by a most curious accident. His gun went off on his back at 1/2 cock–& his hand happened *just to be* passing by the muzzle!

The girl Driscoll is at last committed for trial before the Supreme Court. The 22d are going to have some theatricals & Rex has got to take Cookesley's part & also to write the overture & train the string band for the music of the burlesque "Villikins & his Dinah."[4] He will dine at the Mess tomorrow night. Oh! *wouldn't* it be nice if *you* could come & keep *me* company.

... Your ever loving sister

My old darling—J. H. E.

LETTER

70

S. John's Day. [27 December] 1868
Fredericton N.B.

My dearest Dot—

After thanking you all 1000 times for the jolly letters we got when the mail *did* come–I think I will tell you how we spent our

242

Xmas. It did not *promise* very brightly – for the cold which seems to hang so unaccountably about me turned out to be a sort of epidemic variety of influenza – i.e. influenza without any cold in the head, but feverish discomfort & a sort of throat affection something like mumps in a mild form outside & swelling within also – in fact "mumps – lumps – & dumps" about sums it up! – "Everybody" has had it, & I couldn't help laughing to hear that Dr. Odell[1] says it is the "mild weather" that is so unhealthy at this season of the year; because our "mild" weather has been a delicious, fine, fair, moderate season, when one could be warm without being buried in wraps, & rather colder than your very "hardest" winter moments! Well – we sent for the doctor at last – & I was very feverish one evening and my dear old man was more good I think than he has ever been yet. He sometimes becomes quite a bungle bear from anxiety if my little finger aches; but when I really *was* unwell he *was* so good! – I found I could eat no dinner, so I put my feet in hot water & retired to bed under innumerable blankets with an admirable result. I got awfully warm & comfortable – & dozed to the tune of Rex's music downstairs – he coming up at intervals to give me tea – & medicine – chiefly kisses! I was no more feverish – & am well over it now & much wanted to go to Church today, only as Mr. Shortt observed "the more care you take the sooner you'll be quite well." So I did not get to Church on Xmas Day, but that was our only drawback; for the dear old Boy was so awfully kind – & we were so jolly & comfortable that we had a delightful day. On Xmas Eve we were sitting on the landing by the dumb stove, when (very late) a ring came at the door & a parcel was put into Rex's hands by an unknown "party." It was (I will make a proper sketch of them.) a a *very* pretty plated coffee pot – & ditto butter cooler – with a note to the effect that some members of the choir begged him to accept this little Xmas gift as a very  small mark of their gratitude for his kindness in taking so much trouble with them. This was rather a pleasant beginning to Xmas –

wasn't it? (Rex had previously dressed the house with some "prick-ing" thoughtfully sent by Mrs. Medley, & had carried me round the house in my nightgown to see the effect – I being supposed to be "in bed." And I had had some fun sending Hetty shopping – for our turkey & various odds & ends of Xmasings.) On Xmas Eve also "Peter Poultice" our indian brother gave us a call – & Rex took the opportunity to buy me a pair of bead worked moccasons – like those I sent Maggie – the 1st smart pair I have had. Then I sent *him* up the town to his favorite "store" to buy a piece of music as a Xmas box from me to *him*, & he returned with "Israel in Egypt" – & an American Stereoscope for *me*. Then Miss Parker sent me some knitted things, & altogether we had a good deal of pleasant excite-ment – Rex going out at intervals to business — carol practice – rehearsal &c. &c. &c. when I took to the novels which Mr. Shortt had kindly got for me as a supplement to his medicines! Then in the evening the old boy went downstairs & played "Christians Awake &c." lovelily with all kinds of stops & different effects – & I sat upstairs by the dumbstove, & was not entirely in Canada – as you may fancy! He did this for me last year – When he had done he came up again, & said he hoped he would play that for me every Xmas Eve wherever we were even when he was an old man & his old fingers trembled on the keys. It was after that the testimonial came. Then the R.C. bell began to chime for midnight mass – and Hetty went to bed, & Rexie read the Evening Service with me as Xmas Eve passed into Xmas Day.

In the morning – Rex brought my breakfast to bed, & strangely enough on Xmas Day came our 1st news of "the Scheme." The new order of things is to begin here on Jany 1. We are to remain here at present – Rex taking all the Departmental work which has hitherto been shared by other officers, & being in fact alone here. This is sure to mean more £.S.D. eventually, but the pay and rations are not to be altered *in anyone's case* in January. The "financial year" of the army begins in the Spring, & all the arrangements must con-tinue pecuniarily – on the old system till the new estimates & vote are given. It really is *very* good news, for we had had some fears of being moved to Halifax – & might very possibly have been sent to the West Indies – but you know I had had a sort of dim, wild, un-

likely hope – that the next change might be an order Home – &
"Ecclesfield" just rushed over me so unbearably that after hiding it 2
or 3 times when he came in with tea & things to me, I *couldn't* hold
out – & when Rexie came in & began to talk about it I broke down &
had a "regular good cry."– I knew it was very selfish, for *he* thinks
me quite Home enough – & in fact *has* no other ties, & likes travelling, & prefers being abroad: & I fully expected him to be
vexed – though keep it back I couldn't. But oh! he was so kind! I
never loved him as I have done since. He sympathized & comforted
me, & in fact just made me feel all right again: & after that we had
the jolliest of days: and sent both man & maid out to enjoy *themselves.* P.M. The Bishop called, & brought Rex a beautiful ruler with all
kinds of measurements on it. Then we had a very swell dinner – (I
was downstairs) & sat over the fire with novels in the evening! I
must add about the Scheme. It *is very* good news. Thus: – *All* military movements are wonderfully uncertain – & as Rex said –
"We *might* be ordered Home in the Spring" – but going on the
"probable" line of events, we were pretty certain to be kept on
foreign service for 2 or 3 years (the foreign terms are very seldom
long now – & Rex has had a great deal of foreign service) – & it is an
immense thing if we spend it – in a place we like so much –
with nice friends – a lovely & healthy climate – easy duties – sole
charge – with no worrying "Head" over Rex – & after all only about
a fortnight from England. Then we know already that under the
New Scheme besides the pay of a man's rank, there is a certain
extra pay to sole charges. But what we shall get under the new
arrangements nobody knows till May. Tell the Mum also that I
asked Rex long ago whether if there were any financial posts in
England connected with it – the stirring up of interest might get
him one – but he said & says – that just now is the last time to worry
the authorities – but when everything is fairly settled down and the
grand crush of general business subsided we might make special
application for any post that seemed likely. Now as our policy is to
sit quiet – we certainly have every reason to be thankful that we
have so desirable a station at which to rest on our oars – for health,
comfort, & economy. Fancy if we had been ordered to Halifax! in
this weather! – & with all the expense of moving only just to get

away from our friends here – to a place we don't like so well! – Monday [28 December]. We got another letter from Halifax this morning. Rex is to do the duty of 5 Departments!!! so they ought to give him something for it! – It will not involve so much extra work as you would suppose, & Rex is very much pleased about it. He says the position is a good one in reference to the Control Department. All this is not very scientifically told, but it is the general result of it, as far as my untechnical ears gather it from Rex's remarks! – I am to add that though no change will probably take place in anybody's pay &c. till the new (financial) year i.e. Spring, yet we may hear news as to how it is to be before then. I am at this moment waiting for the Bishop with whom I am going to communicate with the "Loyalist Ladies." They are 2 *very* old ladies who live in a cottage opposite. Their father was one of the loyalist Americans who left the States to settle in Canada when the States rebelled – I mean in the *old* American War. They were some of the 1st settlers in Fredericton. The 2 sisters are a single lady (Miss Bailey – not the unfortunate do!) & a widow (Mrs. Emmerson) They call me their "little neighbor" – and are pleased to look very favorably on me, & they like me to come when they receive the Holy Communion which they do from time to time, as they never go out now. I accuse Rex of a penchant for Miss B. & a flirtation from his dressing room window. *She* is awfully old – 90 – something – but *on dit* that she does not like it to be supposed that she is so old. However she likes me, though I *was* injudicious enough to enquire how the 1st French Revolution affected this Province from her experience! We have had some *very* cold bright weather since the "mild" days to which Dr. Odell lays our epidemic; & the cold coming suddenly on a thaw, froze the melted snow as it poured from the roofs & made a fine display of icicles. (You are not accustomed to icicles hanging right over the upper windows – I suppose 4 or 5 feet in length) I tried to sketch some as I lay in bed – but they are very difficult; only I reflected that if I can't sketch icicles, it is very little use my going to sketch the frozen waterfall above the Nashwaak Cis – as I want to do!!! I am *very* sorry tell the dear Mum that being unwell has prevented my finishing my story: but it would neither have been good for me nor for the story to write when I was seedy. I am *very* impatient to be at it, so she may be sure it will come as soon as I can manage it. Tell her I read "Childhood in Art"[2] again one day when I was in bed with *great* pleasure. It is awfully good. Tell her too from me that I hope & trust she will not fidget at my having had a little influenza attack in company with all my neighbors—such as I might have had any- where. I tell you—because I think it better than keeping anything back—but if *she* is worrying 10 days hence—when I shall probably be snowshoeing, or perhaps dancing at a ball, I shall leave off com- municating such small ailments per:Halifax Mail!!! I am sorry too she thought the *murder* weighed on my mind— I think it weighed more on our *tongues*. You know news is scarce here, & then we military people were naturally indignant. But it is to be remem- bered that perhaps *one* reason why it was managed so very badly was that no such case (no capital crime) had blackened the calen- dar of this place within about 30 years. Rex won't let me write a bit more—he says I'm to be idle & I wanted to write several letters!!

However "'Usbands will 'ave their way"—

... Goodbye darling old thing. I wld like to see your dear old faces!

Ever your loving sister
Juliana Horatia Ewing.

Voice of Rex from the DumbStove upstairs
"Now Jow—*are* you done?"

LETTER
71

[From AE]

Fredericton. 11 Jan. 1869

My dearest Mum,

I am quite sure you will believe *strictly* every word I say about Jow; and I think, at the same time, that unless I *do* say a few

247

words, you will be fancying that she is ill, because I have advised her not to write more than a few lines to-day. The strict, unadorned truth is this, then. There has been a nasty type of influenza prevalent, with low feverish symptoms; the result, it is supposed, of an unusually mild winter. Jowie had a rather bad "go" of it about Christmas time, and got over it, all right. She had not, however, *completely* recovered her usual amount of strength, when, in the middle of last week, there came to us what the residents call "the January thaw"–(it happens every year nearly–only, last year being a severe winter, there was none then.). The temperature rose some 15 degrees, the air felt soft and mild, the snow and ice melted, the houses dripped with water (exteriorly)–it was like spring coming. Of course, Jowie opened every window in the house, to enjoy the freshness, and the thorough ventilation; and when I came in from my duties in the forenoon, I found her drawing rather injudiciously near one of the open windows. I took the alarm at once, but, unfortunately, it was too late; she had caught a fresh cold. The day before yesterday, she was influenza-ish, and I nursed and coddled her into convalescence; to-day she is quite free from everything but weakness, and just a *remnant* of a stiff feeling in the throat (*really and truly* this is *all*); but I do so want her to get back her full strength quite "at one go" so to speak, that I have begged her only to write you the merest line. I have no doubt she might write you a long letter without bad effects, but I want to err on the safe side this once. (Only my *excess* of precaution, which you, her mother, understand, *almost* as well as I!)

The mail only reached us *this* morning–*ten days over due*–had to call at Newfoundland, with a Governor![1] We are *much* pleased with the get up of Mrs. O. Jowie must say the rest. Best love to all

Your afft   Alexander Ewing.

[JHE's Continuation]

My darling Mum

My outrageously careful Ogre will hardly let me say a word – as he tells you! In the present state of delayed mails I think if I had been less well I should not have told you of my little relapse – because I *could* not give you the worry of "waiting" to hear that I was all right again. As it is I have at least the merit of judiciously timing my little breakdown "between posts"!!

Please tell Bell I am *utterly delighted* with Mrs. O. It is one of the most refined, delicate "get ups" I ever saw. There are one or two printer's blunders devised especially for this edition – but n'importe. I will write to him next mail. It is lovely!

Tell dear Dina I *do* congratulate her on the possession of Michelet![2] – & thank her – Eleanor – Brownie – Steenie & yr dear self & Dot for all your contributions to this welcome mail. Rex & I have been splitting over Happy Thoughts. Rex performed the Lancers figure on the lawn across the room as he read!!![3]

Hector has been with me a great part of today – when Rex reads the Bible he wags his tail imagining it addressed to him . . . .

Goodbye darling Mum
Your loving Judy.

LETTER
72

Septuagesima. [24 January] 1869.
Fredericton.

My darling Dot.

Many many many happy returns of your birthday you dear old thing! (I cannot remember your exact age.[1] I wish some day somebody would send me a list of the birthdays & ages of the family!!!!) The 2d now since we left Home! –

It was a delightful Mail this time. "Long looked for, come at last"–is our "mortar" now, as Mrs. Gamp would say, for the passages seem very slow at present. Then the intermediate letters did not come betwixt & between, they arrived *with* the Halifax mail. *Why*–I have ceased to hope to discover. The time before they broke the gap nicely. But both batches were most welcome! One set dated "Xmas Eve"–& the other "New Year's Day." You seem to have had a very nice Xmas, & by this time you know that *we* had a very happy one in our small way. It does not do to dwell on the thought of what it would have been to be one of the family party at Home–& indeed nothing could be more ungrateful–when we were so happy together *here*, & then get such happy accounts of all you *there*. . . . The theatricals went off very well. There were 3 pieces. "An ample Apology" (a very amusing farce for 4 actors.) "Vilikins & his Dinah" (burlesque, music arranged by Rex.) & "Taming a Tiger" (which is our old friend with the parts of Dolly & Arabella cut out). Mr. Backhouse who acted the lady in the Ample Apology was *1st rate. I* never saw a man do a lady's part one 10th part so well. It & the burlesque were the most successful. I don't think the Tiger was as good as our own–though the get ups were good–but there was hardly a laugh, & Rex "can't see any fun in it"—!!!!! They acted well–but too *tamely* & this, with the withdrawal of "the females" gave a *sameness* to it– It was like one long interview between the 2 men–& they moved about so little, it really got *dull. One* scene they much excelled us in–where Jacob watches the fishpond scene from the window. Mr. Woolsely as Jacob–was admirable. I don't care much for burlesques–but Vilikins was very amusing. Rex was admirable as "Grumbleton Gruffin" the father of Dinah–& his "get up" was certainly equal if not superior to the rest–which after all my anxieties was comforting.[2] After the 3rd night there was a "supper" at the Mess which Rex attended, & where his health was proposed in a long speech, & "He's a jolly good fellow" was sung to one of the airs in the burlesque with all the verses & with such unanimity in time & tune as the memories & musical abilities of the party allowed!! Mrs. Carey (22d) said to me the other day "An opportunity offers for you to become permanently attached to the 22d. The band say that if they only had Mr.

Ewing to teach them always—they *would* practise!" I said *my* objection was that Bandmasters' wives are not "received" in military society (which N.B. I think a great mistake) She further told me that they said Mr. Ewing always knew *who* it was that played the wrong note when any mistake occurred—(no compliment to Wichtendahl the present bandmaster—that it shld be a wonder!) & the last practice Rex told me that when he had occasion to say to one of the men in the middle of something "That F— *sharp* if you please!" he saw a smile go round among the bandsmen who were looking on. One admirable result has accrued from all this—which seems a funny result from a burlesque practice. You must know that the military service here is rather a scandal. Mr. Coster who is Chaplain is *un*ritualistic to slovenliness (though a kind good man) They don't use Ancient & Modern—though it is prescribed—they always have a mutilated service—& the music is *awful*—one loud trombone being *the* feature, and as the band were attached to their own style, & none of the officers take any interest in it, (& those officers who kneel & behave well at the Cathedral services—with that extraordinary shamefacedness or whatever it is of Englishmen—never kneel, or give to the offertory, or do anything they ought to at the "Soldier's Service." So it is a literal "Church *parade*" & by all accounts a far from seemly one!)—hitherto it has seemed hopeless. But there has been a stir among the dry bones—& the queer old Col. has issued orders to Wichtendahle to amend the music. Now his English is of the poorest & his knowledge of *Ecclesiastical* music—nil, but the band have rescued themselves, by suggesting to Mr. Coster that "if Mr. Ewing would undertake it" all wld go right. So as Rex says, there is "one more iron in the fire," & I rejoice to see the thin edge of a wedge I have long desired fairly inserted!!

Rex is very busy still. There is a good deal more to do now—at least a great variety of things. He & Major Cox now have to make inspections together so Major C. was up the other day, & sat with me all the afternoon—Rex being out. As he had been having laryngitis—the 60 miles here & 60 miles back to S. John in a sleigh in one of our "cold spells" can hardly have been beneficial! The day he & Rex had to "inspect barracks" the wind was so bitter that Rex's cheeks got scorched—& were red, swollen, & *hard*. They are coming right however. Another man with them, requested Rex to do him the civility of telling him how his ears looked – as he could no longer feel them! – *I* am just keeping indoors till this "nip" is past – for there is no sunshine just now – & nothing to tempt one to face the cold. Zebbi Cox sent especial word to me to enquire how the Mum was. I wish she lived nearer – it would be a great pleasure to *me*, and she says to *her*. He is clever & crotchetty, which I believe is characteristic of Engineers (they are said to be always either "mad – or married – or methodist." I can *just* trace a soupçon of all 3 in our friend! he *is* crotchetty – a *very* devoted husband – & "serious" in that rather unorthodox style characteristic of military men) His mind is one of that type in which "suppositions" & "propositions" & queries of all kinds are always seething to the surface, so when we meet (which we do by his always calling when he comes up professionally) we generally talk for hours. On Friday some of the questions raised were "Will a wave of barbarism ever sweep away the Civilization of Europe as former Civilizations have been swept away?" I thought *not*, & gave my reasons. "Do savages – & people like the indians here – respect and admire us for our superior cleverness, & our civilization, for instance does a *railway* adequately impress them?" Again I thought *no*, & gave my reasons partly based on the Legend of Sologne[3] – tell the Mum!!!!!! & partly on the study of my "brother Peter." We had also a little Colenso[4] & Irish Church – lightened by afternoon tea!! & I consulted him professionally as to the safety of our hall stove!!

(N.B. Hetty has been out, & tells me it is "quite warm." So perhaps the "nip" is past!)

We are going to dine with the Maunsells on Wednesday, & to have our own musical parties some time before Lent.

Major Graham has got his brevet rank & is Colonel now.

Mrs. Medley is *much* better.

There was a fire the other night, but the new *steam* fire engine does wonders.[5] The old things were like so many garden syringes.

Driscoll reappeared in town the other day & was very abusive to the soldiers on guard at Govt House – but he has been withdrawn from Fredericton once more we are happy to say.

There is talk of some private theatricals now, in which I suppose – I shall probably join.

We are at a very low ebb for altos. This morning there were
only 2 on the decani & none on the cantoris side: so Rex had to sing
Tenor with the decani & Alto with the cantoris!!!

No Scheme news: & this is all the Fredericton news I think.
No – by the bye! – Did I ever tell you of "Kethro the Barber" – He is
an Englishman – an odd pomposo kind of man – awfully conceited,
& with a bee in his bonnet (he has been in confinement) – but not a
bad fellow. He sang tenor in the Choir – but somebody else singing
a solo he considered *his* – he withdrew to the Baptists (or some
other body) The Bishop called to remonstrate – & dwelt on the sin
of leaving the Church for a personal pique &c. Kethro argued with
his usual crackiness – one part of his learned defense being "After
all, my Lord, you know the Bible shows us there were sects in the
Early Church. Why, there were seven Churches of Asia!" There are
lots of good stories of his sayings, & he is a well known character.
Well. Last mail brought out a new ensign to join the 22d who is
reported to be a university man – a little inclined to "set everybody
to rights." On the last night of the theatricals Kethro was present in
a front seat, which suggested to some of the youngsters in the 22d
the following joke. One of them said to the new ensign – "You
know our colonial dignitaries here are very different to that sort of

thing in England. You mustn't expect to see the sort
of men who fill these posts at Home. You wouldn't
think now, that that was our chief Justice?" (point-
ing out Kethro.) Eventually he was introduced to
Kethro under that title – & Kethro who has that sort
of wit which often accompanies a loose tile – took
the joke admirably, & kept up a long and affable
conversation with Mr. White. As he is very talk-
ative & opinionated in his line – it must have been
splendid. At the "latest advices" Mr. White is still
deluded![6] –

"Peter" has made Rex a lovely baton of white
wood – merely from my description & the roughest

of sketches— The heavy end is weighted by a carved figure of an indian with his feet on a moose head—& a beaver climbing up his back.

My dear—did you ever get the 4 photo.s I sent to *you*. Gabe's portrait among them. The *Mum* thanked me for the little photo.s & adds "Did I ever thank you for the beaver's house &c." I hope she hasn't taken *your* photo.s Surely I wasn't such a goose as to have sent her *duplicates* of the beaver dam. Eh? I should like to know how it is.

. . . The burlesque party are going to be taken, & when they are ready I will send a copy [Plate 14].⁷ *We* are going to be done instanter!!!!!

Our dear love to all—& special love to Maggie & Frank. Of course they get the news from you. Your most loving sister

Judy.

LETTER
73

Sexagesima. [31 January] 1869.
Fredericton.

My dearest Mum.

As the mail is still not heard of, the intermediate letters this time were doubly welcome. If it is any help towards solving our postal problems—know that the latest Halifax letters were dated Jan. 1. & that those (Dot's & yours) which came by the intermediate mail were dated Jan 8. & (oddly enough) had no *route* direction (I mean there was no "viâ" anything on the envelope.)!!!! Of course we cannot tell whether any of our letters *were* lost in the "City of New York" especially as the slip of newspaper you sent had no date: but as far as we could calculate—I do not think my *story* can have been with that mail.¹ Even if it were, it would only involve *trouble*. For I make rough & final copies of everything I send across the uncertain ocean!!!!—so I cld write it out again, though I would rather not! . . .

I told Mrs. Parry how you sympathized with her. *Her* mother, also, is a great advocate of chloroform, & will be very indignant.[2] However, Mrs. P. herself is particularly flourishing just now — & the 2 latest cases among the ladies of the regt have been such remarkably good precedents, that I tell her this ought to cheer her. The first time I walked with Rex to his office, (according to my morning custom), after I got well, I received quite an ovation from the Parrys. I think I told you that I often turn in there for a chat on these occasions — They live just opposite to Rex's office, & as we leave our house about 9, the Parrys are generally at breakfast, Parry in uniform with a travelling clock at his elbow that he may not be late for parade! Hector jumped on me as if we had not met for years — & I had a supplementary breakfast, & afterwards spent most of the morning with Mrs. P. Friday last was a charming day. One of our clear, brilliant, cold & sunshine days. I was out almost the whole day & enjoyed it greatly. For it has been rather provoking lately that the weather has not been nice — dull — raw — bitter days when really it was not wisdom to go out for anyone but *very* tough individuals — & staying indoors with stoves & double windows is not pleasant for any length of time. First I went "up the town" with Rex — & with him over his "stores" (the ones newly put under him — with barrack & hospital things — amongst which it was curious to see some dozen & 1/2 iron "dogs" — belonging to the officers'

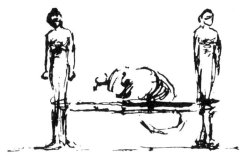

quarters before the days of stoves. They were very pretty. 2 female figures. Then I went into Mrs. Parry's. Then I went to see Mrs. Medley, & as she was going out driving, the Bishop proposed that he & I shld have a walk, so away we went — to the Post to ask after

the Mail – to my doctor's to ask how *he* was, for he has been ill – &
back again. Then we met Rex on his road to the photographer's, so
with him we retraced our steps up the town & saw the proofs of the
2 groups from the burlesque – of which we hope to send you
specimens by this mail. I think we ourselves are to be done (in our
own characters!) next week. We also send a local 'notice' of the
theatricals – in which (I think) they do no manner of justice to Mr.
Wolsley. . . . Since Dot admires the heartsease on Mrs. O. I hope
she is aware that the idea was *mine*. That I choose the color, &
material of the binding – & said that I wished the name to be in the
middle, & on the side of the book, & in a wreath of heartsease for
which I gave Bell a little rough sketch. *I* would have preferred it if
Bell had kept the block for *my* books, but one cannot expect
everything to go exactly as one wishes – especially with the Atlantic
between us. He complained to me of the expense of the block
(£10.10.0 I think) – but I suppose he will charge half of that to Miss
Jones' book.³ However I have nothing to do with that – though if I
had had my choice, I think I would have been satisfied with less pay
for this edition to have my binding to myself!!!!!

I am sending you 2 fairy stories – for yr editorial consideration.
They are not intended to form part of "The Brownies" book – they
are an experiment on my part – & *I do not mean to put my name to
them*.⁴ Please remember this. You know how fond I have always
been of fairy stories of the Grimm type. Modern fairy tales always
seem to me such *very* poor things by comparison & I have 2 or 3
theories about the reason of this. In old days when I used to tell
stories to the others – I used to have to produce them in considerable numbers & without much preparation, & as that argues a
certain amount of imagination – I have determined to try if I can
write a few fairytales of the genuine "uninstructive" type by following out my theories in reference to the old traditional ones.
Please *don't* let out who writes them (if you put them in – & if anyone cares to enquire!) – for I am very anxious to hear if they elicit
any comments from your correspondents to confirm me in my
views. In one sense you must not expect them to be original. *My
aim is* to imitate the "old originals" – & I mean to stick close to
orthodox traditions in reference to the proceedings of elves –

dwarfs – nixes – pixies – &c. & if I want them – to use such "common properties" of the fairy stage – as unscrupulous foxes – stupid giants – successful younger sons – & the traditional "fool" – with much wisdom under his folly (such as Hans in Luck) – who suggests the court fools with their odd mixture of folly & shrewdness. *One* of my theories is that all real fairy tales (of course I do not allude to stories of a totally different character in which fairy machinery is used – as your Fairy-Godmothers[5] – My 'Brownies' &c. &c.) – that all real 'fairy tales' shld be written as if they were oral traditions taken down from the lips of a "story teller" – This is where modern ones (& modern editions of Grimm – vide "Grimm's Goblins"[6] – otherwise a delicious book) fail, & the extent to which I have had to cut out reflections, abandon epithets, & shorten sentences, since I began, very much confirms my ideas. I think the Spanish ones in A.J.M. must have been so obtained – & the contrast between them & the 'Lost Legends'[7] in this respect is marked. There are plenty of children who can appreciate The Rose & the Ring – the Water Babies – your books – & the most practical & suggestive dreams of Andersen. But (if it can be done) I think there is also a strong demand for new combinations of the Stepmother – the Fox – the Luck Child – & the Kings – Princesses – Giants – Witches – &c. of the old-traditions. I say combinations advisedly, for I suppose *not* 1/2 of Grimm's Household Stories have "original" plots. They are palpable "réchauffés" of each other – & the few original germs might I suspect be counted on one's fingers even in faery-lore & then traced back to a very different origin. Of course the market is abundantly stocked with modern versions but I don't think they are done the right way. This is however for the Editorial Ear – & to gain your unbiased criticism. But above all – don't tell any friends that they are mine – for the present. Of course if they *did* succeed – I wld republish & add my name.[8] But I want to be incognito at present. 1° to get free criticism. 2° to give them fair play. 3° Not to do any damage to my small reputation in another "walk" of story writing. I do not in the least mean to give up my own style & take to mere fairy tale telling – but I wld like to try this experiment. I shall explain this to Bell as I am going to write to him. By the bye don't tell him that I am *greedy* about my binding. It's done now – & no use bothering. I shall send more tales soon–& I hope better ones. Last night I finished the Water Sprite one[9]–& when we were in bed Rex asked me what it was about. Now he generally likes to read things for himself–& you know I am not successful in imparting ideas of my own stories (in my own style I mean) so I was rather elated by his hearing the story all through as if he were a little boy & (to my astonishment!) being delighted with it. He said it "just suited him." I must add that during the last few words of the *other* tale he fell fast asleep!!!!!!! But so far he "wants more"–which is satisfactory! What does Bell give you per 1000 for editions of your 3/6 books? Pray don't tell him I have asked this–or he might think I am dissatisfied with his arrangements with me *which I am not.* I only asked for curiosity.

We are going to have a musical party next Monday–so I am rather busy. *Feb. 2.* The mail still not in. We *may* get it tomorrow. You may expect 2 more tales by next mail–but don't take them unless you like them of course.

Our dear love to all. I mean to write Maggie next, tell her with my best love.

I have some lovely narcissus out. One stem has 8 flowers at the head. I hope my rooms may have a "faint aristocratic odour" (if not overpowered by the near neighborhood of the kitchen!) next Monday. Ever dear Mum

Your most loving daughter
Judy

LETTER

74

Quinquagesima. [7 February] 1869.
Fredericton N.B.

My darling Dot.

I began a letter to you the day before yesterday & now I cannot find it. Sometimes things get *so* lost, that one's only chance of finding them is to assert superiority by doing without them. It is the old

story of finding your silver thimble by buying a brass one, & I have
no doubt my commencement will now turn up. Since I wrote it I
have had a tooth out!!! Tell the Mum this, & she will find one more
item of consolation for our separation, when she thinks of being
spared the sight of my previous paroxysms of toothache, as well as
the final *screewaunds*. You know I had some neuralgia as part of my
seedyness the other day, & we kept thinking this might be neuralgia
also. At last on Friday, (when I was in the thick of my calculations
for a party of 30 on Monday!) it got *werry* bad, & the dear little
Bishop came ploughing through the deep snow to say that I might
have the close sleigh if I wld like to go & consult Dr. Dow the
dentist. So I wrote to Dr. D. who appointed 3 P. M. but about 2 when
I was lying very miserable on the sofa he drove down himself—saying he cld not bring me out on such a day. (we have had
heavy snowstorms) I must tell you how blest we are in this respect,
as in so many others, not to be anticipated in this out of the way
land. We have a first class dentist. Though he *advertizes*—like the
Jew Mozelys[1]—& is a little french looking Yankee—& a stump
orator who (after many personalities freely exchanged in the public
street before an enlightened audience) crushed his opponent once
(in Rex's hearing) by the withering hit "Why the very teeth in his
mouth are mine, & *not paid for!*" though in fact he is the very anti-
podes of Hanover Square in his style[2]—he is fully all that Mrs.
Medley told me. She said she had been under the 1st men in London
& Paris—& that Dow beat them beyond all comparison.[3] He usually
uses Nitrous Oxide (Laughing Gas) to deaden your pain—but being
'out of' this he brought chloroform—gave it me in the neatest manner—took out my tooth (I felt *nothing*) & Rex said it was a perfect
triumph of dentistry— The instrument was no sooner in than the
tooth was out. He says "The pain is *so* bad—that an operator cannot
be too quick, & my aim is to break the nerve at once." One of the
last things I heard him say as I dozed off was "I'm pretty well *posted*
in chloroform—before we got the gas, I always had it for my own
teeth." You must imagine the Yankee accent!—

Monday [8 February]. My deary, The cares of a supper for 30 &
the adjustment of our small rooms really leave me no time for
a long letter—especially as Rex's *one* object is that I should

"rest"!!!!!!! He has written the loveliest little song to Miss Proctor's words "A doubting heart"![4] He did it just after breakfast this
morning.

Hector's nose is out of joint as I tell him now freely. But (as I
also tell him) he is still the Son and heir! Mrs. P. has got a little girl.[5]
A very fine one. She got through it in the same splendid style as
Mrs. Chauncey & Mrs. Carey—was ill a very short time—& everything is couleur de rose. As this seems to be in the season—I hope
to hear equally good news of dear Maggie before long. I shall not
send the photo.s of the theatricals *today*—as I want them for my
visitors tonight— Programmes of the music for our party are being
written out in splendid style by Rex's hospital sergeant who has a
fist "like print." My toothache has prevented my writing out the 2
other fairy stories—but they will come shortly. The weather is *very*
fine, & the snow "packing" so as to be lovely to walk or snowshoe
on. Hector is spending the day with us—& our party confusion—
upsets him nearly as much as the reign of Gamp & Co. at the
Parry's. Rex wants to know if I "have done." I'm sure the Gardens
of Hesperides were not better guarded than my health is. Tell the
Mum "Grandmamma's throat"[6] was written a year or two too
soon— She shld have waited to see maternal anxieties reproduced
in an over anxious (because so good & loving!) husband. Yours
(under orders to stop)

Judy.

LETTER
75

20. Feb. 1869. Saturday
(to go on Monday. 22.)
Fredericton N.B.

My dearest Mater.

I hope you were not too much excited by my letter to Dina! Rex
was quite vexed with me for having said so much. He said you

would feel as if there were really a probability of seeing me in the Summer–& then be doubly disappointed if we were *not* ordered 'Home. But in the 1st place, you have always been so awfully good about it, (from the parting day when *you* were the brave one–though *I* was beginning life with my dear old Boy–down to your present philosophy about my colds &c. &c. out here), that I sent my letter–in spite of all. I think, too, I judged you by myself, & to *me*–the little excitements of a possible move–are so many "breaks" in the time; & reminders that sooner or later we may hope to be "ordered Home." If there were any other evils connected with our being out here–except that we cannot see you all as often as we wld like–it wld be different. But as we are so truly happy here, & *you* are so happy that *we* are happy–I think you would like to hear of all our ups & downs and bits of news–even if they some-times come to nought.

Monday. 22d. I have been so busy (domestically) today; that whether I shall be able to finish copying out the "Nix in Mischief,"[1] is very doubtful I think–& Rex has no time to help me now. Not having sufficiently scraped the snow from our roof, this morning we have had a "general thaw" in the house & the wet has been pour-ing into my pretty drawing room!! The more modern houses are better built in reference to the snow–with deeper eaves &c.– I feel rather ashamed of myself—but my successive colds about Xmas-tide stood in the way of explorations into outhouses, woodsheds, & cold cellars; & general ice & snow investigations!! And my dear old man's genius is more towards "Literature & the Fine Arts" (as poor little Mrs. Shore said!) than towards domestic provenience!!– *I* manage "man & maid"–& as I said–I *do* feel ashamed of myself now the wet is dripping in. Our man did do that side of the house to which the "fire ladder" is attached–but (not being a resident or a bricklayer!) he "funked" going down the other side with a rope, & everybody's ladders almost–are frozen to their houses, & after trying to borrow one–I suppose I got one of my colds or something & forgot about it. "Hinc illae" &c. &c. !!!! Rex wanted to do it him-self this morning–but though *he* doesn't mind sliding down a roof with a rope & shovel, his wife would "reether not"–that he did so! However, we have got a ladder–& Kendal has accomplished the work, & only broken one window pane!!! & I have been "having out" the cabbages–apples–jams–&c. lately–to see what were "good" & what rotten–tearing the sheets down the middle (where they are beginning to wear) & seaming the sides together for the centre that they may wear evenly–&c. &c. &c. But the *more* one housekeeps (tell Dot!) the more immortal becomes the Duke's motto!!! I thought I had *nearly* complied with it when I plunged into the coal house the other day, & made Kendal bring out all the rotting artichokes which his irish predecessor had thrown there till a 'convanient' season for storing them properly in the cellar–besides fragments of carpet–newspapers–&c. & insisted that the garden spade should *not* be used as a coal shovel! I duly instructed him that the refuse shld be put on the rubbish heap till we could have our Spring bonfire–& retired, not sufficiently warmed by the argument to do without a fire any longer. He is a very nice, good humoured–steady young fellow–but (as Hetty emphatically observes) 'rather *soft*'–& he simply devised a perfectly fresh "irish corner" within sight of the dining room window, where the coal dust & rotten vegetables do *not* ornament the "soft white ermine snow"—!!! As it is several feet deep–I can easily have it remedied. But you see just now I am rather busy. I have a good deal to *do*, & my old boy won't let me *over*do. We have no news, except that if anything can be guessed of *our* movements–it seems possible that Rex will be in 'sole charge' of N. Brunswick, (Control: and Supply Departmentally speaking!!!!!). If so–we shall be stationed at S. John. N.B. Next to Home–I wld like to remain here. Next to *that*–I think S. John. It has many advantages. It *is* a very uninteresting town–& I wld *like* to see Montreal or Quebec (the latter especially.) But after all–unless you have lots of tin–you see no more of the general features or particular lions of a country by being quartered there–than one necessarily wld see the British Museum or the historical lions of Britain by being stationed at Halifax Yorkshire–instead of Halifax Nova Scotia. We have never been to "Grand Falls" yet–though it is *the* lion of this station. It wld cost about £5, & all being well, we mean to treat ourselves in Spring, & could do this from S. John almost as easily as hence. Mr. Dowling says it satisfied him on the whole–better than Niagara. Of course the latter is on a larger scale–but its surroundings are so cockneyfied now–that you get little idea of what it was before it became a recognised lion. "Grand Falls" still pour down –surrounded by rocks & forests as of old–& I can well believe that *size* at Niagara does not repay you for the want of suitable accessories to its grandeur. Now if we were moved to Quebec or even a pretty & healthy W. Indian station–we must lose (pecuniarily) by "3 moves" within 2 years–& this materially diminishes the benefits of cheap living in Fredericton–& we are not likely to find another station nearly so cheap! If we go to S. John.—living & rent are not *very* much dearer– The expense of moving–a trifle to what it wld be even to Halifax.– We could *take* some of our things instead of selling them for an old song when all the 1/22d. "sell up" also— The *Coxes* will probably be unaffected by the change–& that would be very nice, (to be near Zebbi I mean.) We quite *liked* S. John the last time we were there. I saw dear little gardens in the outskirts–& I do think the sea breezes did me good in the 2 days we were there. *Living* is dearer–but the shops are better & cheaper (in the "dry goods" line¹)– The climate is *damper*–but with *sea* damp–& is cooler in summer & warmer in winter than here– The lovely "steam" from there to Fredericton in Summer–only costs a few shillings–& if we *do* go–the railway will probably be finished by that time²–& (as Rex says) we might "run up for choir practice"–& go back– To *that* I do look forward–for the line I suspect will be lovely–running through these lovely woods–& by this beautiful river! *If* we go— & *if* we spend the rest of our foreign term there–& *if* you would lend me Dina during the summer–it wld be infinitely more convenient for *that*. She wld come *direct* & as S. John is much "gayer" than Fredericton–I think she wld really enjoy it–& come up & see our old home as well. Fredericton wld be under Rex all the same; & *he* wld be obliged to come from time to time. Once–Fton was the Headquarters–& might possibly be so again. Really no one knows anything. We *may* be sent anywhere to do anything–but I am quite prepared for anything that has been suggested yet–to really *like it* I mean! I am feel-. ing quite brisk & strong again–& awfully happy! *If* S. John is to be our home this summer–my aquarium will become a *sea*:one I

fancy! & if I were to get at all "over roasted" by the heat (or Dina either if she were here) a few streets & a *ferry* will bring us to the fashionable bathing place of the neighborhood – where people from here go to refresh themselves after the summer heat. If Eleanor persuades *her* mother & I have both, we will have great larks!!! & *you* shall be rewarded with *beaveeds*. But this is all "ifs and ands" — I hope I am right in telling you all our news as we hear it. But you & I generally understand each other — & what I wld like – I think *you* will dear dear Mum! — If today had been fine, I think we should have gone to be photoed, but it is dull. I have been very busy "gardening" among my indoor plants: but on that subject I mean to write Miss Thompson a long letter at once – so will spare you! Let me boast that I had 29 flowers in one pot of Polyanthus Narcissus (Soleil d'Or). I do so enjoy faddling with them! It is past 3 – & I must condense my news into the form of "our carpet bag" in the Era – & the de omnibus rebus of the local papers.[3] These are *vilely* vulgar in style – & generally very aristocratic in topic – thus — "the Queen is becoming ritualistic" – "The Princess Royal feels strongly on the rights of women question" "An heir to an English peerage has forged his brother's name for (indefinite no. of dollars!) and *cleared out.*" —— & so forth!!!
Well:

The inhabitants of Fredericton are very flattering in their re-grets at our departure.

Miss Parker proposes that Mr. Ewing be elected Governor by universal suffrage.

Two other ladies propose that Mrs. Ewing be bullied into bully-ing him to take Holy Orders & become the Bishop's Chaplain. (It is thought that one of these who has a squabble with the present holder of that office wld not object to see "Vice So & So. super-seded!" – but this is scandal)

Rex has gained 3 chest notes since he came to New Bruns-wick – & is now the principal Alto of the Cathedral: & has a 'lovely voice.'

His wife "always said so."

Mrs. Ewing made a "moose steak pie" on Saturday night – rather successfully.

On the same day Miss Parker brought *Mr*. E. a mould of the "particular"–to be eaten entirely by himself– It was in the shape of a *rabbit!*

The snow is 8 feet deep in the streets of Montreal & already much deeper than last year–*here.*

We hope to see a splendid "freshet" when it breaks up–for as there is no chance of being tolerably dry–we may as well be remarkably & famously wet!!

Mrs. Medley is better–but (I think) *very* fragile. It is complicated. I think she wld *like* a letter from you–if you like to write.

> Our dear dear love
> In haste– Your loving
> Judy.

(*How about my Diary?* Was it ever sent?)

I shall try the Thursday Mail this week I think to dear old Maggie.

Mrs. Parry getting on famously.

LETTER

76

Fredericton. New Brunswick. Canada.
Feb. 23. 1869.

My dear Miss Thompson.[1]

I know you will sympathize with me in the joys & sorrows of my window garden during this long & severe winter. Not that it has been anything like so cold as the last year's was, but I mean that the length of Canadian winters & the intensity of the frost make indoor gardening very different to what it is at Home. On the other hand anything *green*–growing–& sweet is doubly & trebly welcome when every trace of one's garden is buried 4 or 5 feet deep in snow – & the ground is frozen *so* hard that you know that there is no getting at anything that you did not take up in the Autumn (or even a bit of garden mould) till May! – *I* have been much more successful this year than last. 1st – Our little house will keep out the extreme frost – & the other one we lived in last year – would not. (we used to carry the hyacinth pots up to bed with us – put them round the stove – & bury them in dressing gowns &c. but the poor things were frozen & thawed – over & over again!! 2dly – Last year I bought my bulbs here, & they were not first rate I think. This year (the Bishop was kind enough to bring them – &) I got them from *Carter &*. *Sons* at Home. They were not kept *dry* enough – & when I got them mould had begun. I lost *all* the aconites – & anemones – & almost all the snowdrops & crocuses – but my hyacinths & narcissi – & tulips were none the worse – & have been most successful. I only lost *one* bulb – (a hyacinth) by a sharp frost. I planted them in leafmould & sand just as I used to do at home – kept them in my dress closet in my room for their *dark* month, & brought them out by degrees into my "forcing house."!!!! This is the tiny "landing" at the top of the stairs. It has a window – & what is called a "dumb stove" – i.e. a "drum" or box of iron through which the pipe of the hall stove runs – & which thus warms the upper part of the house. The

My Forcing-house.

window is very near it, & on the window sill I *force* my bulbs! But every night–I have to move them from the glass (though we have double windows)–as if a "snap" of increased frost came, I might lose them one & all. Our house is very warm, & they would probably be safe 6 nights in 7–but if one doesn't do it always one is apt  to forget on the cold nights–& I have lost one hyacinth–my only rose–& some other things already, besides my poor Calla Ethiopica which was just looking grand!! 3dly Mrs. Medley is such an admirable gardener that I get many hints from her. I do wish you *could* see *her* window gardens! She has long narrow boxes (I think I shall try them next year) just painted green. Two iron supports (wood of course wld do, but you can buy the iron ones for screwing on, & they are prettier) are just screwed on to the woodwork of the windows–& a shelf or ledge of wood (also green) laid on them. On to this the box is put–& lifted backwards & forwards as is needful. The pots are just sunk in the box with saucers beneath & moss round them. She has variegated sweet geraniums–kept *very dwarf* in pots & lycopods (like the "stag's horn moss" on the moors) which was got in the autumn & which is not growing, but still looks wonderfully green–(& will freshen up by soaking a night in a pail of water) The *flowers* this year have been hyacinths, tulips, narcissi, crocuses, scillas, lachenalias, & cyclamens, with little bunches of *lichen*, & some red "highbush cranberry" berries dotted about (*not* growing) The boxes are quite narrow–only holding one pot in width, & just the length of the window sill. She has no greenhouse–pit–or any*thing* that you & I had not at Home–& she doesn't line her boxes with zinc–or buy "forcing cases" or do anything expensive or out of *my* reach–which makes her hints more valuable to *me* than book receipts. She rears, & coddles all her bulbs, seeds, cuttings &c. in the windows of her bedroom, the Bishop's study, & the landing; & has not even a gardener or any garden but a very narrow strip in front of the house shaded by trees, & facing east. When you look at *my* illustrations–I fear you will think of Barr and Sugden's Catalogues, & how easy it is to *draw* "Zinnia Elegans Flore-pleno" the size of a prize dahlia & correspondingly rounded in outline & full in quill; & how far from easy we found it to produce similar specimens in the garden!!² So I will give you one or two statistics. I only treated myself to 3 polyanthus narcissi (all "soleil d'or") & put the 3 bulbs into one pot – They sent up 4 stems – & I have counted 29 blossoms. I had one *exquisite* blush single hyacinth (name lost) which sent up a stem with 18 very large bells: the same bulb has now sent up a second stem with 9 bells quite as large as the others. I have pressed one of the 2d lot against my penholder – & from point to point the spread petals are as wide as the line I have drawn. In

the same pot was a single white *faintly* tinged with yellow (*Rousseau*) Also very fine. The first stalk bore 18 bells – & the 2d seems to have 30 – but I can hardly be *certain* yet – they are so closely packed. That makes 75 bells from the 2 bulbs in one pot. I only had 9 hyacinths – they have certainly *fully* repaid me. *I* never had such blooms as some of them, I think. I lost one – gave one away – & the other 7 have been a great enjoyment to me. Now that we have

My Greenhouse.

given notice to leave our house in May – I have no *garden* to consider – so I brought everything I have to the windows, & commenced Spring forcing as soon as I heard the news; for I may as well enjoy them as *pot* plants. Our house is taken already but I hope the next tenant will be civil, & let me take the wild flowers & ferns &c. &c. that I stored in my little flower patch last summer. I have a large patch of Sweet Williams from Ecclesfield seed too – in the kitchen garden! It is one of the inconveniences of military life – that one may be moved *just* as one begins to settle down – & get a

home about one. This is a small cross however!— And we have so
many comforts & blessings, that I do not complain. We know
nothing whatever of our movements except that if we remain *here*,
we shall probably go into quarters. There I should probably have a
sunny aspect & a verandah before my windows—which I mean to
hang with flowerbaskets & fill with plants. In summer it wld be
really pretty. For it looks upon the green where the bands play—&
on the river—& the big willows where tree fireflies float about like
sparks of fire—after sunset. I am now forcing on my few things—
that I may make cuttings from them in good time, & increase my
stock: for plants &c. are very dear here: & as we do not know *when*
we may move (nor where) I spend as little ready cash as *possible* just
now—since we might want it all at a few weeks' notice to pay my
journey expenses, & furnish our *3d move!* I fear there is no chance
of our coming Home—but we know nothing.

I had lovely major convolvulus last year, & yesterday—walking
on snowshoes in my garden (The snow is nearly up to the top of the
palings, & I walked over my latest sowing of *peas*—across the top of
the peasticks!!!)—I saw some of the seed vessels still hanging from
the house. I wonder if the frost has killed it—or whether the seeds
wld grow. I shall put one or two in this & you shall try, & when you
write—you shall put one or two seeds from your own stock of seeds
into your letter, if you will, & we will make one link between
Grenoside & New Brunswick!

I am proud of my bulbs—but am perverse enough to be *more*
proud of an English primrose that is coming into bloom—& of 2
cuttings struck in a *bottle*, because I broke them off a beautiful
fuschia at a time not orthodox for "gardener's cuttings"— I have
had such comfort & beauty from the store of moss I laid up before
the winter. It is wonderful how it *revives* in water—& adorns my
flowerpots. If we have a box out in Spring—I will have some from
Home—& I should like a contribution from Greno Wood!

Your always & affat [JHE]

Rex's best regards to you, & mine to Hannah & her husband please.

Alas! I fear the seeds *are* spoilt.

LETTER
77

March. 2. 1869

Darling Mum

What a disgraceful scrap! I enclose the Nix. No mail yet. Expected on Thursday.

The H. C. Vessels sound *lovely*. Do not send anything to us till we have news of our movements – & as yet we have none. Ought we not to see the inscription for the plate before it is engraved? As to the *spelling* of the words I mean. I am not sure I have got Magaguadavie right yet!! [AE's hand: "*'Maguaguadavie'* A.E."] How pleased the parson *will* be & the people also. Thank Father & you again & again for the prospect of Hallamshire[1] & yr book – We have not the most distant idea as to our movements. Absolutely no more time.

Your ever loving Judy.

I have written to Maggie & Miss Thompson.

N.B. If Mrs. O. "takes" – I shall be desperately tempted to throw some ideas that float in my head into that form – for a 2d series. It just suits certain of these ideas – I mean it comes natural to me to evolve them in that "chatty" style.

Nous Verrons! but what do *you* say?

Don't *announce* me though. . . .

LETTER
78

6. March. 1869. Fredericton

My dearest Mum.

. . . I should have devoted this morning to "mail" matters, but that I had to give it up to Mrs. Parry. As a girl her *back* was weak – & neglected so far as to need 3 months recumbent rest – leeches &c. &c. when the doctor *was* sent for! She got *splendidly* through her confinement on the whole, but has (I *thought*) been overdoing herself – & only my enquiries got out of her that she was suffering from *acute* pains where the leeches were applied years ago. So I made a point of going to Mrs. Medley after Morning Prayers (who is confined to the house – but better) & taking counsel with her which ended in my going up the town, & seeing Mrs. Parry fairly at rest on a sofa & extracting a promise that she would try to nurse her baby lying down, & discipline that young person to her convenience, instead of sacrificing herself to "Baby's" acquired habits. That she kept her shoulders flat for 9 days – was no thanks to the Dr. — but a sort of haphazard tradition combined with *my* & *her* "cookery books" warnings!! [1] The Dr. said "9 days! that old wife's 9 days! *Why don't they say* 19?" . . . "and he told me stories of 2 women who worked in *hop gardens* (I think)" says poor Mrs. P.! "and whose babies were born in the field, & what *they* did, &c. &c. &c." *I* could have told *him* of the Chinese – & of a woman whose baby was born in the street below the officers' quarters – When the husband saw she could go no further he walked on, the little stranger was welcomed without pincushions – as a medical moralist might observe – & the officers sent down a few old clothes &c. When she was a little rested – the Mamma took her young hopeful (I believe in Rex's flannel shirt), & joined Papa. But my limited intellect fails to · see the application to Mrs. Parry's case – *unless after carefully ascertaining* that she was both *strong* and *fanciful*!! On her part, it seems doubtful whether she told him she had ever had a weak back – not

271

knowing that it bore on the subject. Excuse my being in rather a *hot* mood! I retract all that I said as to the unpracticality of *poor* people in particular – only however to feel it (doubly distilled) in reference to all classes. One must begin much higher up, & (*pace* the Saty Rev. & Pall Mall!)[2] even with the superior sex!!! Allow me to add that I have (since I wrote to Maggie) – got Mrs. Spain as well as Mrs. Dwyer "on my mind" – & you will forgive the Gampy tone of my letter. Mrs. Parry seems very cheerful – & now she can rest with a quiet conscience – I hope will be none the worse. But I got Capt. P.'s promise not to let her touch a box in "the move" – & I hope Mrs. Medley will get to her tomorrow if not sooner. But we have had some high winds, & Dr. Ward will not let Mrs. M. go out in them – as she has been bothered with palpitations (like yours) & he says the *wind* is apt to make it worse when she is weak. She has been having teeth stopped too – but looks better I think. So you see, dearest Mum, I have some excuse for spending my morning out – but shall possibly write again on Thursday by New York. No news of our moves yet. We are well, & very happy, & very busy! . . .

Goodbye my darling Mum – Our *dear* love to all.

Your own loving daughter J. H. E.

. . .

LETTER

79

[11 March 1869]

My dearest Dot.

This *is* "vile" paper! — and I did flatter myself that at last I had got some fit to write upon! I was quite ashamed to send that letter to the Mum, when I found how "disgusting" it was! But strawpaper, & thin note paper (such as one gets in 1/- or 9d packets at Home) are not to be got here – If I had not been so much hurried – I should not have inflicted the warmth of my feelings about Mrs. P. on her – either: but I had had to spend my whole morning over it – & (besides being "pressed for time") – could hardly turn my head to anything else before post time.

We have no news; & the uncertainty of everything – "What to do with our houses – & where to go when we have done with them" – is the topic of the day with "the military" here. *Our* house is taken. do. the Parrys – The Careys *hope* they may not have to move on May 1. (They live in little Mrs. Shore's house – & it depends on her trustees &c. –) *If* they are left in peace till the Regt goes they have asked the Parrys to go to *them*. If not – there is some talk of Careys & Parrys taking our old house (which has had no tenant since we left it) together; & we have "put in" for a garret if needful! – There was a garret with a *lovely* view & a splendid "studio light" — which we used to call "Charlie's Room" — when we joked about having the whole family out, & "putting you up." It *would* be funny if we were to go back to it for a bit!! But "if ifs and ands were pots and pans" in New Brunswick – we should one & all retire from the uncertainties of military movements & make large fortunes in "hardware stores" — for they certainly abound just now!! as to us. *If* we are kept here – *if* there is a much reduced garrison in Fredericton – *if* we go into quarters – *if* the 1/22d do not get off before May – & make room for us – & *if* Mr. Wetmore is turned out of *his* house – & must come into this & nobody asks us to stay with them — we very likely may share a house with some of the others. But we may be sent to S. John – *or* some other part of Canada – or *anywhere*. One *cannot* guess – but Home seems the *least* likely thing now. Where in England the 1/22d is to be stationed no one knows. Mrs. Graham told me "We all say it is going – where we want it to go – so *I* say *Limerick*!" Mrs. Chauncey's sentiments are that she doesn't care where the Regiment goes to — "I know where *I* am going! – *straight home*.[1] But oh Mrs. Ewing! the river never *will* open this year!" It probably will open with a tremendous "freshet" — as the snow fall has been so much greater than last winter. The view from Charlie's room would be splendid!!

... Rex wants me to come out – deary – & the intermediate mail has not come – & there is no official news from Halifax. But I want to try this American (Thursday) Mail. *We* were photoed yesterday – & hope to see "proofs" tomorrow. *We*=Rex, myself, & the

Bulldogue. He sat *splendidly!* My good man is walking up & down after the manner of roaring lions – & fidgetty dragons! It was 25° fahr warmer last night than the night before – our fires are out – & R. wants me to be the same. It promises to freeze again – but is *lovely* now

Our dear love
Your own loving Judy

He *WON'T* let me go on!!!!!!!!

LETTER
80

15 March. 1869.

My dearest Mum –

As Rex – too justly! – observes – "you would hardly know what it was meant for" – i.e. – this scratch at the top of my letter. It is out of all drawing & was only meant to give you an idea of the depth of snow in "our grounds" — I have long meant to do a sketch from our dining room window this winter. A=the Kitchen wing occupying the same relative position & having an east aspect as that at Home—only with no upper story. B=that pure blue sky popularly appropriated to Italy! C=roof of the wood:shed gleaming with deep snow. D=icicles glittering brighter still. E=the fence I made last summer. All the rest is snow about 4 or 5 feet deep with roads cut through it–making jagged outlines where it is thrown up in banks. But you must be tired of hearing me rave about the beauties of the snow!–

Now I must tell you that our photo.s turned out very well–but Rex wants us to send all together–which we mean to do when we get the snowshoe ones (this week–) As yet we have only got proofs of the Hector group– But the dear old thing sat splendidly. This paper makes one *irate*–which is perhaps unreasonable as one has not to pay more than 100 or 150 per cent (as a general rule) above english prices. Certainly I tried to the other day to get some very common white note paper–such as one gets in England in ^{S}1/- 5 quire packets–& it was ^{S}2/6 *a quire*. Which is 750 per cent– But then one could have written on both sides–which is desirable!!!!!!!!! Joking apart (not that it is a joke!) whatever else we get from Home when we *do* have a parcel–we must get some decent stationery. It is a necessary of life, in somewhat large quantities, to us: & at present I believe we could have arms, crest, & monograms in plain–colored–& gilt stamping & most other paper luxuries, for the money we invest in stuff that is so disgusting to write upon–that one shudders to think what it must be to read!!!! However–till we know something of our future–it is no good having boxes out from England. But do not think that I am indifferent to what I inflict on your dear eyes! No mail yet. And it is not likely to come in before this letter departs. I am quite anxious to know how you like my fairy tales. I have thought of rather a pretty introduction to them, I think; but I fear my style in *that* would betray me. But I cannot decide till I know how you like them. How you will *scream* when you see the photo of the Bulldogue! I think when I come Home some day I shall try my hand on a series of sketches of true incidents in his life. I send you a nice little paper about Magaguadavic, & will get some more from Mrs.

Hannington. Mr. Dowling was here yesterday, & told us–that when he read Mr. H. the bit about the Communion Vessels from the Mission Life[1]–he got awfully excited (he is a delicate, rather excitable man), & was unspeakably pleased. He is a very unassuming, hardworking man, & the paper is utterly *uncooked.* I *think* he worked himself at the church–& neither the needs nor the labors of the people are overstated or colored in *any way*, as far as our observation goes. I think I will send you one of his service lists for this year, & one of Mr. Dowling's that you may understand them–remember that in many of these settlements–there are neither rich people–nor *paupers*–& the people in great part support their ministers by the Offertory. The few really "poor" (such as would receive alms from the Offertory in England) are so from accidental causes–& are–as Mr. Dowling says–so few that he himself can relieve them & attend to them. The necessaries of life are cheap & plentiful– If you want a house–you can fell the wood & build it &c. &c. Those who really have no money to give "Parson" give him a sack of oats–a few potatoes &c. &c. You may also remember–that these churches are often many miles apart–2 of Mr. D.'s have 25 miles of backwood roads between them! I mean to get some more papers for you to give away, & also a photo. of Mr. H. to show–& when I can, I mean to sketch the site, which is very beautiful. . . . We have no news–& look anxiously for it. Almost all of us are to turn out in May–& no one knows when or where to go. *We* shall *probably* be kept in Canada but cannot say! — I am having my boxes mended &c. &c. & making ready for a start, which *may* be only for a destination a few streets away–or may be for Europe– Asia–Africa–or Australia!!!! Meanwhile the Choral Society Concert is coming off–& Rexie is very busy therewith. Mrs. Parry & Mrs. Medley are both *much* better– It is *lovely* weather just now–clear–bright & beautiful. My flowers are really very jolly. I have 7 hyacinths on their last legs–some lovely tournesol tulips–&

such a poor primrose!! It looks out on the snow & seems too much astonished to think of growing!!!! *2 or 3 seeds* of stocks asters or anything Dot has popped into a letter are always acceptable! — No intermediate letters came this week & I am *longing* for the mail! — I mean, if all be well, to send you a parcel by the 1/22d when they go home.

(*Rex's P.S.* Jowie *is* looking better at last. She ate *a whole pudding* a few days ago! And is obliged to eat meat 3 times a day as well! N.B.

Rex)

[JHE's Postscript]

I didn't know what he was going to put!!! "the pudding" is a standard joke against me!!!! Why *cannot* one *laugh* on paper?

LETTER

81

Fredericton. 17. March 1869.

Our very dear Mum,

When your dear letters came this morning (those of Feb. 14. & of Feb. 26) – answering so much that I asked yesterday – & asking for the very thing I sent you – I more than ever regretted the too-provoking delays of the Mail! But, on the whole, I am consoled by being so thankful to get your 2d letter, when you were evidently so much more your dear *self* than on Valentine's Day. It seems strange enough that "nice mild weather" – fine, open, soft, tempting days that persuade one that Spring is come! – do not seem to be healthy in any part of the world, when they come too soon, & intrude on Jack Frost's share of the year. As I told you it really *did* amuse us to hear the old observations reported in reference to this Canadian winter, whose "mildest" days are so much bitterer than your most "severe" ones. And yet our comparatively mild midwinter—seemed to produce as much illness as yours. Low fever, typhus, colds, throats & so forth. Neuralgia too—in plenty. You poor dear Mater!—I do grieve that you should have your anxieties about my health *still*, & at all this distance. But you really *must* recall how *very* little illness I have had since we parted, & I must say that I think—if anything—*I* have had a smaller share of the "green winter" ailments than you at Home seem to have indulged in. You seem all of you to have had something. But you *are* very brave & good! . . . As to the Dentists—they are *wonderfully* good out here! And the Science—seems at last to be making rapid strides. I had the Chloroform on a handkerchief & it was Duncan & Flockhart's[1]—& *in remembrance of you*—I saw to the window sash being "ready for action"—but the utter absence of solemn hocus pocus & the ineffable odours of the dentist's parlour—are great tranquillizers of the nerves! Afterwards I had very similar "1st sensations"—on the other side of my mouth—& as these are all the teeth that Woodhouse patched up when Dina & I were in town, it seemed only too probable that they would go together. So I set my face as flint—& called on "Dow & Ellis" at their own "office". *Do* you know the orthodox dentist's parlour at Home? the nightmares of mahogany sofas—tables &c.—the ornaments bought with the wages of torture, the arm chair that looks as if it came out of Foxe's Book of Martyrs—the volumes of Sermons that fail to console—& the volumes of Punch that are powerless to distract?— — — — Well. It *is* an agreeable change to have to screw up one's courage in a totally different sort of place. High—airy—whitewashed rooms— with screens—light wood american chairs—& 2 sharp eyed intelligent little men who look neither severe, nor professional, nor mysterious, who do not swear that they are not going to hurt you—but *do* declare that they do not think that they or any other dentist ought to do so; & that in a few years dentistry will be painless. It does seem to be progressing with rapid strides—& I believe many of the late discoveries are already in England. "Sponge gold"[2] for stopping—(& one may say—*making* teeth—if you have ever so small a fragment of a tooth—given insensibility to pain & it is to be made into a solid sound & smooth one.) Nitrous Oxide Gas—is "safe" for anybody, & its action so speedy that it seems made for dental operations more than for the prolonged suffering when chloroform can be used.

So in a little while your provincial dentist in Sheffield will either have to be more skillful in his work & more moderate in his prices – than the 1st men in London – or some Yankee adventurers will take the bread out of *his* mouth & put teeth into his customer's!!!!! The moral of which is that I hope yet to know your dear old self indifferent to the toughness of Barlow's Beef!!!!![3] Now I have such heaps of things to talk about that I will only add to *this* subject – that Dow was as positive that nothing was needed in the way of stopping &c. &c. this time – as he had been certain the time before when he pronounced my tooth hopeless. He says the old gold stoppings (he praised Woodhouse's work, tell Dina) make the nerve feel the changes of temperature & cause a little discomfort now & then – *nothing more.* I leave you to imagine the relief!!! I *do* think the other tooth affair helped to pull me down, as well as the influenza. Tooth worries affect one generally – in a degree one hardly perceives at the time.

Now about "All Saints" Magaguadavic.[4] Poor Mr. Hannington is in an indescribable state of delight & gratitude. He called to see me the other day, but unfortunately I was out. But he himself proposed (to Rex) that he should write a letter of thanks – said he "wanted to do so" – (N.B. Hector's nose almost on the paper! He sends love to Grandma' Gage. I said "I'm writing to yer Grandma' Gage. If you send love – wag your tail!" I need hardly add the immediate tattoo!) — Well – Mr. H. told Rex that one evening he was in very low spirits & depressed about matters, when Mr. Dowling took Mission Life & read the bit about the Communion Vessels – & told him. So if so very unexpected a help could have come at a moment more happy than another – that was the moment! I think this will please both you & the children. It seems so nice for a bit of comfort to have come just when all looked dark. This is all for your private ear (or to tell by word of mouth) however. You see I had sent you this nice unpretending little paper – but it does not contain the "latest advices" – & one is in the Bishop's hands for correction. *He* gives the altar (butternut wood I think.) Mrs. Medley the colored cloth. Mr. Pearson – (assistant minister at the Cathedral

& Sub Dean) the Font. *Ecclesfield* the Communion Plate, & there seems a prospect of the fair linen cloth, (a nice plain one can be got for 5 dollars,) & I will tell you how, for it was the reason why I missed Mr. Hannington – & have been busyish – ever since. Mrs. Medley told me she had promised to collect the 5$ & meant to do so. Now I have been waiting to see what *we* could do, so I offered to collect it, & am trying to do so by $1/- subscriptions among the *military* people. For I think we have such "privileges" here as few military stations offer – & ought to do something to help those who so very much benefit us. We could not attempt any *large* thank offering just now when we may any of us be moved any where – any time – with expenses equalling X i.e. – an unknown quantity!! But we purpose to put the 5$ into the Easter Day Offertory. Paper money *is* useful on these occasions as it goes neatly into an envelope (provided the banks remain sound!!!) If I cannot get all I hope for – Rex & I shall make it up ourselves – so you may consider the *linen* provided for. Calling on one of the ladies to beg, I found that her husband had just given her £70 (a not quite expected legacy from an old aunt) & she (*Saty* 20 March. Evening) My dear Mum *she* (i.e. Mrs. Cookesley) has just sent me a 5$ note with the message "use this as you like, for the Church you spoke of – or otherwise" – Is not that good news? *She* did not tell me how much her husband had given her, but I heard it from Mrs. Parry. Do not print Mr. Hannington's account till I give you the latest news. I mean to do so by the Portland Mail – which *may* reach you sooner than this. I am going up to the Dowlings after Easter, & then hope to send you photo. sketch & everything; & when I can describe the place &c. &c. your little report will be so much more complete. The old Master of Rolls was so much pleased with the straightforward little paper that he sent five dollars towards the general subscription list. Mrs. Medley tells me that old Mr. Hannington dined with them on Sunday, & is *very* much pleased by the interest shown in his son's mission. I do not think there is much fear of "Popery" in Mr. Hannington's epistle. He is a native (i.e. a "Bluenose"=a New Brunswicker) – & I mean to send you his photo in which I think you will find nothing more alarming than a want of robustness. It was *his* little baby that I drew in its coffin – you remember. I fancy among settlers fast losing their old civilization & Xtianity in the backwoods—that the Pope does less harm than the Devil; & that one can appreciate the Spirit in which *our* Bishop welcomed the Presbyterian Minister to one of the South Sea Islands;[5] better perhaps than at Home where the difficulties & dangers are of another kind. However–I do not know. I am more & more convinced of the miserable *economy* (so to speak) of starting any good work on any but the true principles. C'est le premier pas qui coûte. However——make your mind easy. I do not think Mr. Hannington is extreme in any direction. Everybody gives him a good word for hard work & personal character, & I think he is none the worse for not seeming to be a *pet* of *any* clique. I got the Bishop's imprimatur as to the needs & worthiness of the object. Mr. Halcombe wants him (the Bishop) to write some New Brunswick papers for Mission Life –but he seems to hesitate.[6] But I shall have another talk with him. *I* think it wld be better to wait till the Consecration of the Magaguadavic Church for any but a *brief* remark. But I will collect all I can for the Portland Mail. My darling Mum–what do you mean by saying "encourage me." Do you dislike my discussing the Mission Army Scheme? If you do–you dear, good, beloved old Mater or do not like anything I ever say or do to you,–GOD forbid I should ever say or do it again! But mission papers have so wonderfully improved lately, & mission work in the Church of England has been so terribly mismanaged–such a weak point, that one is *truly thankful* to see *it* coming in for a little improvement in these stirring times. I honor with all my soul every effort in that direction, & for that very reason feel anxious to get trustworthy conclusions from experience of a plan so novel as the Mission Army. It is *Yankee-ish* in its tone, (& one gets a little surfeited with Yankee vulgarity here!)–but the Yankees, on the other hand, often progress where we stand still, & certainly one has no right to condemn hastily *any* efforts to revive interest in an undoubted duty, which we have undoubtedly neglected. But I really wanted to *know* more of its working. I suppose I bear it an extra grudge, because I–& Rex–& everybody else I think!–regret that your talents are frittered away in a *quantity* of work, which could be done quite as well by lots of people who never could get up the *quality* of the things that have made your name.[7] However I really *do* mean to raise that question, because I want you to take up Nat. History again – not in a mere occasional paper hurriedly done – but *really* & (don't be astonished!) *with me*. I have got hold of an old book & a new pamphlet, the former – a Scientific Manual Godfathered by the Admiralty – with *delicious* papers suited to the capacities of young middys &c. to instruct people whose duties carry them about the world how to use their eyes for the benefit of science. The "Botany" instructions are by Sir W. Hooker[8] – & they all tell me heaps of things I wanted to know. The pamphlet is Yankee, from an American Society – & equally useful. It is wonderful how *strong* the natural taste for nat. science is when it is inborn, however long it may lie dormant. It will do *very very* much to reconcile me to a longer exile from Home, if I see my way towards "collecting" here. There are directions for the best way of collecting seeds, tubers, &c. &c. of native plants – the time of day to look for fresh water shells & so forth. You *may* have *me* yet as a Nat. Hist. Contributor under the title of Nez:Bleu!!!!! But all this next mail, & *thereafter*.... No news yet. But some must come ere long. Meanwhile we get happier & happier. Give *my* grateful earnest thanks to the Ecclesfield M.A. for letting their affectionate memories of me influence the direction of their mission charity. I quite enjoyed the little notice. It is Butter-worth certainly – But you couldn't expect *boys* to be *quiet*. Please remember though, that not even for Mr. Halcombe can I ever consent to have my name printed in any *general* (not local as Ecclesfield or Sheffield papers) paper – maga – or report with any comments or adjectives that I have not first seen. I will not lend one penstroke towards dragging the first hopeful missionary maga. of any importance back into the false style which has been the greatest bane hitherto of efforts to help the cause of England's greatest duty. It is terribly pleasant to be flattered by those one loves – as I love you – & Ecclesfield – But beyond the precincts of Home – it is as wrong as absurd (as I see it.) My "interest" in All Saints is exactly \$4.50^{cts} less at present than Mrs. Cookesley's – £5 odd less than the interest you & the Ecclesfield M.A. have taken in it for my sake, & £4 less than was taken by the individuals who subscribed to give the "soldiers" a tea. I am obliged to be explicit because I know if the M.A. wanted the report put into Mission Life your loving heart would blind your judgement & good taste. But if it is done – never mind.

X   X   X   X   X   X   X   X   X   X   X

— Wait till you see my collections!! I mean to send some contributions to X   X   X   A.J.M.?   X   X   No.   X   X   X   X   Mission Life?   X   X   X   X   NO

Last Sheet

—— but to your Museum!! If only the 1/22d stay on a bit – a hornet's nest – some lichens &c.

What did you mean by saying you had written to Capt. Parry? He is *here*.

Sir James Carter is coming out in May, perhaps. *If* he comes to S. John direct, I dare say he would bring me something – particularly for Aunt Jane's sake. How sorry I am she has been ill! – *Otherwise* send nothing till you hear again – & I will send a list *next* mail. You shall have more stories soon. Make any suggestions in *pencil* on the proofs that you like. (I presume Hoffmann has started. I want that.) Please present a Mrs. O. to the Ecclesfield Library from me if not in it already & I will send a bit of paper to gum in it. Our dear dear love. I shall write to congratulate the Govr on Hallamshire. I can hardly yet *believe* I am to have it!! & if you knew my delight when I found *you* meant to give me Harvey's life![9]

Easter Monday. [29 March] 1869.
Fredericton. N.B.

My darling Mater –

In spite of this feeble failure, I won't waste another sheet. It was begun to give you some idea of what an Easter Day we had. After some very stormy weather & sunless Days – we had I fancy *quite* as warm a day as you can have had. Lovely over head – thermometer at 50° *above* zero – & then at night the most exquisite moon & starlight, with a *lovely* "Aurora" all *broken* about the horizon. These  exquisite nights – when the snow is on the ground – in this clear, bracing atmosphere, do make the walk home from the Evening service *very* enjoyable sometimes, & make one long for some of you to see it all. The Cathedral never looks more beautiful I think. – You know how the stained windows illuminated from within look? – & how that effect, & the fabulous brilliancy of the moonlight combine into a scene that (disgusting as it is to confess!!!) reminds one of —— the theatre!

You know – you poor, dear, greedy old Mum! – that I owe no end of letters to the dear good girls – & *promised* one to the Pater but I have no heart to write to anybody else when you are "in the lows." This you certainly were about March 5. & (once more) I have *that* consolation in not getting the intermediate letter till the Halifax mail, that it was so much less cheerful than the 12 Mar. one which it accompanied. I fancy I have discovered a "dodge" about the United States letters. Those that come from *London* do *not* miss— But ones from the country are apt not to arrive till the Halifax ones come. Such is the Carey's experience. So next time send the U.S. ones a day before the proper time–& let us see if that covers the difficulty. You are *very* dear and good about our ups & downs, & it makes me doubly regret that I cannot reward you by conveying a perfectly truthful *impression* of our life &c. here to your mind. I trace, in your very dearness & goodness about it–in your worrying more about discomfort for me in our moves than about your own hopes of our meeting at Home–how little able one is to do so–by mere letters. I wish it did not lead you to the unwarrantable conclusion that it is because you are "weak & old"– that you do not appreciate the uncertainties of military house- keeping–& can only "admire" the coolness with which I look for- ward to breaking up our cosy little establishment, just when we were fairly settled down. You can hardly believe how well I under- stand your feelings for me, *because I have so fully gone through them for myself.* I never had Dina's "spirit" for a wandering life–anymore than her talent for making babyclothes. And it is out of the fulness of my experience that I *know,* & wish unspeakably that I could con- vey to you–how *very much* of one's shrinking dread, has all the *un- reality* of fear of an *unknown evil.* When I look back to all I looked forward to with fear & trembling in reference to all the strangeness of my new life–I understand *your* feelings on my behalf better than you think. I am too much your daughter not to be strongly tempted to "beat my future brow"–much more so than to be over hopeful. Rex is given that way too–in his own line; & we often are brought to say together how inexcusable it is when everything turns out so much better than we expected, & when "GOD" not only "chains the dog till night"–but often never lets him loose at all! Still–the natural terrors of an untraveled & not herculean woman, about the ups & downs of a wandering homeless sort of life like ours are not so comprehensible by him, he having travelled so much, never felt a qualm of seasickness, & less than the average of home sickness–from circumstances. Then men are seldom able to give those descriptions to places & people that convey comfort in such little domestic points. Long as Rex has lived in Colonies, I could give you more details & "points" to set your heart at rest in 1/2 an hour than I ever could 'get out of' *him* myself when he most wished to please me, & when they would have spared me a good deal of worry. It is one among my many reasons for wishing to come Home soon, or else to have someone out soon–that one chat would put you in possession of more idea of our passing home–the nest we have built for a season, & the wood it is built in, & the birds (of many feathers) amongst whom we live than any *letters* can do. I do *so so* grudge *any* needless wear & tear on your dear nerves & strength just now. Perhaps what comforted *me*–may in the same foolish feminine way comfort *you*–so I will tell you an anecdote of myself. *You* can imagine the state of (far from blissful) ignorance of military life–tropical heat–Canadian inns &c. &c. &c. in which I landed at Halifax after such a sudden wrench from the old Home–& such a very far from cheerful voyage, & how dreary & desolate the discomforts of the overcrowded "Todger's" (by far the best hotel of the place) did feel, & how I burst out crying when I saw clean tea & toast for the first time, & how little I appreciated (as a consolation) Rex's assurances that I did not "know what heat was," & all the anecdotes of the summerheat, the wintercold, the spring floods, the houses, & the *want* of houses, the servants & the want of servants, the impossibility of getting anything & the ruinous expense of it when got!!!! —which people pour into the ears of a newcomer just because it is a more sensational & enter-taining (& *quite* as stereotyped) a subject of conversation as the weather & the crops. The points may be (isolatedly) true; but the whole impression one receives is alarmingly false! Then it so happened that the 3 military households to which I was 1st intro-duced–the McKinstry's & Routh's at Halifax (McK. the officer put in arrest afterwards by Strickland. R. Strickland's predecessor) & our predecessors *here* gave me rather a false impression. Mrs. McK. & Mrs. Hackman were both dark–melancholy–rather 2nd rate looking ladies – one if not both W. Indian (Mrs. H. never "went out" here at all) & their small houses had "parlours" as depressing as yer brother 'Enry's[1] *before* it was painted & papered!! Old R. a fine looking old fellow with a bonny, good, kindhearted noisy wife & 8 children in the extreme of scramble & muddle & hospitality just 'moving' & Mrs. R. proportionately full of cookstories were *thoroughly* kind, but he told old stock military stories of 15 year's service in "furrin parts" &c. &c. till my courage nearly failed me – & coming home with Rex a little bit of my fears escaped me. I shall never never cease to feel grateful for that one bit of indulgence, as I told him (much to his amazement!), when he told me *not* to fidget myself about *it* or anything else I heard – for that besides the fact that these were regular "senior officers'" anecdotes of a bygone state of things – long terms of service &c. &c. — whenever from my own experience I disliked the life & wld prefer to leave it – he would throw it up & come home at once & get something else to do – Because I was all he had, & as my happiness was his *only* object – & what would be the good of his staying in a kind of life I didn't like. It lifted the whole nervous weight *at once*. And I can only say that my 'experience' is so totally different from my fears, & from the cook stories of the "profession" – that I do not mean to request him to leave Our Department at present!!!!! No doubt moving & planning – must grow more & more irksome with a large family & all the involved questions of "the boys'" future & the girls' manners & education & so forth. But to us as we are at present it is really little more than something to talk about, & a variety to the monotony of life. Now you see how freely I tell you the truth. I have no more "gift" for being a Lady Baker than yourself, but 1. *So far* we have had comforts in abundance – healthy climate – plenty of friends – indeed *everything* but the sight & sound of our old friends & people – & much as we like this little house – one does not regard it as one would regard a real Home however small. No news this mail. But we are all very jolly & comfortable! – my plants are coming on capitally – & I am fairly longing for Spring to botanise. Dr. Adams sent me another of the papers of the "Smithsonian Institution" & you may hope to receive Diatomaciae – scientifically dried! I have been so full of trying to comfort you about myself that

I have left no time to say lots that I had to say. Especially about Mission Life. Don't fidget about *that* till I *have* time to "explain my meaning." My grudging you to the *human* topics of this exciting age is at the root of it all. *I* am very hopeful instead of hopeless for our race & the Church & (don't laugh!) everything & everybody. There is so much marked improvement – in *reality*, enquiry, knowledge & general interest – huge as the blunders also are – that one thanks GOD & takes courage – But meanwhile the Harveys of life – the writers of Parables – are not to be *made* even by a zealous & active age & you have not strength both to enter into the lists of political religious & social controversy & to write Parables.

Oh dear! I must stop!! Alas alas!
Well & happy. You shall have
Rex's song – photos – & my stories very soon
Your loving Judy –

I hear of a dear little notice in Feb or March of Mission life – of the C. Vessels.[2] I have not got it yet though. Our subscriptions not quite finished yet. Mr. Dowling getting me some papers.

A photo enclosed. *My* stare accidental!

LETTER

83

288

April. 3. 1869.

My dearest Mum.

As you perceive – "the floods are out" – & it is not supposed that the river can much longer stand this continued thaw & rain. An ice freshet is anticipated. I dare not *wish* it, as it is uncharitable towards our friend Mr. Barker (of Nashwaak fort, & the priest's ring – memory) – whose property gets much damaged on these occasions: but if it *does* come – I think the "John Gilpins" aspiration is permissible – "may I be there to see!" I fear we hardly shall see it – being so far from the river. In other respects our position is a desirable one – when blocks of ice & masses of escaped water come dashing along regardless of expense. Not that much damage is done in Fredericton I fancy. Isolated farms & barns at points near the river – sometimes get carried away or blocked up in a "jam," but it does not deluge the town much I think. These backstreets get much wetter, however, in the "general thaw" than a high road like that which ran past Reka Dom. And there has been much more snow this year than last – so we have a little river up to our front door (now elegantly bridged over!) – where we dug out our snow road. I mean to make a sketch before it is all over if I can. It has been delicious overhead – mild & spring like. Today it rains steadily – & I think the river *must* go soon! The 22d wld gladly feel as secure in reference to their going – or staying or doing anything definite. But all is *in nubibus.* Major Cox wrote to Rex yesterday, & mentioned a "report" that there were to be no troops at all in N.B., adding that the Genl. had "recommended" to Govt to leave a company for S. John – & one for Fredericton – but had not yet had a reply. He begged his name might not be used in connection with *on dits* on the subject. So only Rex & I are the wiser – & it amounts to nothing. It hardly seems likely the troops will be withdrawn till the Alabama matter is settled, & I suppose the Govt itself cannot tell beforehand how soon that will be[1] – Of course if there are *no* troops here – we shall go also – but whither we know not. It is *probable* we all think, that we shall hear something next mail if not sooner. But in all this uncertainty there is nothing the least unusual – or even avoidable that we know of, & the personal inconvenience to us is so much smaller than it might easily be that one only talks of it for chat. Every profession has its stock grievance – small incomes & many "calls" is the clerical one, long journeys & disturbed nights is the doctor's, uncertainty & so forth *ours*! It *is* rather a heavy grievance to people with large families – but *we* are in very 'light marching order' & so long as we are in healthy places, able to be together, & have a not too distant prospect of seeing Home again – our grievances are very minute indeed! – As Furtiva (Miss Parker=Furtive Pathar – a Hebrew point)[2] said to me the other day (in reference to *bonnets*) – "Oh! but don't you *enjoy* 'contriving' & feel so proud of it – Like the old woman whose pudding cost her nothing – 'for she had a little meal by her in the house.'?" – My Easter bonnet certainly *was* a case in point. I had been very busy just before Easter with various things, & had not prepared any change in my costume. But when Rexie asked me what new thing I had for Easter Day – I felt rather ashamed of having been reading Mr. Trevor's "Story of the Cross"[3] to the Loyalist Ladies – collecting for Magaguadavic – &c. &c. &c. & not making myself creditable for my old man. So, late on Easter Eve, I made a very elegant little bonnet to take the place of Maggie's – which cost me only a strip of black velvet – I having "a little meal in the house" – in the "shape" of the identical black vel-

vet covered shape I had at Southsea (& afterwards covered with crape when in mourning!) On this is posed Aunt Fanny's white point lace triangle, & my 2 blush roses & black velvet & lace lappets cross in front. It is considered very becoming! combined with neck velvet of that cerulean forget me not blue which goes so well with blush pink. We have not yet contrived to get photoed again. Rex never seems to have time. And now he won't let me send the ones that *are* done to his people. I sent them vi et armis to you. But he was afraid you would think I looked ill because of the queer strain & stare I gave over my shoulder. You know we sacrificed ourselves to the bulldogue – & as soon as I had calmed *him* the man drew up the slide – Rex muttered "look at the camera"– I daren't move *myself* but twisted my *eyes round* & gave an agonized stare (dreading that the bulldogue would shake!)–hence my "anxious gaze." I had calculated that the noise of the slide going up would fix Hector's attention–make him think there was a rat or something to be "fetched out"–& I was very proud of the result– He has never been taken decently before [Plate 15].[4] I shall send you the other one–which wld have been good of Rex if he had not shaken– In the other his head was put in the vice. I stood still enough without [Plate 16]. I doubt if we shall be able to be taken on the snow *now*–so we mean to be taken in our snowshoeing costume indoors. Monday 5. *On dit* a telegram last night to say the 1/22d goes home in May. No news for *us* yet, except that Monk & Uniacke at Halifax are promoted (no £.*S.D. extra* yet you know.) & will probably stay there. This makes it unlikely *we* should go *there* which we are glad of. I had a carpenter in the other day & had all the boxes–locks &c. looked over & put to rights. After which I paid him–so *that* is done with. Now we are making a catalogue of our books–& I think of having a back & moveable front, made to one of my bookshelves, so that I could *pack* the books in it & take it about with me. It *is* such fun contriving & planning sometimes, that I *do* feel not having one of the girls to go over it with me! My dear old man has not the ghost of a mechanical genius, & is equally pleased whatever I do or do not perform! (One. P. M. The poor old dear has just got back to his dinner, & is off again in consequence of a fire bell. It is wonderful how 'used' one gets to fires–but, for one thing, some of the alarms have lately turned out "Young Fredericton's" chaff!! He has come back, & can't see a symptom–even of "smoke"!! — We leave "Aunt Judy's Cot"–on May. 1. but before then I mean to have various boxes of books–summer clothes &c. locked up in the Hospital stores so as to have very little to do at the last. Whether we shall set up house alone–or with some other people–here or elsewhere; as yet we don't know. Mr. Dowling has opened *his* house to us–& we shall probably have other hospitable offers till we *know* something. It really seems likely that we shall hear soon *now*. Meanwhile my darling Mum, I have *not* much time to enter on any of the subjects I have started with you. Don't be in a hurry to decide on anything I *have* said till I have time to explain. I must tell you that on Maundy Thursday [25 March] I heard that some of the Costers were ill & going in late, I found Mrs. C. in bed – Clara ditto with inflammation of the lungs – Robin an invalid – & Charlie convalescent – & the 'Maiden Aunt' almost speechless with cold, administering doses & applying turpentine counter irritants in a depressed frame of mind. Consequently after Good Friday Morning Prayers I laid hold on Charlie & Harold & kept them till bed time – (or rather evening service time –) & gave them some of your little "mission" books to keep their noisy boots from the invalids. The result of which is that they are 'off' on the subject – Harold has already made a banner, & Charlie has already accused somebody of having an eye to the *cakes!!* So yesterday, Mrs. Coster began to ask me about it. *She* had had a sort of prejudice against the American idea – as having a flavor of "cant" she said – but liked your little papers so much she wanted information about it. I told her it was just what I had written home for – and she should hear the result. She does not think it will do for a tea to be a necessary part of the programme here. Indeed her children already "save cents" for the offertory without any such inducements – but the Bishop does not publish his offertory accounts, so people hardly know *what* it is going to – & the boys are taken with the Mission idea. Anyway I think I shall get a small sum from them for the Magaguadavic affair. I got a letter from Mr. Hannington which I mean to send you – only *too* grateful. He is coming down this week & wishes to write his acknowledgement to your young soldiers. He says – "You have assisted & strengthened our hands very much – you don't know *how* much —" & "I would then like to send an acknowledgement to the Children of Ecclesfield, and give any further information you may think interesting or encouraging to them." It seems odd – but I believe the interest you & yours have taken in these poor settlers will do more to rouse their *neighbors* to help them than if the Bishop had pounded away for a year. The Costers had never even *seen* the "appeal." (They are *generous* to a fault – I only speak of the local ignorance & indifference). Probably if Canada took up the Grenoside question, a few rich manufacturers at home wld discover that some Yorkshire filecutters were rather in want of "Church privileges." It is very *natural*, & is a strong argument in favor of helping missions even where one's home needs are great–the novelty of the field gives a juster estimate of the needs & importance of the matter....

You may expect some lichens & Brownie's book &.. &c. by the 22d. N.B. I have a Nat. Hist. Convert among the ensigns I hope. He is going to shoot me some lovely birds if he stays.

Some more MSS. shortly– Don't begin the Tales till I see proofs please.

Our dearest love
Your own loving bairns
A. J. H. E.

LETTER

84

April 10. 1869

My dearest Dot

I owe you & Dina 1000 letters–but, as you know, I had things to write to the Mum about, & we have been 'busy' as usual. The Mail came in today, & I got Home letters of 2 dates–as usual; for the intermediate ones did not arrive when the other United States letters came. (I mean that the mess got papers &c. so it was not that the mail failed) But I believe the only way is for you to post them a day earlier (the intermediate letters) than you have hitherto done–and put viâ United States–or whatever it is on the envelope.

... I *do* sympathize with you in reference to your axiom about interfering with "lovers & musical geniuses!" Perhaps one 'corps' *is* as troublesome as a body of singers–a corps dramatique. And one fears that so long as plays & concerts are not exclusively made up of principal characters & solos–the management of either will not be altogether a sinecure. The people here do now repose the most wonderful confidence in Rex, & have sunk many oldstanding 'points'–& several claims to be AI. in deciding on various matters have been utterly waived since we came here. Still both the Choir & more especially the Choral Society have occasional storms. The

293

latter has (to the universal delight of everyone concerned), got rid of the german conductor & Rex was appointed to his place by acclamation. I must do Rex the justice to say that he did all in his power (he was accompanist) to help Wichtendahl along – give him hints – interpret his broken english – &c. &c. but he really took very little interest in the Society when he found that it did not pay as an advertisement for pupils – At any rate he was so ludicrously careless & unsatisfactory in every way that it has been a marvel that the people have held together as well as they have. A quarrel (on *business* matters) with the Committe brought matters to a head – & Mr. W. sent in his resignation. (He & *Rex* are perfectly good friends.) There have been 2 nights under the new baton, & the people are delighted. "We" are to give a concert shortly & you shall have a programme. Rex is writing a thing with an "invisible Chorus" on the words of Miss Proctor's "Vision." Old Roberts (basso profundo) is to take the 1st part (solo) – half the chorus is to take the mourner's song "on the stage" – Mrs. Rowan (soprano) is to take the 2d part (solo) & the other half of the chorus will sing the Angels' song "behind the scenes."[1] I am to be with the party in front so as to hear the invisible chorus. It seems so strange to have so much to do with concerts & choirs here – & not to be able to have any of *you* in them! I want the ladies to be dressed in uniform & hope it may come to pass. We shall probably all be in white – with different colored ribbons for sopranos & altos. All the ragtag & bobtail varieties of Yankee fashions will look awful in a 'corps' of any kind in public – & something of the uniform kind was done at a 'methodee' concert in the town the other day. The Sopranos being in black with white cloaks – & the altos in some shade of red. It would give a much more artistic & respectable effect to us I think, for we are not all of the "higher walks" of society & some rather striking 'fashions' might otherwise be anticipated. However I do not know if we shall manage to carry it out. No news by the mail. I am rather disappointed – as we hoped for some. I am sorry for the poor Spains too. We & they have given up our houses – & they are both taken. Meanwhile the S.s. depend on *our* movements (or at least on the facts on which *our* movements will depend) & they have several little bairns, & have only been here a few months. You see the 1/22d do at least know that in all likelihood *they* will move very soon – & move Home. But we don't know whether we shall move – nor yet where to. Spain is a wonderfully handy man! (He has the Lucknow Relief medal. Crimea with 3 clasps – Alma, Inkermann, & Sevastopol – & the Turkish do.) & bears the best of characters. His love affair was very romantic – & began before the Crimea. She was in place with a lady whom she afterwards nursed into her grave & to please her she "fubbed off" poor S. more than once. (as to the marriage – they were engaged & corresponded through the Mutiny) To save her from having to wash with the rough soldier's wives at Aldershot – they took in a lot of shirts to make – & *he* began by hemming & eventually learned to stitch these, so as to help her.[2] He is a great relief to *me*, when wearied with inconsequent irish, & our present good but goosy orderly – for I can send a message or trust him to *pack* without "doing it myself"!!! I have also now got hold of an R. Engineers carpenter, who is going to carry out my idea of turning our bookshelves into moveable ones, so that I can *pack* the books *in* them. Rex has made another brilliant suggestion on his own account i.e. that the *front* of the bookcase shall (on the inner side) be painted so as to form a musical blackboard!! I had "a little meal in the house" in the shape of some deal which I had had for the top of my writing table in Reka Dom. The shelves are (as they stand) of the commonest construction. Deal – no backs &c. I *stained* them myself, with some stuff Capt. Parry gave me. I soon saw that "no back" is very false economy *here*, as — given a fire – how much spare time would one have to empty 2 bookcases? Whereas with backs – a very few seconds would suffice for 2 men to tear them up at B. & carry them out on their backs, books & all. When I had decided on this – I thought also of making a moveable *front* (to be screwed on) with protective bits at the 2 ends: & this is to be put in hand at once. It

will give us no *extra* luggage (as the books must go somewhere!) & we shall have a bookcase ready wherever our tent may be pitched – (to say nothing of a musical blackboard!) Mail Day. – &

oh! my dear – such a lovely – sunny springlike one – that I fear I *must*
go out – & cut short my letters. . . . I begin to doubt if there is *much*
chance of our remaining here – but no one knows. I *revel* in the
Spring & feel quite up to anything. My dear dear love to all, & my
friends may hope for some letters viâ Portland. I quite long for news
of my poor dear old Maggie – but really the success of mothers &
babies just now seems quite remarkable. If Master or Miss Smith
proves as engaging as the little Carey – I shall take to it as I have
never taken to a "long clothes" individual yet. The latter mite is a
dear little soul – & never frightened of *me*. Parry junior – is not
lovely so far – & I neglect my duties in the *Keetchy Keetchum* department in reference to that cherub! But Mrs. P. is in *great* force
again – Ditto Mrs. Adams & *her* bonny baby. Ditto Mrs. Fallon &
her prodigy (she has never had a living child – or successful illness
before.) I have my eye on a "sweet" thing in moccassons for the
nephew or niece tell Maggie.

I find I have no time to write a separate note to

My dearest old Mum.

Please accept this P.S. I think it is just as well L. of L.T. got in when
it did. *Do not* print the fairy tales please. We will wait & see – I
think it is likely you are right. Anyway I know they demand improvement. Mrs. O. is very likely to take a further shape someday.
But I would *like* to continue the Brownies, Land of Lost Toys &c.
series if I can – & shall bend my mind to that. No reliable news – but
the lovely Spring makes me feel in the highest spirits & up to anything. . . . Capt. Carey has gone to Niagara with sketching mate-
rials & 3 lessons from me!!

Clara Coster is coming to stay with me for 2 or 3 days – She is so
pale & feeble & cannot eat – I am going to "put her up" somehow – & give her fresh air – which everybody is afraid of here – especially if they have delicate lungs & bad appetites – They inhale
carbonic acid gas & bad drains for the former – & take calomel &
something that goes by the awful name of *Pod* – . . . . to improve the
latter. *We* sleep with our windows open – when the thermometer is

below zero. It is so gloriously *dry*. I have two geraniums in flower &
my plants rejoice my eyes. We all seems to wake up like dormice in
Spring. Goodbye you dear old Mater.

Your loving Judy.

LETTER

85

Our House in a "Northern Light—"

Fredericton N.B.
April. 17. 1869.

My dearest Father

Many many happy returns of your birthday on the eve of which
I am writing. I wanted to adorn your letter—but I fear have not succeeded. The illustration is by way of giving you an idea of the finest
"aurora" I have ever seen— I have been a little disappointed with
the want of color in the auroras I have seen here hitherto—& they
have only occupied part of the heavens—but on the 15th from 8 to

297

9 P.M. (with *us*) the above was visible, & poured from the zenith to the horizon–north, south, east, & west. In the west the rays were beautifully colored & the sky looked as rosy as after sunset *or* a fire in the woods. Against this the "young moon in the old moon's lap" over the dark chimney tops of the Rectory, was certainly a lovely sight. The magnetic storm seemed to *rage* in some places, & the general brilliancy faded from time to time, & then burst out again in vivid streams at particular points. It began in the south & passed northwards–not a usual thing *here*. In fact it was altogether more like an Australian Aurora Rex says. *The* lovely (or rather *grand*) feature was the corona at the zenith above our heads. *It* changed as ceaselessly as the rays–sometimes obscured–a dark mass would suddenly *rift* with an effect like one of Martin's boldest imaginations in his Milton.[1] The rays were sharpest near the corona–& then again near the horizon. It was like standing under a tent of celestial proportions–where the curtains showed light & shadow as they rustled. Occasionally in the West the rosy tent was mixed with greenish & yellow rays–never very brilliant that we saw. But we did not see it at the *very* best I believe. Mrs. Coster's sister sent a boy to tell us & out we turned into the street in rugs cloaks & indian

coats. I crowned my furs with Maggie's sofa blanket, put Rex's indian coat on-to Clara Coster (who is staying with us.) & Rex adorned himself with an old military cloak. I fancy many of the neighbors thought *us* the sight of the evening. It was a colder night than we have had for a while, & ever since the grand aurora–we have been literally 'looking out for equals' instead of which, we have had the loveliest weather. Today was like an english early summer's day. We sent Herbert Lee on to the Bishop–& *they* turned out ditto ditto, & the Bp. said he had not seen such an one for 20 years.

I got an english Churchman by the U. States mail today–but no

letters. We are still quite without news in reference to our movements. The poor 1/22d people are selling up one after another.
Dr. Adams on Thursday. The Parrys on Monday— Then the
Grahams–Chaunceys–Tyackes–Monks–Cookesleys &c. &c. At
any rate we *are* fortunate in not having to sell off our few 2s & 3s
with them— If *only* we knew who was coming–one might secure a
few things for them!! The Nashwaak is "out" today–& the S. John is
expected to "go" tomorrow. The river does generally go on a Sunday–& after all our expectations of an ice freshet it seems likely to
depart in all peace & quietness. I think this is the last day of even
the most foolhardy traffic on the snowroads for 1869. One or two
dark blots on the river–surrounded by *crows*–remind one that 2 or
3 horses generally fall victims to 'dangerous' spots toward the
Spring. Wonderfully few human lives are lost on the whole however, & medical men–indians–farmers &c. to whom it is very inconvenient when the river is neither safe for passage–nor clear of
ice–do cross at wonderfully critical times. When the river is
clear–nous verrons. The regiment *may* go—or it may not. This is
the extent of our knowledge. The latest "chaff" is what Capt.
Cookesley retailed to me today. "So *we* (1/22d) are going–but Medlen, Shortt, & Ewing, are to be left behind. Medlen to look after the
place, Shortt to look after Medlen's health, and Ewing to pay them
both." "Medlen" is a little man belonging to the Engineer Dept–a
Clerk of Works. Shortt is the "Staff" doctor, & has no connection
with the regiment. I need hardly say that this *is* chaff.

No more time– *News* by next mail we hope. Your loving dau.

Judy

86

April. 19. 1869 Monday.

My dearest dear old Mum.

Your letter (viâ U.S. April. 2.) arrived today just in time for me to answer it by the mail which leaves this afternoon at 3. So it was a really "intermediate" letter this time. And such a jolly one. So well written & lively, it quite cheered me after one or two mails in which I fancied you rather depressed & unwell. I am sure you may offer to "punch the heads" of all the high church publishers in London & elsewhere – & indeed – threaten *mine* across the Atlantic – & welcome if your dear old self will only feel well & energetic enough to do it. Oh! how I would like a laugh with you over it. I have not been made so happy by a home letter for a good bit. When I feel anything that I want to "have out" with you – I feel so inclined to plunge into it, but though the knowledge & remembrance of how you & I eventually always did & do understand each other (whether we agree or not.) is strong within me, sometimes this long parting, the distance – the mails that absorb nearly 6 weeks in taking home *my* ideas & bringing back your reply & so forth — deter one. There is more that is strange & odd in my share of our separation than you can feel. Sometimes I have a vague feeling as if on any points where I fancy I could bring my experience here in any way to bear on home affairs – that perhaps it might feel like interference of a married sister – or some of those wonderful family "unpleasantnesses" which seem to occur in other families sometimes – & which are so difficult to understand till (I suppose) one has been in the position. You know I feel *just the same* – & cannot feel as if I belonged the least bit less to the old house than I used to do. When one moves about so – one makes no rival *Home*, however happy one may be. – However the fact is that we have received notice that the letters must be ready earlier than usual today in consequence of the state of the roads–& I think I will send this even *before* the appointed time in case of accidents–so I can only add a few words. I earnestly hope Fröhlich may be secured for Nursery Nonsense at any sacrifice. ~~I do think it would pay in the end.~~ –No, I see what you mean. But for a good large bonus I think you might let Fröhlich do it himself. Or for an agreement duly drawn up to give you so much on each edition. Would Bell not speculate in publishing it, & employing Fröhlich?[1] It seems a pity it could not have been done so in A.J.M. – *Pictures* are certainly the weak points of the firm somehow. I feel it–for I must have my *child's* book well illustrated. (The Brownies &c.)[2] But I will write to Bell about this. You have done admirably in re. Mrs. O. & the german lady, & I shall wait for further news. Do *not* print the fairy tales. I have 2 or 3 *schemes* in my head.

"*Mrs. O. (2d series.)*" Fatima's Flowers &c. &c.

"The Brownies (& other Tales)" Land of Lost Toys, 3 Xmas Trees. Idyll &c. Boneless. 2nd Childhood &c. &c.

"The other side of the World." &c. &c.

"*Goods & Chattels*" (quite vague as yet–)

"A Sack of Fairy Tales" (in abeyance)

(A Book of *Weird queer* stories) (none written yet)

"Bottles in the Sea." "Witches in Egg Shells."

"Elephants in Abyssinia" &c.

And, (a dear project) a book of stories chiefly about Flowers & Nat. Hist. associations (*not scientific–pure fiction*)

"The floating gardens of Ancient Mexico." The Dutch Story.

"Immortelles"–

"Mummy Peas"–&c. &c. (none even planned yet.)[3] (an indian brother has called & I have not 5 minutes more.)

Adieu you dear dear old Mum– More another day. My love to Steenie–& I think he is *quite right* anent his collection. I will help him.

Your loving–Judy

87

Rose Hall.[1] Fredericton N.B.
8 May. 1869.

My very dear Mum.

This is our new nest – about which more presently – it is a lovely summer resting place – we take it by the month (we pay a little more than £2 a month:) – & there seems a fair prospect of our not having to move at any rate for 2 or 3 months – but there is no certain news for anybody as yet. It is believed that the "Serapis" left England on May Day – & proceeded to Quebec – from whence she is to come to S. John & take the 1/22d &c. home. I do feel very proud, my dear old Mater, of having given *you* advice worth listening to. I got your 2 latest letters together yesterday (the Halifax mail much earlier than we have had it lately). Also a charming letter from Liz – ditto with seeds from Miss Thompson. It was a delightful mail – I am only impatient for news from Butterthwaite – though very very glad to have such flourishing accounts of dear Maggie. The bairn means to be a Mayflower I suppose! – [2]

... Weeks ago I asked Mrs. Medley if she could tell me where to get one of the "hornets' nests" of the country, such as she has been in the habit of sending Home to her "collecting" friends, for I want to send one to your Museum by the 1/22d. She said "*I* will get one, & send it to Mrs. Gatty from myself – or rather to the author of Parables from Nature – that is how I like to think of her –" (or words to this effect.) *Still* I have not said how fresh & charming your Parable[3] is – I "vished there wos more of it" – as much as Mr. Weller could have desired. If it hangs on hand for a month or 2 longer – I shall send you all I can observe & "make a note of" as to the lovely orchidaceae of these parts – Anyway I shall do this, for they are *very* lovely. It seems a shame there should not be a botanical draughtsman among us all. How beautifully true & simple are Isaac

Sprague's illustrations to Asa Gray's "Lessons in Botany" – & "the Manual."[4] I told you that I had begun some figures of the ferns here, by a laborious & very primitive tracing process – which however made an unmistakable portrait of my first attempt: Struthiopteris Germanica. I lost it in moving into "Aunt Judy's Cot" – & was thereby disheartened & did no more. But I have found it again, & mean to continue the series. If our wandering lot should send us drifting about in at all an uncertain way when we *do* move – & I have an opportunity – I may send some things of this kind Home to be taken care of for me. Things, I mean, that suffer in frequent changes. . . . *Thank you* for refusing to publish my tales without my leave & corrections. It was as well for (even if I put them in) it seems to have been forgotten that they are to have an introduction; for which I have got a very pretty idea, I flatter myself. But I think you have enough fairy tales at present; & I must try & get on with a successor to "The Land of Lost Toys."[5] Oh! I have so much to talk about I hardly know where to begin – or when to leave off. However bedtime breaks this ramble off for the present. Tomorrow is dear Maggie's birthday — I hope some nice news is coming across the Atlantic from her – GOD bless her! – Goodnight dear Mum.

May. 10. Monday. We get more & more pleased with our present arrangements. It is a great point to have big airy rooms in the hot summer here. I wonder if I can give you any idea of our sitting room. Well – imagine the Page Hall dining room. Fancy a door *opposite* to the bay window – & that bay window with a *south* aspect – looking into a garden & shaded by a verandah. The middle compartment of the bay window opening to the ground at pleasure. I did work so hard to make the bare room look habitable before Rex came back from S. John! Well. I got a stand of flowers into the window (middle compartment.) ditto into the 2 other compartments of the bow. Our round dining room table with crimson cover then fills up the recess of the window – & is a very well *lighted* table for drawing &c. The fire place as in P. Hall – & white marble mantlepiece with Ecclesfield – the Claude, & Raffaele above it – & the cherubs – bronze clock & japan ornaments – between fire place & window – the harmonium – Regie's chair – *my* picture – & Mendelssohn – crimson chinese scroll &c. Opposite the fire the pianoforte with the old oil painting & Tennyson above *it*. Our round *drawing* room table in the middle of the room. Sofa & armchair on opposite sides of the fireplace. Between the window & *piano*–the writing table–with knickknacks–You &c. on the other side of piano music stand–another table–"Light of the World"[6] &c. On one side of the door a dark colored chiffonier–surmounted by dark bracket–& Joan of Arc. On the other the red *divan* & the turkish inscription above that. In the recess where at Page Hall there is another *little* window we have an ottoman with dear Maggie's Afghan blanket–&c. Our bedroom, above this, is large– with 3 big windows–& R.'s dressing room–is not much smaller. So far–we get on à merveille with the Ruells– Mrs. R. is all civility (& gentility) & they are really very kind. Mr. R. has offered me the use of a hotbed to raise annuals–a plot of ground in the garden for flowers–has placed his boat at my disposal–& sent me the 1st radishes &c. I have tasted this year–& the only mushrooms I have had since I left home!!!!

Tuesday [11 May]. As usual, I have to end hurriedly dear Mum. But I have been trying to get things fairly settled. We have *no notion* when or where we may be moved! Our dear dear love

Your loving Judy.

LETTER
88

[ca. 17 May 1869]

My dearest Dot.

I hope by this time your visit at Butterthwaite has come to a happy conclusion. I am very anxious to hear. What a Whitmonday! At least it is pouring & dull, with us. I wonder what weather you have at Ecclesfield. Very fine, probably. I had begun a birthday letter to dear old Brownie to whom we are sending the big volume of Marx's School of Musical Composition[1] as a present–(By the 1/22d) They are under orders, & will be gone in a day or two we expect. No news for us yet. Rex will be very busy getting them off. We expect a company of Highlanders 72d in their stead.² What *we* shall then do we know not. I shall be very glad if we have not to move into barracks for I have *just* "got straight"–as they say–blinds up–toilette covers washed–carpets down & pictures up–& plants in the windows &c. &c. & the effect is charming–

... Did I ever tell you of the Bishop's present to Rex–2 huge splendid volumes of anthems &c. by Purcell &c. published by the Mollett Society–with an inscription on the 1st page

To
Alexander Ewing–from his sincere friend John Fredericton. In remembrance of many happy hours–spent in the Service of the Church of GOD.

... I hope to send news by the next mail, but as yet all is in the clouds, & one is almost weary of saying so. Meanwhile we have charming rooms–& I feel inspired towards writing in this quaint old place.... Mr. H. sent me some *bear*, & I "rendered" down the fat & made bear's grease & am sending you some–by the 1/22d!! with a few other trifles

Your loving JOW.

LETTER

89

May. 31. 1869

My dearest Dina.

We are going to Halifax, but do not exactly know when. We have asked for a little "leave"–but I have my doubts about Rex being spared, & mean to be "ready" for a move at early orders. I would *like* a quiet two months here *very* much– It is far away the bonniest & coolest summer abode we have had, & has inspired *one* 'plot' for the new vol. of Mrs. Overtheway already – but it is so long since I have had time to write – & I have only just got my rooms pretty & bright & now to pack my kit & march again does take a wonderful amount of time! –

We have been in an indescribable whirl for the last week or 10 days – & I have had flying parties of the poor 1/22d – dining – having tea, working, resting – calling – & swarming in & out ceaselessly. Rex has been worked off his feet almost – but the embarkation was carried through triumphantly — Bear – Bulldog & all.[1]

Now they have taken into their post office heads – to send off the mail earlier than usual – but after this week there *may be* peace for awhile. We were up at 4 for about 3 mornings – & they had lovely weather for embarking. The Concert went off splendidly[2] – & from that night onwards – the departure of our friends took all our time. We feel it very much – & the desolate look of the broad sweep by the blue river – & the green trees – where not one speck of the familiar *red* relieves the scene is felt by everybody. The last batch went on Friday morning. We were there between 5 & 6 & went on board – gradually the Careys – Chaunceys &c. &c. arrived & came on. (I had been packing with the Careys & Tyackes till lateish the night before) – The crowd got thicker & thicker – the day was lovely – & about 6 – the beautiful band crossed the old green with "Goodbye Sweetheart, Goodbye." I broke down utterly – got a kiss from Mrs. Carey & the bairns – Capt. Chauncey ran after us for a handshake – & we went on shore – You have never seen the redcoats clustering over a white vessel for a farewell – as she swung round in the sunlight with "Auld Lang Syne" – on the band & our 2 years' friends waving & cheering – to the last wave of the drum major's wand – it was overpowering enough – Rex went back to work – & I went to the Cathedral for 7.30 (A. M.) Litany – where we prayed for Her Majesty's 22d Regiment – the women & the children in *very* choky voices. Our turn will come soon I suppose.

Now they are fairly gone – You may expect some more respectable letters from me. I suppose we shall be at Halifax for a good while. And now we know our destination things can come to

306

us. (I suppose the Rosses have *left?*) I shall send a letter on Thursday viâ New York I think. Not a moment more.

Your ever loving Judy

LETTER
90

Rose Hall.
6. June. 1869.

My darling old Mater

... I take in the "sense" of "Madge & the Baby" coming to see you —(& I suppose the sounds take care of themselves!!!!) but I cannot *realize* it. And yet by this time I suppose he is my Godson!!! I must have a photo. of him, & Maggie. I could not get his shoes in time for the departure of the 1/22d & indeed have sent nothing by them. They were loaded – & sent off in a hurry. We have been living in an amazing whirl of late. Halifax will have at least one merit. We shall get our Home letters sooner & more certainly. It will make two or 3 days' difference. We don't know yet when we go – & this is such a lovely summer's nest – that I hope Strickland will be able to give us a month's leave. Then we shall *probably* get away at the end of July – or beginning of August. Tomorrow morning at 5.30 I start with Rex for Eel River – (about 60 miles up the river. We speak of it as if it were a walk to Chapeltown!!) There is a military outpost there which he has to visit, & we shall put up at the "public." On Tuesday we come down – Rex comes home – because of the Choral So.'s practice – but I only come as far as "Crock's Point" where Mr. Dowling will meet me & take me to Douglas for a visit. On Wednesday he will drive me to Prince William whither Rex meanwhile will have come – & Mr. Hannington will take us to the settlement to see the Church – & that I may make the sketch – & get his letter & send you a little account of it. We come down together on Friday. Mrs. Cox was down for a couple of nights last week – &

spent the time with us – We took her out in our canoe, & she enjoyed herself very much I think. Fredericton is looking *very* bonny
just now – but oh! we miss the red coats – As Rex says the Rifles
look as if they were in mourning for the 1/22d. There is only a
company of *them*. Capt. Tufnell & Mr. Warren were with us this
afternoon – & Capt. T. began quoting "Alice" to our great delight, &
exchanged sentiments on the subject of the Cheshire Cat &c. He
then went off on "Happy Thoughts" –

By this time the Bulldogue must be approaching Gt. Britain.
Rex wears his picture in an old locket of mine tied to his watch
chain, – & we have not at all got over his loss! I think of setting up a
tortoise! – "I vish a Poodle!" – We 'peak vords to all the dogs we
meet – & they generally 'peak vords to us. When we have *no*
representative of the beloved race – Rex barks & whines & "does
dogue" for me. This morning he brought his toothbrush in his
mouth – & snuffed & whined just like a bulldogue!!! ...

We are working for another concert on July 1. The 1st gave
universal delight.

My dear love to the dear old girls & the dear old boys. Tell
Steenie I hope *the* Collection will profit by my visit to Eel River.

... Tell the Mission children of Ecclesfield – that I think their
example really has stirred up help for All Saints Maga: And the
S.P.G. is withdrawing more & more from the Province.

We are bitterly regretting the possibility of Mr. Dowling having
to go. He *cannot* manage his enormous work without a curate now.
The people will raise 200 dollars per annum – if 200 more can be got
from without – I hope it may be raised; he is such a capital – hard
working – unaffected – educated – earnest man. I fear I must say
goodnight you dear dear Mum – for with a prospect of getting up at
4.15 one wants *some* sleep!! Hoping & praying this will come to you
& find you better – I am & Rex is – Your loving AJEwing.

LETTER
91

14. June. 1869.
Rose Hall
Fredericton N Bk

My dearest Mother –

... We have at last had a John Gilpin jaunt in our honey-moon – & it *has* been enjoyable – & at every place we have hoped & prayed our old Mum might be well enough thoroughly to enjoy hearing of it all. It has been one drawback of the "sole charge" that whilst other military couples have come & gone on trips into the country, Rex has been tied here for these 2 years – except for a couple of business trips to S. John – on one of which I went with him – (in 1868.) But the contractor for the board of the men on look-out for deserters to the States,[1] stationed at the outpost on Eel River, having fortunately chosen this lovely season for failing to ful-fil his contract – Rex had to go there on *business* & I accompanied him for pleasure! –

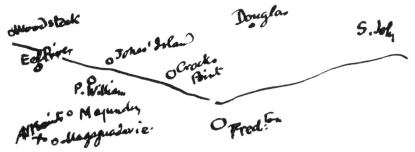

The thing I wanted to accomplish was seeing "All Saints" &c. &c. & it is done – & we have had Royal Weather – & enjoyed it more than I can tell you. Rex had to go back to Fton once, but he re-turned to me – & we got out to Lake Magaguadavic & saw it all. We have been away all the week – & as there are no railroads – & very rough driving roads – & the distances are great, our time has been pretty well spent in travelling & I could only make rough pencil notes for colored sketches. But we were so much pleased, & I should so like to give the Ecclesfield Regiment some idea of the place & people – that I think of writing *you* an account of our trip & sending rough colored sketches to illustrate it. This might be read to them in the School if you like; but none of it, please, to be printed without my revision. One of the mission clergy here annoyed his people very much once by what he had said at home, which got reprinted in Yankee style in a local paper, & was more personal than pleasant. They are all "Home" people – & have English relatives & associations and keep a wonderful interest in the old country. If you think well I would also give you a short little account for Mission Life which might save you labor just now.[2] I may as well tell you that I had a good talk to Mr. Dowling (who is *very* intelligent & large minded) about the Mission Army. He told me that he himself had had our feeling of prejudice against it, & found himself "coming round" – He said he went to one of Dr. Twing's own meetings in N. York – His final idea is, "I *feel* I am softening – it *certainly* supplies a want – I *think* certain peculiarities came from the Yankee *style* & want of *taste* – & I began to see from Mrs. Gatty's papers that it might be done differently. I should like to hear what E. Clarke does with it[3] — if I fairly saw my way I shld start it here *at once*." — Mr. Hannington who is as impetuous as he is hard working, & drives, rides, poles a canoe, starts a mission army, builds a church, & botanizes with equal impetus, started *his* Magundy Regiment – only a day or two before we were up there. He said "I thought what was the good of telling them of what had been done for *them*, if they were not stirred up to do as much as *they* could." So the Magundy scholars are enlisted – As we drove past the school the children were coming out – & Mr. H. pointed out one lad (he looked about 11 or 12 or less) who had hauled & driven teams & worked for the Church. But to go back. We had never been "up river" before, except 10 miles or so in canoe – The "boats" only run in the spring & autumn freshets. We left here at 5.15.A.M. & got to Eel River about 2.P.M. (60 miles or so). It was lovely, though the "black fly" hardly left us alive! We spent the night at the inn – took the boat again on Tuesday morning & came *down river*–48 or 50 miles down–landed at Crock's Point, where Mr. Dowling met me in his "wagon" (the 4 wheeled "gig" of the country)–& Rex went on to Fton for the Choral Society's practice. At Douglas we had some dinner, & in the afternoon Mr. D. having to visit a sick man in his Keswick district, he, I, & Mrs. Dowling squeezed into the waggon, & drove 18 miles through *lovely* country, on *such* a beautiful evening. I saw the Keswick Church (to the Consecration of which Rex went in the winter of 1867) a *very* nice little one. Coming back poor Mr. D. had "hard times" of it, me & his wife, for we had brought a trowel, & we found "ladies' slippers" & other treasures not so common close at hand–& it seemed very doubtful if we could get home before dark–though it is Mid-summer!! Old "King" Mrs. D.'s dogue was with us & enjoyed himself greatly– When we came in–we found Mr. Hannington en route home from a drive in *his* wagon. People exercise un-limited hospitality of its quiet kind in the coun-try, & he stayed all night. We *meant* to go to bed very early but we ended in sitting up rather early!

in the study, discussing–Tennyson, Handel, Miracle Plays, Jeremy Taylor, Table Turning, &c. &c. &c. &c. Somebody promised to "call" Mr. H. who had to drive 15 or 16 miles to Jones' Island where Rex was to be deposited by the morning boat from Fredericton. Happily he called himself, for we were all too thoroughly done up to wake early. We did not breakfast till 1/2 past 8 I think, then Mr. D. & I talked mission matters awhile, & then Mrs. D. & I went out & botanized till a *little after* dinner time, & then she & I got in the wagon. (He was too much knocked up to come & wld not leave his sick man–) packed my traps, took King, bid Douglas ADieu–& drove to P. William. It is about 16 miles, & as we had a "wait" at the ferry we did not get there till 8.P.M. when the Hanningtons & Rex had almost given us up– They had got a roast turkey for us–& we had a capital dinner & were much refreshed but so sleepy all the evening–that I discovered as in a dream that Mr. Hannington was prizeman for Botany at the College here–& that he exhibited to me a very ingenious press – gave me some splendid specimens of brown trillium. Again we all faithfully promised to 'call' each other & rolled into bed. We started off again next day – (Mr. H. having been up early packing the lunch.) & after prayers & breakfast Mr. H. & I packed into *his* wagon – Mrs. Dowling and Mrs. H. into the Dowling's – Rex rode the spare horse — & away we went. It was a 20 miles' drive & part of the time the sun was very hot, & I had to take off my grey cloak & put the table cloth round me to turn the sun. On the road Mr. H. gave me a full account of the Magaguadavic affair – & told me lots of interesting stories. *He* is a native you know. I mean of one of the old "settled" families. He is very excitable & impetuous, & is in the highest state of gratitude & pleasure at the interest taken in his new church. It is indeed a most *worthy*, & *reasonable* subject of effort these mission parishes make to prevent our own *emigrants* from becoming *heathens*. And the work is no joke sometimes. I am grieved to say, it is knocking Mr. Dowling up in *his* mission to such a degree that if he cannot get help for a curate he is going to resign. He wants 400 dollars (considerably less than £100 a year) & poor as the people are, they have resolved to raise 1/2, if it can be met. Mr. Hannington is looking much better than he was, & he is "uplifted" to a degree about All Saints. As we crept up the last hill (through country more like our moors, saving that the hills & slopes are covered not with heather but the illimitable forest) he wildly begged me to shut my eyes. I kept them closed till we were on the summit and by the church. It looks down on —— "Killarney on a larger scale" says Rex – the distant ranges not so high in proportion – but a wide wide beautiful Lake, dotted with fir covered islands deep down in the valley below the church – on the other side it looks down on an *ocean* of unbroken forest – softening into purple & blue with distance – but "woods, woods, woods," against *this* background far down the little quaint, white:painted Magundy Church shines like a star.[4] Near it the tumbledown house where is the School, and the Magundy Regiment. Around the Magundy Church is a churchyard (if you knew how often settlers bury their people in their own gardens &c. &c. as if they were their old horses or pet dogs, you wld know the value of the sight!!) full of white stones & with clumps of

S. Bottes . Magundy

the apple green osmundas on the graves. All Saints will be a very pretty Church (N.B. it is not built of *logs* but of wood like the houses & very pretty) It is roofed in & is to be consecrated in September. One grave is already in the Church Yard – among the wild strawberry blossom & the fern – that of a very good girl & a communicant. We picnicked in the valley below [   ] the mosquitos & the lovely trees! Then we went on to the Lake & it *is* lovely. The shore is gleaming white sand – (*porphery* says Mr. H. & it is lovely stuff, I brought a handkerchief full to put in my aquarium) out of the sand grow blueberry plants. Mr. H. "whipped off" his shoes & stockings & walked about so along the shore. When we returned our horse had escaped – & the men had to hunt for him. I dug up flower roots with dogged persistency, though the mosquitos & black fly bit me till I rushed madly to the lunch basket, grabbed the butter, smeared my face & hands all over – & — went back to the trilliums!!!! Tell Steenie I saw 14 different species of fern that I knew in that one drive – & I got pitcher plants (full of rain water!) &c. &c. Well – we got our horses – Mr. H. rode – & Rex drove me – When we got back to All Saints I went over it – & oh! dear Mum, we have really felt very very grateful to have been allowed to have *any* hand in helping it – It certainly does "sanctify the gorgeous waste around"[5] – Mr. H. told me when the roof was fairly on they all raised cheers, & he jumped so high in his excitement that they all fairly laughed at him – excited as they *all* were. While he was away I went back into the Church to use it as a house of prayer for once, for the strange sad feeling is we shall probably never see it again. Coming out I found *Rex* had been adjuring the old iron grey "Dolly" on the subject of men & beasts praising the Lord. He is delighted & he & I are to give the Prayer Desk. One of the people had prepared a tea for us at Magundy–so we did not get home till nearly midnight–& 2 miles in the dark through woods do seem *uncommonly* long!— Next day we drove to the river bank–canoed to Jones' Island–took the boat & came home. We have been very busy on Saty & today–but I am going to confab with Mr. Adams at Govt House next Thursday. (He is Private Sect. to the Govr) for he used to do amateur scene painting for his regiment before he left the Army–& I want to make some rough effective colored things from my sketches for you to show the children. We expect to go to Halifax in a month or 6 weeks at latest.

Our dear love to all–my godson included (if he is to be mine!)

Mr. Hannington's photo. letters &c. &c. will come with my sketches if I manage them.

Your loving children AJHE.

. . .

LETTER

92

5 Sunday after Trinity. [27 June] 1869
Fredericton N.B.

My dearest Mum.

You are so good in appreciating the striking uncertainty of military moves, & in not building upon any 'possibility' of an 'order home'—that we risk the disappointment you may feel if it all comes to nothing (as it did last time it was upon the cards) & tell you that it does seem unlikely that Rex will be detained in Halifax–& that it is just possible that our faces may be turned homewards. There is no order yet about it, you understand, nor, I suppose, shall we know where we are going till we get to Halifax–

Then we might be sent Home, *or*—anywhere else. But Rex's services do not seem to be required at Halifax. *So* please, send *nothing* to *us personally*, but if a chance occurs of getting the Communion Vessels to Halifax or S. John by private hand, they may be directed to the Bishop. We will look out for such an opportunity ourselves, and All Saints will not be consecrated till September at the very earliest. For this same reason (our *possible* homecome) I shall 'wait a wee' to see if I cannot bring my own sketches & account with me!!!

Oh dear! It does *not* do to *think* of. I try not to speculate. Indeed I can but humbly & thankfully await GOD's will about what certainly would be so *great* a happiness to us both (to us *all*!) that it seems almost more than our share– We are so very happy, & we have had such a pick of a station, & *you are better*——that to get Home just now— However I won't talk about it anymore, for it is better not. 'Wan *Gott* will!' & meanwhile one wld be basely ungrateful to worry–& I know your dear unselfish Mother love is almost satisfied with the knowledge that I am well and happy, & enjoying life with my old man & our perennial "dogue."

For we have another, though the Bull Dogue's photo hangs at Rex's watch chain–in one of my old lockets that used always to be 'on duty' among Regie's flames in old days! *Trouvé* is the name of Hector's successor.[1] Cos for why we found him locked up in one of the barrack rooms when I was with Rex on one of his inspections. He is a 'left behind' either of the 1/22d or the 4/60th rifles–we do not know which. He has utterly taken to us–& is especially fond of me I think. He is a big black fellow–between a Newfoundland & a retriever. In the 'Sweep' line, but not so big. He is wonderfully graceful & well mannered (barring a trifling incident yesterday when he got into my little cupboard, ate about 2 lbs of cheese, & all the rolls, & *snuffed* the butter. And another trifling occurrence today. We chained him on to the sofa, which, during our absence, he *dragged* (exactly as the dogs dragged *Mons. Jabot's bed*)[2] across the room, upset the ink on the carpet, threw my photo book down by it, & established himself in Rex's armchair. It was awfully ludicrous, for the other day he slipped his collar, & *chose the sofa* to lie on, but because he was tied to the sofa with full permission to use it–he

315

chose the chair! & must nearly have lugged his own head off. He does wonderfully little damage with his pranks – there were wine glasses, bottles, pickles, &c. in the cupboard when he got the cheese, but he extracted his supper as daintily as a cat, & not a thing was upset! Oddly enough, when we are with him, he never thinks of getting onto cushions & chairs like that blessed old sybarite the Bulldogue. But if we leave him tied up, he plays old gooseberry with the furniture. I had been fearing it would be rather a practical difficulty in the way of his adoption – the question of where he shld sleep – but he solved it for himself. He walks upstairs after us, flops on the floor, gives 2 or 3 whines, & goes gracefully to sleep. In the morning he shakes himself & comes to see if I am awake, gives a few short sighs & puts his great soft paws on the bed & *grabs* at me. We don't let him on, even as an outside passenger (he is *too* big) then he goes round to Rex, licks both our faces copiously, after which he sometimes lies down again & has 40 winks more. When I go into the next room for my bath, he gets much excited by the sound of splashing water, & does not at all like remaining 'on the wrong side of the door' – In fact he has something of *Jim's* partiality for being with every member of the family at once!

[AE's Note] (The poor old dear, this beautiful Sunday morning, in the bright calm sun, very early, before any of us had moved, was heard flopping the floor with his great tail, dreaming a happy dream, we presumed) *Rex*

June 28. I see Rex has added another anecdote of the 'oldy manny.' I wish you could have seen him lying in perverse dignity in the armchair with the sofa attached to the end of his chain like a locket!!! We keep him in very fine discipline as to behaviour at meals — but he is constantly assured also that Grandma Gage will be utterly *pervious* to his *paw*! It *is* so big, & soft, with a brownish tinge on it. We tell him his Grandma's heart & *plate* will be at his disposal after the first pleading pat! But the very name of Gma Gage is demoralizing & he takes liberties on the strength of *you* already! I have some writing on hand but it will not get off this mail, for I am *so* busy packing! & another concert is on Friday next & what nights are *not* practice nights I hardly know. I *do* try to forget what is not out of my heart & thoughts 10 minutes in the day! – If it is fairly decided that we are to stay in Canada – or go to X or Y, or Z – I shall be busy enough house hunting & so forth to forget the disappointment, but when I have no guide to my packing but the hint of Home – & am spending hours in R.'s absence packing such a box for Home station – & such an one for Ecclesfield – it is difficult to realize that when I get to Halifax all may have to be rearranged for Kamskatcha! —

In all this lovely weather – these moonlight nights as I plan – & pack – or sing – or garden – at musical meetings or the early cathedral service — the hope that is so near & yet so far runs under everything, like a brook. . . . . in the Shroggs![3] And I am such a selfish beast I am only exciting you about it. However, if it is not to be, I shall soon be busy enough, and you will be glad to hear what new sights may be before us. We expect to leave Fredericton in 2 or 3 weeks (about a month) for Halifax, where we shall learn where we are to go.

I begin my packing early to avoid fatigue.

Also I mean to sell all my furniture.

Your ever loving daughter
Judy

. . .

LETTER

93

Bishopscote. July. 6. 1869.

My dearest Father.

I have a long letter – almost finished – to you at home – but we have been dining here, & the Bishop has given me this to write to you with, & to prevent my having to go home before service. I have not long – & people are talking round me.

317

Please send the Communion Vessels by the first opportunity to
Andrew Brown Esqr
37 Paradise Street
Liverpool
addressed to the Bishop. Mr. Brown is the Bishop's agent – & the
Vessels will come out with his things.
Send nothing to us – if you have not already done so —
I hardly know how to write it — but – thank GOD! — I believe
we are really coming Home. But you must bear in mind the un-
certainty of all military orders, when all is said & done.

Mr. Strickland arrived unexpectedly by the night boat yesterday. Sat up discussing all things in earth sky & sea till between 2 & 3
this morning – & avows no objection to our going Home except
that he wanted us at Halifax himself. It really *is* his doing, & I shake
in my shoes when he growls that he had been looking forward to
having us there – & that he could keep us if he chose.

But I do not think he will. And his kindness is wonderful – only
equalled by his curious un"chief"-like candour. Only an hour or
two ago he said to me – after a grumble about our not going to be at
Halifax — "However – just now my idea is, anyone who can go
Home *should* go, & look after his own interests."

It is all in GOD's hands – where we are thankfully willing to
leave it – but when we *do* dwell on the idea of seeing you all in the
flesh this autumn – (*Perhaps* in August!) we feel like "Colin's" wife –
    "I'm downright dizzy wi the thocht
    In troth I'm like to greet."[1]
Now — for I must finish off — this is how it lies.

We *may* be sent *anywhere*: but are most likely at present to be
sent home.

If we are sent Home – we shall probably sail *during the month* of
August.

Goodbye & a thousand loves & blessings
Yr loving daughter
Judy.

I hope the *news* will compensate for a short letter. . . .

94

(July. 11th. Sunday. This is the letter I began & did not get home to finish. I sent you a scrap from the Bishop's instead.)

July. 5. 1869.
Fredericton NB.

My dearest Father –

I got the letter with your bit in it this morning, the day after the Halifax mail. As to solving the riddle of the postal arrangements here, it is hopeless, and now we are no longer interested in the matter, it is hardly worth while taking any trouble about what the residents do not care to have altered.

So far as any military moves can be counted upon; – we do now seem to be justified in considering *Home* as our next station! Thank GOD! thank GOD! – We hardly know how to feel grateful enough for such a sunny lot as ours has been, so far. Only 2 year's foreign service – & that in so good a climate – & so nice a place – & with such kind friends – & then Home again to the dear old nest. – I hope we may show ourselves grateful, by being contented if, after all, we should be sent somewhere else! – Of course, you must remember that this is *possible*. But allowing for that, I think you may hope to see us in the flesh, GOD willing, this autumn. After Mr. Strickland first mentioned the possibility, *Rex* adjured me not to set my heart on it, & *I* made a great show of taking the idea *loosely* & lightly; but gradually we met on the common ground of planning this & that for Home – & giving vent to our feelings in references to Trouvé & Grandma' Gage. Then Rex made another desperate rally against dwelling on it; but I rebelled: for I said we might as well have the enjoyment of the *hope*, & all the more if that was to be *all* we were to have, especially as we have far too many solid blessings in being together &c. &c. to behave very badly if we were disappointed. This morning came a note from Strickland saying we might now consider England as our destination before long, & referring us for Department news to a letter which he (*failed to*!) enclose! In the afternoon I went to Church–& Rex had to go to a wonderful *reunion* at the American Consul's house–(The A.C. also keeps a hardware store–& we buy our knife powder of him!)–to celebrate the Day of the Declaration of Independence.[1] It was convivial and complimentary. After various speeches it was proposed to sing "Hail Columbia" & "GOD save the Queen"– There were a good many Yankees besides the Consul–but nobody *knew* Hail Columbia– *Mrs.* Consul & *Miss* Consul were sent for, & still no one could Hail Columbia with Columbia's own National Anthem– So finally the "Star Spangled Banner"[2] or some such effusion was sung–after which GOD save the Queen was sung & found familiar to all!!!! When Rex returned he found a telegram to say that Strickland was coming up by tonight's boat–& here we are (nearly II.P. M.) waiting for him– He is coming to see about various matters in reference to winding up the station. When it is 'wound up' (in about 3 weeks we fancy) we shall go to Halifax–& I fancy it will not be very long before we proceed Home. Tell the dear dear Mum– we are bringing the Member for York County from the Black Dog's Parliament to see Grandma Gage. Since I last wrote we have "moved" again. I begged Rex to let us come into 'Quarters'–& now he likes it very much. It was an awful day for our "flit"– It *poured* & *poured*, but we got very little damage done, & escaped without colds ourselves.

Between 2 & 3 A. M.–Mr. Strickland has just departed to his inn, having sat here discussing all things on the Earth for hours! He had just begun to develop to me his theory of "circles"–when I was obliged to suggest as an illustration of his idea that all things go in circles, that it was so with the hours! One began in the morning & worked round to morning again– On which he drew out his watch & found the position exemplified!!!

July II. Sunday. I send you this old letter dear Pater, as it contains some news you have not heard. The Chief was amiable to the Nth power. He was charmed with the Medleys– The lunch there was very successful. Several people were asked to meet us. Mr. S. took in Mrs. Medley & the Bishop–me–& there was a good deal of fun & pleasant chat. Miss Holbrook much agitated about the middle of lunch — "Oh, Mr. Strickland! *Was* it *you* who took away our *flag?*" Strickland's humourous face was quite a sight! "Well I declare," he said, "if there is an old flag anywhere about you shall have it." "We'll hoist it every Sunday" – Miss H. quaveringly promised. Of course the talk went off as to the old question of the Colony & the imperial policy – annexation &c. &c. & Strickland got into one of his political speeches – At the point when he was laying down — "You've constant & increasing facilities of communication whereby you can express your wishes & sentiments to the Home Govt — " the Bishop broke in with the serio-comic face he can pull from the other end of the table — "You see Sir, we feel Mr. Ewing could express our wishes & sentiments for us so well – if you w!d leave him for the purpose." Somebody else said – "Oh yes leave us Mr. & Mrs. Ewing & the flag & we'll be quite satisfied – " but the Bishop added – "If you'll give me Mrs. Ewing – I'll compound for the flag." Strickland is wonderfully *frank* with us, & we certainly owe him thanks for unbroken kindness – He & Rex were never off their feet hardly whilst he was here – but he let us go to the Choral So. practice on Tuesday Evening. He had all his meals with us, & was very polite to Trouvé. He went off on Wednesday morning. I was not sorry, though I like him very much, but I had a good deal on my hands, & had barely got over the fatigues of moving in, & it has been close, & *damp heaty*. On Wednesday evening I had the Cathedral Choir – & the members of Rex's Friday class to tea, nearly 40 people – After Strickland's departure, I went into the market & secured a lot of the wild strawberries which are just beginning – butter &c. – borrowed china & glass of my friends & all went off very successfully. The music (it was a practice) was very good. I wish you could hear the movement from Rex's anthem of "When the Lord &c." —— "He that now goeth on his way weeping." Mrs. Rowan sings it beautifully & the chorus of "They that sow in tears shall reap in joy – " was really fine. In reference to what you said about Cocks – it is one of the many reasons why I shall be so glad to come Home just now.[3] I want Rex to publish on his own hook before his things are pirated here. For really there is a good deal of his music known & sung here now. . . . July has been altogether an exciting month to us. The paper I send will speak for itself as to the 2d Concert which was *most* successful[4] – I only wanted some of your dear old faces to reflect *my* pride & pleasure at the way the people *heaped* praise & applause on my old boy's head. Old Roberts broke down in reading the address–which I now keep in a sacred drawer. It is a most elegant affair tied with red ribbon. But *the* upsetting thing was when the little Bishop left the audience & came trotting up on to the platform. He had known nothing about it, & his 'say' was of course all impromptu, & the paper does it no manner of justice (we have no Robt Bootterworths to do reporter here!) When he turned his loving old face on Rex to bid him goodbye–it was – – – – –well what the whole thing was–almost more than one cld bear. We are going to scramble in another concert before the month is out if all be well–& we suspect there is to be another "demonstration" then!! I must write a line to the girls. Dearest Pater. Your loving dau: J. H. E.

LETTER

95

Monday July. 12. 1869.

My darling Dot –

I can hardly write for the excitement of our prospex! *Fancy*————seeing you all so soon! And yet we work steadily on, & keep our minds as prepared for disappointment as we can.

As I told the Govr, July has been a wonderfully exciting month. I have never spoken of the Church Society's meeting–which was very interesting. The Synod assembled here this year–& black coats replaced the red ones.[1] But taking them all together, the Bishop may be proud of his clergy. Especially among the younger ones there are some *admirable* men–& the work they do for set-tlers from Home cast upon the sea of wilderness & forest–is surely "written in Heaven." But you shall hear all *when we meet!*

(What a when!) I ought to say that the subs: begun at the meeting was started by poor little Dowling offering 20 dollars towards the deficiency, & one mission parson after another skinning flints by offering the same sum. However some laity joined & the next day at the meeting–the feeble fine old Master of the Rolls tottered in among the members–& with a common impulse they all rose. He sat down by the Bishop & said nothing, & the impression prevailed that he had not *understood* about it (He is breaking up & paralytic–the last of the real fine upright *gentlemen* of the place) Presently he tottered out again–but he had left an envelope with 200 dollars on the table![2]—

Well, all the Church affairs have been *one* exciting interest. Then my "flit" in pouring rain. Oh! I *never* had such a time! After the 1st load had left what *did* my old man do, but keep Spain at the barracks, & send me word he wasn't coming back! And there I was with crockery–glass–kitchen dishes &c. &c. &c. to pack! I packed tumblers & claret glasses–basins & dishes–till my brain spun round–& Mrs. Spain could do nothing but *talk* & laws-a-deary me–& ketchee the "dear babe" till I could have *shaken her* with pleasure. However–we *got off*–& dear old Rex had kept Spain to make roaring fires to dry blankets &c. &c. & it was truly wonderful how little damage was done–I soon had the new rooms furnished–and our "long drawing room" is quite pretty. Only now I am daily stripping it, for I pack a bit every day almost–& most of my pictures & brittle knickknacks are packed. I must tell you that there shines before my eyes a possibility almost *too* good to be true. *On dit*–that "the Crocodile" is coming out again with emigrants to New Brunswick. *If* so–& *if* the time shooted–I know the General would give me a passage Home in her. It wld save *us* my fare–& Govt Rex's–by mail–& the difference in comfort– – – – – – – – – as between a village sickroom & the moors for fresh air–& space! She is a *splendid* transport built for hot climates. It wld make me almost look forward to the voyage–& it wld be no small matter to save the money, for I fear we shall sell our furniture for next to nothing. It is a *drug*!!! Meanwhile I ought to tell you that it is *possible* (though I hope not likely) that we may be detained by Rex having to remain to conduct a worrying suit between Govt & an awful snob of a contractor here– It is a long story–in which a *key* is involved. Strickland informed the said Contractor in no very measured language what his opinion of him was, when he was here.

However we hope for the best.

Please tell the Mum I send the fairy tales. I have decided *not* to write an introduction to them for the magazine. I wish no author's name to be put to them. But the *set* to be called *Old fashioned fairy tales*. Could not Bell get a foreigner to illustrate them?[3] The 2d rate English artists have no soul above the present day, & the latest thing in boy's knickerbockers.

Beg the dear Mum to keep very well for us – Our dear dear love to all – especially the blessed boys – & old Dina & every one – I go mad to think of hugging you all.

Best love to Miss Thompson, of course. I got her letter – & the seeds are sown long long since!!! Your loving Judy.

LETTER

96

S. James. [25 July] 1869

My darling Mum.

There is no special news – except that this is probably the last Halifax mail by which you will hear from us at present. Our hopes as to the "Crocodile" seem dashed to the ground – & the mail by which we want to leave is the "City of Cork" – We have asked to be allowed to go by Boston instead, but have had no answer to the application. If we *are* allowed – it will involve 36 hours of rough sea passage to Boston (*very* nice boats – but the Bay is *choppy* & rather trying to bad sailors) & a *little* more expense, but then we see

Boston, & go home by Cunard Line. If not—we shall probably come by the City of Cork – all right enough only she is a *slow* coach. She is the next Halifax Mail after the one that takes this letter. She is coming out this time, & Mrs. Maunsell's Mother & Sister are coming in her, on a visit to the Maunsells. But she is a *slow* vessel so you must not fidget if the mail seems late – She is *the* slow one of the line. Once the Crocodile sent her letters home by the City of Cork – & sailed herself 24 hours later & got home *48* hours sooner, & had to wait the 2 days for the letters she had sent by the mail before sailing herself!!! However it is a fine season – & fine westerly breezes often blow just now – which would send her home pretty quick independent of her steam! – But I think we shall probably come by Boston. I have no doubt Strickland wld willingly keep us till another mail – but *I would rather not.* I want us to *get off* – & run no risks of being detained – & as to sickness & discomfort – one can bear a good deal *going Home!* Besides it would be convenient to me in many ways. I want to go in the middle of the month – & before the equinoctial gales. . . . I am *very well* just now, thank GOD, & do an amount of work in the summer heat that surprises myself. But it has been a very cool Summer for Fredericton — a great comfort to me. The hardest part of my packing is over. I have packed my dessert china — I hope safely – all my pictures, & almost all the books & knickknacks. I was casting wildly about yesterday for means of packing my pretty (dozen) dessert plates when my eye fell on Aunt Anne's silk lined work basket. I unsewed the pincushion – emptied the basket – & the plates *exactly* squeezed in. I laid silk & soft things between each – till it was full, packed the remainder in another basket, strapped them with leather straps, & *shook* them well experimentally! They are now packed in a box with blankets & soft winter clothes – & will, I hope, be safe. *Moths* are what I live in dread of for my clothes. . . . I don't see how I *can* mind the voyage much this time! Every day that we "win through" will be one day nearer to the cab on Sheffield Lane of which we are always talking, & I never shall realize the delightful fact till we are positively Homeward Bound. Then it is such a comfort that Rex is always well & strong to help me.

Monday [26 July]. My darling Mum. We are really so awfully

busy – I know you will excuse such a scrap of a note. Keep your mind easy now till we telegraph from Liverpool — ! . . . we shall probably come by Boston – but there is no saying – & Strickland has not answered our application yet. I pack, & pack, & pack. But the most is done. Sir James Carter is expected on Tuesday, & we are to meet him on Wednesday Evening.

We had a charming expedition to the Oromuctoo River the other day. We went down by the 9.A. M. steamer to the mouth of the Oromuctoo – Then we took out our canoes – & paddled 4 or 6 miles up – & had a picnic lunch; we paddled back in the evening – & turned off to tea with some people who live near the river. Then we played croquet &c. & finally met the steamer at 10 P. M. pushing off to meet it in a "way boat" – with a lantern to advertize our approach. I am so very busy today dear dear Mum – forgive a short letter – The weather is lovely – but warm – Trouvé lies & pants. I tell him that when he reaches England – his nose is to be *black-leaded*, his teeth brushed with orecanut paste — & his tail & ears put in curl papers – to fit him for presentation to his Grandma' Gage.

Rex's best love
Your ever loving dau:
Judy.

LETTER
97

Aug. 1. 10 Sunday aft Trinity 1869
–Stone Barracks.[1] Fredericton. N.B.

My darling Dot.

We are here still, as you perceive; & indeed, are not much nearer any definite idea as to the *when* & *how* – of our move, than when I wrote last week. The sale of the Government Stores is advertised for the 8th which is something,[2] & Strickland says he shall see about a convoy for the Govt furniture &c. that is to go to Halifax as soon as possible – When the stores are sold – & the others shipped, there is nothing to detain Rex here — "departmentally" speaking. The mail most *convanient* wld be the next Halifax do. (that is so far as we know)–but she is the City of Cork–& we wld prefer to avoid her. She is bringing the mail this time from Home–& is awfully late. She is an awful old slow coach–& an odd 48 hours or so tacked on to the usual time is a serious matter when one suffers so wretchedly at sea as I do. Besides, I know the Mum wld fidget–try as she might, if the mail were late, though it is her nature *to*–having no very strong steam power– We *may* be detained till the next mail–& come so. But we have now asked if we may go *viâ Quebec*. It will cost a little more but not much–& seems well worth it– We should see Montreal & Quebec–& the country as we pass through it. We shall be tantalizingly near Niagara if we do go so: but even so small a detour to a "lion" costs a good deal, as Regie & I felt when we went to Brussels–but not to Waterloo!– However my heart will be so much more with Ecclesfield Dam–or S. Nicholas' Brook–than the Falls of Niagara that I shall not be in the least disappointed. Moreover, I shall have quite enough to do if I lionize Quebec & Montreal after a bit of sharp sea tossing en route–without further tiring myself before crossing from Quebec to Liverpool. We gave up the Boston idea–because the Cunard steamers do not call there *going back* (they really "run" between N. York & Liverpool). They only *bring out* people to Boston. Sir James Carter told me this. He came out viâ Boston & means to return viâ Quebec. He is a dear old man. *Very* nice looking–fresh, white haired, soft voiced, courteous, of the voluminous-silk-handkerchief–silver-snuffbox–low pumps and silk-stocking-date, delightfully antithetical to the democratic free & easy style of society on this side the Atlantic. I shall have a little mischievous enjoyment of his calmness & irreproachable pumps tomorrow night at Govt House, as contrasted with our hospitable but plebeian Governor. We dine there to meet him. Last Friday we met him at the Coster's–on Wedy. at the Wards. He asked a great deal about Aunt Jane (Cumby) & said how pretty she used to be. We still live in a whirl, & in fact I have little hope of rest till Home. I really shall want a week's sleep "straight on end." However the amount of domestic details I have had to see to, & the paucity of time for head-work–has not done me any harm. Everybody says "How well you

are looking. I hope Mrs. Gatty will see you looking as you are now."
I hope she will, but seasickness takes off one's bloom for a bit, so if I
do *not* look fat & fair & ruddy (which almost is my present condition) she must remember I have been so. And there's one consolation about mal de mer – One soon recovers when one gets on
to steady land once more. This summer has been much less hot
than the last – & I have really been very well, I am thankful to say.
Only now & then I get a little bit tired of the ceaseless unrest – & so
does my poor old man – but ——— Home is at the End D.V.!! The chief
heads of our present occupations besides Rex's business – are
"going out" – having people here, packing & unpacking, domestic
ups & downs, music & so forth by day, & fires by night. Last Monday the matter of mischief got into *Spain*'s head in the shape of
some marvellous crotchet or other, & he deliberately "struck work"
(in his private capacity as *our* domestic) & said he had "rather not"
bring up the dinner!! Rex has had an awful lot of bother with the
"roughs" here in reference to the grounds of the Barracks into
which they are always trying to come. Rex has two sets of Barracks
with grounds &c. &c. & lots of Govt stores to take care of – & no
sentries – or soldiers, & a local force of 2 policemen worse than
useless. On Sunday last we found as we thought that the boys had
got into the balcony & stuffed up the wards of the lock of the mess-
room which we use as our drawing room, so we got in another
way, & when we went to Church Rex locked up all the upper part
of the place & took the keys with him, which that unspeakable
goose Spain considered a reflection on his *honesty*! with a whole lot
more bosh which has been seething in his head, because Rex has
fastened up various gates &c. a process having no more connection
with the Spains than with you. But the irishman's toe having been
trodden on, you cld no more get reason into his head than if it were
a "brass knob with nothing in it."³ I doubt if they quite enjoyed
nobody being the least angry but themselves. Rex simply said "Well
that settles that – " & told him he & his family could move into quarters that afternoon. (He is to live in one of the Barracks & take
care of it.) He tried successive grievances as to his "quarters,"
(which was quashed by his having liberty to occupy the whole
barracks, if he chose to be responsible for any damages he & his

family commit.) Next day Rex gave him liberty from the office that he might settle into his new rooms–but he presently returned to enquire what he was to understand by his services not being required that morning–was he "suspended"–Did Rex mean to report him. (Rex loquitur) "GOD bless your soul, man, do try & keep such ridiculous fancies out of your head." Since then they have got settled, & Mrs. Spain has paid me an affable visit, to borrow a jacket pattern & fetch her flat irons!– My present maid ———is a man. Coffee by name–late of the 15th. He is a dear old soul–& a capital waiter, & he & I do the domestic arrangements with much satisfaction & ease. He comes early in the morning & goes away after tea, cuts the wood, goes to the market for me–makes the bed, empties the bath, cooks under my directions, & waits like a professional. He is very economical, intreats me not to get too much meat in at a time & suggests that if we "take" the butter "pretty aisy" it will "*muster*, till the next week–" but of potatoes he is lavish & feeds Trouvé on them. Of course he is irish. We were just in the 1st blush of the change on the Tuesday when the Misses Wilmot came in from Oromuctoo & I had to have them to tea & take them to the Choral So: I rushed out & bought sardines, marmalade, eggs &c. Bessy Roberts (who was staying with me) ran home like a brick, & borrowed some cups, & we made a very jolly little spread– Wedy. to the Wards. Friday the Costers & to meet the Bishop at the boat. Saturday choir practice &c. also a workwoman in the house 2 days & ceaseless unpacking of evening clothes & repacking of things. Tomorrow Major Cox comes up–we dine at Govt House– Tuesday a private concert of the Choral So. & Testimonial to Rex– Wedy Capt. Mackenzie & Mr. Sparkes come back & will have to "feed" with us as before–& I suppose the next week *may* see us off—or–it may not!– Our own sale is yet to come off & the round of P.P.C.⁴ visits–no small item.

   Tuesday. & my birthday!–

I must scribble a bit more before the post goes out. We got your letters yesterday— It is no good bothering about the mails *now*. We have got no letter yet in which you allude to the idea of our coming home–and neither of those we got had any *viâ* at all on them. But we enjoyed them very much. The Govt work gets on apace – & I still hope we may get Home by the end of August or beginning of Sepr. *Probably* viâ Quebec – but it *may* be by a good steamer from S. John. The latter plan wld be much the cheapest – though a little longer as to sea passage. The Acadia which is on her way out, & will return soon is a very fine vessel I believe. We will telegraph from Liverpool when we arrive. We had a pleasant dinner party last night – & the evening "fire" was on the other side of the river. Last Saty there was a bad one in the town[5] – & we hear it has been suggested in certain disreputable quarters that the Park Barracks[6] wld be well *burnt.* So we sleep with one eye open & the deaf ear downwards!!!!! The P. Barracks are *not* the ones *we* live in. Tonight the Choral Society are going to give Rex a testimonial.

I have accidentally discovered that it is a *Cup.* We are very well – happy & busy – & *longing* to see you all!

Your ever loving
Judy.

LETTER

98

10 August 1869.
Fredericton N.Bk.

Our very dear Mum –

We would fain spare *you* the uncertainty which is the shadyside of our wandering life. But (as we often have reason to say) 'one can't have everything.' And you are such a dear, good, reasonable Mum! – Up to yesterday afternoon we hoped, & believed that this very day we should begin the journey that, please GOD – is to end in the old nest – but it is not to be for a little bit yet. We hope, however, that it *is* only deferred for a few weeks. We felt rather 'knocked over' yesterday evening, but all right today – I *had* rather dwelt on the joy of sending you a telegram from Liverpool in place of a letter across the Atlantic — but still we feel keenly enough how

much—how very much—we have to be grateful for—& *if we are
allowed to go Home this time*—I shall make few grumbles as to
route—vessel—or anything else—I promise you!! I must tell you the
history of this week— On Monday [2 August] came Major Cox—
& we entertained him at meals. Coffee & I managed domestic matters—Rex worked hard at Govt work, & I packed ceaselessly.
On Tuesday evening the Choral Soy. gave a small concert—where
Sir James Carter sat smiling in the front ranks & Major Cox sat
meditative by the door! After the Hallelujah Chorus—The Bishop
came forward & in the name of the Society gave Rex a silver cup &
a watch chain. The cup is very light & artistic—very pretty indeed &
beautifully engraved with an inscription on one side, & a "design"

of musical instruments on
the other— The chain is
simple & pretty. The peo-
ple were awfully kind, &
are forever bemoaning our
departure. On Wednesday
Mr. Sparkes & his son, &
Capt. Mackenzie & his
bride came up (The 2 offi-

cers to be present at the sale of Govt Stores) Capt. M. was jollier
than ever—& his wife is *charming*. We are great allies, & they took
rumbletumble tea with us as they found it & Capt. Mackenzie
played with Trouvé such wonderful antics that we have proposed to
get up a "show" to which Rex is to perform appropriate music! You
wld have laughed to see us all dashing about the mess room scream-
ing & laughing & setting the dogs on each other, & playing the most
wonderful games! Mrs. McK. is *very* bonny. A fair Swede—with
exquisite blond hair—& a sweet face. He is *very* clever & amusing!
On Thursday the sale began, & Rex got a telegram from Strickland
to tell him to wind up the station at once & proceed to S. John to
await orders. Meanwhile the General had telegraphed to the Govr
that a raid was expected of Cuban filibusters, & a gun boat was sent
down to S. John.[1] Rex told me this with orders to *keep dark* which of
course I did. He was a good deal worried as it looked so like work
on the frontier for him—& I began to speculate on packing him a

separate "kit." He telegraphed to Strickland on Thursday evening "Am I to come with wife & baggage–or light kit," but we got no answer till next day & only to be in readiness for a move! So Rex worked like a horse & said it was a simple duty to sell our furniture & be ready– On Friday it poured–& *no* sale cld take place– The Mackenzies stayed on & we got a letter (several days older than the telegram's in date) refusing our application for any route but the mail. On Saturday it was fine–our sale was advertised for 12.A. M.² — Coffee was to call us at six–but we had to get up without him–& he got drunk. ("He wldn't be an irishman if he didn't fail us at a pinch" says Rex!!) Bessy Roberts was staying with me–& we washed pots, & rubbed up tin-articles, &c. &c. & set out everything in front of the barracks– It was an awfully bad sale–for there have been sales *ad nauseam*, & trade in the town is at a very low ebb. Altogether it came to more than we hoped from the ludicrous prices bid—about £34. Our dear indian brother Peter–bought our *drawing room chairs* & gave full price for them!!!! *Where* he will put them in his hut–he best knows!!!! The Mackenzies went away. Our barrack sergeant had bought our bed, & offered to lend it to us till we left–so we slept in barracks–& on Sunday breakfasted with Mrs. Roberts–& had dinner & tea with the Medleys. The Cuban idea seemed to be passing off–& we expected to go by this mail–& made ready to leave on Monday afternoon. Sunday seemed to come in inconveniently–but we strictly did nothing & the rest was good. On Monday early we set to work–Rex to finish off the station, I to fasten up every box–have the few dirty things washed, pay bills, & make ready our "steamer" portmanteau & bags. R. telegraphed that the work wld end that day & asked if he were to come on & go Home by the Mail. We 'fed' at the Medleys. Coffee continued muddled, & he & Spain had a quarrel! —— At 3.P. M. Spain brought a telegram "Please remain at Fredericton till further orders."–& he & Coffee began to abuse each other like Billingsgate–& report each other to Rex–who got in an awful rage–as you may fancy–& pitched into both of them. It was rather a blow, for we have sold every stick at disadvantage–& have now to live at a boarding house—"till further orders." We have been sleeping here & we had breakfast today with the Medleys–but she is not well, &

they cannot have us anymore – & we are feeding at the hotel. If no more news comes today we shall move into a boarding house till we go. (This is Tuesday. 10 Aug.) We went to church yesterday afternoon & Rex played the organ, & everybody is very kindly glad we are kept – but we really cannot pretend to be! We still hope to be off next mail, & if we do get off then, we shall be very thankful. We are both very well thank GOD, & the weather is lovely, & anyway the packing & sale are *over*. We hope not to draw on my little nest egg with *Bell*. But if we are kept long, & put to much expense – Rex will have to draw on him as we agreed. It is *very* pleasant to get a kind word & a hearty regret, from every tradesman one pays off, & every friend we say goodbye to. I think we know every decent body in the place – & people say we seem to be *part of Fredericton*. Poor dear Mrs. Medley broke down so bitterly in congratulating me on going home to *my Mother* – "She will be so proud of you both – & the love you have won here –" & the poor soul sobbed – & did I *not* sympathize! –

My darling old Mater. I forgot to tell you that Capt. Mackenzie took Trouvé with him & he & the canoe are to start this week by "The Pacific" for Liverpool – addressed to Mackenzie Smith Esqr

> Kent St. Mills
> Liverpool

Beg Frank for our sakes to bespeak Mackenzie's good offices for him. The Pacific is a sailing vessel.

I am bringing some indian work for you all – & am trying to get an indian rosary for Aunt Horatia!! . . .

We are very jolly – Our dear dear love to all

> Your ever loving daughter
> Judy.

12th Sunday after Trinity.
Aug. 15. 1869
Fredericton N Bk —

My dearest Dot.

We have not yet got any letters from you by this mail – because they were sent to Halifax I suppose – we hope to get them to-morrow. I am afraid you will all be terribly disappointed that it still *is* a question of *letters* between us – but I still hope for Home this year. At the same time one must face the fact that these threats of Cuban & Fenian difficulties out here may well make the authorities fancy they have been clearing out the stations a little too rapidly, & if more soldiers are stationed at S. John – *we* shall probably be stationed there also; & the chance of Home once passed; one cannot tell when it may come round again. The whole of the 78th *have* been ordered there within the last week or two –, & the order *countermanded*.[1] We hear *nothing*, & consider it good policy to keep quiet. If however it does end in this, you must remember that we like S. John very well – have friends there – & the winter is less trying than at Fredericton. But I still utterly refuse to realize the idea of Xmas anywhere but at Home this year!!!! We are very jolly again, and having a rest which is very pleasant. I am afraid my letter to the Mum last week was rather dismal, but we were a little bit *floored* after working so hard to get off at once. Above all, let her try to be prepared for anything – if we *do* get off, you will probably know nothing of it till you get the telegram – & I do not want the Mum to be *startled*. For her conservative mind was still open to being "flustrated" by a telegram when I left Home!!!!!! (*We* get more telegrams than letters!) Bless her! — After all Trouvé did not go – which vexed us. They made a muddle of bribing the ship's officers, & he is not crossing the Atlantic in the Pacific as we hoped! However, till we know our fate, it is perhaps as well. We are in sort of lodgings, & are very comfortable – & it is not ruinous by any means. We have a very pretty sitting room with a bookcase of books belonging to a deceased medical man of the place[2] – A very miscellaneous but entertaining collection. We are going pretty steadily through them – or rather *creaming them* – so to speak! – Our skimmings so far include Jesse's Gleanings & Whewell's Principles of Morality – The Poems of Herrick – Horatius Bonar & Keats, Ellis' Women of England & Catlin's N. American Indians, Soyer's Cookery & the Tracts for the Times – a book on Acadie &c. &c. &c.[3] We have a nice bedroom & dressing room, & the wittles is good. I must tell you, my old duck, that I have been trying to get some pretty birds for feathers for you & Dina – but so far Peter has been very unsuccessful – but something I must bring you. I thought plumes wld be nice for your hats. We had a great scene with Peter yesterday. Rex has 2 guns you must know – a rifle, & an old fowling piece – good enough in its way but awfully *old fashioned* (not a breechloader) & he determined to make old Peter a present of this, for he is a good old fellow – & does not *cheat* one, & we had resolved to give him something, & we knew this wld delight him. I wish you *could* have seen him. He burst out laughing, & laughed at intervals from pure pleasure, & went away with it laughing. But with the childlike *enjoyment* (which negros have also) the indians have a power & grace in 'expressing their sentiments' on such an occasion which far exceeds the attempts of our "poor people" – & is most dignified. His first *speech* was an emphatic (& *always slow*) "*Too* good! Too much!" & when Rex assured him it was very old, not worth anything &c. &c. He hastily interrupted him with a thoroughly gentlemanlike air almost Grandisonian – "Oh! Oh! as good as new to me. Quite as good as new." They were like 2 Easterns! For not to be outdone in courtesy, Rex warned him not to put too large charges of powder for fear the barrel should burst – being so old. A caution which I believe to be totally unnecessary, & a mere hyperbole of depreciation – as Peter seemed perfectly to understand! He told me it was "The first present I ever receive from a gentleman. Well – well – I never forget it, the longest day I live." The graceful candour with which he said "I am very thankful to you–" was quite pretty. I must tell you that Rex now bitterly regrets that we did not take up the indian dialects earlier. I was very much bent on it when we first came, but he then thought it not feasible & I gave it up. The *capacity* of their organs of speech seems very great. They have Hebrew gutturals & wonderful sounds like the nice distinctions of chinese throat sounds, & the Greek *th ph* & *ps* in their own language–& do not seem to have the least difficulty with any of our consonants. They speak english capitally, slowly, & with a faintly foreign *tone* that is attractive, & totally without the *slurs* & *skips* & *misaccents* that make many of our own provincial dialects *vulgar*. Please give my love to Aunt Horatia when you have the chance–& say that it will not be my fault if she does not soon possess a rosary of indian workmanship. I have been at my friend about it for a long time, but have suspected a disinclination on his part as he knows I am not an R.C. but perhaps now he will do it. I have also ordered a wooden *cross* for Charlie of indian work–which has also not yet been accomplished!–

One thing that upset me a good deal the other day–I must tell you. I was worried enough that Coffee chose the particular day of the sale to get drunk–but if that had only been all!– Among all the things he *failed to do*–he exercised (by his own account) a very unnecessary energy in putting out our *tea pot* (the Heads' dear present!) to be sold. *Where* he put it–if his tale be true–I suppose he can't remember now–but it is *gone*—& *not sold*—we have got nothing for it & I fear no chance of recovering it. I cried like a fool about it– I was so upset & vexed–& one gets so *weary*–of liking people–& treating them kindly, & being so horribly cheated. And the Heads' dear gift too!— However I don't like thinking about it!—

... I am sorry to say that Mrs. Medley is very far from well. I suspect she will be ordered Home–though no one speaks of this as yet.

Monday [16 August]. Still no news–but your letters came this morning. Oh! dear, it *is* sad disappointing you all. But I feel hopeful yet– So far the 78th *are not* moved to S. John, & if there is no further cuban alarm–I do not see why we should not get off. Strickland knows how anxious we are to do so–& is friendly. We keep our boxes packed, & are resting from our labors. I am drawing ("instead of washing pots" growls my Bungle Bear!), & Rex progresses steadily with the library of the late Dr. Robb. Trouvé is coming back to us this evening, & we are going down to the boat to meet him. (By the same token, we are just off– R. says I must get ready. It is after 10.)

Tuesday [17 August]. No news whatever. And Rex says I ought to tell you that he does not think there is any likelihood of our coming Home at present. I *hope* he is a little *hopeless*! But so he says. And he does not like me even to speak of it. He is so sorry about the Mum's disappointment. He offered *me* to come home alone, but of course I shall not unless I see real grounds for thinking he will follow & *then   not then*–I think. The idea is to save me the passage in the equinoctial gales. But I mean to stay with him. I cannot in my own heart give up hope, but it certainly does not look very bright. What does seem really unnecessary is the *mystery* about it all. There seems no reason (& R. says there is no departmental etiquette) to hinder Strickland from *telling us* whether or no we are likely to go Home. But Rex says *he* cannot *ask* any more! I think we must surely have *heard* something by next week–at any rate, and as that is the regular mail, you will not have long to wait for news I hope.

I have got the rosary for Aunt Horatia. Oh, dear! How I have hoped to bring my little souvenirs myself!!! But one must be patient.

Prince Arthur is on his way out, I believe. I suppose we shall see him now!– Trouvé is with us again. . . .

I think I must stop– I wish I had had more cheerful news to communicate– But as long as we are all alive & well–we thank GOD –& look "immer vowarts"–

I keep my eyes on the mails of the season. Rex & all black appearances notwithstanding!

> Goodbye my duck– Your ever loving
> though rather low spirited Judy.

337

By what vessel did
you send the Communion
Plate? You never told us!

LETTER
IOO

Tuesday. S. Bartholomew. [24 August] 1869.
Fredericton.

My darling old Mum.

I *did* think we would have some news to send you by this mail – and it is provoking to report ourselves "as you was." Not one line of a letter has Rex ever received in explanation of the orders he got by telegraph a fortnight ago – nor a hint as to our future. We do so bitterly regret the worry for *you*. But one must not complain when one is spinning out the time in the loveliest phase of a fine climate – with the hope still unextinguished of spending Xmas at Home. (For we must hope on till we hear the contrary!) We have heard side wind rumours too, of one of "our" officers going Home from Bermuda where his wife's health has not been good – and if Strickland keeps us from going there we must not fidget at a little delay. Some days since Rex wrote to him – saying he was utterly "in the dark" – but wld Strickland mind just telling him thus much – wld it be safe & advisable for him (Rex) to go away for a few days' holiday to Grand Falls, adding that if it wld delay by one hour any chance we might still have of getting home, he would not dream of it. &c. &c. To this came a telegram consisting of 2 words – "Stand fast." This was last Saturday. Since when – not one syllable have we had. I freely confessed I *hoped* from it. I thought it might mean "Keep quiet, I am trying to get you off this mail," — & I think Rex hoped a little also. But all hope for this mail is over now. We could not possibly catch it but by going down this afternoon & catching the boat at night to cross the Bay of Fundy. And there has not been a word. We hope we shall get a *letter* tomorrow from

Strickland which may give *news*, though we have now no possible hope for another fortnight. I wish this letter could be kept till to-morrow that you might hear the news, but it cannot be! *If* we get Home by the next mail (& what earthly excuse there is for keeping us we cannot conceive, as Rex has nothing to do, though he may not leave the place!) – it very likely will be the City of Paris we think. She has just brought out Prince Arthur, & has made the very quickest passage on record – 6 days & 17 hours!!!![1] It is wonderful. She must be a good boat, even allowing for "Royal weather" & a 'putting on of steam' for the Prince, & I do hope we may get off then, for we *might just* escape the equinoctial gales! We were at the Bishop's last night, & Mrs. Medley was very sympathetic about *you*. Indeed, dear Mum, we *do* regret having to add *suspense* to your ail-ments – but at any rate it is no small blessing to think of us as well, comfortable, & happy; which we pray GOD is also the case with you all, & wait patiently till He sees fit to bring us together again. I have full confidence in Strickland's friendliness towards us, & that he is doing as he believes to be best, & he well knows how anxious we are to get Home.

Now to pleasanter subjects — My dear dear old Mum. *The Communion Plate has arrived!* & I *am* so glad to have seen it, as it might have crossed us on the road! – (They have charged awfully for the transit. £2!!) We are paying the Bishop – & can settle with you afterwards. It is splendidly solid & fine, & the gilding of the chal-ices is beautiful. How *charmed* the people will be! & we are all so glad it has arrived in time for the Consecration. The inscription is beautifully cut, but who *did* "correct the proofs"? The alms dish is called a *Paten!* & 2 *plates* are also enumerated. Paten is the old word for the plate or plates on which the bread is put. And, as there are 2 cups or chalices – I suppose the 2 small dishes are the plates or patens. The other – like all the *big* dishes in communion sets – is to receive the alms when they are brought by the collectors to the minister. However the Magaguadavic settlers will not find *that* out; & will they *not* be proud!!! I am longing to see Mr. Hannington's face! After all we *may* be here for the Consecration. It would be nice to have been at the first using of your children's beautiful gift. I *do* feel *so* proud!!! If we find we are likely to be *long* delayed, or sent elsewhere, I shall *send* my drawings &c. of Magaguadavic. We may be at the Consecration ourselves. If not – I have engaged Mr. Dowling to send you an account of it. Mr. Hannington has had a severe loss since we were up there. His parsonage has been burnt down[2] – but his ever-energetic parishioners are building him another. It certainly is true that the more people do & give the more still they seem willing & able to give & do!! I shld like to see the queer old face of Mr. Henry (the settler with whom we had tea at Magundy, one of the chief helpers at Magaguadavic) when he sees the Communion Plate!! By the bye — if I send a little account for *printing – I do not wish to be paid for it* – & I *think* it wld be better in Mission Life than A.J.M. But as you think well. We treated ourselves to a drive the other day. Took our luncheon with us, & spent the day "in the country" — We were in some woods where an old woman met a young *Bear* a few days since. I had got out of the "wagon" (anglicé country carriage of peculiar make) & was getting ferns &c. &c. when I heard a rustling & a sound that made me think the Bear was there, for it was just the place where he had been seen. I rather wanted to see him – but Rex called me, for he had heard the sound & came to the same conclusion!! So I got in & we drove off. Rex did not want me to stop, for fear it shld be the Mother Bear who might have been savage & devoured me!!! That is our nearest approach to a "wild beast story" since we came to these parts! We have paid off nearly everything of our bills in the place – & are glad to find that though our things did not sell well – we shall have enough to bring us Home without drawing on Bell. It is more expensive living in hotels, of course, than keeping house – but it is a rest – & the difference is not great. I suppose now we shall be here whilst Prince Arthur is here – & meet him & the Govr Genl – & Lady Young at Govt House. I feel like any fat old country dame going up to London "to see the Queen" – for I have never set eyes on one of the somewhat numerous members of the Royal Family. What the poor young gentleman will do with himself at Govt House *I can't think*. The Govr is a strict Methodist – & doesn't allow dancing & as he is neither literary nor artistic (except in being rather musical & a good florist) the rooms are woefully *unsuggestive*! & it is all *I* can do to keep awake there! He is coming next week – & I must make myself a bonnet! & (oh me!) *unpack* some clothes! Your loving dau. Judy

P.S. Do not fidget dear dear old Mater. You will have us for Xmas yet I hope & believe. We are having lovely weather, & I may get a few more Autumn tints before starting. We hope for a few more *drives* too. We are having a nice bit of *rest*, which may make me all the fitter for the sea. I have got the indian cross for Charley – a pipe of peace for Regie – & moccassin slippers for Brownie – & a minia-ture canoe for Stephen. I hope they will like their things. My best love to Miss Thompson (I am bringing *her* a souvenir) & all old friends – & dear Maggie & Frank – & the Dot & Dina – Peter is still trying for *plumes* for the latter.

Our dearest & best of love (I have an indian spectacle case of large dimensions for the dear pater!!) ———

LETTER
101

Fredericton
14. Septr 1869

My darling Mater.

Our orders from the General have not arrived – & in fact we have heard no syllable since I wrote last. But we still hope to be Home by this mail. Though one is obliged to warn you that it is not quite a military certainty! – It is trying to me to be all this time without a line from Home, but it was only natural you shld hope that letters wld be superfluous! I hope & pray you are all well. It feels desperately like the way we have waited through fortnight after fortnight for each mail hoping for a letter or a telegram telling us to start — & all in vain! But we do *think* we shall get off this time. If we do, it will be the "City of Baltimore" I hear. A very good boat. I think if we have a good passage we ought to get in at the end of the first week in October – or early in the second. I mean about the

6th or 8th. We have very pleasant weather just now – though it has been much the reverse. Prince Arthur's visit went off very well.[1] There was a large evening party at Govt House – & everybody was presented – & he shook hands with everybody, & was very bright & pleasant. He is a very nice looking young man with a very dignified graceful manner. I had not the honor of any conversation with him!! But I had a good look at him, for he was on the steps receiving the fireman's "deputation" when we arrived, & then he shook hands with us of course when we were presented. He made himself very popular at the balls where he has been I believe, but our Govr being a Methodist won't give balls – so there was none here.

Rex & I are just going a drive — it is a lovely day. Farewell calls. Oh we *shall*, we surely *shall* be with you soon!

So glad you like the fairy tales. I hope you are keeping my *incog.*

Your loving
A.J.E. & the
Dogue!

[AE's Postscript]

Please to understand that *I* have hurried her away from her letter; the trap being at the door.

We are coming by next mail, unless we are countermanded.

AE

CODA

They are come! They came Monday evening & that night we had for a couple of hours the whole family in the house – 8 children, 2 sons-in-law, and the Grandchild. Dear Julie is almost entirely unchanged except in being a great deal stronger & they are happy as people can be in the world. The excitement is far from over for I can hardly believe she is here when I see her! She has brought a souvenir for you & us all. . . . Rex looks *much younger.* . . . The state we were in all Sunday & Monday can't be told. We got a telegram from Cork Sunday morning. The whole village was up in arms on Monday & they were [greeted] on Monday by *all* the children bursting into the grounds full tilt and crowding all round the front to see them alight. The chaos and excitement were overwhelming & yesterday when Undine was going round her district people were *wild* to see Julie.

(Mrs. Alfred Gatty to Mrs. Horatia Elder,
Wednesday [6 October 1869] [HAS 43a])

ABBREVIATIONS

AE	Alexander Ewing
AJM	*Aunt Judy's Magazine*
BOT	*The Brownies and Other Tales*
CMA	Children's Mission Army
CO	Colonial Office
HAS	Hunter Archaeological Society, Sheffield Central Library
HQ	*Headquarters*
JHE	Juliana Horatia Ewing
MD	Miscellaneous Documents, Sheffield Central library
ML	*Mission Life*
MP	*Monthly Packet*
MOR	*Mrs. Overtheway's Remembrances*
NBRFA	*New Brunswick Reporter and Fredericton Advertiser*
OED	*Oxford English Dictionary*
OFFT	*Old-Fashioned Fairy Tales*
PANB	Provincial Archives of New Brunswick
PAC	Public Archives of Canada
SPCK	Society for Promoting Christian Knowledge

Appendix 1, The Mails

Between 1867 and 1869 a number of changes were made in British and Canadian contracts for the conveyance of transatlantic mail, and a knowledge of these changes is essential for a clear understanding of what JHE means when she refers to the American mail via New York, the Halifax mail, and the mail sent by the Quebec Route.

American Mail via New York

The first regular transatlantic mail service began in July 1840 in accordance with the provisions of the 1839 contract between the British Admiralty and the British and North American Royal Mail Steam Packet Company (of which Samuel Cunard was part-owner). The contract stipulated that the mail was to be conveyed monthly in winter and bi-monthly during the rest of the year, from Liverpool to Boston via Halifax. The agreement also included the provision that during the months the St. Lawrence was open, Cunard would carry the mail on to Quebec, but in 1845 this branch service was dropped, to the displeasure of the Canadian government. By 1852 the Cunard service to the coast of North America had become weekly throughout the year, with ships leaving Liverpool each Saturday and sailing alternately directly to New York and to Boston via Halifax. During the late 1840s and early 1850s the American Collins Line offered direct competition, and after Collins' failure in 1858, the British Inman Line, which sailed twice weekly from Liverpool, sought a contract to carry mail to Halifax, New York, and Philadelphia; nonetheless, the British government continued to subsidize Cunard at increasingly higher rates.

However, by November 1868 when the United States and Great Britain signed a new postal convention which reduced the letter rate from 1s.2d. per 1/2 ounce to 6d. and book post from 3d. to 1d. if less than 1 ounce, the British government had taken steps to lower the annual subsidy of £173,000 paid to Cunard by opening the bidding for mail service to the United States to public competition. In October 1868 the tenders of the Cunard, Inman, and North German Lloyd lines were accepted, and in December the contracts were signed. Cunard ships were to sail every Saturday from Liverpool to New York and every Tuesday from Liverpool to Boston via Queenstown. Inman ships were to sail every Wednesday from Liverpool to New York via Queenstown, but in February 1869 the sailing day was changed to Thursday. Both Cunard and Inman were to provide ships having a speed of 12 knots per hour; both contracts were for seven years from 1 January 1869 and terminable on not less than one year's notice. The yearly subsidies to Cunard and Inman were respectively £70,000 and £35,000. The contract with the North German Lloyd Line, which also began 1 January 1869, was terminable at any time on six months' notice; the line was paid 1s. for every ounce of letters, 3d. for every pound of newspapers, and 5d. for every pound of book packets. The North German Lloyd ships sailed every Tuesday from Southampton to New York and were required to make the passage in not more than 276 hours April through October and in not more than 300 hours during the rest of the year.

In early 1869 average passage time westward for Cunard's fast Saturday ships was 11 days, 4 1/4 hours; for his slow Tuesday ships, 12 days, 12 1/4 hours; the average time for Inman ships was 12 days, 20 1/2 hours, and for North German Lloyd ships, 12 days, 8 3/4 hours. No specific sailing days were assigned to the sailings from New York, but the Cunard ships usually left New York on Wednesdays and Thursdays, sailing directly to Liverpool via Queenstown; the Inman ships usually sailed for Liverpool via Queenstown every Saturday and every alternate Tuesday, the Tuesday ships going via Halifax.[1]

Halifax Mail

Halifax had served as a mail depot since 1840, when the Cunard Line began its transatlantic mail service between Liverpool and Boston via Halifax. In 1866 the British government decided to concentrate the mail exchanges between the United Kingdom and the United States upon New York beginning in January 1868. To allow the dominion government time to make new arrangements for Canadian mail, the British government made a temporary arrangement with the Inman Line to convey mail fortnightly between Halifax and Queenstown for six months from 1 January 1868 at £375 sterling for each voyage. Later a contract was entered into with Mr. Inman for a continuance of the fortnightly service between Halifax and Queenstown for three years from 1 July 1868, at the rate of £312 10s. sterling for each voyage. Both contracts specified that Inman ships were to sail from Halifax alternate Fridays; the contract of January 1868 set alternate Sundays as sailing days from Queenstown, while the contract of July 1868 allowed a choice between alternate Saturdays or Mondays. In 1868 the average westward passage time was 10 days, 20 hours; the average passage time eastward was 9 days, 2 hours.[2]

Quebec Route

When Cunard dropped service to Quebec in 1845, the inland Canadian provinces lost their regular transatlantic mail service; consequently, efforts were made to establish a Canadian mail line. The tender of Hugh Allan of Montreal was accepted in 1852, and in 1853 he contracted to provide service between Montreal and Liverpool, and Montreal and Glasgow. This mail run, subsidized at an annual cost of £45,000, began in 1856, with ships sailing fortnightly during the months the St. Lawrence was open and monthly during the winter, when the mail was landed at Portland, Maine, and then sent by way of the Grand Trunk Railway to Montreal. By 1859 service had become weekly throughout the year, and the yearly subsidy had been raised to £55,000. The Union Act of 1 July 1867 further increased efficiency by bringing postal service throughout the dominion under one administration. During 1868 daily mail runs were established on the St. John River route to Rivière du Loup, from which point the mail was carried to Quebec by the Grand Trunk Railway, which in that year also began to run special Montreal-Quebec and Montreal-Portland trains to insure rapid conveyance of mail from the Allan Line ships. The mail ships of the Allan Line sailed from Liverpool on Thursdays and from Quebec and Portland on Saturdays. The three-year contract, signed 23 March 1869 for £54,500 currency a year, specified that westward passage should not on an average exceed 14 days and eastward passage should not exceed 13 days. In 1869 the average crossing time from Liverpool to Portland was 11 days, 23 hours; that from Liverpool to Quebec was 9 days, 15 hours; the eastward passage from Portland was 10 days, 15 hours; that from Quebec was 9 days, 16 hours.[3]

Appendix 2, The Scheme

During the 1860s, successive attempts were made to centralize control of the civil branches of the British Army. In 1864 a committee was appointed to consider the system of supply, and the following year, Lord De Grey implemented its findings when he recommended to the Treasury that the administrative departments be brought under some unified direction, but no immediate action was taken. In 1866 Lord Strathnairn was asked to head a committee to inquire into the subject of army transport, and having done so, he recommended that all administrative services—Transport, Barracks, Commissariat, Purveying, and Stores—be brought under a single system of control. On 27 June 1867 in the House of Lords, he stated that "all these departments are under the War Office, and their duties bring them into constant relations at military stations with . . . the troops and their commanders. But these relations are not defined by any rules or organization. The result is friction ... amongst the departments themselves and undefined, doubtful subordination to the Commander-in-Chief.'"

Strathnairn believed that a solution might be reached by appointing an officer who represented the double authority of the War Office and the commander-in-chief, and who, "acting under the General Commanding, ... should carry out all War Office Regulations required for the service relating to the administrative departments." Consequently, in December 1867 the War Office proposed to the Treasury the appointment of a controller-in-chief, with a position comparable to that of a permanent undersecretary of state, at a salary of £2,000 a year. This appointment was concurred in, and on 1 January 1868 Sir Henry Storks became controller-in-chief of the newly established Control Department of the War Office.

In March 1868 Storks presented his proposal for the reform of army organization to the Treasury, but he was asked for further information, and because the Treasury had not endorsed the War Office proposal concerning the power of the controller-in-chief in financial matters, the control system was not introduced in Ireland on 1 April 1868 as Sir John Pakington, the secretary of state for war, had proposed. On 28 April 1868 the Royal Warrant for the constitution of the new department was issued; on 29 June 1868 the Treasury offered a series of modifications to the War Office proposal, which Pakington accepted but which gave rise to great controversy in both Houses. The most important matters of debate were the recommendations that the controller-in-chief receive a salary of £1,500 a year, that he be appointed without the rank of undersecretary, and that a financial officer, who was to receive a salary of £1,500, and a deputy also be appointed.

On 16 July 1868 discussions in both the House of Lords and the House of Commons focused on the questions of whether the financial officer and his deputy were to be officers of the Treasury or of the War Office and on the relative power of the controller-in-chief and the financial officer. (The decision to divide the responsibility between these two men, who owed allegiance to different departments, was in part responsible for the brief life of the control system.) These discussions slowed down the implementation of the scheme, but by 11 March 1869 the secretary for war, Edward Cardwell, was able to report to the House of Commons that Ireland, Gibraltar, Aldershot, the Cape, the Straits Settlements, Nova Scotia (which as a command included New Brunswick), Newfoundland, Bermuda, Barbadoes, Grenada, and Australia, were all under the new control system, which would soon further extend throughout Great Britain and to all other colonial stations.

The question of the relative power of the Horse Guards and the War Office, which lay behind the July 1868 controversy over the degree of authority to be wielded by the controller-in-chief, became a more open and more prominent issue in the discussions of army reform which took place in 1869 and early 1870, and were ended on 28 June 1870, when the Queen signed an order-in-council which made the commander-in-chief a subordinate to the secretary of state for war, thus opening the way for Cardwell's far-reaching army reforms of the 1870s, the most important of which were the introduction of short-term service, the abolition of the purchase system, the formation of a veteran reserve, and a total reorganization of the governing structure, which by 1875 abolished the control system and brought all branches of the army under the tripartite authority of the commander-in-chief, the surveyor general, and the financial secretary—all of whom served under the direct authority of the secretary of state for war.[1]

Appendix 3, Knickerbockers

[JHE writes:] Going out [to Canada] in Autumn—a good stock of *woolens* will be very useful—as english material is better than Canadian. The children should have coarse red—or linsey wolsey large knickerbockers made to go over *all their clothes* out of doors—on this pattern. 1 & 2 perfectly straight legs. 3 the middle

piece—a square to be folded at the line & put in thus. It is all gathered into a band & opens at the 2 sides & all the petticoats are stuffed in— Ladies wear them

out of doors over everything except crinoline & outer skirts. Strong warm protection against the cold will save much in sickness & worry. (JHE to Eleanor Lloyd, 16 September 1870 [HAS 65])

Appendix 4, The Bear

[JHE writes:] I knew the pet bear of the 1/22d in Fredericton well. We were both young in those days! We both lived by that beautiful river, the S. John. *He* lived at the foot of an old willow-tree – a very fine one – which he barked completely –

to make a Bear Baby House of. That indefinite lump marked A shows the sort of place he curled up on in the tree. He was very lonely, & I suppose became mixed in his mind, for he took to a little black lump-of-soot of a retriever pup, & I think thought it was a Baby Bear. (I *hope* it was *Trouvé* [see L92, n1]). When the soldiers brought him his bread & milk in a W.O. pail & he dipped his nose in & ate his breakfast, the wee pup sat & gazed hungrily at him, & hopelessly at the tall pail. One day I saw the bear see this, & he put down his nose, all dabbled with the bread & milk to the Pup & the Pup ate it off his nose. When I saw him in Aldershot *my heart was broke intirely.* I had some difficulty to hear where he was – & then I found he was kept in a place he could hardly turn round in by some outhouses in the permanent barracks – an unsheltered corner in the sun! Poor Dear! He looked *so* miserable, & they said he was "dangerous" – & I think *I* should have been dangerous after his experiences of life!! They have his head now as a mess ornament I believe! – . . . I see no cruelty in giving an animal a short life & a merry one, & then a bullet in his noddle. But the bitter life from caresses to carelessness & to neglect, should be trodden by none but human pilgrims, who can finger the sharp edges of their scallop shells & think of immortality! – (JHE to "My dear Giant," n.d. [HAS 65])

Appendix 5, The Brennan Case

During an evening stroll on 8 October 1868, John Brennan, a private in the 22d Regiment, and Miss Elizabeth Driscoll were approached and threatened by two men. Fearing danger to Brennan, Miss Driscoll ran for help to the home of Private John Watters of the 22d Regiment and then on to the Exhibition Barracks, where she told her story to Sergeant Carter and Corporal Scully. Returning with them to where she had left Brennan, she found the young man unconscious and mortally wounded. He was immediately taken to the hospital, where he was examined by Dr. Adams, 22d Regiment Surgeon, and shortly thereafter he died without regaining consciousness.

The verdict of the corner's jury, based in large part on evidence given by Miss Driscoll at the coroner's inquest on 9 October, was "that the said John Brennan was maliciously and wilfully murdered ... by John Shaughnessy and John Driscoll" (NBRFA, 9 October 1868) – Shaughnessy being a young man who had taken a fancy to Miss Driscoll, and John Driscoll being her brother and Shaughnessy's friend. The brutal murder enraged the soldiers, who on the nights of 9 and 10 October broke store windows and beat some of the citizens of the town.

Rioting was principally occasioned by one of the sergeants, who in our hearing said that if he had his way, the Regiment would sack the whole b——y town. We also saw him forming his men in line and giving them the word to charge, when they rushed down the street beating young and old indiscriminately, and halting in front of Mr. Hatt's store demolished some of his windows. (NBRFA, 16 October 1868)

On the morning of Monday, 12 October, the preliminary investigation began, the mayor presiding; J.L. Marsh and George Gregory appearing on behalf of the Crown; and Charles Fisher for the prisoners. At this hearing, Elizabeth Driscoll revoked the testimony she had given at the coroner's inquest, insisting that darkness had prevented her from recognizing either of the two men who called out to her as she walked with Brennan, though she admitted that she had thought she heard the voice of John Shaughnessy and had warned Brennan against him (NBRFA, 9 and 16 October 1868; HQ, 14 October 1868). In summarizing the evidence given at the inquest, the NBRFA, 16 October 1868, recounts the following incident, which occurred when Elizabeth Driscoll told the defence lawyer, Charles Fisher, that "'Persons might have passed on the street without my seeing them.' (Here Mr. Fisher made a slip and asked – 'when you passed your brother and Shaughnessy –,' and he corrected himself.)"

The preliminary investigation continued on 13 and 14 October. On the morning of 14 October, Mayor Needham read Miss Driscoll's previous testimony to her because "he had been told she wished to confirm the evidence she gave on Friday at the Coroner's Inquest, which contradicted that given by her on Monday before him, when she did not think she was under oath" (HQ, 14 October 1868). When he asked her if her previous evidence "was correct or not ... she replied 'part of it is'" (NBRFA, 16 October 1868). Mayor Needham warned her "to be very careful or she might place herself in a very precarious position" (HQ, 14 October 1868). When she was about to speak, her mother, who "accidentally" had been allowed to interview her while she was being held in jail as a witness, motioned to her, and Miss Driscoll then said she did not wish to change her evidence (*NBRFA*, 16 October 1868). She was warned by the mayor "to reflect before the day of trial on what she had said," and she was then remanded to jail (*HQ*, 14 October 1868).

In the 23 October continuation of the preliminary investigation, Mrs. Mary Watters testified that when she had asked Miss Driscoll who had killed Brennan, she had answered "my brother John and John Shaughnessy" (*HQ*, 28 October 1868).

On 9 November the case came before the Nisi Prius Court, Judge Fisher presiding; council for the Crown, M. Weldon and H. Tuck; for Driscoll, A.L. Palmer; for Shaughnessy, C.H.B. Fisher – the nephew of Judge Fisher. On 10 November Elizabeth Driscoll testified that darkness prevented her from seeing who set upon Brennan, but that while walking she "heard a voice [and] imagined it was that of John Shaughnessy." She insisted that she "never saw [the accused] that evening" (*HQ*, 11 November 1868), that she did not remember what she had said to Mrs. Watters, and that she did not remember "anything that took place that night." She further asserted that she did not remember whether she had given evidence in the case before, but if she had, she had not known what she was saying (*NBRFA*, 13 November 1868). When on the morning of 11 November 1868 she was examined further, she claimed she could not remember her statements made under oath at the coroner's jury or the preliminary investigation (*HQ*, 11 November 1868). Mr. Tuck then requested the court to have the witness committed for perjury. Judge Fisher asserted that "he had never read the depositions, and consequently could not know in what particulars her present evidence differed from former evidence. . . . He thought the case should first be examined by a magistrate" (*NBRFA*, 13 November 1868). Friday, 13 November, was set for this examination. The defence then called a number of witnesses who testified to the "sobriety" and "unimpeachable character" of John Shaughnessy (*HQ*, 11 November 1868). Mr. Timothy Driscoll, John Driscoll's father, swore his son and John Shaughnessy were in the company of himself and his son Patrick on 8 October from morning until they went to bed at his house, about 8:30 in the evening (*NBRFA*, 13 November 1868).

Both Shaughnessy and Driscoll were found not guilty, a verdict which dissatisfied the local newspapers:

> Looking at all the circumstances of this case, never before have we been so impressed with the impotency of British law as upon this occasion. The very Jurymen who pronounced the acquittal will not hesitate to say that British law has in this instance failed to vindicate the cause of justice and righteousness. . . . It cannot be forgotten that when unavenged, the case of poor young Brennan to-day may be the case of any one of us to-morrow. If perjury and murder, can stalk hand in hand, who then is safe. . . . Brennan is dead, not killed by one blow, but murdered by many blows, and there is very little doubt while the girl was at his

side. . . . And she must have recognized the murderers, for bursting in Mrs. Watter's door she screamed "they've killed him, they've murdered him; Brennan is killed, my brother John and Shaughnessy have killed him." She swears to this before the coroner's jury; she recognized them both. . . . Then the mother had an interview with her in the gaol, and when next examined she has no recollection of her brother, but still swears to Shaughnessy. Finally, before court and jury she swears she saw nobody at all, and this evidence must be accepted. (*NBRFA*, 13 November 1868)

We are credibly informed that [the prosecutors] were not aware until a day or so before, that they were to conduct the prosecution; that they had no consultation whatever with Messrs. Gregory and Marsh who appeared for the Crown on the examination and were acquainted with all the local circumstances; that they never held converse with the witnesses to know what they would or could prove, previous to putting them upon the witness stand; that they never held any communication with the principal witness, Elizabeth Driscoll; that they allowed one witness to hear the evidence of another in Court; and allowed the father of the girl to stand up in front of her all the time of her examination, attracting her attention. Shaughnessy, it is generally believed, was prepared to turn Queen's evidence, but whether this would have been a correct procedure we are not prepared to state; certain the experiment was never attempted. In brief, it would be hard to convince this community that the proper authorities, whoever they may be, are not guilty of gross negligence and culpable of indifference in the management of the whole affair. (*NBRFA*, 20 November 1868)

Local papers further expressed displeasure over the way Judge Fisher responded to the request that Elizabeth Driscoll be indicted for perjury:

It was really monstrous to hear His Honor, in reply to Mr. Tuck's appeal for an indictment for perjury against Elizabeth Driscoll, say that, as he had not read the depositions, he was not satisfied that there were grounds for taking that summary step. By saying so he has placed himself in an inextricable dilemma. He either did or did not read the depositions. If he did not he was derelict in his duty; if he did he said what was not the fact. But he said on Tuesday, at the opening of the Court, that he read the depositions on Monday night, so that he either spoke not the fact on Tuesday or on last Wednesday. That he did read the depositions on Monday night is presumptively proved by his detailing shortly the facts of the case to the Grand Jury; but, granting that he did not really read them – though he said he did – his ability to detail the facts of the case, shows that the statement that he carefully abstained from the papers was incorrect. (*HQ,* 18 November 1868)

After a series of postponements, which as *HQ,* 18 November 1868, said, "look badly," Elizabeth Driscoll was brought before a magistrate and arraigned for perjury. On 25 November 1868, represented by Mr. Fisher, she appeared before Mr. J.P. Penley, J.P., who postponed the case until 2 December, because Mr. Marsh, who had been hurriedly called to conduct the prosecution, arrived in the courtroom to find "that the witnesses were not present, that no preparations had been made for the defence, and that the very depositions and papers were missing, carried off to St. John or hidden away in some pigeon-hole of the House of Assembly" (*NBRFA,* 27 November 1868). The case was heard 2–3 December, and she was committed for trial before the Supreme Court in May 1869 (*NBRFA,* 4 December 1868). In May the Grand Jury "failed to find a true bill against Elizabeth Driscoll" (*NBRFA,* 14 May 1869). A final news item closes the Brennan case:

"IN MEMORY OF."–The officers of H.M. 22nd Regiment have erected in the Roman Catholic Cemetery a monument to the memory of Pt. Brennan, who was murdered in our streets last fall under circumstances too painfully familiar to our readers.– It is a shaft of Italian Marble, about 8 feet high, work executed by Milligan of St. John, and bears the following inscription:

THIS MONUMENT.
Was erected by the officers of the 1st Bat,
22nd Regiment, to the memory of
Private J. Brennan, 1st Bat, 22nd Regiment,
who was foully murdered on the 28th October,
and the assassins allowed to escape.

Beneath are the Latin words,

"Deus Omnia Videt."–God sees all

The officers made the *slight mistake,* so we are informed, of having the monument placed in the first instance over the grave of a certain unobtrusive citizen named Brennan, who died several years ago peaceably in his bed, and had never troubled Coroners or Courts in either life or death, nor ever created a sensation in this or any other community. Round this grave the officers were congregated with mournful expression when apprised by a comrade of the real Brennan of their "slight mistake." (*NBRFA,* 30 April 1869)

354

Another "slight mistake" was made: the murder occurred 8, not 28, October 1868.

Appendix 6, The Scovil Affair

In November 1868 St. John suffered a series of commercial disasters. The *NBRFA*, 20 November 1868, reported that "the failure of the Commercial Bank, and the flight of the Cashier, defaulter to the extent of $90,000 at least, is overtopped by the failure of Mr. S.[amuel] J. Scovil, with liabilities over $350,000." Scovil was agent of the St. Stephen's Bank, which was, therefore, also threatened with ruin. On 21 and 26 November, meetings of his creditors and depositors were held, and it was learned not only that he had assigned the majority of his property to T. Barclay Robinson and to his brother, the Reverend W.E. Scovil of Kingston, but also that he believed that his creditors should be preferred to his depositors. Having been taken prisoner by the sheriff, he was confined to his own home in the company of his friend Major William B. Robinson. Robinson helped him escape but Scovil was arrested in Kingston on the night of the 26th (*NBRFA*, 27 November 1868). Subsequently, Major Robinson was arrested and committed to trial for his part in the affair (*NBRFA*, 4 December 1868), but on 18 December he was acquitted because the testimonies of the two key witnesses, the sheriff and Mrs. Scovil, who was also William Robinson's sister, were directly contradictory (*NBRFA*, 18 December 1868).

It was proposed that Scovil be charged under the Absconding Debtor's Act, but the fact that Scovil was being held in Kingston jail complicated matters. In the 4 February 1869 hearing in St. John, Judge Watters ruled that he could not adjourn proceedings to Kingston in order to obtain evidence from Mr. Scovil because "he had no power to hold judicial proceedings in King's County which had been commenced in the County of St. John" (*St. John Morning Journal*, 5 February 1869). No further information appears in St. John papers, but the conclusion of the episode may be guessed from Richard Lewes Dashwood's contemporary comment:

> The laws [of New Brunswick] are also favorable for swindlers, the common dodge being to make over your property to your brother or wife, get into debt as much as possible, and then bolt to the States. There have lately been several serious defalcations among cashiers of banks; the worst of it is, that in such a case, according to the law of the country, it is merely a breach of trust, and the thief−which undoubtedly he is−cannot be criminally proceeded against. (*Chiploquorgan; or, Life by the Camp Fire* [Dublin: Robert T. White, 1871], p. 207)

Appendix 7, Kethro the Barber

[AE writes:] The principal, (and, generally, the only) Tenor in the Fredericton Cathedral (*Cantoris* side of the) Choir when I was first connected with it (1867) was a hairdresser and dealer in sensational illustrated Yankee newspapers, named Moses Kethro. His advertisement, headed with the quotation

"'Tis a glorious charter, deny it who can

That's breath'd in the words 'I'm an Englishman'"

occupied a perennial place in both the weekly newspapers. He had some good powerful notes, though no great compass, and he sung in a pothouse style, trying to make as much noise as possible, considering the choir merely as a vehicle for individual display, and imagining that the world revolved round his little tenor solos as a centre. The Bishop was very kind to him, used to doctor him when he was sick, and try to keep him straight. He was *not* straight, poor fellow. When the Bishop first saw him, he was in the Lunatic Asylum at St. John. The Bishop was visiting the institution, and the resident Doctor knowing his Lordship's musical taste, told him he had a patient who was "a beautiful singer." Kethro was produced, and sang (the Bishop said) the *whole* of "For unto us a child is born", (by which I suppose was meant a kind of resumé of that chorus.) Having done thus, he said "Ah! my Lord, I wish I were singing in your choir."

In due time, this wish was granted, and Kethro, being discharged from the asylum, came to Fredericton, and sung in the Choir for many years.

He had a grown-up son, also a hairdresser, who behaved badly to him – or, at all events, they disagreed, and the son set up an opposition shop. The father went back to England, in hopes of doing better there. I think he told me *Bath* was his native place; but he found it very difficult to realize his ideals there. He told me there was "no opening for a tenor," and that he could not achieve the same position "in society" as he could here. The real fact is that at one time he accepted an engagement to *shave the dead* at some hospital.

So he came back to Fredericton, and re-entered the choir.

In 1868, Mr. Wichtendahl, then Band Master of the 1/22d, was added as a Tenor to the Cantoris side of the choir. He had a better, and much more cultivated voice than Kethro; and sometimes, (but very rarely) got a solo. The Bishop, in kindness to Kethro's foible, and knowing that he had not many interests or enjoyments in life, gave him most of the solos. But his jealousy of Wichtendahl was great and dire. He used to strive to "sing him down" – and made all the noise he could, (in piano passages and all). About this time, his health seemed affected, and his voice was weaker than before. He would open his mouth sideways, and *seem* to be roaring like a bull, but not always did a corresponding volume of sound come out. One memorable Sunday evening, he sung "till he was sick"; i.e. he so exerted himself, in efforts to outdo Wichtendahl, that he got faint, and had to go away.

All this could not fail to have a most ludicrous side—but I am not only ridiculing it. The fact was, the Bee in his bonnet, which had never altogether ceased buzzing, was waking up again into activity; yet not to any really serious extent.

He withdrew from the Choir. The Bishop, always kindly interested in him (as in every-one), on enquiry, found that he had entered into negotiations with the Presbyterians, who wanted a "Precentor" and also with the Baptists, who required a tenor for some purpose. (These were paid or salaried posts; whereas the Cathedral Choir is an unpaid one.) In justification he said to the Bishop: "You know if you were offered Nova Scotia, you would better yourself by taking it; & you would be quite right."

"But" said the Bishop "I shouldn't be leaving my *church*, as you are doing!"

"Bah!" said K. "*Church?* There have been divisions from the beginning, as were told in the Bible. *Weren't there seven Churches in Asia? And something wrong with every one of them!*"

This was the end of it. Altho Kethro fell to the ground between the two stools and neither went to the Presbyterians nor to the Baptists, he came not back to the Choir. Dr. Ward succeeded him on the Cantoris side, and I became 1° Tenor on the other, in his stead.

Fredericton, 23 March 1869.

In connection with the above, I should add, that Kethro was, last winter, seated in state as a spectator at our (the Garrison) Amateur Theatricals, when Rhoades of the 22d told White (the latest fledged Ensign, just out from home) that K. was the *Chief Justice*, and introduced him to White as such. Kethro kept up and enjoyed the joke. ("Commonplace Book" [HAS 78])

Appendix 8, Model Dental Establishment

[From *NBRFA*, 17 December 1866] On Wednesday last we had the pleasure of visiting the Dental Rooms of Doctors Dow and Ellis, of this City. These gentlemen seem determined to keep pace with all the improvements of the day in their particular line. They have recently imported from Boston a complete and we should think perfect apparatus for the manufacture and administration of the celebrated nitrous oxide, or *Laughing Gas*. The patient inhales from a silver mouth-piece this pleasant and agreeable oxide, and while experiencing the most delightful sensation, the tooth is removed. The restoration is almost immediate. We have been informed by Doctors Dow and Ellis, that thus far the success of its administration has been perfect.

We also saw in this establishment a magnificent dental chair manufactured in New York. It is solid mahogany, elegantly upholstered with all the improved modern appliances. Dr. Dow says that such a chair and Nitrous Oxide are luxuries in a Dental office.

Specimens of mechanical Dentistry in the shape of teeth on what is called a vulcanite base or plate, was exhibited to us. The most eminent Dentists in the United States are now using this article instead of Gold Plate.

A beautiful and convenient apparatus for applying the newly discovered agent called Rhigoline, or Spray, for preventing pain in slight surgical operations was shown us at the same time. It effectually *freezes* the part to be operated upon, and deadens all sense of pain during the operation, while one of its chemical properties is such that no hurtful results attend the freezing process. The establishment is well worth visiting.

Appendix 9, Cuban and Fenian Difficulties

Since the fall of 1865 there had been fears that Irish veterans of the American Civil War who had joined the Fenian brotherhood would invade Canada as a means of inaugurating war with Britain. In 1866 two raids took place, and though in both cases the invaders soon recrossed the border, the volatile situation was taken seriously by American, Canadian, and British authorities. In response to the Fenian threat and at the urging of the Canadian government, Britain reluctantly supplied reinforcements. But in December 1868 the new Gladstone government embarked upon a course of withdrawing troops from the colonies as part of far-reaching army reforms. Edward Cardwell, secretary for war, was opposed to maintaining British troops in the colonies in peacetime unless the colonies contributed significantly to underwriting the expense, and he also believed that withdrawal of troops from foreign stations would induce more men to volunteer because they would then spend more of their service time in Great Britain. Gladstone had long believed that the very presence of British troops in Canada enticed the Fenians to attack across the border. The withdrawal of British troops was opposed by the Duke of Cambridge, a firm imperialist and the commander-in-chief of the Army, and by the Canadian government, which feared not only Fenian raids but also a possible invasion by United States forces as a result of the still unresolved *Alabama* affair (see L83, n1). Gladstone and Cardwell were, however, determined upon a policy of reducing British troop commitments to the colonies, despite the fact that the threat of a Fenian attack so increased in July 1869 that plans were made to call out 1,500 militia men in Ontario and Quebec and to ready the Canadian gunboats for action. On 17 July 1869 the prime minister, Sir John A. Macdonald, wrote to the governor general, Sir John Young, suggesting a series of precautions, among which were the recommendations that "Sir Hastings Doyle should . . . be put upon the alert so that he may reinforce the Garrison at St. John, as far as he can from Halifax," and that "the Admiral be requested to keep watch at St. John with the two fold object of preventing an attack from the Fenian invaders, and the sailing of a fili-bustering expedition against Cuba from that Port." Macdonald wished all "necessary precautions" to be taken "with as little public notice as possible," and in a letter of 24 July 1869 to Young, he reiterated his belief that "we will not be attacked, and I am satisfied that the United States Government will act in good faith." This confidence was upheld by subsequent events: St. John remained quiet and no Fenian attacks occurred during 1869. On 12 February 1870 Young was informed that all British troops in Canada would be withdrawn except for 1,500 men left to garrison Halifax as an imperial station. No Fenian raids had taken place since 1866, but the tension, which had remained high, increased in May 1870, when the Fenians twice briefly crossed the border into the province of Quebec, and this new evidence of danger delayed the final British withdrawal until 11 November 1871, when the last troops left the citadel at Quebec.[1]

Notes to the Introduction

1. Alfred Gatty (1813–1903) and his wife Margaret, *née* Scott (1809–1873); of their ten children, eight survived infancy:

    Margaret Scott (1840–1900)

    Juliana Horatia (1841–1885)

    Reginald (1844–1914)

    Horatia Katharine Frances, "Dot" (1846–1945)

    Alfred Scott, "Brownie" (1847–1918), who later changed his surname to Scott-Gatty

    Undine Marcia, "Dina" (1848–1930)

    Stephen, "Steenie" (1849–1922)

    Charles Tindal (1851–1928)

2. A[ndrew] Leith Adams, *Field and Forest Rambles* (London: Henry S. King & Co., 1873), p. 3.

3. William T. Baird, *Seventy Years of New Brunswick Life* (St. John: Geo. E. Day, 1890), p. 29.

4. To Mrs. Davenport, 29 April 1867 (HAS 57).

5. To Eleanor Lloyd, 29 May 1867 (HAS 65).

6. The disease from which Mrs. Gatty died was not diagnosed, but the fact that she suffered periods of loss of muscle tone interspersed with variable remissions suggests that she was a victim of multiple sclerosis.

7. 23 April 1867 (HAS 57).

8. To Mary Gatty, 5 November 1868 (HAS 44).

9. Quoted in Christabel Maxwell, *Mrs. Gatty and Mrs. Ewing* (London: Constable, 1949), p. 227.

Notes to the Letters

LETTER

I

1. Built in 1861 the Cunard *China* was the first large screw-steamer to cross the Atlantic.
2. In 1865 Juliana and her brother Reginald holidayed for two weeks in Antwerp.
3. Two Gatty servants.
4. Thomas Wilkins (1831–1897), Dr. Gatty's curate at Ecclesfield, 1857–1867; perpetual curate of St. Michael and All Angels', Neepsend, Sheffield, 1867–1894.
5. *Aunt Judy's Magazine* (1866–1885), published monthly by George Bell, 1866–1883. *AJM* was edited by Margaret Gatty until her death in October 1873, then jointly by JHE and her sister Horatia until 1876, and then by Horatia alone. All members of the Gatty family contributed to *AJM*, and most of JHE's work first appears there. Though never a financial success, the magazine had a reputation for high quality, and the work of some important authors, including Lewis Carroll and Hans Christian Andersen, appears in it. The "short thing" to which JHE refers is "An Idyll of the Wood," *AJM* 3 (September 1867): 257–66.
6. "Reka Dom," Russian for "River House," was the name of a house which Juliana had seen in Topsham, Devon, in 1862 (see L25, n1); this house was the inspiration for "Reka Dom," the 4th chapter of *MOR*, *AJM* 5 (July–November 1868); the Ewings also named their first house in Fredericton "Reka Dom."
7. Mrs. Todgers and Bailey junior, in *Martin Chuzzlewit*.
8. JHE and AE received Holy Communion at All Saints' in Margaret Street, London, on 2 June, the day after their wedding.
9. Fredericton's Christ Church Cathedral was consecrated 31 August 1853. The basic plans, modeled on St. Mary's Church, Snettisham, were by Frank Wills; the tower, sanctuary, and furnishings were designed by William Butterfield (see L4, n8).
10. Halifax became an imperial military and naval post on 21 June 1749. The 1867 festivities began with a salute of 118 guns.

11. AE's dog; his memorial tablet in the Ecclesfield vicarage garden reads:

In Memoriam
Trot
D-Dec. 3, 1875. Aged 11 years.
A gentle heart-a faithful friend lies here.
A dog-but yet to me a dog most dear.

12. JHE's sketches of this woman are reproduced from Horatia K[atharine] F[rances] Gatty, *Juliana Horatia Ewing and Her Books* (London: SPCK, 1885), pp. 48-49. The originals were JHE's 1867 birthday present to her sister "Dot" (see L18).

LETTER
2

1. The Ewings arrived in Fredericton on 28 June 1867.

2. Fredericton became a Cathedral City in 1845 by the terms of Bishop Medley's Letters Patent.

3. The 15th Regiment was stationed in Fredericton, June 1862–October 1863. In *Chiploquorgan; or, Life by the Camp Fire* (Dublin: Robert T. White, 1871), Richard Lewes Dashwood, who served in New Brunswick in the early 1860s as a Captain in the 15th Regiment, writes: "The withdrawal of troops from Canada will cause an unprecedented fall in the matrimonial market of those 'sections.'. . . Canada has proved more fatal to celibacy than any other country where troops are stationed, including even England" (p. 211). The 22d Regiment was stationed in Fredericton, April 1866–May 1869.

4. Government House, designed by J.E. Woolford and built in 1826, was the residence of the lieutenant–governors of New Brunswick until 1893.

5. The Ewings' "Reka Dom" was situated on land now occupied by houses at 50 and 58 Waterloo Row. Demolished about 1910, the eighteenth-century building had once housed Fredericton's first inn, The Golden Ball.

6. Andrew Leith Adams, M.D., M.A., F.R.S., L.L.D. (1816–1882), surgeon of the 1/22d Regiment for twenty-five years, retiring with the rank of deputy surgeon-general in 1873, when he was appointed professor of zoology, the College of Science, Dublin. He held that chair until 1878 when he became professor of natural history, the Queen's College, Cork. He wrote three books on natural history, including *Field and Forest Rambles*, which describes the flora and fauna of Canada.

7. William Brydone Jack, M.A., D.C.L. (1819–1886), appointed professor of mathematics, natural philosophy, and astronomy, King's College, Fredericton, in 1840. In 1860 King's College became the University of New Brunswick, and in 1861 Professor Jack became president; he retired in 1885.

8. In the 1850s fears were voiced that seepage from the Old Burial Ground, located in the centre of town, was contaminating Fredericton's ground

water. Nothing was done until the 1870s, when new cemeteries were established upriver from town.

9. George Montgomery Campbell (1831–1871), English born and Cambridge educated, was appointed professor of classics, University of New Brunswick, in 1861. He and his wife, Sophia (see L6, n1), had four children: Henry (1859–1933), Herbert (1861–?), Annette (1863–?), and Rachel Mary (1867–?).

10. "Reka Dom" was a quarter mile downriver from Christ Church Cathedral.

11. Avery's Landing—named for Ebenezer Avery, who owned the Golden Ball Inn ("Reka Dom") in the early nineteenth century—was the farthest downriver of Fredericton's eleven landings.

12. Possibly the wooden garage that still stands on the property at 58 Waterloo Row.

13. AE served in the 1860 North China campaign and in the 1862 campaign against the T'ai-p'ings.

14. From *HQ*, 17 July 1867:

> Lost
>
> A Small Deal Box, containing a Hand Sewing Machine in a Mahogany Case.
>
> The above box was not very distinctly addressed, and it is thought it may have been accidentally removed with baggage from the Steamer "David Weston," on Friday 28th June, 1867.
>
> Anyone who may have found it is requested to send it to Mr. Ewing, Commissariat Office, Fredericton.

LETTER

3

1. See Appendix 1, "The Mails."

2. "Distant Correspondents; In a letter to B.F., Esq., at Sydney, New South Wales."

LETTER

4

1. Andrew Straton Phair (1821–1875), whose family had held the position since 1800, was Fredericton's postmaster, 1845–1875. Beginning in 1863, manuscripts and printers' proofs were to be posted at printed-matter rate—one cent an ounce. The ruling was intended to promote the production of literature.

2. A reference to Mrs. Gatty's "Cook Stories," first published in *MP* 16 (August 1858): 152–83, and then in *Aunt Judy's Tales* (London: Bell and Daldy, 1859), pp. 48–76. In this sketch a family of children, pretending to be grown up, ex-

change stories about the vagaries of their cooks.

3. *L'Histoire de Monsieur Crépin* (1837) is one of several of comic albums, including *L'Histoire de Monsieur Jabot* (1835), written and illustrated by Swiss schoolmaster Rodolphe Töpffer (1799–1846).

4. Nineteenth-century slang for *stealing.*

5. J.H. Walsh, F.R.C.S., *A Manual of Domestic Economy: Suited to Families spending from £100 to £1000 a Year* (London: G. Routledge & Co., 1857).

6. Millicent Marples (1827–1880), schoolmistress of the Infant School, Ecclesfield.

7. Sir Charles Hastings Doyle, K.C.M.G. (1804–1883), served as lieutenant-governor of New Brunswick, 1 July–18 October 1867, resigning to become lieutenant-governor of Nova Scotia. Doyle entered the army in 1819, rising through the ranks to major-general in 1860, when he was posted to North America. He assumed command of British troops in the Atlantic area in 1861 and during the 1860s displayed great skill in dealing with issues arising from the American Civil War, the threat of Fenian invasion, and Confederation. He was promoted lieutenant-general in 1869; in 1873 he resigned the lieutenant-governorship of Nova Scotia and returned to England, where from April 1874 to May 1877 he commanded the southern district at Portsmouth. In 1877 he was promoted general and placed on the retired list.

8. John Medley (1804–1892) graduated with honours from Wadham College, Oxford, 1826; ordained deacon in 1828 and priest in 1829; curate of Southleigh, Devonshire, 1829–1831; vicar of St. Thomas, Exeter, 1838–1845; prebendary of Exeter Cathedral, 1842–1845. On 4 May 1845 Medley was consecrated bishop of the new See of Fredericton, to the endowment of which the Colonial Bishopric Council and the Society for the Propagation of the Gospel had heavily contributed. It is likely that the choice of Medley as bishop was the result of the influence of his friends John Duke Coleridge and W.E. Gladstone, who were treasurers of the Colonial Bishoprics' Fund. Known to be closely associated with the Tractarian movement and a friend of Keble and Pusey, Medley was opposed from his arrival in June 1845 by the Low Church party and by Loyalists, whose views were frankly Erastian. An enthusiastic supporter of the revival of interest in Gothic architecture, Medley brought the plans for Christ Church Cathedral with him, and on 15 October 1845 laid the cornerstone, using as the initial building fund the £1,500 presented to him on his departure by the bishop of Exeter. A man of strong will, Medley steadfastly pursued his goals, and though as the years passed, he met less opposition, it never totally dissipated. His influence remains apparent in the Maritimes: his taste continues to be reflected in church music; many of the Gothic churches designed by his son Edward Shuttleworth Medley still stand; and Fredericton's cathedral is, as he believed it would be, the spiritual centre of the diocese. In 1879 Medley became metropolitan of Canada. His first wife, Christiana Bacon, died in 1841, leav-

ing him with six children; in 1863 he married a long-time friend of the family, Margaret Hudson (1821–1906).

9. Consecrated 2 February 1864, the Church of St. Mary the Virgin, New Maryland, southwest of Fredericton. JHE's diary reveals that on Tuesday, 13 August 1867, the bishop made good his promise (HAS 41).

10. Samuel Wilberforce (1805–1873), bishop of Oxford, 1845–1869; Charles John Vaughan (1816–1897), vicar of Doncaster and rural dean, 1860–1869; William Thomson (1819–1890), archbishop of York, 1863–1890.

11. Edward Mayrick Goulburn (1818–1897), dean of Norwich, 1866–1889, and author of many books of sermons and devotions. The reference is to "On The Low Standard Of Personal Religion Now Prevalent, And The Causes Of It," *Thoughts on Personal Religion*, 2 vols. (London: Rivingtons, 1862), 1:1–17, which takes its inspiration from I Kings 22:34. Goulburn speaks of how all too frequently "the sermon is thrown every Sunday into the midst of the people very much as the arrow which found out King Ahab was darted into the host of Israel." The minister submits to the "temptation . . . to be general and vague in both doctrine and exhortation," with the result that "the discourse being meant for nobody in particular . . . hits nobody in particular."

12. Bishop Medley's ornately carved and polychromed staff is in Christ Church Cathedral.

13. The restored Loyalist graveyard, situated between "Elmcroft" (No. 7, Elmcroft Place) and the St. John River, is reached by the access road which runs parallel to the river bank. "Elmcroft" was the home of the Hon. Neville Parker (1798–1869) and his wife, Elizabeth Parker, née Wyer (1799–1886).

14. In a letter to "My dearest Dot," 27 September 1865, Juliana tells of visiting the Museum in the Hague, where she and Regie saw "the 'Royal Cabinet' of curiosities." "Regie was quite at home among the 'relics,' & I am ashamed to say has stolen a bit of horsehair from Barneveldt's chair" (HAS 62). Jan van Olden Barneveldt (1547–1619), Dutch statesman and patriot.

15. Probably the 3rd revised edition of *Manual of the Botany of the Northern United States* (New York: Ivison, Phinney & Co., 1862).

16. "The greater part of the 'Canada' Flour which has been received in the market is unsound. Our merchants attribute it to the bad harvest of last Fall, but do not anticipate a recurrence" (*NBRFA*, 9 August 1867).

17. The Barker House, which stood at the corner of Queen Street and Barker House Alley.

LETTER

5

1. A distinctive bend in Mill Road, Ecclesfield, explains its nineteenth-century name.

2. In 1836, Keble, Pusey, and Newman began work on the *Library of the Fathers*

of the Holy Catholic Church Anterior to the Division of the East and the West. Medley and the Reverend Hubert Cornish produced the 4th volume of the series: *The Homilies of St. John Chrysostom, Archbishop of Constantinople, on the First Epistle of St. Paul the Apostle to the Corinthians,* translated with notes and indices (Oxford: John Henry Parker, 1839).

3. The first Lambeth Conference, or Pan-Anglican Synod, 24–27 September 1867, was called by the archbishop of Canterbury in February 1867 to promote greater unity in the Anglican Communion, but of the 144 bishops invited, 68 refused to attend, many of them – including Medley – doing so because the agenda had not been established. By the middle of September, after much argument, the subjects for discussion were decided upon, but on the second day of the conference, the programme was changed at the urging of the bishop of Capetown and his supporters, and the rest of the proceedings were dominated by the Colenso controversy (see L72, n4).

4. Mrs. Alfred Gatty, *Parables from Nature,* published in five series (1855–1871), are brief narratives for children, which use scientific observation to illustrate moral and religious truths.

5. Although Rex wrote the music for "Jerusalem the Golden," people assumed his famous kinsman, Alexander Ewing (1814–1873), bishop of Argyll and the Isles, 1847–1873, was the composer.

6. Thomas Kerchever Arnold, *The First Hebrew Book* (London: F. & J. Rivington, 1851).

7. In 1867 the legislative library held some 8,000 volumes and was housed in the old Provincial Hall, a wooden structure which stood on the present site of the Legislative Assembly Building.

8. "A Catalogue of the Books in the Library of the Cathedral Church of Fredericton, 1853," restricts library use to clergy and divinity students, and requires annual dues of 2/6 "to provide fresh Books."

9. Ten of the twelve issues of the monthly magazine *Nature and Art,* published 1 June 1866–1 June 1867, include illustrated articles "On Sketching from Nature" by Aaron Penley (1807–1870).

10. John James Blunt, *Undesigned Coincidences in the Writings Both of the Old and New Testament, An Argument of Their Veracity; With An Appendix Containing Undesigned Coincidences Between the Gospels And Acts, And Josephus* (London: John Murray, 1847).

11. James Duffield Harding, *Lessons on Art* (London: David Bogue, 1849).

12. The two-volume edition of 1861–1865, which reprints Series 1–4 in 8°, the earlier editions being in 16°.

13. In his "Introduction," Macé says, "We will study first, piece by piece, the exquisite machine within ourselves.... We will see what becomes of a mouthful of bread which you place so coolly between your teeth" (Jean Macé, *The History of a Bit of Bread, Being Letters to a Child on the Life of Man and Animals,* translated and edited by Mrs. Alfred Gatty [London: Saunders, Otley, and Co., 1864–1865]).

LETTER
6

1. Sophia Campbell (1831–1893), only daughter of the Hon. John Simcoe Saunders, long-time member of the Legislative Council and senior justice of the Courts of Common Pleas for York and Sunbury counties. Saunders was the brother of Arianna Margaretta Jekyll Shore (see L7, n9). The child in arms was Rachel Mary, born in 1867; the little girl was Annette, born in 1863.

2. Margaret Inches (1824–1901) lived with her husband and five children at what is now 102 Waterloo Row – a few doors downriver from the Ewings.

3. Rex composed the music for "Jerusalem the Golden" in the late 1840s, but when it was printed in *Hymns Ancient and Modern* (1861), he was serving in China and so could not protest the editor's decision to change the time from triple to common, an alteration which Rex believed vulgarized his composition.

4. Sir George Job Elvey (1816–1893), composer of sacred music and organist at St. George's, Windsor.

5. The Reverend Henry Master White (1821–1892), vicar of Masbrough, Yorkshire, 1865–1870.

6. Charles Coster (1831–1879), son of Archdeacon George Coster (1794–1859), was assistant minister at Fredericton Cathedral and master of the English department at the Collegiate School. In 1851 he married Grace Holbrooke; their children were George (1852–?), Clara (1854–?), Robert (1857–?), Charles (1860–?), Harold (1861–?), and Grace (1871–?). JHE taught in the Soldiers' Children's Sunday School.

7. John Pearson (1829–1910), sub-dean of Christ Church Cathedral and missionary at New Maryland, New Brunswick, 1864–1875. Fanny Pearson (1830–1909). The Missionary College of St. Augustine, Canterbury, was established in 1848 to train men for service in British dependencies.

8. See L4, n7.

9. Charles Fisher (1808–1880), a member of the Legislative Assembly of New Brunswick, 1837–1850; attorney-general and leader of the government of New Brunswick, 1854–1861, except for a brief period in 1856. During his time in office, many constitutional, political, social, and economic reforms were enacted, but in 1861, when he was implicated in a crown lands scandal, he was forced to resign, first as party leader, then as attorney-general, though he retained his seat in the assembly until 1864. Re-elected in 1865, he was a delegate to the London Conference of 1866–1867, where the final details of Confederation were hammered out. On his return he successfully ran for the dominion Parliament and also resumed his position as attorney-general of New Brunswick; in 1868 he was appointed a puisne judge of the Supreme Court of New Brunswick and judge of the Court of Divorce and Matrimonial Causes.

10. The home of Bishop Medley, "Bishopscote" – now greatly altered and re-named "Beauregard" – is at 79 Church Street.

11. "Fredericton presented another claim to the title ["The City of Fire"] on Friday night or early Saturday morning [August 30–31]. . . . the buildings in the rear of the City Hotel, and connecting with the City Hotel stables [were] all ablaze, while great blazing cinders borne by a stiff wind went floating off meteor-like into the darkness. . . . In an incredibly short space of time the block bounded by Queen and Campbell Streets and Phoenix Square from the line [through the alleyway to the Hotel]. . . was one blazing mass. . . . The greater part of the labour. . . to the discredit of the citizens. . . fell upon the military, who worked not only their own engine at the river, but No. 1 as well. General Doyle himself directed the efforts of his men." It was estimated that the fire destroyed more than $20,000 worth of property (*NBRFA*, 6 September 1867).

12. Small notations – dots and strokes – which indicate punctuation, pronunciation, and stress in written Hebrew.

13. "Cherry pie" is a common name for heliotrope.

LETTER

7

1. Shortly after their arrival from England, Archdeacon George Coster (1794–1859) and his wife, Eleanor, were burned out three times in four months.

2. A[ndrew] L[eith] Adams, *Wanderings of a Naturalist in India, the Western Himalayas and Cashmere* (Edinburgh: Edmonston and Douglas, 1867). The *Saturday Review* 24 (20 July 1867): 92–93, describes the book as "genuinely interesting, accurate enough to satisfy the man of science and simple enough to please the general run of readers."

3. Bertha Jane Adams (1837–1912) wrote more than ten novels and several collections of stories, essays, poems, and plays. After the death of Dr. Adams, she married the Reverend R.S. de Courcy Laffan.

4. Loring Woart Bailey (1839–1925), professor of chemistry and natural science, University of New Brunswick, 1861–1900; professor of biology and geology, 1900–1902; a charter fellow of the Royal Society of Canada, 1882.

5. William Henry Harvey, M.D., F.R.S. (1811–1866) – professor of botany, University of Dublin, and author of a number of important books on phycology – became acquainted with Margaret Gatty in 1850, when she wrote to him about her interest in seaweeds. They became close friends, and in 1855 he named *Gattya Pinella* in her honour. He revised and corrected the proofs of her *British Seaweeds* (London: Bell and Daldy, 1863), which is a simplified version of his most famous work, *Phycologia Britannica: or, a history of British Seaweeds*, 4 vols. (London: L. Reeve and Co., 1846–1851).

6. Dr. Joseph Wolff (1795–1862) was born a Jew in Bavaria, but became a Roman

Catholic in 1812; then, after a few years, an Anglican. In 1821 he began more than twenty years of travels in the Near East and India as a missionary to the Jews and Muslims. He was a frequent house guest at the Ecclesfield vicarage, where with the help of Mrs. Gatty and her daughters he wrote his autobiography, *Travels and Adventures of the Rev. Joseph Wolff*, 2 vols. (London: Saunders, Otley, and Co., 1860).

7. Sarah Thompson (1818–1875), a neighbour and good friend of the Gatty family.

8. For years Margaret Gatty collected sketches of sundials and their mottoes, and with the help of JHE's friend Eleanor Lloyd, she drew 377 examples together in *The Book of Sundials* (London: Bell and Daldy, 1872). Item 124 reads:

> IMPROVE THE PRESENT HOUR, FOR ALL BESIDE
> IS A MERE FEATHER ON A TORRENT'S TIDE.

May be read at Fredericton, in New Brunswick, Canada, as the motto of a dial which is placed on a wooden shaft that is shaped like a ninepin, and stands in the garden of the late Mrs. Shore.

9. Arianna Margaretta Jekyll Shore (1792–1868), daughter of the Hon. John Saunders Shore (1754–1834), Loyalist settler and chief justice of New Brunswick, 1822–1834.

10. See Appendix 2, "The Scheme."

LETTER
8

1. Before her marriage and move to Canada, JHE published three of the five stories which form *MOR* (London: Bell & Daldy, 1869). Completing the remaining two stories occupied her during her first year abroad. "Ida," "Mrs. Moss," "The Snoring Ghost," "Reka Dom," and "Kerguelen's Land" first appear serially in *AJM* 1 (May–July 1866), 2 (December 1866); 2 (January–February 1867); 3 (June–October 1868).

2. St. Mary's Indian Reserve.

3. The inexpensiveness of pirated editions struck JHE early on arrival. In her diary entries of 25 and 26 June 1867, she notes that she bought "a complete Tennyson for 90 cents!!" and "a very good Elia for ^{d}6!!" (HAS 41).

4. Friedrich Heinrich Wilhelm Gesenius, *Hebraische Grammatik*, first published in 1813 and frequently reprinted.

LETTER
9

1. Edward Shuttleworth Medley (1838–1910) emigrated to Canada with his father in 1845, but at fifteen he returned to England to study architecture for three

years under William Butterfield. After graduating from King's College in 1862, Medley entered holy orders, serving as canon, 1863–1865, and rector, 1865–1872, of Christ Church, St. Stephen, N.B. Medley is remembered for his distinctive contribution to New Brunswick church architecture, especially for his church in St. Stephen. In 1872 Medley returned to Britain, where he lived the remainder of his life.

2. Henry James Saturley, who preached the sermon, describes the chain of events in a letter home. See 31 October 1867, "My Dearest Mother" (PANB, MC 300 MS 18/14).

3. Alice, *née* Coster (?–1873).

4. Sir James Carter (1805–1878), appointed to the New Brunswick bench in 1834; served as chief justice of New Brunswick, 1851–1865.

5. "We regret to learn that the Rev. Edward Medley (son of the Bishop of the Diocese), a young and talented clergyman of the Church of England, stationed in St. Stephen, died recently in England, whither he had been sent by advice of his physician for the benefit of his health. His death is deeply lamented by his parishioners, affording a good index of his devotedness and piety" (*NBRFA*, 27 September 1867). *HQ*, 6 November 1867, publishes a letter from the "deceased" in which he states: "The report was circulated by a person in England whom I have every reason to believe intended more harm to me than he was able to accomplish."

6. Probably Jane Cumby (1798–1886), daughter of JHE's paternal grandfather by his first wife, and therefore the half-sister of JHE's father.

7. Carter married Emma Wellbeloved in 1831; Mary Ann Elizabeth Miller in 1844; and Margaret Spencer Coster in 1852.

8. HAS 84 contains the table of contents for JHE's Canadian watercolour sketchbook. The description of page 7 reads: "Fred. N.B. From 'the other side.' R & I having crossed the horse ferry he studying Gesenius! N.B. He says I have made him look like a 'lumberer' wh[ich] is rather true – The Cath[edral] to the left. The other spire is the Methodist Meeting House. . . . A little further to the left stands our home, but it is not in the sketch." Copies of this sketch, "Fredericton from the Nashwaak Septr. 27. 1867," are in MD 2689 and in Wakefield District Library Headquarters 7/99083.

9. Set within the "College Fence," the College Grove covered the hillside descending from the University of New Brunswick's Old Arts Building.

10. In Ecclesfield, various parish clubs supervised by the members of the Gatty family met on Mondays.

11. In "An Idyll of the Wood," the captive thrush is provided with "fresh turf and groundsel, besides meal-cake." The nature of the "mistake" is not apparent.

12. In 1867 "Book Post" from England was 3 pence for each packet not exceeding 4 oz., 6 pence for packets 4 to 8 oz., and so on, rising at a flat rate of 3 pence for each additional 4 oz. An issue of *AJM* weighs approximately 3 oz. Gregory's, a Fredericton bookstore, advertises that any English magazine

may be ordered at the rate of 30¢ to the shilling (*NBRFA*, 24 April–15 May 1868); at this time an issue of *AJM* sold for 6 pence in England.

LETTER
10

1. Francis Pym Harding (1821–1875), served in the Crimean War, promoted colonel 1858, commanded the 1/22d regiment 1866–1875, promoted major-general 1868. Harding held office as lieutenant-governor of New Brunswick, 25 October 1867–14 July 1868.
2. Dr. Henry Ward (1825–?).
3. Mounted under the gable of the Soldiers' Barracks, this badly worn dial is presently concealed by the building at the corner of Queen and Carleton Streets. In the late 1860s the area between the Soldiers' and the Officers' Barracks held no significant buildings, and Carleton Street had not been cut through from Queen Street to the riverbank. Accordingly, the area then might well have been called the Barrack Square or Barrack Yard.
4. The archbishop of York, William Thomson, who married Rex and Juliana, gave them a Bible and a prayerbook as wedding presents.
5. Sarah Peters Rainsford (1830–?). On 19 April 1870 she married George J. Bliss (see L35, n7).
6. *The Ten Commandments, the Lord's Prayer, etc. In the Maliseet Language.* Printed for the Micmac Missionary Society (Halifax, Nova Scotia, 1863).

LETTER
11

1. Dr. and Mrs. Aveling were long-time friends of AE and the Gatty family; it was in the Aveling home that AE and Juliana first met in 1856, and in 1866 Mrs. Aveling acted as a confidante of the lovers. In 1867 the Avelings were living at 5 Howard Street, Sheffield.
2. Sheridan, *The Rivals*, act 5, sc. 1.

LETTER
12

1. Lemont & Son, Fredericton merchants, exhibited "a collection of Indian curiosities, beads and beadwork," in the triennial Exhibition of the Manufactures of New Brunswick, held in St. John the week of 11 October 1867 (*NBRFA*, 11 October 1867).

2. A moated Saxon mound still exists in what in the Gattys' time was the north-east corner of the vicarage grounds at Ecclesfield.

3. The levée was held 17 October 1867 in the Legislative Council Chamber (*NBRFA*, 18 October 1867).

4. William Hayden Needham (1810–1874).

5. Lemuel Allan Wilmot (1809–1878) (see L49, n4).

6. See L10, n1.

7. Margaret Gatty, "These Three: A Parable from Nature," *AJM* 3 (October 1867): 331–37.

8. Juliana's "The Brownies: A Fairy Story" first appears in *MP* 30 (December 1865): 658–701, and then in *BOT* (London: Bell and Daldy, 1870). In 1915 Lord Baden-Powell derived the name and the activities of the junior branch of the Girl Guides from the title and subject matter of this story.

9. JHE did not write such a tale, but later Mrs. Gatty did: "Nursery Nonsense No. 1. – 'The Cat Washing the Dishes,'" *AJM* 6 (January 1869): 183–85. Joseph Wright, *English Dialect Dictionary* (London: Henry Frowde, 1898), establishes that this expression was used in North Lincolnshire.

10. Jim and Rough were Gatty dogs; their memorial tablets in the Ecclesfield vicarage garden read:

Jim
Died Nov. 3rd 1869.
Aged 20 years
"Thou Lord
Shalt Save
Both Man
And Beast."

Rough
The Best of Dogs
Died 7 June 1874
Faithful Unto Death

LETTER

13

1. "Three Christmas-Trees," *AJM* 4 (December 1867): 80–88.

2. Between 1861 and 1866 Charlotte Mary Yonge, editor of *MP*, published five of Juliana's stories: "A Bit of Green," *MP* 22 (July 1861): 80–91; "The Blackbird's Nest," *MP* 22 (August 1861): 188–97; "Melchior's Dream," *MP* 22 (December 1861): 614–42; "The Yew-Lane Ghosts," *MP* 29 (June 1865): 601–33; and "The Brownies: A Fairy Story." The first four of these stories are among the seven

which make up J.H.G[atty], *Melchior's Dream and Other Tales* (London: Bell and Daldy, 1862).

3. Edward Simonds (1820–1873) farmed a 2,000-acre estate which lay *down*river from Fredericton, below Mill Creek on the south shore of the St. John River – about a mile from Reka Dom. Edward and his wife, Frances (1820–1898), had five daughters who survived infancy: Ann (1844–1917), Fanny (1846–1918), Helen (1850–1872), Elizabeth (1849–1927), and Louisa (1857–?). That part of the highway which begins at the foot of Forest Hill was first laid out as the road to the Simonds' home, "Ridges."

4. Shandrydan: "A kind of chaise with a hood. In later use, a jocular designation for any rickety, old-fashioned vehicle" (*OED*).

LETTER

14

1. John Henry Thomas Manners-Sutton (1814–1877), lieutenant-governor of New Brunswick, 1854–1861.

LETTER

15

1. George Bell (1814–1890) was the son of Matthew Bell of Richmond, in the North Riding of Yorkshire. A bookseller, printer, and occasional publisher, the elder Bell was a friend of Margaret Gatty's father, the Reverend Alexander John Scott, D.D., vicar of Catterick, and it was from this long-term friendship that George Bell's relationship with the Gattys stemmed. In 1832 George Bell went to London, and about 1838 he established his own publishing company, which over the years grew to moderate size, specializing in publications of an educational and serious character. In the mid 1840s Bell began to commission and publish the series of school books which became known as the *Grammar School Classics*. He was the publisher of the *Journal of Education*, 1847–1854, and of *Notes and Queries*, 1850–1863. In 1854 he entered into a partnership with Frederick Daldy, which was dissolved in 1872, when the firm became known as George Bell and Sons. In 1864 Bell and Daldy bought the publishing branch of the business of Mr. Bohn, taking over the stock and the copyrights of the "Libraries." As the publisher from the 1850s of the Aldine Series of Poets, Bell established a reputation as a publisher of poetry; among the poets whose work appeared under his imprint were Adelaide Anne Proctor, Richard Garnett, William Allingham, Thomas Ashe, Andrew Lang, and Robert Bridges. In the field of theology, Bell published the work of such men as J. Erskine Clarke, C.S. Vaughan, and William

Whewell. In addition to publishing many books for children, Bell published *Aunt Judy's Magazine* from 1866, the year of its inception, until 1883 (see L1, n5).

2. Despite these instructions, "J.H.E. (Fredericton)" appears at the end of "Three Christmas-Trees," just as it appears three months earlier at the end of "An Idyll of the Wood."

LETTER

16

1. St. Anne's Chapel, in the upper part of Fredericton, was the first of Bishop Medley's many church-building projects.
2. AE's father's death in 1855 left his family impoverished. Rex, then twenty-five and studying music in Germany, chose to make a career in the army and served in the Crimean War.
3. In planning to follow the £250 budget, JHE is setting up reasonable expectations, for the "Table of Expenditure" in *Domestic Economy* is calculated to cover the needs of parents and four children. The table suggests the following annual estimated expenses: Butcher's meat and bacon, £30; Fish and poultry, £7; Bread, £14; Milk, butter, and cheese, £16; Grocery, £18; Italian goods, £3; Green grocery, £10; Beer, £10; Wine and spirits, £8; Coals, £12; Chandlery, £7; Washing, £15; Rent and taxes, £31/5; Clothing, £31/5; Wages and incidental expenses, £18/15; Illness and amusements, £18/15 (p. 606).
4. *Great Expectations*, ch. 34.

LETTER

17

1. Jonathan Abbott Pasquier (1826–1884), genre painter, watercolourist, and illustrator, whose work appeared in many periodicals, including *London Illustrated News, London Society, Quiver, Sunday Magazine,* and *Beeton's Annual,* in addition to *AJM* during the 1860s. Joseph Wolf (1820–1899), popular painter and illustrator of animals and birds; special artist to the Zoological Society. His work was admired by the pre-Raphaelites, by Darwin, and Sir Richard Owen; Landseer stated that Wolf was "without exception, the best all-round animal painter that ever lived."
2. Elisha Kent Kane, M.D., U.S.N., *Arctic Explorations: The Second Grinnell Expedition in Search of Sir John Franklin,* 1853–55, 2 vols. (London: Trubner & Co., 1856).
3. Canada's first parliament convened 6 November 1867.

LETTER
19

1. Emily Elizabeth Roberts (1846–1884), usually known as Bessy.
2. See Appendix 3, "Knickerbockers."
3. Sir William Tyrone Power (1819–1911) was commissary general-in-chief from 1863 to 1869, when he became director of supplies and transport in the new Control Department; in 1876 he was appointed agent-general for New Zealand.
4. Jean Macé, "War and the Dead: A Dramatic Dialogue," *AJM* 1 (October 1866): 367–71. "Popular Tales From Andalucia, As Told by the Peasantry" are translated by C[aroline] Peachey from the Spanish of "Fernan Caballero," pseudonym of Cecilia Francisca Josefa Arrom de Ayala, who went among the peasantry to collect these tales; the first installments appear in *AJM* 3 (August–October 1867).
5. Apparently never written.

LETTER
20

1. Lewis Carroll, "Bruno's Revenge," illustrated by F. Gilbert, *AJM* 4 (December 1867): 65–78. "Emblems"–a monthly feature of *AJM* in its first years–are brief moral essays by Mrs. Gatty. R.A.E., "Scaramouches," 3 (June–July 1867), tells of five of "the naughtiest children that were ever seen or heard."
2. On 1 January 1868 the Inman Line took over the Halifax-Liverpool mail run.

LETTER
21

1. JHE perhaps recalls the first line of Ambrose Philips' "To the Earl of Dorset," *English Poets*, ed. Chalmers (London, 1810), 13:117: "From frozen climes, and endless tracts of snow."
2. *Bombastes Furioso*, a one-act burlesque tragic opera by William Barnes Rhodes (Dublin: W. Tyrell, 1819), concerns General Bombastes' thwarted love for Distaffina, who dismisses him in favour of the already married King Antaxomines. "Kafoozalem," one of many comic, pseudo-oriental songs popular in the mid-nineteenth century; author and composer unknown. The one-act farce *Done on Both Sides*, by John Maddison Morton (London: S. French, n.d.), tells the story of the poverty-stricken Whiffles family's

machinations to arrange a marriage between their daughter Lydia ("the pretty one") and the supposedly wealthy Mr. John Brownjohn.

3. Built in 1692 and abandoned in 1698, Fort Nashwaak stood at the junction of the Nashwaak and St. John rivers, opposite Fredericton. In October 1696 Father Simon—a Franciscan missionary at Meductic, a village on the St. John, about four miles above the mouth of the Eel River—brought thirty-six braves to defend Fort Nashwaak.

4. Theodore Edward Dowling (1837–1921), rector of Douglas, 1861–1871; rural dean of Fredericton, 1868–1871.

5. St. Paul's, Upper Keswick, consecrated 2 January 1868. Designed by Edward Shuttleworth Medley, the church was built by the congregation, since the Church Society could provide no help. *HQ,* 8 January 1868, comments on the consecration service: "Nothing could have been more hearty than the singing. This was no doubt owing, mainly, to the accompaniment on the Melodeon by Alexander Ewing, Esq., the composer of one of the most popular Hymn-tunes of the day—'Jerusalem the Golden.'"

6. W.H. Tippet (1814–1874), rector of Queensbury for twenty-five years.

7. *English Dialect Dictionary* gives "scrawmy," a Yorkshire term meaning "lanky, straggling, spreading."

8. Worksop is twenty miles southeast of Ecclesfield.

LETTER

22

1. Frank (1853–?) was one of the sons of Dr. James Robb (see L99, n2) and his wife, Ellen Maria, *née* Coster (see L35, n5).

2. Though in November 1867 the 74th Highlanders, then stationed in Dublin, were warned for New Brunswick, they were in fact ordered to Gibraltar in February 1868.

3. Charles Dickens and Wilkie Collins, "No Thoroughfare," in the 1867 Extra Christmas Number of *All the Year Round.*

4. The Burbot, *Lota maculosa.*

5. Mary Nameria Jacob (1820–1904) (see L35, n8).

6. Named after the German soprano Henriette Sontag (1804–1854); a knitted or crocheted cape, tied about the waist.

LETTER

24

1. The House of Assembly, or Provincial Hall, built in 1802 and destroyed by fire in 1880, was a wooden building of Georgian design, which stood at the site of the present Legislative Assembly Building.

2. The word may be "lip."
3. Sheridan, *The School for Scandal,* act 3, sc. 3.

LETTER
25

1. In December 1862, Juliana visited the home of her friend Elizabeth Ella-combe, daughter of Henry Thomas Ellacombe (1790–1885), rector of Clyst St. George, Devon. In a letter to her sister Maggie, Juliana speaks of a visit to Topsham: "It is a most singular little old town, a dutch settlement in bygone days and in the old part the little dutch houses remain.... One of the houses now belongs to some people who lived near a russian river and they have painted the name of their russian home on the gate post of their English one, Reka Dom. The River house! – It is a most curious little bit and renews my longing for Holland and Denmark!!! – Just don't burn this re-membrance of the place, for I may want to refresh my memory about it" (HAS 62). Topsham provided inspiration not only for JHE's "Reka Dom," but also for *The Miller's Thumb, AJM* 11 (November 1872–October 1873), which ap-pears in book form as *Jan of the Windmill* (London: George Bell & Sons, 1876).
2. "The Old Rectory," 734 George Street, built in 1833 for Archdeacon Coster, after he and his wife were burned out three times in four months. In 1873 this Georgian brick structure became the childhood home of Sir Charles G.D. Roberts, his brothers, and his sister.
3. 729 Charlotte Street, the home of Charles G. Coster.

LETTER
26

1. The discovery of paraffin in 1830 revolutionized illumination because it was both safer and gave a much brighter light than earlier fuels. Following the discovery of petroleum in Pennsylvania in 1859, paraffin became inexpen-sive, and hundreds of American patents for paraffin lamps were issued in the next decade, but paraffin lamps were not used widely in England until about 1869.
2. JHE misheard the surname, which is "Polchies."

LETTER
27

1. Mary Gatty (1808–1892), Alfred Gatty's sister.

LETTER
29

1. Although the word *coasting* first appears in England about 1855 (*OED*), the term apparently remained uncommon there. In *Chiploquorgan*, Dashwood describes a St. John winter scene with boys on "small hand-sleighs": "This amusement is called 'coasting;' and in winter appears to take the place of the marbles and peg-tops of the boys at home" (p. 4). *Troboggan* is one of the many early variants of the now-standard *toboggan*.
2. JHE's diary, 23 December 1867: "Sarah went off to get married" (HAS 41).
3. JHE's older sister, Margaret, was engaged to Francis Patrick Smith of Barnes Hall. The Smiths were an important Ecclesfield family.

LETTER
30

1. Rampike: "A tall, dead tree, especially one that is blackened and branchless from being caught in a forest fire" (*Dictionary of Canadianisms* [Toronto: Gage Educational Publishing Ltd., n.d.]).
2. Dr. George Roberts (1808–1878), principal of the Collegiate School for forty years; he and his wife, Emily Goodridge (1810–1891), were the parents of five children who survived infancy. Their son, George Goodridge Roberts (1832–1905), rector of Fredericton, 1873–1905, was the father of the writers Sir Charles G.D. Roberts (1860–1943) and Theodore Goodridge Roberts (1877–1953). The daughters of George and Emily Roberts were Emily Elizabeth (1842–1884), who married Sam MacDonald; Mary Hyde (1844–?), who married John Robinson; Agnes Kelland (1847–1926), who married C. Sterling Brannen; and Lucy Octavia (1849–?), who married William H. Howard.
3. Bouillons are flounces or puffed folds.

LETTER
31

1. "The music-loving portion of our community will be pleased to learn that there are very favorable indications of the establishment of a Choral Society in Fredericton. An interim committee of gentlemen, whose names provide no insufficient guarantee of success, have taken the matter in hand, and advertise a public meeting of those interested in the Society, to be held in the Madras School House, on Wednesday 1st April next." The names of George

Roberts, Alexander Ewing, and Theodore Wichtendahl appear in the accompanying advertisement (*NBRFA*, 27 March 1868).

2. AE's serial, *The Prince of Sleona*, *AJM* 1 (May 1866)–2 (April 1867).

LETTER

32

1. James C. McDevitt (1823–1897), for forty-six years rector of St. Dunstan's Church, Fredericton.

2. The "Correspondence" column of *The Guardian*, 5 February 1868, carries a letter from H.W. Barker requesting "contributions of hymns and tunes for the Appendix to *Hymns Ancient and Modern*."

3. A four-stanza poem, translated by JHE from the Danish of A. Oehlenschloeger, *AJM* 1 (July 1866): 187.

4. Rat leather, used in the fabrication of the thumbs of kid gloves, was also sold for repairing leather items.

5. See L35, n8.

LETTER

33

1. J.A. Pasquier provides nine of the ten illustrations for *MOR*, including the illustrations for "Reka Dom."

LETTER

34

1. Dr. Thomas Fisher (1801–1867), for over twenty years assistant librarian of Trinity College, Dublin; an old mutual friend of Dr. Harvey and Mrs. Gatty.

2. In the final version of "Reka Dom," the bibliophile landlord of Reka Dom rents the house to the heroine's father because he knows "an Elzevir from an annual in red silk." The Elzevirs were seventeenth-century Dutch printers, famous for their editions of the classics.

3. *HQ*, 8 April 1868, announces "a very successful meeting" held 1 April for the purpose of setting up the Fredericton Choral Society; "the Bishop was unanimously elected as President . . . Herr Wichtendahl, the Band Master of the 22d Regiment, was chosen Conductor, A. Ewing, Esq., D.A.C.G., Accompanist."

LETTER
35

1. Charles (see L6, n9) and Amelia Fisher, *née* Hatfield (1819–1890) had four daughters. Juliana probably refers to Jane Paulette (1841–?), Frances Amelia (1844–1905), and Clara Ariana (1848–1897). In mid-life Jane married, but Frances and Clara died spinsters.

2. Mrs. Medley remembered JHE's description of the Fisher girls. On 25 November 1896 she wrote to Mrs. Horatia K.F. Eden, *née* Gatty: "[Jane Paulette Fisher] who afterwards became [Lieutenant-Governor John James Fraser's] wife was a member of our Choir, a flibberty-gibbet in dress, & wearing all sorts of colours – Judy described her & her sister very neatly in a few words – 'They looked,' she said, 'as if they had been dipped in sticky stuff & rolled in finery'!" (HAS 71).

3. The Prince of Wales toured British North America and the United States, July–October 1860.

4. Harriet Martineau Garrison (1838–?), a niece of William Lloyd Garrison (1805–1879), came to Fredericton from Sheffield Parish, Sunbury County, where her father was a merchant and a schoolmaster.

5. Ellen Maria Robb (1819–?), the eldest daughter of Archdeacon George Coster, and her husband, Dr. James Robb (1815–1861) (see L99, n2), were the parents of nine children: Charles (1844–?), Frederick (1846–?), George (1848–?), Edmund (1849–?), James (1851–?), Frank (1853–?), Harriet (1855–?), Arthur (1857–?), and Katherine (1859–?).

6. William Carman (1804–1885) and his second wife, Sophia Maria Bliss (1828–1886), were the parents of the poet Bliss Carman (1861–1929).

7. George J. Bliss (1824–1888) and his first wife, Susannah Mary Dibblee (1833–?), were the parents of Susan (1853–?), Elizabeth (1855–1877), James (1857–?), Samuel (1859–?), Helen (1861–?), Frederick (1863–?), and Henry Lewis (1866–1918).

8. Edwin Jacob (1793–1868), president of King's College, 1829–1860. He and his wife, Mary Jane Patterson (1803–1866), had six sons and two daughters. Disappointed in his expectation of being appointed bishop when the See of Fredericton was established in 1845, he became increasingly difficult and was the centre of a long conflict culminating in 1859 when King's College became the non-denominational University of New Brunswick. At this time the chair of theology, which he had held for thirty years, was abolished, and he was demoted to professor of classical and moral philosophy. As a result of his continued opposition to change, he was pensioned off in 1861, but he had to be forcibly evicted from the university premises. When her father was compelled to retire from his professorship, Mary Nameria Jacob (1831–1904) was his only remaining student. She lived out her life in Fredericton and is buried

near her parents at Stone Church. A dedicated churchwoman throughout her long life, in 1899 she was made deaconess for her work in missions along the Nashwaak and the Miramichi, and many stories are told of how, even in deep snow, she regularly walked the railroad tracks to reach the mission stations.

9. Jane Parker (1824–?), eldest daughter of the Honourable Neville Parker, died unmarried.

10. Dr. Henry Ward's first wife was Fanny Augusta Coster (1834–1866); on 9 July 1867 he married Louisa Isabella Street, the eldest daughter of John Ambrose Street (1795–1865) and Jane Isabella Hubbard (1799–1883).

11. George Edmund Street (1824–1881), noted for his Gothic architecture. In June 1868, after eighteen months of controversy, he was nominated sole architect for the Law Courts in the Strand.

12. JHE undoubtedly requests the change to avoid duplicating the name of her Fredericton neighbour the Reverend John M. Brooke (see L49, n5).

LETTER
37

1. Mrs. Shore died 20 April 1868 and was buried 23 April 1868.

2. Margaret Scott Gatty and Francis Patrick Smith were married on 14 May 1868.

3. The first regular meeting of the Fredericton Choral Society, held 21 April 1868, was presided over by Bishop Medley (*NBRFA*, 24 April 1868).

4. Hiram Dow (1825–1884), born in Wheelock, Vermont, was for many years prominent in Fredericton political and medical circles.

LETTER
38

1. The Ewings' second home, "Aunt Judy's Cot," is at 746 George Street.

LETTER
39

1. At times Mrs. Gatty's degenerative disease incapacitated her right hand.

2. JHE's song, which parodies Isaac Watts' "The Sluggard," probably takes its primary inspiration from Lewis Carroll's parody of Watts in *Alice's Adventures in Wonderland* (1865): " 'Tis the voice of the Lobster."

LETTER

40

1. In "Reka Dom" the heroine takes a bed filled with lilies of the valley for her own garden plot.
2. Elizabeth Bailey (1770–1876) and Ann Emerson (1786–1873) lived at 745 George Street.
3. JHE's guess is wrong: the Loyalists first settled in Fredericton during October 1783.
4. Dr. Samuel Cooke (1723–1795), who became ecclesiastical commissary to the bishop of Nova Scotia in 1790, was drowned 23 May 1795, when his canoe overturned in the St. John River.
5. For Bishop Medley's position on the question of free seats, see his address on the occasion of the laying of the cathedral cornerstone, 15 October 1845, in William Quintard Ketchum, *The Life and Work of the Most Reverend John Medley, D.D.* (St. John, N.B.: J. & A. McMillan, 1893), p. 71.
6. In 1848 William Hunter Odell (1811–1891) and a Mr. Jones fought a duel. Bishop Medley insisted that neither man could receive Holy Communion until six months after he had publicly apologized, which Odell refused to do. Consequently, he and his family began to attend St. Anne's, which was a mission church and, therefore, not under the bishop's jurisdiction.

LETTER

41

1. Miss Emma Raymond Partelow (1828–1897), later the wife of James S. Beek (1814–1907).
2. The carpenter was undoubtedly Charles Moffitt (1821–1905), whose diary entries for 28 and 29 April 1868 show that he worked on the place (PANB F-593).
3. From late May until 19 June 1861, Juliana visited the Symonds family, and in her diary entries for those days, she often refers to meeting Major Edward Cox in the homes of various acquaintances in the neighbourhood; the visit to Hurst Castle occurred 30 May 1861 (HAS 41).
4. The 4th Battalion of the 60th Regiment moved from London, Ontario, to St. John, New Brunswick, in May 1868.
5. In 1865 Sir George Grove formed the Palestine Exploration Fund Movement to promote exploration of the Holy Land and thereby advance biblical scholars' geological and archaeological knowledge of the area. Lieutenant Charles Warren, of the Royal Engineers, conducted the second expedition of the PEF and in 1868 excavated in and around Jerusalem; his drawings ap-

pear in *Plans, Elevations, Sections &c., Shewing the Results of the Excavations at Jerusalem,* 1867–70 (n.p., n.d.).

6. Maggie's and Frank's Paris honeymoon was attended by more than usual difficulties: "they arrived without incident at the railway station in Paris. British-like, he could not speak French and had no desire to do so. His attitude was that if they did not understand good, plain English, it was time they learned to. They hired a cab to convey them to their hotel, but the driver had been celebrating. Instead of taking them to their destination, he drove them round and round a square. Argument being useless, F.P. Smith took the driver off the seat and (putting him inside the cab) mounted the box with his wife beside him and drove on. A gendarme stopped them and demanded explanations. Neither understood a word the other said. F.P. climbed down from the box and continued the argument on the pavement. The gendarme tried to arrest him and found himself on his back in the gutter. Another gendarme came to his comrade's aid and shared his fate. F.P. was at last over-powered and he and his bride spent the night in a cell. The following day the British Embassy succeeded in smoothing the authorities down sufficiently for the 'mad Englishman' and his bride to be released" (J.R. Fisher, "The Smiths of Barnes Hall," *South Yorkshire Historian* 3 [1976]: 36–37).

LETTER
45

1. Wolf did provide the illustration of two nesting albatrosses for "Kerguelen's Land," *AJM* 5 (October 1868): 339.
2. J.G. Wood, *Homes Without Hands* (London: Longmans Green and Co., 1865).

LETTER
46

1. Sir Edward Strickland, C.B., K.C.B. (1820–1889), served in the Crimean War, 1854–1855; in the British army of occupation in Greece, 1855–1857; in New Zealand, 1864–1866; and in Nova Scotia, 1869–1874. He became deputy controller, the highest ranking control officer in Nova Scotia, in January 1870.
2. Although her primary interest was taxonomic, Mrs. Gatty raised money for charity with books of pressed seaweeds, arranged attractively and captioned in layman's terms.
3. A picture frame, the sides of which extend beyond the corners to form crosses.
4. *AJM* 5 (June 1868), devotes only pp. 67–74 to "Reka Dom."

LETTER
47

1. JHE uses the trillium as the basis of her legend "The Trinity Flower," which first appears as "The Blind Hermit and the Trinity Flower," *MP*, n.s. ii (May 1871): 490–97, and later as "The Trinity Flower," in *Dandelion Clocks and Other Tales* (London: SPCK [1895]), pp. 30–42. The JHE memorial window in St. Mary's, Ecclesfield, includes a trillium among the flowers that form its background.
2. *Nature and Art* ceased publication in June 1867.

LETTER
48

1. Anna Jane, *née* Mooney, and Colonel George Joseph Maunsell (1836–1906). An officer in the British Army, Maunsell had been attached to General Grant's staff prior to becoming adjutant general of the New Brunswick militia in 1865. During the 1866 Fenian invasion, he was engaged in the defence of the western frontier.
2. Twelve miles upriver from Fredericton (see L59, n5).
3. The first edition in the Osborne Collection of the Toronto Public Library is bound in green cloth. AE's hymn tune does not appear in this or in later editions.
4. Like the June issue of *AJM*, the July issue devotes only eight pages to "Reka Dom." Succeeding issues print considerably longer installments of the work.

LETTER
49

1. Halfpenny's 1878 map of Fredericton shows a rifle range along the southwest border of the Race Course and Exhibition Grounds, where military reviews and sporting activities took place. Presumably, "the Camp" was in this area.
2. In *A Charge to the Clergy of the Diocese of Fredericton, delivered at his Eighth Triennial Visitation, in the Church of St. Paul's, Portland, St. John, June 30th, 1868* (Fredericton: Henry A. Cropley, 1868), Medley argues that clergy should accept the dissolution of church-state ties.
3. We have been unable to trace Dr. Marnerais or to find evidence that he translated any works by Mrs. Gatty or JHE. In the 1860s a British writer could prevent the publication of unauthorized translations only in countries

with which Britain had reciprocal copyright agreements: Germany, France, Belgium, Spain, and the States of Sardinia.

4. Lemuel Allan Wilmot (1809–1878) took office as lieutenant-governor of New Brunswick on 23 July 1868; he was the first native-born man and the first non-conformist to hold this office, which he retained until November 1873. As a member of the Legislative Assembly, 1835–1851, he was active in the movement for responsible government and devoted much energy to attempts to liberalize King's College and to establish a non-sectarian school system. As attorney-general, 1848–1851, and a puisne judge, 1851–1868, he supported the causes of Confederation and common schools. He zealously worked for the Fredericton Methodist Church (now the Lemuel Wilmot United Church), of whose Sunday school he was superintendent for more than twenty-five years. A powerful and popular speaker, Wilmot gave many public lectures on such topics as the historical accuracy of the Old Testament, the flaws in Darwin's theories, and the dangers of alcohol. Though an opportunist in his political life, Wilmot never hesitated to express and to stand by his religious convictions.

5. Isabella Stewart Brooke (?–1882), married John M. Brooke (1800–1882), who came to Quebec from Scotland in 1840 and in 1842 accepted the call to St. Paul's, the Presbyterian Church of Fredericton, which he served as pastor until 1874.

LETTER
50

1. The Irish Church question dominated the proceedings of Parliament from the spring of 1868 until July 1869, when the bill disestablishing the Irish Church was signed into law. It was one of the major issues in the general election of November 1868, which resulted in the resignation of Disraeli and his ministry.

2. Mary Elizabeth Braddon, afterwards Maxwell (1837–1915) was one of the most popular of the "sensation" novelists of the 1860s. Remembered today chiefly for *Lady Audley's Secret* (1861), she published some eighty other novels.

LETTER
51

1. Jonathan Eastwood (1824–1864) served as Mr. Gatty's curate, 1848–1854, and remained a close friend of the family.

LETTER
52

1. "The Happy Family," by Hans Christian Andersen, tells of the domestic bliss of two old white snails who live in a deserted garden where the burdock leaves are so thick that they seem capable of overgrowing the world.

2. The Reverend William Morley Punshon (1824–1881), a remarkably eloquent Wesleyan lecturer and preacher, was a native of Doncaster, fifteen miles northeast of Ecclesfield. Ordained in 1849, he ministered in England until 1867, when he became president of the General Conference of the Wesleyan Methodist Church of Canada. Re-elected five times to the presidency, he exercised supreme control over Methodism in Canada between 1868 and 1872, and during this time he preached and lectured to large crowds in nearly every important town in the Dominion.

   Mr. Punshon arrived in Fredericton the week of 21 June 1868 to preside over the Wesleyan Conference; on 23 June he gave a public lecture, on 28 June he preached, and on 1 July he was the most notable guest at the festival held at Evelyn Grove (Lemuel Wilmot's home, corner of Regent and Aberdeen) to raise funds for painting and refurbishing the Fredericton Methodist Church. The festival, scheduled to coincide with Dominion Day, began at 2:00 P.M. and featured music by the band of the 22d Regiment; in the evening, the grounds were illuminated and fireworks were shot off (*NBRFA*, 26 June, 3 July 1868).

3. On 10 August 1868 Tom Thumb, born Charles Sherwood Stratton (1838–1883), appeared in Fredericton with his party, which consisted of his wife, Mercy Lavinia Warren Bumpus (1841–1919), her sister Minnie Warren (1850–1878), and George Washington Morrison McNutt (1848–1878). It was frequently rumored that "Commodore Nutt" and Minnie Warren would marry, but he died a bachelor. In 1877 she married Major Newell, known as General Grant, Jr., who had joined the troupe in 1874; she died as a result of complications in childbirth.

LETTER
53

1. Gatty slang for *seaweed*.

2. There is no evidence that JHE completed this story.

3. Rex was posted to Constantinople in 1855 and returned to England in the autumn of 1856.

4. Gabriel Acquin, about ninety years old when he died 2 October 1901, was a figure of local interest in Fredericton for over half a century. An Abenakis

Indian and chief of the Malicetes, "Chief Gabe" had in 1847 cleared and fenced fourteen acres on the north shore of the St. John – a site which later became St. Mary's Indian Reserve. He made at least three trips to London, attending the Colonial and Indian Exhibition (1886) and travelling with Captain Paul Boynton's water circus (1892). In *Chiploquorgan* Richard Lewes Dashwood describes an 1865 hunting expedition guided by an "Indian hunter named Gabe, a well-known hunter at Fredericton" (pp. 124–31); see also Carole Spray, "Gabe Acquin and the Prince of Wales," *Will O' the Wisp: Folk Tales and Legends of New Brunswick* (Fredericton: Brunswick Press, 1979), pp. 27–32.

LETTER
54

1. The first edition of *MOR* was priced at 4s. In 1868 George Routledge and Sons was publishing numerous colourfully illustrated children's books, priced from 6d. to 3s. 6d.
2. Heron's Lake, now called Killarney Lake, three miles north of Fredericton.
3. William Buckmaster & Co., Tailors and Army Clothiers, 3 Burlington Street, London. In the 1860s members of the firm made annual North American business trips.

LETTER
55

1. In August 1868 Dot, Dina, and Brownie attended Stephen's graduation ceremonies at Winchester.
2. Caroline J. Dowling, *née* Wolhaupter (1840–1889) was the daughter of Benjamin Wolhaupter, who built and originally occupied the house later known as "Bishopscote" – the home of the Medleys. Mr. Wolhaupter and his daughter were close friends of Bishop and Mrs. Medley.

LETTER
56

1. The sketch which originally headed this letter is missing. The reproduced sketch is from H.K.F. Gatty, p. 23. See Appendix 4, "The Bear."

LETTER
57

1. In 1836 Archdeacon George Coster urged the establishment of the Church Society. This was "the first systematic attempt in a British Colony for more

full and efficient support of its own church.

2. A loosely formed settlement stretching along the south bank of the St. John, eighteen miles upriver from Fredericton.

3. Magaguadavic – a rural settlement twelve miles southeast of Prince William.

4. In the May 1868 *Mission Life* Mrs. Gatty urged the formation of an English Children's Mission Army to be modelled on the American Domestic Missionary Army, founded in January 1867. The children's annual dues of one shilling were to be contributed to the Society for the Propagation of the Gospel, to the Church Missionary Society, or to any special missionary fund approved by the clergyman of the parish. The first "Regiment" of the CMA was established in Ecclesfield in June 1868, and the movement continued to grow for several years.

LETTER
58

1. Edward Arthur Wellesley Hanington (1844–1917), ordained priest in 1867, the same year he married Margaret Susan Drummond MacLean (1844–1919). Their first child, Georgia Fanny Wellesley, died at eight weeks of age on 22 September 1868 and is commemorated by the altar window of St. Clement's Church, Prince William, of which Hanington was rector, 1866–1877. Hanington became canon of Ottawa in 1897.

LETTER
59

1. Horatia Elder (1808–1882), Margaret Gatty's sister.

2. In 1859 Horatia Elder became a Roman Catholic.

3. *The Insurance Plan of Fredericton* (1888) shows a priest's residence, a convent, and St. Dunstan's Church on Brunswick Street between Regent and St. John Streets.

4. The Cathedral of the Immaculate Conception.

5. St. Anne's Church, reconstructed following a fire, is in French Village, Kingsclear Indian Reserve #6.

LETTER
60

1. Elizabeth S. Tucker, *Leaves from Juliana Horatia Ewing's "Canada Home"* (Boston: Roberts Brothers, 1896), tells more about JHE's wallpapering adventure (pp. 23–25).

2. Predicting the qualities of one's future mate by examining the size, shape, and taste of a cabbage plant pulled by a blindfolded person on Halloween was widespread in northern England and Scotland. In Scotland it was customary to steal the cabbages used for divination.

3. John Newton (1725–1807), sailor, slave-trader, co-author with William Cowper of *Olney Hymns* (1779), and rector of St. Mary's Woolnoth, London. When he was nineteen, Newton deserted ship, was arrested by a military patrol, and marched through the streets of Plymouth, England, to the town guardhouse.

4. See Appendix 5, "The Brennan Case."

5. *Family Jars*, a one-act farce by Joseph Lunn, first performed in the Theatre Royal, Haymarket, 26 August 1822; *Twenty Minutes with a Tiger*, a farce, adapted (probably by Francis Cowley Burnand) from the French and first performed at the Theatre Royal, Drury Lane, 29 October 1855.

LETTER

61

1. A tablet set in the wall of the Ecclesfield vicarage garden reads:

Hic Jacet
Carolus Edwardus
"Pretender"
Asinus, Alacer
Impiger Honestus
Victor Ludorum Alipes.
Anno Obit XL imo
A.D. XI. KAL:Feb
MDCCCLXXXVI
1886

The donkey, which pulled a shay, was purchased because Mrs. Gatty's increasing physical debility made walking difficult; his name reveals her characteristic sense of fun: she is laughing both at her husband's hatred of the Jacobite cause and her own romantic attachment to it in her girlhood.

2. Mrs. Gatty put a tie for Rex in with the other things that she asked Bishop Medley to take to the Ewings.

3. T.H.E., "The Trials and Troubles of the Kettle Family," *AJM* 5 (July 1868): 181–88, tells of a family whose children are plagued by Old Dordell, the diabolic spirit of procrastination.

4. All illustrations for *MOR* appearing in *AJM* are included in the first edition of the book.

LETTER
62

1. Wolf's illustration is the frontispiece of the first edition. In later editions Pasquier's "Mr. Joseph" becomes the frontispiece, and Wolf's illustration is returned to the text of "Kerguelen's Land."

2. In the first edition, as in the version published in *AJM*, the final word, *remembrances*, is not capitalized; in later editions this error is corrected. "Maunder" is probably a reference to Samuel Maunder (1785–1849), compiler of numerous dictionaries and texts on grammar and spelling. No addition concerning "the bird understanding the men" appears in later versions of the text.

3. On 29 October 1868 Elizabeth Simonds married the Reverend William Sterling Neales, whose brothers were engaged to Emma and Julia Simpson, the daughters of Fredericton's first mayor, John Simpson (1795–1863), Queen's Printer, and his wife Rebecca (1804–1844); JHE is obviously confused about the identity of the "fat old" woman. On 27 October 1868 Emma married the Reverend T. Neales; Julia later married W. A. Balloch.

4. *Pickwick Papers*, ch. 54.

LETTER
63

1. Burning two nuts side by side was a Halloween rite of augury. In the north of England, quiet burning betokened a happy wedded life, but in the south, the bursting of the nuts foretold marital bliss. On Halloween, prophetic tokens such as coins, buttons, and rings were concealed in a pot of porridge. Cabbage stalks used in the divination rites were placed above the door in the belief that the Christian name of the man or woman who first entered would be the same as that of one's future mate.

2. JHE's chief bridesmaid was her sister Margaret, who married a year later.

3. Edward Young, *Night Thoughts on Life, Death, and Immortality* (1742–1745).

4. No work by JHE appears in *AJM* 6 (January 1869).

5. John Frederick Tayler (1802–1889), lithographer and etcher, noted for his hunting and hawking prints. On 17 November 1882 JHE writes to Mrs. Medley, "Do you remember, when Fredericton was our home, and when everything pretty from old England did look so very pretty! – how on one of those home visits from which he brought back bits of civilization – the Bishop brought *me* a "chromo" of dogs and a fox which has hung in every station we've had since?" (HAS 65).

6. Charles Thomas Longley (1794–1868), archbishop of Canterbury, 1862–1868, died 27 October 1868; he was succeeded not by William Thomson, archbishop of York, but by Archibald Campbell Tait (1811–1882), bishop of London.

7. "Kerguelen's Land," the last chapter of *MOR*, appears in *AJM* 5 (October 1868): 333–47.

LETTER

64

1. "A round game in which a narrative of the meeting of a lady and a gentleman, their conversation, and the ensuing 'consequences,' is concocted by the contribution of a name or fact by each of the players, in ignorance of what has been contributed by others" (*OED*).

LETTER

66

1. Louis Spohr (1784–1859), whose works, including his oratorio *The Last Judgement*, led many in the nineteenth century to value him above Beethoven.

LETTER

67

1. "A fire on Monday night destroyed the barn and workshop of Mr. James Agnew, situated at the lower end of Charlotte Street" (*NBRFA*, 27 November 1868).

2. *Cook's Excursionist And European And American Tourist Advertiser*, 5 September 1868, states that "First Cabin Return Tickets are now issued by Mr. Cook, at Reduced Fares, between London, Manchester, Liverpool Or Glasgow, And The United States & Canada. Either Way, Available By Six Lines Of Steamers, At Fares varying from 20 Guineas to 30 Guineas, Allowing Passengers to return at any time within Six or Twelve Months."

LETTER

68

1. See Appendix 6, "The Scovil Affair."

2. Ran in *All the Year Round* from 4 January to 8 August 1868; published in volume form by Tinsley Brothers, July 1868.

3. George MacDonald, *Alex Forbes of Howglen* (London: Hurst & Blackett, 1865).

LETTER
69

1. In *The Pickwick Papers*, ch. 15, Count Smorltork says that "the word poltic surprises by himself."
2. "The Land of Lost Toys," *AJM* 6 (March 1869): 259–64; (April 1869): 323–40.
3. "There is considerable sickness in Fredericton during the present season, a sort of epidemic which has the general appellation of 'a cold' affecting very many" (*NBRFA*, 4 December 1868).
4. Frances Cowley Burnand's one-act burlesque, first performed 8 November 1855 at A.D.C. Rooms, Cambridge (see L72, n2).

LETTER
70

1. Dr. George Mountain Odell (1818–1892), younger brother of William Hunter Odell.
2. Mrs. Alfred Gatty, "My Childhood in Art," first published in *MP* 8 (May–June 1857), and then in *The Human Face Divine, and Other Tales* (London: Bell and Daldy, 1860), pp. 63–146.

LETTER
71

1. On 5 January 1869 the *City of Manchester* arrived at Halifax after a stormy sixteen-day passage from Liverpool. Among the passengers was Sir Anthony Musgrave (1828–1888), governor of Newfoundland, 1864–1869.
2. Jules Michelet (1798–1874), prolific French historian.
3. Francis Cowley Burnand, *Happy Thoughts*, a series of comic sketches appearing in *Punch* from 23 June 1866 to 27 April 1867, and then published in volume form by Bradbury, Evans & Co. in 1868. Chapter 3 recounts the struggles of the hero to concentrate on writing while dancers perform "the bowing figure" from the Lancers.

LETTER
72

1. Dot was born 10 January 1846.
2. George Roberts, *An Ample Apology*, first produced at Princess's Theatre, 13

March 1865; Frances Cowley Burnand, *Villikins and His Dinah* (see L69, n4);
Taming a Tiger, a slightly shorter version for private theatricals of *Twenty
Minutes with a Tiger*, a one-act farce, probably also by Burnand (see L60, n5).
The Lady in *An Ample Apology* is Mrs. Clasper, who is the innocent victim of
her husband's jealous rages and a young man's infatuation. *Taming a Tiger*
revises *Twenty Minutes with a Tiger* to omit the parts of Dolly, the housemaid
and wife of the servant Jacob, and Arabella, the daughter of the "tiger," Mr.
Chili Chutnee, and the beloved of Charles Beeswing. In *Taming* the meeting
between the young lovers is necessarily omitted and the scene of Mr. Beeswing catapulting into a fishpond after a scuffle with the enraged father is
described in a monologue by Jacob rather than, as in *Twenty Minutes*, in conversation between Dolly and Arabella. In *Villikins*, Master Grumbleton
Gruffin's refusal to let his daughter, Dinah, and Villikins marry, causes the
lovers to drink poison and die, though they are miraculously revived by his
announcement that were they alive he would let them marry. Grumbleton
Gruffin has three solos and also sings in a quartet and two trios, the music
being taken from popular songs of the 1850s and earlier. Burnand's farce is
an adaptation of the operatic farce *Willikind and Hys Dinah* by J. Stirling
Coyne, first performed at the Theatre Royal, Haymarket, 16 March 1854.

3. Mrs. Alfred Gatty, "A Legend of Sologne," *Legendary Tales* (London: Bell and
Daldy, 1858), pp. 1–90. Having met a child and an old man who show no
amazement at the extraordinary because they lack knowledge and experience, the narrator rejects the proverb "only fools wonder" and decides instead that "only the wise . . . wonder for . . . only the wise . . . know where
the earthly possible ends" (p. 10). He reads that from midnight of Christmas
Eve until noon on Christmas Day, animals in Sologne can speak. Later, he
dreams that he journeys to Sologne with his pets, certain that at the appointed time they will declare their admiration for him, but instead, they tell him
he is selfish, inadequate, and stupid.

4. In 1861 and 1862 John William Colenso (1814–1883), bishop of Natal, 1853–1883,
published commentaries which revealed his unorthodox views on eternal
punishment and biblical inspiration, thus arousing the concern of conservative churchmen. Consequently, in 1863 the metropolitan of Capetown,
Robert Gray (1809–1872) convened a synod of the South African bishops,
which declared the Church of South Africa independent of the Church of
England, deposed Colenso, and established the new See of Maritzburg,
whose bishop was to replace the bishop of Natal. Colenso appealed to the
privy council, arguing that the bishop of Capetown had no jurisdiction over
the bishop of Natal, and won his case in 1865. The controversy thus centred
not on the latent issue of heresy, but on the question of a secular court's
authority over the church. Gray, refusing to acknowledge such authority,
excommunicated Colenso in 1866 and attempted to have him condemned by
the Lambeth Conference of 1867; this attempt was frustrated, but a private

paper condemning Colenso was circulated at the conference. In 1868 W.K. Macrorie, Gray's choice, was consecrated bishop of Maritzburg; thus until Colenso's death, there were rival bishops and church factions in Natal.

5. In April 1868 the Fredericton City Council approved the purchase of a steam fire engine (*NBRFA*, 24 April 1868). The engine arrived in early September (*NBRFA*, 11 September 1868), and though initially jeered by the hand pump crews, the "little giantess," nicknamed the "Alexandra," showed her might when she extinguished a fire in early December (*NBRFA*, 18 December 1868). "The Steamer's praises were in every mouth" on 11 January 1869, when "for four mortal hours" through 1250 feet of hose, she poured water on a fire in a barn holding three tons of hay. The jealousy of one hand-pump tender was such that he tried to uncouple the suction hose of the steamer (*NBRFA*, 15 January 1869).

6. See Appendix 7, "Kethro the Barber."

7. The tinted photograph, "Amateur Theatricals, Fredericton, 1868 [1869?]," the York-Sunbury Historical Society Museum, Fredericton (Accession 5405), shows from left to right Mr. Woolsley, Mr. Ewing, and Mr. Hammersley.

LETTER
73

1. From the *Sheffield Daily Telegraph*, 29 December 1868: "On the arrival of the mails in Liverpool on board the City of New York, from Halifax, it was reported that a bag, containing mails, and supposed to be from 'Fredericton, Cork, viâ Halifax' was washed overboard and lost, almost opposite the Rock Lighthouse. The river police are at present in search of it."

2. After convincing her doctor to administer chloroform during the birth of her ninth child in 1851, Margaret Gatty became an advocate of the drug, which she called "Angel's food."

3. The Osborne Collection copy of the first edition of *MOR* bears JHE's heartsease (viola tricolor) design in the centre of its cover. The reference is to Gwynfryn, *Friends in Fur and Feathers* (London: Bell and Daldy, 1869); Bell did not use JHE's device on the cover of Miss Jones' book, but he did use the same designs in the corners of the covers of both publications.

4. *BOT* includes "The Brownies," "The Land of Lost Toys," "Three Christmas-Trees," "An Idyll of the Wood," "Christmas Crackers," "Amelia and the Dwarfs," "Timothy's Shoes," and "Benjy in Beastland."

5. Mrs. Gatty's *The Fairy Godmothers and Other Tales* (London: Bell and Daldy, 1851) contains "The Fairy Godmothers," "Joachim the Mimic," "Darkness and Light," and "The Love of God."

6. *Grimm's Goblins* appears as Parts I–VI of *Fairy Books for Boys and Girls* (London: George Vickers, 1861), the first of Vickers' "New Illustrated Periodicals."

The series came out in weekly penny numbers which were later bound as complete volumes. Most of the illustrations are by Hablot K. Browne, and all are engraved and printed by Edmund Evans. While the majority of the tales in the collection are from Grimm, the anonymous translator/editor includes French and Norse tales, as well as some which are probably his own creation. The translations are unreliable, which is understandable since the intention, as stated in the "Preface," is to improve on previous collections which, "if not entirely frivolous, are often vulgar in language and gross in details, thus rendering them unfit for home purposes and the education of children.... In *Grimm's Goblins* everything of such a character has been sedulously excluded" in the hope the book will be "one of the most innocent as well as one of the most entertaining volumes in any language" (M.E. Brown, "Vickers' 'New Illustrated Periodicals,' 1861, with Special Reference to *Grimm's Goblins*," B. Phil. thesis, Oxford, 1974).

7. "Popular Tales From Andalucia" (see L19, n4); Mary Senior Clark's "The Lost Legends Of The Nursery Songs" (*AJM* [May 1868–August 1869]) develop the stories hinted at in popular nursery rhymes.

8. The first eight of JHE's fairy tales appear in *AJM* between November 1869 and September 1870; all except the fourth, "The Hillman and the Housewife," which is signed "J.H.E.," are anonymous, but in the table of contents inserted into the bound volumes of *AJM*, they are grouped under the heading "Old-Fashioned Fairy Tales by Juliana Horatia Ewing." Seven of these tales are collected with eleven others in *OFFT* (London: SPCK [1882]); to this book JHE adds a preface in which she explains that her intent is to use "ideas and types" which occur "in the myths of all countries" and to avoid "discursive or descriptive" writing, because household stories "should be written as tales that are told." She also defends fairy tales as "the most valuable literature for the young."

9. "Kind William and the Water Sprite," *AJM* 8 (November 1869): 33–37, and later in *OFFT*, pp. 93–102.

LETTER
74

1. Guilliaume Moseley, a Sheffield dentist.

2. In July 1865 Juliana had major dental work done by Alfred James Woodhouse, 1 Hanover Square, London.

3. *NBRFA* prints occasional articles on topics such as Dr. Dow's "Model Dental Establishment" (see Appendix 8), his removal of a large uterine tumor, and the performance of his 191st successful harelip operation (*NBRFA*, 2 October 1868). Dr. Dow was active in politics: between 1861 and 1882 he contested every election for York County member and was successful three times out of eight.

4. "Where are the swallows fled? / Frozen and dead, / Perchance on some bleak and stormy shore. / Oh doubting heart! / Far over purple seas, / They wait in sunny ease, / The balmy southern breeze, / To bring them to their northern homes once more. . ." (Adelaide Anne Proctor, *Legends and Lyrics*, 2 vols. [London: Bell and Daldy, 1858], 1:40–41).

5. Amy Mary Parry, daughter of Georgina Mary and Frederick William Best Parry, was baptized 26 March 1869.

6. "Grandmamma's Throat," which first appears in *MP* 21 (June 1861): 581–607, and then in *Aunt Judy's Letters* (London: Bell and Daldy, 1862), pp. 104–38, is the story of a girl who is carefully watched over because she suffers from the family weakness of a bad throat.

LETTER

75

1. "The Nix in Mischief," *AJM* 8 (April 1870): 363–66, and later in *OFFT*, pp. 28–35.

2. Completed in 1869 the Western Extension, connecting Fredericton and St. John, later became part of the Canadian Pacific Railway. Construction began 6 November 1867 when, as that day's *HQ* reports, Mrs. Needham, the wife of the mayor of Fredericton, "with handsome spade, deftly dug out a loosened sod and placed it in a gorgeous wheel-barrow [and] His Excellency [Lieutenant-Governor, Colonel Francis Pym Harding] wheeled the barrow gracefully along the plank and returned. The cannon spoke out, and the Band played the 100th Psalm."

3. "Our Carpet Bag," an irregular feature in the *Era*, an English weekly paper, contained verses, aphorisms, jokes, and gossip about the great. "De Omnibus Rebus" was a similar column in *HQ*.

LETTER

76

1. See L7, n7.

2. *Zinnia elegans flore-pleno* is Gatty-family code for baffled hopes. In the February 1864 issue of "The Gun Powder Plot," the family nursery magazine (HAS 76), Juliana writes:

Hot Fire on the Grenoside Quarter

When first I saw thee advertised
There seemed such truth about thee,
So highly were a few seeds prized

I did not dare to doubt thee,
I saw thee grow, yet still relied
Still clung with hope the fonder;
And thought whatever failed beside
My zinnia'd be a wonder.
    But go! deceiver go!
The heart whose hopes could make it
Trust Sugden Barr & Co.
Deserves that thou shouldst break it.

E'en now, altho' thou art in bloom
And not a flower is double,
And not a plant is worth the room,
Altho' I took such trouble,
Thy meagre petals are not half
    So pretty as a daisy's,
Sometimes I weep, sometimes I laugh
The sight my poor mind crazes.
    Go! Go! 'tis vain to curse
It is no use to scold thee:
Hate cannot wish thee worse
Than my poor eyes behold thee.

In JHE's gardener's alphabet, "Garden-Lore," *AJM* 17 (March 1872): 290–92, the last entry reads: "Zinnia elegans flore-pleno is a showy annual, and there's a coloured picture in the catalogue; but – like many other portraits – it's a favourable likeness."

LETTER

77

1. *Hallamshire: The History and Topography of the Parish of Sheffield, The County of York, with Historical and Descriptive Notices of the Parishes of Ecclesfield, Hansworth, Treeton, and Whiston, and of the Chapelry of Bradfield*, by Joseph Hunter, F.S.A., A new and enlarged edition by The Rev. Alfred Gatty, D.D. (London: Bell and Daldy, and Sheffield: Pawson and Brailsford, 1869).

LETTER

78

1. In *Domestic Economy* Walsh writes, "every woman who wishes to regain her health entirely, *without any discomfort or drawback*, should never raise her

shoulders off her pillow for nine days after her delivery" (p. 559).

2. The *Saturday Review*'s anti-feminist reputation was heightened by its anonymous publication of Mrs. Lynn Linton's vitriolic article "The Girl of the
Period," which caused so great a furore that in the same year it was published as a pamphlet and given the leading position in a volume of thirty-
seven essays, all from the *Saturday Review* of 1867–1868, entitled *Modern
Women and What Is Said of Them* (New York: J.S. Redfield, 1868). These
essays, not all of which were by Mrs. Linton, support the *Saturday Review*'s
long-held insistence that women are by nature intellectually inferior to men,
and all castigate modern women for failing to see that their innocence and
delicacy, which unfit them for independence, impose upon them the role of
guardian of the sanctity of the home. JHE somewhat unjustly implies that the
Pall Mall Gazette was equally anti-feminist. The greater moderation of its
views appears in such articles as "The Higher Education of Women"
(6 January 1869), which asserts that though on the whole "men. . .[are] remarkable for sense and the logical faculty, and women. . .for sensibility and
the emotional faculty," much of the "silliness" of women, "which has caused
reasonable observers so much pain of late, is simply the result of defective
training" (p. 11).

LETTER

79

1. The Regiment was sent to Ireland.

LETTER

80

1. *ML*, a magazine devoted to information about the missions of the Anglican
Church, appeared monthly, February 1866 through December 1869, except
for March, May, and June 1866. In May 1868 Mrs. Gatty became editor of the
children's department (see L81, n7). The paper about Magaguadavic does not
appear in *ML*, but *ML* 5 (December 1868), reports that "the Ecclesfield Regiment has it in contemplation to. . .apply £5 of the money now in hand to a
Mission west of Fredericton, New Brunswick, where the settlers are building their own church by voluntary labour, but sadly need some accessories.
Especially it is proposed to supply communion plate from the Ecclesfield
funds" (p. 812).

LETTER
81

1. This firm of Edinburgh chemists and druggists, which in 1847 provided Sir James Simpson with the chloroform he used in his first experiment in anaesthesiology, enjoyed wide fame for the quality of the ether and chloroform it manufactured.

2. Adhesive gold, used for filling teeth and building crowns; though patented in 1853, sponge gold was not widely used until after 1864, when the development of the rubber dam enabled practitioners to keep saliva from contaminating the metal.

3. Thomas Barlow, an Ecclesfield butcher.

4. The church still stands, but was dismantled and rebuilt in the early 1920s.

5. From February 1867 through May 1869 articles on the history of the Anglican Melanesian Mission appear in *ML*. Bishop Selwyn's encouragement and advice to Mr. Geddie, a Presbyterian missionary, is specifically mentioned in the July 1867 and August 1868 issues.

6. John Joseph Halcombe (1832–1910), editor of *ML*. No papers by Medley appear.

7. From May 1868 to January 1869 Mrs. Gatty edited the *ML* children's department, "Little Workers and Great Work." In January 1869 this department is replaced by a column entitled "Children's Mission Army Report," but the title "Little Workers and Great Work" appears again in the March, April, and May issues over brief articles by Mrs. Gatty on the progress of the CMA. In July 1869 the column announces that the growth of the CMA prevents *ML* from devoting further space to its activities.

8. William Hooker, "Botany," *A Manual of Scientific Enquiry; Prepared For The Use Of Her Majesty's Navy: And Adapted for Travellers in General*, ed. John F.W. Herschel (London: John Murray, 1849), pp. 400–420.

9. *Memoir of W.H. Harvey, M.D., F.R.S., . . . With Selections From His Journal And Correspondence* (London: Bell and Daldy, 1869).

LETTER
82

1. Brother 'Enry is the Gatty nickname for the family physician, Henry John Hawthorn.

2. "From Ecclesfield we hear that the sum of £5 12s., out of monies subscribed by the Young Crusaders, has been expended in the purchase of a set of Communion plate (electro-plate) for the use of a small Mission church in a wild

part of New Brunswick, North America." The interest of the Ecclesfield Mission Army was aroused by a "letter from the married daughter of their Vicar, now resident at Fredericton.... [The service] consists of a flagon, two chalices (gilt inlaid), two plates, and one paten. The inscription is as follows: —'Presented by the Ecclesfield Regiment / Of the English Children's Mission Army,/Feb., 1869' " (*ML* 6 [March 1869]: 172).

LETTER

83

1. The general election of 1868 brought Gladstone into office as prime minister in December, and he quickly began to pursue the policy he had stated as early as 1864 of making British colonies increasingly responsible for their own defence. In January 1869 he accepted the proposal of his secretary of state for war, Edward Cardwell, that British troops in North America be reduced from 16,185 to 6,249, all ranks. Of these, 2,000 were to be stationed in Nova Scotia to defend Halifax, which was an imperial station. Despite the objections of the military and the Canadian authorities, in April 1869 Sir John Young, the governor general, was informed that a reduction of at least this magnitude would be carried out.

   The "*Alabama* Matter," which was not resolved until 14 September 1872, arose from the fact that though the British government had proclaimed its neutrality in the American Civil War in May 1861, it allowed the *Alabama* and other Confederate vessels to be built and equipped in British ports and made no attempt to detain them from participating in the war against the Union. The issue, which threatened to lead to war between Great Britain and the United States, became especially heated in 1869, when on 13 April the United States Senate rejected by a vote of 54 to 1 the Johnson-Clarendon Convention, which specified that the two powers settle differences in accordance with the decisions reached by a four-man commission and, if necessary, an umpire. The Senate vote was greatly influenced by a strong speech in which Senator Charles Sumner implied that only by allowing the U.S. to annex Canada could Britain sufficiently compensate for the depredations of the *Alabama*.

2. "One little lady in the choir, who always slid and glided into her seat with an undulating movement, never allowing her garments to touch anything as she went, was called by [JHE], 'Patha Furtiva,' which is the Hebrew for a 'thing which glides' " (Tucker, p. 34).

3. George Trevor, *The Story of the Cross; in Daily Contemplations for the Holy Week* (London: J. & C. Mozley, 1866).

4. We have been unable to trace the original of this picture. The photograph we publish [Plate 15] appears in Tucker, p. 81.

LETTER

84

1. In the poem, angels comfort those who mourn the death of a "gentle maiden" (Proctor, *Legends and Lyrics*, 2:226–29).
2. In 1865 privates were paid a shilling a day, with an extra penny for beer. A deduction for rations left three pence half-penny for personal needs. To supplement their husbands' pay, wives took in work from the wives of officers.

LETTER

85

1. John Martin illustrated Samuel Prowett's edition of *Paradise Lost* (London: Septimus Prowett, 1827).

LETTER

86

1. During 1869 Mrs. Gatty wrote seven brief sketches which she published in *AJM* under the general title "Nursery Nonsense"; none were reprinted. Karl Fröhlich (1821–1898), German silhouette-cutter.
2. George Cruikshank illustrated *BOT*.
3. Of these titles, "*The Brownies* (& Other Tales)" appears as *BOT*. "A Sack of Fairy Tales" may be *OFFT*, and "The Dutch Story" may be *Jan of the Windmill*.

LETTER

87

1. Destroyed by fire in 1882, Rose Hall stood at 176 Waterloo Row. The property was once owned by Benedict Arnold, but it is not certain that he ever lived there.
2. Maggie's first child, William, was born at her home, Butterthwaite, 27 April 1869.
3. Probably "The Cause and the Causer of the Cause," *AJM* 8 (November 1869): 3–17.
4. Asa Gray, *First Lessons in Botany and Vegetable Physiology* (New York: Ivison & Phinney Co., 1857), with over 360 wood engravings from original drawings by

Isaac Sprague. Asa Gray, *Manual of the Botany of the Northern United States* (New York: Ivison, Phinney & Co., rev. eds., 1856, 1862, and 1867), also with illustrations by Sprague.

5. "Kind William and the Water Sprite," *AJM* 8 (November 1869): 33–37, is JHE's next published work.

6. William Holman Hunt (1827–1910), *The Light of the World,* exhibited at the Royal Academy, 1854.

LETTER
88

1. Probably, Adolf Bernhard Marx, *The School of Musical Composition, practical and theoretical.* ..(London: R. Cocks and Co., 1852).

2. No 72d Highlanders were sent to New Brunswick.

LETTER
89

1. *NBRFA,* 28 May 1869, describes with regret the embarkation of the 22d Regiment.

2. The concert was given 24 May 1869 in the new City Hall. The *NBRFA,* 28 May 1869, remarks: "Perhaps the most noticeable part of the evening's entertainment was a weird-like original composition of the Conductor, A. Ewing, Esq., entitled 'a Vision,' which consisted of a bass solo, introducing a pathetic semi chorus, and an exquisitely rendered soprano solo, followed by an invisible chorus in an adjoining room. The whole scene was written expressly for the occasion and notwithstanding its length was rapturously encored." *NBRFA,* 21 May 1869, prints the programme. See PANB, MYO CB9 4 for a leaflet advertising the concert.

LETTER
91

1. "When the [22d] Regiment was [in Fredericton], the American Civil War was just over. The Yankees were very short of instructors and offered British soldiers stationed in Canada two hundred dollars and ten gallons of rum to desert and join them as instructors. To prevent this, small parties of NCO's and men were stationed in block houses on all the roads leading to the U.S.A. These parties had a good time fishing and hunting. They were paid an extra shilling a day and wore mufti. A field officer visited them every month,

paid them out, and left a monthly ration of salt pork, beef, bacon, molasses, flour and biscuits. The soldiers got fresh food by exchange with the local farmers" (Arthur Crookenden, *Twenty-Second Footsteps, 1849–1914...* [Chester, England: W.H. Evans, Sons & Co. Ltd., 1956], p. 26.

2. JHE's account of All Saints, Magaguadavic, does not appear in *ML*.

3. The Reverend Alvi Tabor Twing (1811–1882)–secretary of the Protestant Episcopal Committee for Domestic Missions, "General" in the Domestic Mission Army, and editor of the *Young Christian Soldier*, a DMA publication –spoke at the first review of the DMA, held in New York in the autumn of 1868. In "How Are We Getting On," *ML* 5 (November 1868): 736, Mrs. Gatty announces that the Reverend J. Erskine Clarke (1827–1923), perpetual curate of St. Andrew's, Derby, 1866–1872, and editor of *Parish Magazine, Chatterbox,* and *Children's Prize,* has become "a most welcome convert" to the CMA.

4. The Magundy Church was torn down in 1916, but the foundations of the church may be faintly discerned to the south of the Magundy churchyard, which was restored by parishioners as a 1967 centennial project.

5. Felicia Hemans, "The Cross in the Wilderness," *Poetical Works* (Boston: Phillips, Sampson and Co., 1857), p. 436.

LETTER
92

1. Trouvé is the original of Nox in "Benjy in Beastland," *AJM* 8 (May–June 1870), republished in *Lob Lie-by-the-Fire and Other Tales* (London: George Bell & Sons, 1873), and of Sweep in *Laetus Sorte Mea; or, The Story of a Short Life, AJM* 20 (May–October 1882), republished in book form (London: SPCK, 1885). His memorial tablet in the vicarage garden at Ecclesfield reads:

> Trouvé
> Commonly and justly called
> True
> Found 1869   Lost 1881
> by A.E. and J.H.E.

2. See L4, n3.
3. A wood near Ecclesfield.

LETTER
93

1. From the song "The Sailor's Wife," by William Julius Mickle (1735–1788).

LETTER
94

1. *NBRFA*, 9 July 1869, describes the party at the home of Spafford Barker (1811–1886), United States consular agent at Fredericton.
2. The United States did not have a national anthem until 1931, when "The Star Spangled Banner" was given official status. Throughout the nineteenth century "Hail Columbia" competed with "The Star Spangled Banner" for the honour.
3. In 1869 Alfred Scott Gatty, JHE's second brother, entered into a three-year agreement whereby he promised that for £100 a year he would supply four serious and four comic songs to music publisher Robert Cocks and not publish elsewhere (Mrs. Gatty to Horatia Elder, 20? April 1869 [HAS 43]).
4. *NBRFA*, 9 July 1869, praises the second concert of the Choral Society, 2 July 1869, and notes "that in the midst of gladness there arises cause for sadness and regret... in view of the departure from our midst of Commissary Ewing, the Conductor of the Society, and to whose masterly skill and untiring energy, the Society owes so much of its present proficiency." See also *HQ*, 1 July 1869, for comments on the high quality attained by the Choral Society.

LETTER
95

1. Both the Synod of the Diocese of Fredericton and the Diocesan Church Society met in Fredericton in the last week of June 1869.
2. At the meeting $800.00 was subscribed towards making up the $3,000.00 deficiency of monies available for clergymen's salaries (*NBRFA*, 2 July 1869).
3. All eight of the tales are illustrated by Alfred Walter Bayes (1832–1909), who though born in France, spent most of his life in London. A follower of the pre-Raphaelites, Bayes specialized in illustrating children's books.

LETTER
97

1. The Officers' Barracks, corner of Queen and Regent Streets.
2. In fact the sale was held 5 August 1869. That it occurred at all is somewhat surprising because the British Army required that "all condemned stores should be destroyed or rendered useless" so as to prevent the possibility of their being furbished and re-sold to the Army. The authorities in Halifax

were asked to make an exception in this case because the withdrawal of troops from Fredericton made such fraud impossible. Initially they refused to yield, and during the interim period – to the anger of the townspeople – a great deal of equipment, including blankets and stores, was destroyed (*NBRFA*, 30 July and 6 August 1869).

3. *Little Dorrit*, ch. 23.

4. P.P.C.: *pour prendre congé*.

5. On 31 July a fire in the area of King Street and Taylor's Alley destroyed five homes, adjoining barns, and outhouses (*NBRFA*, 6 August 1869).

6. The Artillery Park Barracks occupied a portion of the block downriver from the Old Burial Ground.

LETTER
98

1. See Appendix 9, "Cuban and Fenian Difficulties."

2. *NBRFA*, 6 August 1869, carries the following advertisement:

VALUABLE FURNITURE, &C.,

A AUCTION

The Subscriber will sell at the Officers' Barracks, to-morrow, SATURDAY, the 7th inst., at 12 o'clock, noon, an assortment of Valuable Household Furniture, &c., belonging to Alexr. Ewing, Esq., D.A.C.G.

    For particulars see Bills.

        J. MYSHRALL, Auctioneer, &c.

Fton Aug 6

LETTER
99

1. In May 1869 the 78th Highlanders were sent from Montreal to Halifax, where they remained until June 1870, though a company was sent to St. John at the end of June 1869.

2. Dr. James Robb (1815–1861), the first professor of chemistry and natural history, King's College. Dr. Robb's residence was probably located at 75 Carleton Street, where he lived with his wife, Ellen Maria, *née* Coster, and their nine children (L35, n5).

3. Edward Jesse, *Gleanings in Natural History*, 3 series (London: John Murray, 1832–1835); William Whewell, *The Elements of Morality, including Polity*, 2 vols. (London: John W. Parker, 1845); Horatius Bonar, *Hymns of Faith and Hope*

(London: James Nisbet & Co., 1857); Sarah Stickney Ellis, *The Women of England, Their Social Duties and Domestic Habits* (London: Fisher, Son, & Co., 1839); George Catlin, *Letters and Notes on the Manners, Customs, and Conditions of the North American Indians,* 2 vols. (London: The Author, 1841); Alexis Soyer, *A Shilling Cookery for the People* (London: George Routledge & Co., 1855); *Tracts for the Times* [ed. John Henry Newman], 6 vols. (London: J.G. & F. Rivington, 1834–1841).

LETTER
100

1. See *NBRFA*, 27 August 1869.
2. The fire occurred 13 July 1869. The building was insured for $400.00 (*NBRFA*, 16 July 1869).

LETTER
101

1. Prince Arthur arrived in New Brunswick 7 September 1869; after stopping in St. John, where he attended a reception and a ball, he proceeded on 8 September to Fredericton, where he was greeted by 4,000 citizens and received by the city council and the mayor. After a torch-light parade through flag-draped streets, the prince attended a party at Government House (*NBRFA*, 10 September 1869).

Notes to the Appendixes

Appendix 1, The Mails

1. Sources: Howard Robinson, *Carrying British Mails Overseas* (London: George Allen & Unwin Ltd., 1964), pp. 135–37, 139–44, 245; *British Sessional Papers, House of Commons*, vol. 34 (1868–69) (*Accounts and Papers*, Session 10 December 1868–11 August 1869), "Contracts entered into by the Postmaster General for the Conveyance of Mails from this Country to the United States, with Messrs. Cunard & Co.; with Mr. William Inman; with North German Lloyd of Bremen; and, Treasury Minute on the subject," pp. 383–99; "Letter from the Postmaster General forwarding Contract for the Conveyance of Mails from Liverpool to New York, *via* Queenstown, with Copy of such Contract," pp. 401–6; "Correspondence between the Postmaster General, the Treasury, and Parties Tendering for the Conveyance of Mails between this Country and the United States (in continuation of Paper, No. 42, of Session 1867–8)," pp. 407–32; "Correspondence between the Postmaster General of the United Kingdom and the Postmaster General of the United States, commencing the 13th December 1867, relating to the Postal Conventions between the two Countries, &c.," pp. 435–42; "Arrivals and Departures, Outwards and Homewards, for the year 1868, of the Steamers of the Cunard and Inman Lines, conveying the Mails between Queenstown and New York, and the Steamers of the North German Lloyd and Hamburg American Steam Packet Company, conveying the Mails between Southhampton and New York," pp. 467–74; "Various Particulars respecting the Mails to the United States, from 1st January 1869," pp. 479–82. U.K., *Hansard's Parliamentary Debates*, 3d ser., vol. 196 (3 May–16 June 1869) (Commons), "Mail Contracts.–Resolutions" (1 June 1869), pp. 1127–59.

2. Sources: *Dominion of Canada, Sessional Papers*, vol. 2 (1869), Sessional Papers, No. 3, "Report of the Postmaster General For the Year Ending, 30*th* June, 1868," pp. 1–360; vol. 2 (1869), Sessional Papers, No. 34, "Mail Service:–Copies of agreements made for the conveyance of mails by the Grand Trunk R.R. and Steamship lines between the United Kingdom and Canada," pp. 1–7.

3. Sources: Robinson, pp. 146–47; *Dominion of Canada, Sessional Papers*, vol. 2 (1869), Sessional Papers, No. 34, "Mail Service:–Copies of agreements made

for the conveyance of mails by the Grand Trunk R.R. and Steamship lines between the United Kingdom and Canada," pp. 1–7; vol. 3 (1870), Sessional Papers, No. 3, "Report of The Postmaster General For The Year Ending 30*th* June, 1869," pp. 3–346.

Appendix 2, The Scheme

1. Sources: J.W. Fortescue, *A History of the British Army*, 13 vols. (London: Macmillan & Co., Ltd., 1930), 13:555–56. U.K., *Hansard's Parliamentary Debates*, 3d ser., vol. 188 (18 June–23 July 1867) (Lords), "Army Transport And Supply Departments.–Observations" (27 June 1867), cols. 586–602; vol. 193 (26 June–31 July 1868) (Commons), "Army–Control Department. Motion for Papers" (16 July 1868), cols. 1265–75; vol. 193 (26 June–31 July 1868) (Lords), "The War Office–Department of Control.–Question." (16 July 1868), cols. 1233–47; vol. 194 (10 December 1868–23 March 1869) (Commons), "Supply–Army Estimates. Supply–*Considered* in Committee" (11 March 1869), cols. 1111–77.

Appendix 9. Cuban and Fenian Difficulties

1. Sources: J. Mackay Hitsman, *Safeguarding Canada 1783–1871* (Toronto: University of Toronto Press, 1968), pp. 192–222; Lester Burrell Shippee, *Canadian-American Relations 1849–1874* (New Haven: Yale University Press, 1939), p. 238. Sir John Young to Lord Granville, 30 July 1869, *Original Correspondence–Secretary of State*. (Dominion of Canada. 1869 May–July Despatches), CO 42/676; PAC B–492. *Macdonald Papers: Letter Books* 12, 1019, 1022–25, PAC. U.K., *Hansard's Parliamentary Debates*, 3d ser., vol. 194 (10 December 1868–23 March 1869) (Commons), "Supply–Army Estimates. Supply–*Considered* in Committee" (11 March 1869), cols. 1111–77. For the most complete account of the Fenian raids, see John A. MacDonald, Capt., *Troublous Times in Canada: A History of the Fenian Raids of 1866 and 1870* (Toronto: Printed by W.S. Johnston & Co., 1910).

Index

Doyle, Sir Charles Hastings, 26, 36, 48, 56, 59, 64, 65, 105, 366
Drawing class, 120, 126, 140
Driscoll. *See* Brennan case

Eastwood, the Reverend Jonathan, 186, 229, 387
Ebor. *See* Thomson, William
Ecclesfield, ix, xiv, xix, 12, 13, 45, 58, 59, 78, 97, 122, 152, 156, 170, 186, 193, 199, 207, 229, 231, 245, 282, 283, 304, 308, 317, 367, 372, 390
Ecclesfield Mission Army. *See* Children's Mission Army
Edge, Mr., 118
Eel River, 307, 308, 309
Elder, Horatia (Juliana Ewing's aunt), 63, 229, 333, 336, 337, 390
Elia (Charles Lamb), 23, 174, 179, 365, 371
Elvey, Sir George Job, 36, 369
"Emblems." *See* Gatty, Margaret, works of
Emerson, Mrs. Ann, 155, 195, 246, 290, 384
English Churchman, The, 234, 298
Era, The, 264, 398
Ewing, Alexander, xi, xiv, 250, 254, 396. *See also* Choral Society
as author, xi, 92, 127, 381
career of, 20, 24, 100, 101, 183, 199, 245, 286, 365, 376
as choir master, 162, 178, 188, 194, 201, 212
as composer, xi, 32, 67, 80, 93–94, 126, 127, 128, 129, 178, 179, 193, 207, 226, 227, 228, 242, 250, 260, 288, 294, 321, 386
military duties of, xi, 7, 12, 21, 28–29, 53, 86, 168–70, 183, 188, 226, 244, 245, 246, 251, 255, 262, 263, 299, 307, 309, 323–24, 326, 328, 330, 331–32
as musician, 21, 28, 32, 36, 38, 51, 52, 66, 80, 91, 94, 95, 101, 123, 128–29, 134, 147, 151, 160, 172, 193, 194–95, 201, 203, 207, 235, 244, 250–51, 321, 331, 333
as translator, xi, 92
works of
"Jerusalem the Golden," xi, 32, 36, 368, 369, 378
Prince of Sleona, The, xi, 127, 381

Ewing, Juliana Horatia, ix, x–xvii, 361
concerns as author, xv–xvii, 53, 66, 69, 75, 80, 93, 97–99, 108–9, 131, 134–35, 136, 150, 152, 166–67, 171, 178–79, 198, 220, 222, 224, 232, 234–35, 240–41, 248, 249, 256–58, 260, 261, 270, 275, 293, 296, 301, 303, 306, 324, 376, 379, 385. *See also* Book Post; Mails; Post office
and bindings, 178–79, 201–2, 248, 249, 256, 257, 396
and copyright, 180, 386–87
and illustrations, x, 81, 93, 134, 167, 222, 223, 224, 301, 324, 376, 377, 381, 385, 391, 392, 403, 406
and sales and income, xvii, 78–79, 98–99, 179, 180, 183, 201–2, 220, 256, 258, 333, 340, 389
as handyman, 149, 161, 172, 217–19, 275
health of, xiii, xvii, 4, 8, 9, 17, 22, 29, 32, 49, 75, 91, 104–5, 107, 109, 132, 144, 145, 146, 147–48, 151, 153, 213, 241, 243, 246–49, 259, 260, 261, 277, 278, 279, 325
works of
"Amelia and the Dwarfs," 396
"Benjy in Beastland," 396, 405
"Blackbird's Nest, The," 374–75
"Bit of Green, A," 374–75
"Blind Hermit and the Trinity Flower, The," 386
"Brownies: A Fairy Story, The," 66, 198, 222, 256, 257, 296, 374
Brownies and Other Tales, The, 256, 296, 301, 396, 403
"Christmas Crackers," 396
Daddy Darwin's Dovecot, xv–xvii
Dandelion Clocks and Other Tales, 386
Flat Iron for a Farthing, A, x
"Garden Lore," 399
"Hillman and the Housewife, The," 397
"Ida," 371
"Idyll of the Wood, An," 9, 12, 30, 53, 81, 301, 363, 372, 376, 396
Jackanapes, x
Jan of the Windmill, 232, 301, 379, 403
"Kerguelen's Land," 98, 160, 166–67, 171, 201, 222, 224, 229, 371, 385, 392,

425